PHOTOSHOP
FOR VIDEO

Richard Harrington

AMSTERDAM • BOSTON • HEIDELBERG • LONDON • NEW YORK • OXFORD
PARIS • SAN DIEGO • SAN FRANCISCO • SINGAPORE • SYDNEY • TOKYO
Focal Press is an imprint of Elsevier

Senior Acquisitions Editor:	Paul Temme
Associate Editor:	Dennis McGonagle
Publishing Services Manager:	George Morrison
Senior Project Manager:	Brandy Lilly
Assistant Editor:	Chris Simpson
Marketing Manager:	Christine Degon Veroulis
Cover Design:	Dennis Schaefer
Interior Design:	Dennis Schaefer

Focal Press is an imprint of Elsevier
30 Corporate Drive, Suite 400, Burlington, MA 01803, USA
Linacre House, Jordan Hill, Oxford OX2 8DP, UK

 Recognizing the importance of preserving what has been written, Elsevier prints its books on acid-free paper whenever possible.

Library of Congress Cataloging-in-Publication Data
Application submitted

British Library Cataloguing-in-Publication Data
A catalogue record for this book is available from the British Library.

ISBN: 978-0-240-80926-7

For information on all Focal Press publications
visit our website at www.books.elsevier.com

07 08 09 10 11   5 4 3 2 1

Typeset by Charon Tec Ltd (A Macmillan Company), Chennai, India
www.charontec.com
Printed in Canada

Dedication

To my parents

Thanks for teaching me about hard work and giving me your love and support throughout the years. The sacrifices you have made for my education and well-being are deeply appreciated. Who would have guessed that all those video games and early computers would lead to this?

To my wife and children

Thanks for your incredible patience and support throughout this project, for your understanding that the long hours and demands of the video industry do not diminish my love and desire to spend more time with you. You are the single most important part of my life.

To my extended family

Your guidance and support have helped with the many twists in life's road. Thanks for helping me get on my feet and stay there.

CONTENTS

Foreword

Given the wide adoption of Adobe Photoshop in professional print and Web publishing workflows, as well as the incredible growth of digital photography in the past few years, it can be easy to forget that the very first version of Photoshop was developed in part by an engineer doing motion picture work at Industrial Light and Magic. Perhaps it shouldn't be surprising that Photoshop has long been an indispensable tool for digital video work.

Adobe Photoshop is the world's most widely used professional tool for image manipulation—regardless of whether those images will be printed in a brochure, linked together in a Web page, or streamed as frames in a video. In fact, it's even finding increasing use in fields as diverse as medical imaging and forensic analysis. How is it possible for a single application to be used in so many different ways? The answer lies at the core of the application, once you strip away Web export options, CMYK printing controls, and other specialized workflow features. What you'll find is a set of powerful tools and commands that allow you to take a collection of image pixels and turn them into just about anything you can imagine.

Photoshop is fabled for its formidable learning curve. I believe that reputation owes more to the extreme flexibility of the application than it does to the challenge of mastering any particular function. There is rarely one right way to do anything in Photoshop. There are sometimes dozens. What Photoshop gives you is a set of powerful imaging building blocks. You're the one who decides how to put those blocks together to build the result you want. You're the one in control.

Of course, having so much control—and so many choices—can be intimidating to the uninitiated. What you need is a guide to help you to narrow the choices to the ones that matter. What are the most valuable functions for the type of work you're doing? What are the key techniques for combining these functions? What's the fastest way to take what's in your head and realize it on your computer monitor?

Before writing this foreword, I conducted a quick online search and discovered more than 500 available books about Photoshop. What's almost as remarkable as the sheer number of books is the variety. There are books written for Web designers, prepress professionals, photographers, and fine artists. There are a variety of books focused on type effects, special effects tricks, color correction, retouching, and portraiture. What I didn't find, however, was a book focused on using Photoshop for digital video.

In fact, motion picture and video professionals rely on Adobe Photoshop every day to retouch frames, design titles, and create sophisticated graphics for animation. They've learned where to find the features they need in Photoshop, how to combine these features to solve the problems they encounter every day, and how to streamline and automate their workflow for maximum efficiency. Over the years, a wealth of tips and techniques have been developed—things you won't find documented in the manual we include in the box.

But now, finally, they are documented in Richard Harrington's new book. If you're just beginning to use Photoshop for video work, then this book will help you get up to speed by focusing on just the things you need to know. If you're already an experienced user, you're still bound to pick up a variety of techniques that can make a difference in your daily work. It's taken a dozen years, but video professionals finally have a Photoshop book to call their own.

Kevin Connor
Senior Director of Product Management
Adobe Systems Incorporated

Introduction: The Gift of Giving

I have been very fortunate to know a great number of talented people. These cutting-edge pioneers worked in small corners of a diverse industry and never received recognition or fame. Fortunately, many of them were generous in their giving of knowledge, never fearing that teaching a young upstart would jeopardize their career or prestige.

When I entered the workforce, the practice of apprenticeship was essentially dead. Due to budget cuts and the emerging digital tools, video and television were being made by fewer people on tighter deadlines. Many people pulled inward, set up small shops, and became fiercely competitive.

Many great tools emerged that let the industry reinvent itself. The advent and subsequent widespread adoption of computer-based editing carried us into a world where even a small corporate video could have visual effects and a rich graphic identity. Soon the tools of the print and emerging web industry were crossing paths with those used for video. Unfortunately, there were few, if any, books in those early days beyond the owner's manuals. Many creative individuals had to struggle with these new tools and spend many late and isolated hours working diligently to climb to the top of this rapidly shifting industry.

But things have started to change. Our industry has become a recognized art form. Students now formally study things like nonlinear editing and motion graphics. When I work with our future peers, the concept of physically editing videotape with two decks or making art cards to shoot with a camera seems arcane and foolish to them. These new co-workers are going to challenge the status quo. All they know is digital; all they have ever seen is visually rich and entertaining television. These students don't define themselves with narrow job titles such as editor, animator, or producer; they want to do it all.

All of these changes have dramatically reshaped the industry. Terms such as *preditor* are emerging (as in producer/editor) for situations where one person is guiding a creative project from start to end, being responsible for completing most of the hands-on work. Even the "traditional" editor is now being expected to create motion graphics, color correct, and understand sound. Because the same computer that can run the nonlinear editing software also runs graphic and sound applications, the editor is expected to grow (sometimes overnight).

So what does this have to do with you? If you bought this book (and thanks if you did!), you are probably working as an editor or motion graphic artist. I am sure that you want to make more visually interesting videos to meet your artistic (and client) demands. You have taken it upon yourself to learn what is often considered the world's best graphic application, Adobe Photoshop. You also need results immediately and don't have time for long-winded explanations or searching through several sources. While you'll find thicker books on Photoshop, it has been my goal to create a book that discusses only the issues facing a video professional. I believe I have succeeded, and I thank the wonderful contributors and editors who have helped shape this book.

It has been my goal to give back to an industry that has been nurturing to me. I sincerely hope that this book makes your job easier and your videos better. Even more so, I hope I can make you faster so you can make your deadlines and get home to see your family and loved ones sooner. Mastering Photoshop takes several approaches; be sure to explore the disc, try every tutorial, and make it through every page (even if you read them nonlinearly). No matter what your experience level, I am sure you will come out better for investing your time.

It has been several years since we released the first edition of this book, and Photoshop has undergone fundamental changes (thank you non-square pixels). I have strived to bring this book fully up to date with the latest changes in Photoshop as well as emerging technologies like High Definition video and DVDs. I've also added in several new topics based on discussions with professionals like you. It has been great to hear feedback and success stories from so many of you at conferences, in a classroom, and online. Please continue to be vocal in your feedback to help this effort grow. I wish you luck, and I look forward to seeing many of you when you manage to get out of your edit and design suites.

Have fun pushing your pixels around.

Richard Harrington
RHED Pixel
April 2007

Acknowledgments

I have worked in several deadline-driven industries: newspapers, broadcast news, waiting tables. . .writing books is harder. I could have never gotten through this without the love, support, and knowledge of many others. I must thank *all* the people who have made things possible for me to write these words. Thanks to the following folks for keeping me on track and helping with the load:

My wife Meghan who was with me in the beginning. You are an inspiration.

My son Michael who reminds me to have fun and live my life.

Paul Temme for the opportunity to write and guidance through the years.

Dorothy Cox for helping me get through so many books and teaching me how to get a book done.

The Staff of RHED Pixel who held it together while the boss went off to finish his books.

Future Media Concepts Ben Kozuch for letting me teach other pros. Marcus Geduld, Jeff Greenberg, and Christopher Phrommayon for providing insight and support.

VASST Douglas Spotted Eagle and Mannie Frances who have pushed me to try new things and reach out to more people.

Technical Editor Thanks to Glen Stephens for tracking both the big and little details, as well as helping me see my blind spots.

Adobe Kevin Connor, John Nack, Daniel Brown, Julieanne Kost, and Jeff Tranberry for being so helpful and listening to my demanding ideas.

Contributors Thanks to my friends and peers who made the time to contribute great tutorials and share advice. There are so many people who believed in this project. I could not have done this by myself.

Trish and Chris Meyer Thanks for paving the way for this book to be written. I appreciate you refining my outline and raising the bar for professional video books.

DV.com My online home. Thanks for your support and resources. To the forum members, thanks for the challenges and keeping me sharp.

The Art Institute of Washington Thanks to Ron Hansen, Michael Davidson, and Alex Buffalo; thanks for encouraging me. Your support has let me contribute to our industry. To my students past and present, you inspire and challenge me.

Apple Patty Montession, Anne Renehan, Abba Shapiro, and Steve Martin for helping me with Final Cut Pro.

Avid Greg Staten for being my Avid guy. The participants of Avid's Master Editor Workshop for showing me how many true professionals are out there.

NAPP for being a great organization and reaching out to video pros as well.

Educators Mt. Carmel High School—for giving me confidence and courage, as well as introducing me to journalism. Drake University—for sharpening my skills and teaching me how to communicate visually. Keller Graduate School of Management—for teaching me the world of business and project management. Special thanks to great teachers like Billy Stone and John Lytle, who helped steer me.

KCCI John Pascuzzi, Dave Legg, Larry Hawk, Jack Tow, and Eric Fishback for teaching me so much about being a pro.

You, the reader for being a concerned professional and improving our art form.

Caffeine Pepsi One, Diet Coke, Coca Cola Blak, Starbucks, and Jammin' Java for keeping me going.

My wife Meghan who is with me in the end. Thanks for putting up with my deadlines and all-night writing. I am looking forward to the challenges and rewards of raising our second child.

About the Author

Richard Harrington has had a long relationship with media. When he was seven, he was grounded for using magnets to rearrange the picture tube on the family's 13-inch color TV. (It works, but don't try it.) He has since gone on to many more interesting television experiments.

The author has surrounded himself with media for his entire professional career. Richard has held such diverse jobs as directing newscasts and producing children's television to managing a video production department and editing award-winning national commercials.

He has an extensive background with many cutting-edge video tools. He holds Adobe Certified Expert certificates in Photoshop and After Effects and has completed Avid's Master Editor Workshop and Avid Certified Instructor Program. Additionally, he was one of the first instructors certified by Apple as a trainer for Final Cut Pro. The Project Management Institute certifies Richard Harrington as a Project Management Professional. He holds a master's degree in project management as well.

The author frequently shares his expertise as a guest speaker at industry conferences and as a trainer for Future Media Concepts. Richard is an adjunct faculty member at The Art Institute of Washington and The American University. You can also find Rich active online at the website www. PhotoshopforVideo.com.

Richard is also the president of a visual communications company named RHED Pixel, which provides technical and design services to a wide range of clients. RHED Pixel creates motion graphics, produces video and multimedia projects, and delivers web-based content, including podcasts.

He believes that we live in a world that is becoming increasingly cluttered with confusing messages. His personal philosophy is "Communicate. . . Motivate. . .Create." He is a firm believer that media can have powerful results. He hopes that this book helps you to create better-looking, more effective videos.

GETTING STARTED

How to Use This Book

"Human salvation lies in the hands of the creatively maladjusted."
—*Martin Luther King, Jr., 1963*

This book is different. I have approached it like an edit session. I have gathered the best source materials. I have "logged the tapes," so to speak, by pulling only the essential information that a video editor, motion graphic artist, or DVD designer would need. I've organized things into bins for you (except here they're called chapters). I've also loaded the system with tons of new effects and powerful tools to help you out. Think of me as the perfect assistant. I've prepared everything for you—now go to town.

This book and accompanying disc can be enjoyed in a non-linear fashion. Work in whatever order you want (or need). I've included a detailed index and glossary to help you through any gaps caused by skipping around. If you're a little rusty, there are expert articles and tips on the DVD to help you through.

I want Photoshop to be fast and easy for you. I also want you to understand it, not just memorize things. While the chapters will often contain step-by-step instructions for certain skills, there is always a clear explanation of both how and why to do things. I want you to get immediate results every time you read a chapter.

I face the same problems you do. I have designed this book so it can live next to your NLE or motion graphics suite. Since space is valuable I have tried to give you the best book out there on making graphics for video. All of the techniques in this book are real-world solutions. You have problems. . .I've got answers.

Iconography

Throughout this book, I have included callout boxes that either present you with additional noteworthy information or direct you toward another resource (the Internet or the included DVD-ROM). The icons associated with these callouts are in the margin.

Key to the Icons

 Web Link. Go online to find out more.

 On the DVD. Resources on the DVD-ROM that are important to the current subject.

 Noteworthy. "Gotchas" to avoid, new terminology, or Photoshop-related skills.

 Technical Tips. Hints and tricks to make Photoshop work for you.

Disc Access

Since this book is exclusively for the video audience, I am assuming you have access to a drive that can read DVDs. If you don't, buy one. There are so many free resources on the disc that the money spent will be worth it.

The book and DVD-ROM are meant to be enjoyed together. Nearly every chapter has its own project files so you can try the techniques discussed in the chapter. Look throughout the chapter for the On the DVD icon to point out much of the bonus content.

You can explore the disc on your own or use the interactive Pixel Browser. The browser helps sort through the 8+ gigabytes of demos, source files, fonts, freebies, tutorials, and source files. You'll find helpful descriptions and a familiar browser environment to view content. For your browsing enjoyment, I've even added a jukebox filled with songs from one of my favorite bands, The Nadas. Be sure to check them out on the DVD as well as visit their website at http://www.thenadas.com.

Installation

- I assume that you are working on Photoshop 7 or newer. If not, download a tryout copy of Photoshop from Adobe's website.
- You will need QuickTime installed to open the video files and view the video tutorials. Download it from Apple's website at http://www.apple.com/quicktime. You need to use version 7 or newer.
- You will need Adobe Reader to open the tutorials and several bonus articles. If you don't already have it installed, be sure to visit http://www.adobe.com to download the latest version of Adobe Reader; it's free.
- In order to use the interactive browser on the DVD-ROM, you will need to have a current version of the Flash plug-in installed. Please visit http://www.adobe.com to download the free plug-in and player.
- In a few instances, I have used Microsoft Office (http://www.microsoft.com). This is for cases where integration with the Office environment is needed.
- There are numerous free plug-ins and resources on the disc. In most cases, you will find a READ ME or User's Guide in the product folder. Consult your owner's manual for installing fonts and other resources; they vary by system. I've included links to most vendor sites; this is the best place to turn for troubleshooting advice.

- If you are having trouble with your DVD-ROM, contact Elsevier Tech Support (technical.support@elsevier.com) at 1-800-692-9010 in the US and Canada, or 1-314-872-8370 outside of North America, for a replacement. This title is a DVD-ROM disc intended for playback in computer drives capable of reading DVDs. It is not for playback in a set-top box.

Mac Versus PC

Adobe Photoshop runs the same on Windows as it does on a Macintosh. The faster your machine, and the more memory you have, the better it runs (regardless of platform). People will always ask, "Why Mac or Windows? What do you recommend?" Here are the facts, as far as this book is concerned.

- The screen captures in this book are mostly from Mac OS X, because of the excellent screen-capture software available.
- My office has 14 Macs and 5 PCs.
- When I edit, I run Avid and Premiere Pro on both platforms and Final Cut Pro on one platform.
- Macs have a longer history with professional editing, so the Mac keyboard commands come first.
- Windows shortcuts are listed, too. In today's world, you need to work cross-platform.
- Don't stress.

MAC	PC
Command	Control
Option	Alt
Control+click or Right mouse click	Right mouse click
Spinning beach ball	Blue screen of death

The Future

As things change—and they always do—I will update. For updates, news, free resources, and the podcast, visit the companion website at www.PhotoshopforVideo.com. If you would like to contribute to the effort by reporting any errors you spot or things I've overlooked, please use the online contact form.

For Instructors

If you are an instructor, I sincerely hope that you will adapt this book to your specific curriculum. I have designed it to be a great resource for advanced courses in screen graphics or video production. This book is based on techniques that I have taught over the years. I am a college instructor, as well as a frequent speaker at industry conferences and training events.

There are several sample files that you can use for demonstration purposes during lessons or lectures. If students own the book, I recommend copying a chapter's files to their local computer. This way, they can save and work with the material.

You will also find an excellent series of articles from http://www.adobeevangelists.com included on the disc. These serve as excellent supplemental material or to fill in points that a new user might not know. This book is written assuming that the reader has completed a "beginner book." If this is not the case, please consult several of the supplemental materials. Be sure to check out the Adobe Evangelist site for more advanced articles on Photoshop and all other Adobe products.

An instructor's guide is available on the Photoshop for Video website (www.PhotoshopforVideo.com). It contains outlines to each chapter, suggested exercises, sample exam questions, and project ideas that students can complete to refine their skills. Additionally, a list of resources for each chapter is also available to help you map the book and disc content to your lesson plans.

As a fellow instructor, you'll understand how much work goes into preparing lessons and sample exercises that are helpful and meaningful. The entire content of this book and DVD-ROM are copyrighted. Owners of the book are granted specific rights as granted in the End User's License or in supplemental licenses provided in each folder. While there are several excellent resources, many of them fully functional or "free," they are for those who purchased the book. In some cases, I have content on the disc that is also available online. I have placed it on the disc for convenience. (Downloading a 12-MB file to 25 lab machines over a network can be slow.) If students do not (yet) own the book, they can access some of the content this way.

If a school distributes copies of the source files, software, plug-ins, movies, or PDFs to anyone who has not purchased the book, that constitutes copyright infringement. Also, reproducing pages electronically or physically is a bad thing. Thanks for respecting my work and that of the project's contributors. Your voluntary compliance with copyright enables this book to be updated and me to keep teaching others. Thanks again!

Qualified teaching professionals can acquire evaluation copies of this book by submitting the request form provided on the Focal Press Web site.

MAKE IT HAPPEN

This book and the accompanying DVD are intended to be a teaching guide, a reference book, and a source of inspiration. It is my hope to make your job easier and your projects more professional looking. To move you towards this goal, I will occasionally take related tangents. Photoshop is a companion to many other applications, so don't be surprised to dip into specific nonlinear editing systems (NLEs) or even After Effects. Photoshop integration is an essential skill in taking your video editing and motion graphic skills to a higher level.

But I'll be honest… Photoshop can be pretty intimidating with its myriad of tools and windows. With hundreds of menu commands, it's pretty easy to get lost. But you need to remember that Adobe Photoshop is the number one selling image editor in the world for good reason. Learning to master Adobe Photoshop is very likely if you take a balanced and measured approach.

Reality Check

Photoshop is one of the most elegantly designed, yet feature-deep pieces of software available. Before you get defensive and proudly stamp your feet in support of Apple, Avid, or Sony, hear me out. No other application has so many tools and processing power combined with the ability to export to multiple formats. Adobe Photoshop is the most flexible program you'll ever work with, but being a master will take time.

Working professionals use Photoshop for a variety of tasks. From graphic designers and Web developers to photographers and scientists, nearly everyone uses Photoshop. Because it is the tool-for-everybody, Photoshop sometimes gets a little crowded. There are so many features (distractions) that have nothing to do with video. I am not suggesting that you write Adobe asking for a refund on unused features. Instead, accept that all you need (and more) is waiting for you. The pros know that the best approach is to learn what you need first, and then dabble with the rest over time.

Honestly Evaluate Your Skill Level

It is OK to be a beginner in some applications and an expert at others. Photoshop requires a "strong bench" of skills.

If you've used Photoshop before, be prepared to change your viewpoint. Video pros often want to understand every bell and whistle in their applications. This obsession is rooted in the belief that absolute knowledge is absolute power. Personally, I don't subscribe to this mindset. Rather, I would argue that speed and wisdom (knowing what tools matter to the video pro and how to get the job done quickly) should be the true goal.

This book is not a catalog of every feature of Photoshop. What it will do is show you the tools that are likely to be used by video artists. The book is squarely focused on both technical expertise and design aesthetics. The book will also dip into some third-party plug-ins and related technologies that may help you.

I will waste no time talking about achieving great four-color printing or how to get faster download times. This is a video book, and you work (or want to work) in the video industry—a fast-paced, deadline-driven, technical industry. I respect that, because I am right there with you, and it is my goal to help you get faster and feel more confident in using the world's best image-editing application.

Suggested Hardware

Photoshop is a great tool right out of the box. However, there are a few things that will help you get more work done. The order in which you add these items on will vary, depending on your work environment and budget. I will not assume you have any of these, other than access to a video monitor in either NTSC or PAL (depending upon your country).

An NTSC monitor.

A second computer monitor. Once you've gotten used to having your palettes open, you'll never be able to go back to opening and closing windows and tabs all day long.

As much RAM as you can hold. RAM has been getting cheaper and cheaper. Fill your computer up with at least 2 GB for heavy lifting.

A FireWire Bridge/DA converter. Photoshop can send out video previews via FireWire, which allow for more accurate judgment regarding color and flicker.

An NTSC/PAL monitor. This lets you can check your work before going into the edit suite.

A scanner that matches your imaging needs. I own four scanners. None of them had a price tag of more than $400, and they all work great for video. In fact, the $99 portable one scanned several photos in this book. Scanners have come a long way in recent years.

For Mac users, a two-button mouse. Because 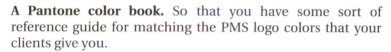ctrl + clicking gets a little old after a while. Many options are available these days, since USB became a common standard between Mac and Windows.

A good set of keyboard and mouse wrist guards. Sore wrists get in the way of what you are trying to accomplish.

A tablet and pressure-sensitive pen. These can be used for both fun and serious work. A little bit of digital doodling can be a relaxing activity. Moreover, a pen is often an easier input device than a mouse or trackpad for realistic brushstrokes and tracing activities.

A Wacom tablet.

A Pantone color book. So that you have some sort of reference guide for matching the PMS logo colors that your clients give you.

A card reader for transferring digital photos. There are multiple format readers available. Get one that is self-powered and supports what you use—such as CompactFlash, Smart-Media, or a Memory Stick.

Keep your Pantone color book in its sleeve and in the drawer. Exposure to light speeds up fading (and reduces accuracy).

Setting Up Photoshop

Success takes preparation. I cannot promise you overnight success, although I can tell you that this book can make you faster and more confident with each chapter you complete. To get the most out of this book, it will help if you and I are operating in a similar environment. I will make suggestions on how to configure Photoshop to operate more like the video editing system that you are used to. So please take the extra time to reset Photoshop.

The LCD (Least Common Denominator) Test

Pick up a combo TV/VCR unit for checking your graphics. These low-cost consumer models are helpful to give you a real-world view of your graphics.

However, if you are strongly opposed to any of these cosmetic changes, skip them. These are merely suggestions to prepare you for success.

Photoshop has its roots as a video and film application. The print—and more recently, Web—industries have claimed it as their own. Now it's our turn. Digital video has emerged as the fastest growing technology area; more and more books and applications are popping up on the shelves, promising solutions for all skill levels. It is my goal to help you reclaim Photoshop and learn to harness its diverse imaging abilities to enhance your video projects.

Setting Preferences

Photoshop has all the tools you need (and many you don't). Let's get started by setting up Photoshop to work with our video applications. First, we'll modify its preferences that control how the application functions. To begin, call up your Preferences panel by pressing ⌘+**K** (*ctrl*+**K**). These Preferences suggestions are based on Photoshop CS3. Most of these options exist in earlier versions of Photoshop, but naming conventions may vary.

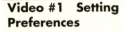

Video #1   Setting Preferences

See the Setting Preferences video tutorial on the DVD-ROM.

General

In the General category, choose:

- Adobe Color Picker, which is a consistent, cross-platform color selection tool.
- Image Interpolation set to Bicubic (best for smooth gradients).
- UI Font Size set to Medium or Large depending upon the resolution of your primary display.
- Dynamic Color Sliders checked.
- Save palette Locations checked.
- Use *Shift* Key for Tool Switch unchecked.

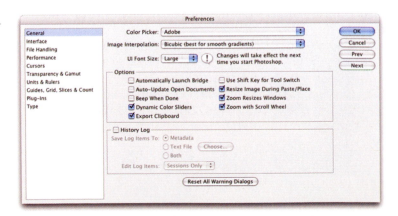

- Zoom Resizes Windows checked.
- Resize Image During Paste/Place checked.
- Zoom with Scroll Wheel checked.
- Click Next.

Interface

The Interface category is new to Photoshop CS3 and groups several important preferences together.

- Leave Show Channels in Color unchecked. This option affects how your channels and images are viewed and diminishes the on-screen viewing quality.
- Check Remember palette Locations to keep your palette arrangements after a relaunch.
- Click Next.

What about Tool Tips?

Older versions of Photoshop have an option called Tool Tips, which you will want to leave on. In Photoshop CS3 this option is automatically enabled under the Interface group.

File Handling

In the File Handling category, you need to make some changes to ensure cross-platform functionality. Even if your shop only uses Macs or PCs, you *will* work with others who are different. Trust me. Be cross-platform compliant when saving your Photoshop files.

- Always choose the Save an Icon and Macintosh and PC Thumbnail options. This will allow you to quickly locate files through visual cues.
- Always append file extension with lowercase tags.
- Set Maximize PSD and PSB File Compatibility to Always.
- Click Next.

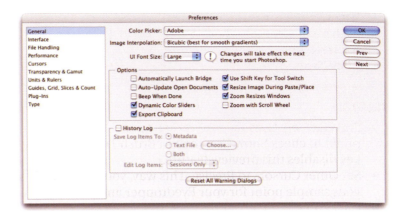

Performance

The performance category is new to Photoshop CS3. It groups several options together tied to managing your installed RAM and graphics card.

- Memory Usage identifies how much RAM you have installed. Photoshop has a minimum requirement of 320 MB, but it's a good idea to choose a number in the ideal range that the program identifies.
- Allow at least 20 history states (levels of Undo). You will vary this number based on RAM and personal experience as you grow less (or more) dependent on undos.
- Memory will generally not be a big deal because you'll work primarily with low-resolution sources in this book. However, if you have extra (local) drives, make Photoshop aware of them. Set your emptiest drive as the First Scratch Disk. Ideally you will choose a drive that is not the system (boot) drive.

Scratch Disk Logic

Already maxed out your RAM slots? A dedicated drive or partition makes the perfect scratch disk. This will greatly improve Photoshop's efficiency in opening large images.

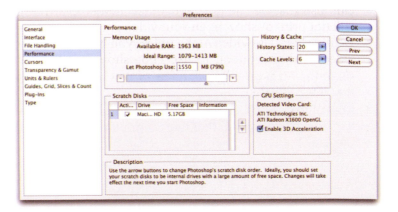

- If you have a robust video card and will be doing a lot of image cleanup, then check the box for Enable 3D Acceleration.
- Click Next.

Cursors

- Set Painting Cursors to Normal Brush Tip. I personally prefer to check Show Crosshair in Brush Tip. (The *Caps Lock* key disables this preview feature.)
- Set Other Cursors to Precise. This way, you can actually see your sample point for your Eyedropper and Stamp tools.
- Click Next.

Help! I Can't See My Cursors

 This is the #1 tech support call to Adobe. If you have the *Caps Lock* key on, Brush Size painting cursors are disabled.

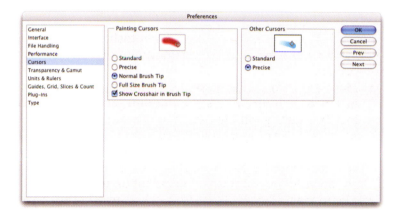

Transparency & Gamut

Under Transparency & Gamut, you can generally leave these options alone. However, personal preferences do vary.

- You can change the grid color if you despise light gray. You can also disable the grid altogether. Remember, the grid will not print or show up in your video graphics.
- *Do not* check Use Video Alpha unless you have an advanced video card and intend to use Photoshop as a live keyer. Chances are there are only a few of you reading this book that are doing this.
- Click Next.

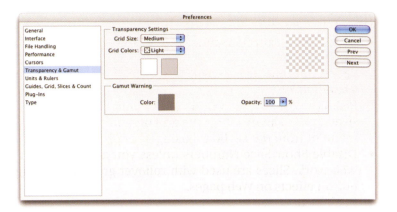

Units & Rulers

Under Units & Rulers, modify Photoshop's measuring system to match video. If you work in a print environment, you can quickly jump back and change your measurement units by double-clicking on the ruler.

- Set Rulers to pixels.
- Set Type to points.
- Ensure that screen resolution is set to 72 pixels/inch.
- Ensure that the Point/Pica Size is set to PostScript (72 points/inch) so that type acts like other video applications.
- Click Next.

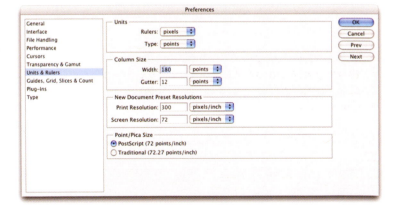

Guides, Grid, Slices & Count

- I find that a Light Red guide is easier to see than the default Cyan.
- Set up a grid using Lines with a gridline every 40 pixels and 4 subdivisions.
- Pick a color such as a dark gray by clicking on the color swatch. You can now turn the grid off and on from the View menu or from the keyboard using ⌘ + " (ctrl + ").
- Disable Show Slice Numbers unless you are doing a lot of Web work. Slices are used with rollover graphics to trigger button effects on Web pages.
- Click Next.

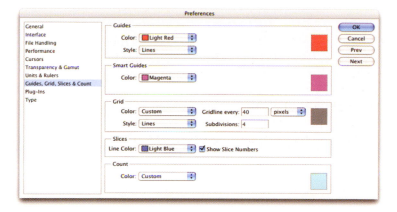

Plug-Ins

- If you need to travel with your plug-ins on a removable drive (for example a freelance assignment) then you can specify an Additional Plug-Ins Folder.
- Click Next.

Get Smart (Quotes)

Use Smart Quotes will automatically insert true, curly quotation marks when you press the **'** (feet) or the **"** (inches) key.

Type

The Type category consolidates several important type options into one area.
- Check the box next to use Smart Quotes if you'll need true quote marks and apostrophes more than foot and inch marks.
- Leave Enable Missing Glyph Protection checked.
- Choose to show Font Names in English.
- Check Font Preview Size and specify a size that you like. The Huge size is helpful if a producer or client frequently sits over your shoulder.
- Click OK.

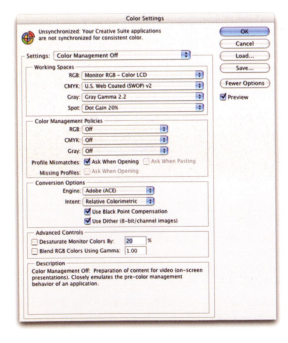

Color Settings

Now it is time to modify how Photoshop handles color and color management. Press Shift+⌘+K (Shift+ctrl+K) to bring up the Color Settings dialog. The default configuration is optimized for Web and print graphics, which can result in color shifts when opening video frames.
- Click the More Options button first.
- From the Settings list choose Color Management Off for consistent results with video graphics.
- Click OK. Photoshop stores preferences when it shuts down. Quit Photoshop and relaunch in order to write your preferences.

Use a Broadcast Monitor with Photoshop

When designing video graphics, it is very useful to view them on a broadcast monitor or television. Starting with Photoshop CS2, Adobe added support for video previews over FireWire. This allows you to perform essential checks for color, interlace flicker, and readability.

Step 1. Ensure the DV device is connected and powered BEFORE launching Photoshop. You can use a camera or a Digital-to-Analog converter that supports either NTSC or PAL and the DV standard.

Step 2. Choose File>Export>Video Preview. The pop-up window will present you with logical choices (you can rollover an item for a detailed description).

Step 3. Choose an Output Mode that matches your hardware (NTSC or PAL).

Step 4. Set an Aspect Ratio for the monitor. If you have a widescreen monitor attached choose Widescreen (16:9), otherwise use Standard (4:3). Photoshop will automatically adjust the graphics to match the hardware attached.

Step 5. Under Image Options you can specify how to handle when the image size differs from the display.

Step 6. Leave the Apply Pixel Aspect ratio to Preview box checked to get the most accurate previews.

Step 7. Click OK.

For subsequent previews, just choose File>Export>Send Video Preview to Device. This will use the last settings you've chosen and bypass the length dialog box. Remember, the only way to see accurate video colors is to hook your machine up to an NTSC or PAL monitor. If this is not an option, you will need to test your graphics with another technique. For more on checking and finalizing graphics, see Chapter 13, "The Road to the NLE or Motion Graphics Application."

Choosing Keyboard Shortcuts

Photoshop has a logical and powerful set of keyboard shortcuts, many of which you'll learn throughout this book. But if along the way, you find one "missing" or "misplaced," feel free to change it. Starting with Photoshop CS, you can customize keyboard shortcuts and create new sets of shortcuts.

Defining or Modifying Keyboard Shortcuts

Step 1. Choose Edit>Keyboard Shortcuts or press ⌥+Shift+⌘+K (alt+Shift+ctrl+K).

Step 2. Create a new set of shortcuts or modify the default set.

Step 3. Select a shortcut type to modify (Application Menus, palette Menus, or Tools) from the Shortcuts For menu.

Step 4. In the Shortcut column of the list, click on the shortcut you'd like to modify.

**An Exclamation Point
Means the Shortcut is
Taken**

 If a keyboard shortcut is
taken, Photoshop will alert
you. Follow the onscreen
directions to resolve the conflicts.

Step 5. Type a new shortcut to replace an existing shortcut or add a new one.

Step 6. After changes are made, the shortcut set will appear with the words *modified*. You can click OK to keep the changes or click the disk icon to save it.

Defining a New Set of Shortcuts

If you want to create a new set of shortcuts, choose one of the following options:

- Create a new set of shortcuts before you edit by clicking the New Set button.
- Create a new set after you've modified shortcuts by clicking the New Set button. This will incorporate any changes you've made.

To save the shortcuts as a file, when you click save, Photoshop CS will navigate to the keyboard shortcuts folder. Name the file and add the extension .keys to the name.

Video's Unique Requirements

Video is a unique creature; it does not enjoy the careful management that other formats do. Web designers have the benefit of designing on computers, for computers. Print designers have precise control during the printing stage, with dedicated professionals calibrating their output devices.

In the world of video, the general population installs $199 color televisions but won't even read the instruction manuals. To make things worse, there's a standards war going on between multiple formats, digital versus analog, standard versus widescreen. Let's just say, your job isn't easy. I want to establish a few key terms immediately to help us move forward. Many of these may seem familiar, so I will keep the introduction short.

Canvas size. This is the area in which you will work. In Photoshop, specify your work area in pixels. It is a good idea to check with the manufacturer of your video software for requirements. These can be found in your owner's manual or on the manufacturer's Web site. You can also check the appendices for recommendations on popular NLE, motion graphics, and DVD authoring programs from top manufacturers.

Standard video is shown at a 4×3 aspect ratio. In the print world, this is referred to as *landscape orientation.*

Aspect ratio. Television is generally a 4×3 aspect ratio, while widescreen is a 16×9 aspect ratio. You will find more information, as well as information on templates, in Chapter 2, "Pixels: Time for Tech."

Image mode. Photoshop supports eight image modes, including bitmap, grayscale, RGB, and CMYK color spaces. For video, work in RGB mode for consistent results with video software.

Bit depth. Also called color depth or pixel depth; a measurement of how much color information is available to be displayed for each pixel in an image. Photoshop users generally work in 8 Bits/Channel mode, because it provides a full set of tools. These 8 bits combine to a total of 24 bits for an RGB image or 32 bits for an RGB image with an alpha channel. Some high-end scanners can capture information at 16 bits per channel. These files are approximately twice the size of their 8-bit counterparts, but contain more detail.

Adobe After Effects and Apple Motion can work with 16-bit images. Starting with Photoshop CS, Adobe now supports layered 16-bit images. However, when working in 16-bit mode, many of the editing tools and filters do not work. You will most frequently work in 8 Bits/Channel mode. Additionally, video editing systems vary on their ability to import 16-bit images. Some will only import a 16-bit image as a flattened file; others will not import it at all.

Luminance ranges. The range of colors supported by video. There are two major color spaces in use for nonlinear edit systems: RGB mapping and 601 Mapping. You should check your system to see which is in use. For more details, see Chapter 2, "Pixels: Time for Tech."

Alpha channels. An alpha channel contains information about all of the transparent areas in your composition. All objects should be on transparent layers when creating an alpha channel. Do not place any of your objects on the background layer. For more details, see Chapter 3, "Why Layers?" and Chapter 4, "What About Transparency?"

Anti-aliasing. Anti-aliasing causes a gentle blending of the colors along the edge of an image. It is often used to reduce flicker. This technique is effective for straight lines and text, to create a smoother composite of foreground and background elements. It is most common for low-resolution output (such as video or Web). There are four different types of anti-aliasing that can be accessed from the Options bar or the Character palette.

Nonsquare pixels. Nonsquare pixels are your own personal demon. These cause more problems for more people than anything else about Photoshop. In a nutshell, computers and Photoshop traditionally work with square pixels (1.0 aspect); most standard-definition digital video works with nonsquare pixels, while high-definition works with both square and

16-bit Archives

If you need to archive an image, a 16-bit scan is the best format. You may have to down-convert to 8 bits for compositing or if your NLE does not support the mode, but at least you have the extra data for future applications.

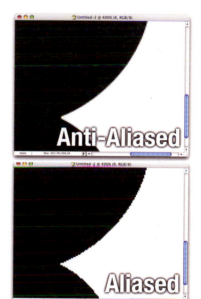

Anti-aliasing helps low-resolution elements containing curved lines (such as text) appear smoother on screen.

Anti-aliasing Essential Information

Anti-aliasing is critical for smooth edges. However, for really small type, leave it off to improve legibility.

nonsquare pixels. Thankfully, Photoshop supports nonsquare pixels, but you will still need a thorough understanding of square pixels. I attempt to squash this problem thoroughly in Chapter 2, "Pixels: Time for Tech."

A Few Basics

Working with Layers

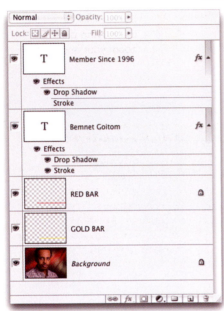

Virtually every modern editing and motion graphics software has added at least partial support for Photoshop layers. Layers enable Photoshop to keep distinct pieces of a design separated (like tracks in a timeline). These efforts are worth praise, but they still do not eliminate the need for saving specialized formats or creating alpha channels. There are times you want layers, and times you don't.

For example, you can import a layered file into Adobe After Effects or your edit system if you want to animate the layers. This is particularly helpful for segment bumpers and show titles. It is also common to import a layered file that contains multiple elements that you intend to use in an editing project. By importing just one file, it is easier to manage media on your hard drive.

So why flatten layers? Do you really want a lower third eating up five tracks of your timeline? What about unsupported/partially supported features like blending modes, clipping groups, and layer styles? Never flatten your design files, but rather choose File>Save As… and specify a new file type. When saving a .psd file as a PICT or Targa file, it is flattened to a single layer, with the option to include an alpha channel.

Additionally, we will go deeply into layer management, masking, blending, and alignment. You should come to appreciate how powerful and flexible a layered file can be. You will work hard for your layers, so do not ever flatten your file and trash all of your efforts. Simply choose File>Save As… and check the As a Copy box to write the file out as a flattened format.

Backing Up Your Work

Your work is what keeps you from enjoying the rest of your life. Do you ever want to have to redo something you've already done? Growing up in Chicago, we were always taught, "Vote early. Vote often." I've adapted this to the Chicago method of file backups: "Save early! Save often."

Saving your work is critical, because unlike many video-editing systems, Photoshop does not have an autosave feature. There is no "attic" or "vault" to help cover you. Saving is your responsibility. Make the act of saving a reflex reaction. Every time you are sitting idle, tap ⌘+S (*ctrl*+S). I often find myself tapping this five times in a row if I am in the middle of a creative thought.

Continue these good habits after the project. Gather up all design and production files, as well as fonts and source materials. Burn them to CD or DVD twice. Maintain two separate project archives so that you always have a copy of the work.

Toolbox

Many tools share space in the toolbox and a keyboard shortcut. Call up the Preferences with ⌘+K (*ctrl*+K) and make sure the Use *Shift* Key for Tool Switch option is disabled. You can now tap a shortcut key (such as M for marquee) and cycle through the tools contained in that tool's drawer. This will speed up your ability to switch tools.

Your hands-on tools are all contained in the toolbox. Similar tools are often nested together. You can access these hidden tools by clicking and holding on a particular tool. Whenever you see a triangle in Photoshop, clicking will open additional options. The first keyboard shortcuts you should master are those for the toolbox. In general, the first letter of the tool is the keyboard shortcut. If you can't remember the shortcut, click on the tool while holding down the ⌥ (*alt*) key to cycle through the available tools.

Not every tool is useful to the video editor. It is important to remember that Photoshop is the #1 image editor for other industries as well. Many of the tools in Photoshop are designed for print, Web, and scientific professionals. A color-coded chart is provided to point out the "video-friendly" tools. Green tools are ones you will need right away, yellow tools will be used occasionally, and video professionals may use red tools infrequently or not at all. You'll also find a copy of this chart on the DVD-ROM.

Next you'll find the foreground and background colors. Many other tools use these colors. The most obvious usage is for the painting tools. Lesser known is that these colors drive the results for many filters. When working with the Artistic, Brush Stroke, or Sketch filters, you will see great variety when switching colors. These colors are often used in painting masks as well.

The toolbox contains a few other useful features for a video editor. Clicking on the Photoshop icon at the top of the box will take you to Adobe Online. This is the quickest way to check for software updates and extensive resources. You can tell Photoshop to check

100% Magnification

Double-clicking on the magnifying glass will zoom your image to 100%.

A Single or a Double

Older versions of Photoshop offer a two-column toolbox. Starting with Photoshop CS3, you can switch between a one- or two-column view by clicking the small triangles at the top of the toolbox.

Mnemonic: Devil's Xylophone

Pressing D will load the default colors of black and white; the X key will toggle between colors.

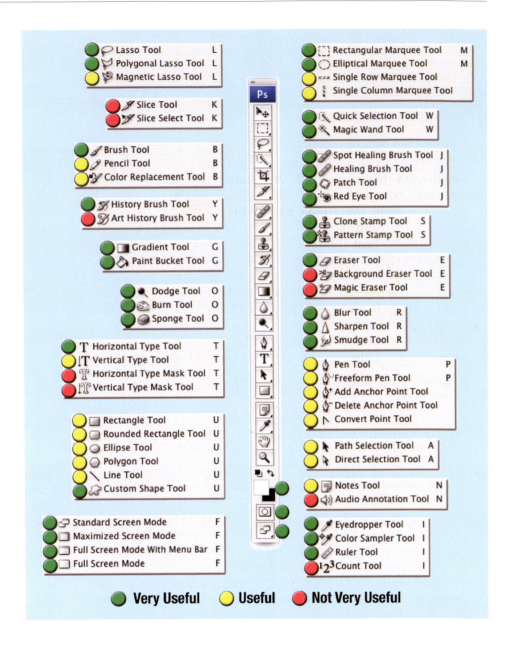

for resources manually or configure it to check monthly, weekly, or daily.

The remaining items will be used in very special circumstances. The Quick Mask mode is useful for creating advanced selections or masks. We'll dig deeper into masks and alpha channels in Chapter 4, "What About Transparency?" Next are the screen mode switches, which change how the workspace is presented.

Palette Popping

One of the biggest wastes of times frequently committed is "palette popping." Many advanced users open and close tools all day long—dragging windows all over the place, closing and opening the same windows over and over. Stop! There are many solutions to this problem.

Temporary banishment. Pressing the Tab key hides all of your tools. Press it again and they come back. Not good enough for you? Using *Shift* + *Tab*, you can hide everything except the Options bar and toolbox. This useful command is best combined with full-screen mode for a video workspace. Tap the *F* key to blank out all other images. Use ⌘+ *=* or *−* (*ctrl* + *=* or *−*) to zoom in and out of your image. Press the *F* key again to cycle and *Tab* again to go back to standard screen mode with menus and tools.

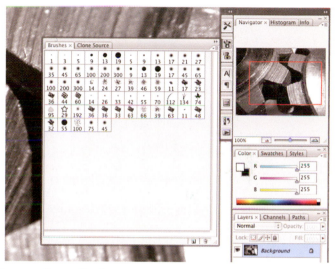

Sitting on a dock. Wish you could keep tools nearby in a virtual drawer? Photoshop 6 brought the welcome addition of the Options bar and its palette well. Photoshop CS3 has further evolved the concept into a dock. You can drag tool tabs to the well or dock, where they are docked as pop-out menus or palettes. Put useful but rarely used tools like the Brushes palette and Navigator here.

A workspace of your own. One of Photoshop's coolest features is workspaces. Like to work with different tools for different situations? Maybe you use the Channels and Brushes palette a lot when masking, but really wish Layer Styles and the Color Picker were there for text work. You can have any combo you want in one click with workspaces. Open the windows you need, and arrange them into the desired position. To save the current workspace layout, choose Window>Workspace> Save Workspace. Enter a unique name for the workspace, and click OK.

To activate a workspace, simply Choose Window>Workspace, and choose a workspace from the submenu. You update a workspace by resaving it with a new name. To delete a workspace, choose Window>Workspace>Delete Workspace. There is, unfortunately, no way to share workspaces with other users or machines, because they are tied to your preference files.

Workspaces Save Time

Workspaces (custom window arrangements) are familiar concepts in several video-editing applications. They can now be found in Photoshop (v7 or newer).

Startup Optimization

Font overload. Upon startup, Photoshop must examine all of the fonts that will be available for the type tools. Large quantities of fonts installed on your system mean long load times. This can cause Photoshop to take longer to start up. If you find the startup time for Photoshop to be too long, remove any unused fonts from your system (see your OS manual), or use a font management program such as Suitcase Fusion. Shareware fonts are often a source of instability as well, due to conflicting font IDs that may confuse your operating system.

Changing the Plug-Ins folder at launch time. By holding ⌘+*Shift* keys (*ctrl*+*Shift*) immediately after launch, the Additional Plug-Ins Folder dialog will appear. You can specify an additional folder from which Photoshop will load plug-ins. Many editors will carry a USB thumb drive with extra plug-ins (although this won't work with serialized plug-ins).

Resetting preferences at launch time. If you would like to reset all of your Photoshop preferences, simultaneously hold down the ⌘+⌥+*Shift* keys (*ctrl*+*alt*+*Shift*) when you launch Photoshop.

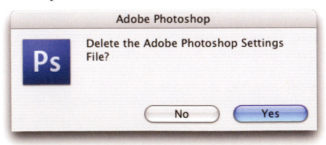

Don't Miss the DVD

Be sure to check out the many great materials on the DVD-ROM. You'll find goodies in every chapter's folder, plus free and trial software. Fully explore the disc for extra articles, tutorials, and training movies. You'll be amazed at how much good stuff is packed in there.

Free Tech Support

If you are a registered owner, you get 90-day tech support for new copies and 30 days for upgrade copies.

Professional Motion Control Photography with After Effects and Photoshop

Documentary-style motion control photography is becoming increasingly popular for use in all styles of video production. Why just show the pictures, static and full-screen? Most editors have traditionally had three options.

The first method involves sending the images to a motion control camera operator. This is an expensive process and must be adequately budgeted for both time and money. The second method involves setting up a camera and card stand, and then shooting the photos with a video camera. This method is prone to keystoning (due to the tilting to avoid light reflections) and does not allow for photo restoration or precise movement. The third method involves importing the photos into the edit system and enlarging (zooming) them. This method produces softening and had very limited results. Many plug-ins have recently been developed that work within edit systems that improve upon this technique, but there is still a better way.

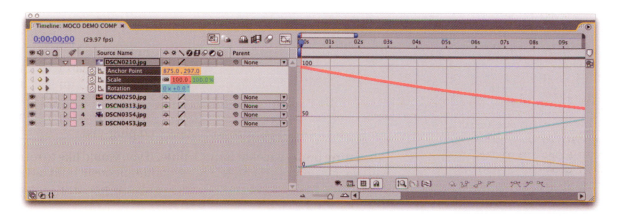

By combining Photoshop with Adobe After Effects, extremely high-quality motion control is possible. In fact, I have produced results that outperform those done on expensive motion control rigs. Everyone knows that Photoshop is the perfect tool for restoring damaged photos. When combined with Adobe After Effects, complex motion is possible.

You'll find Exercise 01 on the DVD-ROM.

PRO*file*: Johnathon Amayo

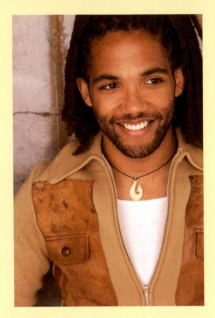

If you ever went to an Avid event during the break of the millennium, you likely met Johnathon M. K. Amayo. As ACSR Program Manager, Senior Instructor for both operational and technical and spokesmodel for Avid's Xpress Pro, Amayo frequently traveled to film festivals, training events and trade shows to demonstrate all fascists of the Avid Editing Software suite. Some even call him Mr. Xpress DV as he was picked to be a "poster" child for Avid's marketing campaign.

Amayo is an accomplished video professional as well. He served four years in the Air Force as Combat Camera. Amayo joined Avid shortly after, but continues to keep his editing feet wet to stay in touch with the craft. Currently Amayo Los Angeles is a workflow & effects specialist for the studios and independent production companies. He's also currently in Production on a new film.

"I work on several entertainment and independent projects in the Boston area. I've worked on 35 mm and 16 mm film projects, as well as some digital video features," said Amayo. "Recently, I've been doing a lot of DV editing."

Early in his professional career, Amayo decided to expand his editing skills. The first complementary program he decided to learn was Adobe Photoshop (version 2.5). This was a natural extension that let him better control the use of graphic and still images with his videos.

"Photoshop is the most complementary software programs for on editor using an Avid system or any other NLE. When you add After Effects, it becomes one of the best value programs. Any user can run them on almost any computer," said Amayo. "An experienced guy can take a thousand-dollar application and compete with million dollar graphic systems."

Amayo stressed the importance of editors branching out: "Learning Photoshop and After Effects can increase your value to a company," said Amayo. "We now have to work with DVD, the Web, and CD-ROMs. Editing is changing because we now have to wear so many hats."

Amayo stressed that experienced pros and even newcomers shouldn't let these demands overwhelm them. Powerful editing tools such as Xpress DV and graphic tools like Photoshop and After Effects are easy to access.

"We're expect to be a jack-of-all-trades and master-of-none. But that doesn't have to be. These programs are available to us early on and they are affordable."

Amayo has relied heavily on Photoshop's powerful tools for matte creation. "I seem to have a flair for creating mattes. I find it cleaner and easier to do it in Photoshop." He suggests cutting a logo or title up into several pieces and then animating it within Avid's timeline. "When I create a title or an effect, I'll often lay it down four or five times… I can then introduce moving fills and other effects."

Despite his personal comfort-level, Amayo said that improvements in Avid's support for Photoshop layers has let him do more and worry less about creating mattes and alpha channels. These improvements were made to make things easier for the editor. However, he still turns to Photoshop for titling effects.

"I really use it for advanced titles… especially since I can import layers into my Avid," said Amayo. "You get more control, and dynamic editing. You can really adjust things with greater control. When I was learning Avid, I decided that Photoshop was the most complementary tool. It's flexible and it's a quick, a very easy program to use. Even today I find it an essential tool when I advise facilities on which tools they should add to their story building suite."

For Film & DV Editors, Amayo says that Photoshop can be useful for fixing tough problems. "Healing and cloning can be very useful for cleaning up frames. It's slow, but a good alternative if you are working on a DV system."

Amayo is a firm believer that most editors need to expand their skill set.

"When you go to big places like LA, especially to a studio, you're likely expected to only know one application and be the best," said Amayo. "But not everybody is going to be able to work there. Most of us are at shops where we are expected to do it all."

2

PIXELS: TIME FOR TECH

When computer graphics are created, they are either raster or vector images. Photoshop supports both types of images, and it is common to mix the two in a single project. Newer versions of Photoshop contain the vector type, giving it the ability to be resized and edited within Photoshop and After Effects. While all graphics for video end up as raster images, a clear understanding of the two categories will help you build, modify, and import artwork.

Pixel by Any Other Name

The pixel is the building block upon which our industry is based. The term *pixel* is a fusion of the words *picture element*, and it is aptly named. The word was coined to describe the photographic elements of a television image. Back in 1969, writers for *Variety* magazine took pix (a 1932 abbreviation of pictures) and combined it with element to describe how TV signals came together. Earlier reports exist of Fred C. Billingsley coining the word at NASA's Jet Propulsion Laboratory in 1965. While the exact origins of the word may be disputed, the meaning is not. Use of the word pixel quickly caught on, first in the scientific communities in the 1970s and then the computer graphics industry in the mid-1980s.

The pixel is the smallest amount of space that exists in our creative universe. Pixels contain color, and these colors combine to form images. Bitmaps (also called raster images) are used for continuous tone or photorealistic images. If you continue to zoom in on an image, you can eventually see the pixel grid that forms the image.

Pixels Build Pictures

Picture elements, more commonly known as pixels, are the building blocks of the video industry. In Photoshop, you will edit pixels when working with your source photos and video frames.

To zoom:
- Use the Zoom tool.
- Press ⌘+= or − (ctrl+= or − on Windows).
- To fill the screen, press ⌘+0 (ctrl+0).
- To view at 100% magnification, press ⌘+⌥+0 (ctrl+alt+0).

Raster   Vector

Go Vector Logo, Go!

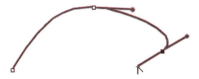

Always ask for the client logo as a vector file. It will give you greater flexibility when scaling. If you own Illustrator, splitting it up is easy.

Vector Type from Photoshop to After Effects

Recent versions of After Effects can convert Photoshop type to vector type. In After Effects choose Layer>Convert to Editable Text

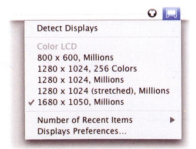

Raster images. When working with raster images, you edit pixels rather than shapes or objects directly. Proper selection techniques are important to get accurate results. Raster images are resolution-dependent in that they contain a specific number of pixels. Therefore, images will lose detail and appear jagged if they are scaled above 100% by a video software application. If you need to scale an object such as a logo or title within an edit or design session, bring it in at maximum screen size, and scale down rather than up. For achieving a documentary pan-and-zoom effect, a wide variety of plug-ins are available for most edit systems. The best solution, however, is to create the effect in Adobe After Effects (see Professional Motion Control "Photography" with After Effects and Photoshop on page 267).

Vector graphics. An understanding of vector graphics may seem out of place to many readers. Traditionally, artists turn to Adobe Illustrator to work with vector graphics. While it is still necessary to use Illustrator for complex vector editing, Adobe Photoshop now provides its own set of powerful vector tools.

Vector graphics are often used for corporate logos and print pieces. Vector graphics are resolution-independent because they are composed of lines and curves defined by mathematical objects called vectors. Vectors describe an image by its geometric characteristics or shapes. These vectors allow the file to be scaled to any size without losing detail or clarity. Adobe After Effects supports the use of vector graphics, and most motion graphic artists swear by vectors for achieving dramatic type effects involving scaling. Vector graphics are best used for shapes or logos, especially if scaling is involved.

Because video monitors represent images by displaying them as pixels along a grid, all vector graphics are rasterized at some point for use in video. Vectors still offer great flexibility, which makes them desirable during the initial design phase. They also are resolution-independent, an advantage if you ever need to take your work into a print environment.

Display Resolution

The quantity of pixels along the height and width of a raster image determines its screen (or display) size. Older computer monitors display 72 pixels per inch (ppi); newer monitors often display 96 ppi or higher. These display settings will often vary, ranging higher or lower, depending on your computer's video card. In contrast, video monitors are not variable. Your video format will use a specific-sized graphic; you cannot pack extra pixels in or change the dimensions of your audience's televisions. I'll go deeper into setting up pixel dimensions and pixel aspect ratio later in this chapter.

In order to get the maximum quality out of Photoshop, you must understand video's limitations. These limitations can be a hindrance, causing flicker on the screen if you improperly anti-alias fine details such as text or thin lines. They can also be a benefit. There are many affordable stock-photography collections available with low-resolution files. Additionally, filters and image-processing techniques are several times faster for video-sized images than print.

It is possible to view many more pixels on your computer at one time than will fit in a standard video frame. For example, a 15-inch monitor can be configured to display 800 pixels horizontally and 600 pixels vertically. An 800×600 image would appear to fill the screen. On a 21-inch monitor configured to the same display settings, the same image would appear to fill the screen, but each pixel would be significantly larger. Changing the monitor's settings, however, could allow more pixels to fit on the screen, leaving empty space around our 800×600 image. However, while most computer monitors support multiple resolutions, television sets generally do not.

Check the display size in Photoshop. You'll usually want to view images at 100%, so that you can make accurate decisions about the display quality of effects. If this is not possible, view in even increments of 50% or 25%, because computers are very good at dividing by two.

Image Resolution

The requirements of print differ greatly from those for video. It is necessary to work with a much higher quantity of pixels to produce satisfactory results when outputting to the printed page. On the flip side, most Web images are too small, as they have been optimized for fast download in a mosaic Web browser.

A common problem occurs when video professionals talk to their cousins in the print and Web worlds. Although all camps speak the same language, some unique terms are used that often result in confusion and extra work by both sides. The most common problem is resolution. Video makers may use the term pixels per inch (ppi); other industries use dots per inch (dpi) or lines per inch (lpi).

Lines Per Inch (lpi)

Talk to a print professional and you'll often hear the term lines per inch. This term derives from the traditional process where images with gradiated tones were screened for printing. This was done (traditionally) by laying film with dots over the image before the film was exposed. These days an imagesetter is used. A higher lpi means means smoother images.

Smart Objects Preserve Vectors

If you choose File>Place to add a vector object to your Photoshop file, it will come in as a Smart Object (Photoshop CS2 or later). This will embed the vector file and give you infinite scaling ability within Photoshop. We'll explore Smart Objects more in later chapters.

Display Size Does Matter!

Be sure to view your image at 100% to make accurate decisions. If your monitor is not large enough, then view in even increments of 50% or 25%.

Right Size Fast

If you have an object loaded on the clipboard, the New Document dialog will automatically size itself to match.

Output Method	Typical lpi
Screen printing	35–65 lpi
Laser printer (coated paper)	75–110 lpi
Newsprint	60–85 lpi
Offset printing (coated paper}	120–150 lpi
High-quality offset printing	150–300 lpi

Dots Per Inch (dpi)

A more common term is dots per inch (dpi), which refers to the number of dots that can fit into a one-inch by one-inch square area. Higher dpi generally means smoother images. Many printers in an average office setting can print 600 dpi or higher. This can lead to very professional-looking images. However, it is essential to remember that dots per inch is strictly a print term that refers only to a physical output. Dots per inch is not used when scanning or describing video graphics.

Video Graphics Have No dpi

There are no "dots per inch" (dpi) with video graphics. All that matters are the total pixels on screen.

Copyright: Krzysiekzpoczty/iStockphoto

Samples Per Inch (spi)

When using a scanner (flatbed or slide), the correct term is samples per inch. This term refers to the number of analog samples taken in order to convert the image into a digital file. A higher number of samples will increase the output quality of the digital file. However, too many samples can surpass the quality threshold for your output devices and simply be a waste of time and disk space. The samples per inch measurement is similar in theory to the sample rate of a digital audio file. The higher the number, the more accurate the sound.

Most scanners will say dpi in their packaging and documentation. What they meant to say is spi. Fortunately, the two numbers are a pretty clean exchange. Just be sure that you look at a scanner's optical resolution (versus interpolated) when shopping. A resolution of 600×600 pixels or greater will suffice for nearly all video work.

Pixels Per Inch (ppi)

The last measure of image resolution is pixels per inch. This measurement measures how many pixels fit on the screen. Because a video monitor is a fixed resolution, increasing the ppi will not improve quality. Rather, it will result in image detail being clipped or an overall softening as the pixels are resampled.

So What are Megapixels?

Start shopping for a digital still camera and you'll be bombarded with megapixels. If you listen to most salespeople, you'll be misled as to what megapixels really are and just how many are needed. You'll need to understand megapixels so you can make smart shooting decisions or instruct those that are acquiring images for your project. A megapixel is a unit of storage and describes the total number of pixels in an image.

In the strictest sense, a megapixel is one million pixels. This is a very common term used to describe just how many pixels a particular camera can capture with its sensors. For example, if a camera can capture pictures at 3872×2584, it is referred to having 10 megapixels (3872 × 2584 = 10,005,248). If you were to print that picture on paper at 300 ppi (pixels per inch), it would roughly be a 13" × 8.5" print.

How many megapixels do you need for video? It all depends on how the pixels are meant to be used. If you plan to do a large zoom or just reposition the photo, all 10 megapixels may be needed. On the other hand, a 1920×1080 HD video frame needs only a 2.1-megapixel camera to capture the minimum required pixels.

Looking for an easy-to-use megapixel calculator? I highly recommend http://web.forret.com/tools/megapixel.

Print Resolution

In print, using too low of a resolution results in pixelization—output with large, rough-looking pixels. Using too high a resolution image increases processing time and storage requirements and slows the output. Video and print pros have very different definitions of full size and high quality.

If you translate a 648×486 television screen into inches, it would be approximately 9×6.75 inches. At 72 ppi, the file size is approximately 900 kilobytes. If you asked a print professional for the same size image at high quality, you would likely get a file in the range of 4 to 60 megabytes. This is because print professionals often use resolutions of 150 to 600 ppi, depending upon output requirements.

Be sure to specify image resolution when working with outside artists and clients, or you will spend a lot of wasted time downsampling images. Print-ready images will quickly eat up your disk space and are difficult to transport electronically due to their large size. Filters and image adjustments take longer on large images, especially if you are used to video or Web work. The only advantage to this extra information is that you can have more control over cropping and scaling of the final photo. Unless I plan on doing dramatic moves on an image in After Effects, I request outside artists to provide me with images at 200 ppi for standard-definition video; this involves the least work for all parties.

Copyright: Jami Garrison/iStockphoto

Copyright: Guy Erwood/iStockphoto

Web Resolution

High-resolution images won't always be your problem, though. With the proliferation of image-rich Web sites, clients are often providing artwork directly from Web sites. While this is a convenient way to find things, it offers many problems. Web images are a low-resolution medium. While Photoshop builds Web and video images at 72 ppi by default, it is rare to find full-screen Web graphics, due to download times. Larger images tend to be sliced up as well, making it difficult to reformat them for video. The worst problem, however, is compression.

Web graphics generally employ three file types: GIF, JPEG, and PNG. These compression schemes discard information; especially color detail, to achieve smaller file size. The Graphics Interchange Format (GIF) is most commonly used to display indexed-color graphics. Indexed color supports only 256 colors and should never be used for video source material.

The Joint Photographic Experts Group (JPEG) format is extremely common. It can be found in Web pages and digital cameras. Most Web images are highly compressed and do not hold up well when reformatted for video. Digital cameras that use at least a 2.1-megapixel system and are set to high or fine quality can produce acceptable results. Be careful when working with JPEGs; they may be set to CMYK or grayscale color modes. It is necessary to convert these to RGB before using them in a video program, or unpredictable color changes may occur.

The least likely format you may encounter on the Web is PNG. The Portable Network Graphics (PNG) format can be used for lossless compression and for display of images on the World Wide Web. There are two varieties of PNG, 8-bit (PNG-8) and 24-bit (PNG-24). These two formats support RGB, indexed color, and grayscale modes, as well as interlacing. Of all the Web formats, the PNG-24 is most desirable (least awful) for video purposes. The file size of a PNG file is significantly larger than GIF or JPEG. This will give you more information to work with. PNG files are very uncommon because older Web browsers do not support them and the large file size deters many Web designers.

Avoid Web graphics at all costs. Both you and the client will be *very* disappointed with the results when using a Web-ready graphic. If clients insist that the Web-ready format is all that's available, dig deeper. Ask them for a business card. If their logo is on that card, then it must exist in a print-ready format (somewhere). Ask who designs the cards or how they get additional cards at work. After a phone call or two, you will have the appropriate .eps or .ai file.

Web Formats are Great...

 Web formats are great... for the Internet! Don't use JPEG, GIF, or PNG in your video projects. If you have to use a Web format, choose PNG-24. It is the most versatile of all the Web formats and even supports transparency.

Get Access to PNG-24

 To access the PNG-24 format, choose File> Save for Web. This great format can store transparency with no need to manually create an alpha channel. Check your NLE or compositing application to see if a PNG file will work.

Salvaging Web Images for Use in Video

One of the worst things to happen to graphic artists was the proliferation of Web pages for corporate clients and associations. Firms are moving virtually all of their assets on to the Internet and have placed such emphasis on their Web sites that they have abandoned or lost track of traditional assets. It used to be far easier to get a high-quality, "camera-ready" ad slick with logos on it. Annual reports or brochures could always be found and scanned as well.

These days you ask for a logo and you get a 200×200 pixel GIF from the client's Web site. These images should be avoided at all costs. No matter what your client says, the logo exists as a higher-quality file. If they have a business card, it exists. There are several approaches you can try before accepting Garbage In.

- Ask if there's an in-house Web department or printer. Call these people and ask for a better logo. While you're at it, ask for a style guide.
- Search the Web site for a press area. Many times high-quality logos are available for download to the media.
- Download an annual report or brochure as a PDF. Often times these are saved at 150 dpi or better (or even as vector files!). A PDF file can be opened and converted in Photoshop.
- Ask for the business card and scan it at as high a setting as you can. If you scanner has a de-screen filter, use it.

So how do you salvage these images? I have seen editors and art departments spend days recreating logos. In larger facilities, this ordeal is often repeated due to poor communication and archives. So always ask anyone remotely experienced in using a computer if they have ever done work for the client before. But if you must "salvage" a Web logo, remember this: Garbage In = Garbage Out. Vector programs as such as Adobe Illustrator—using its Live Trace feature—can help here, but it is very hard to pull something from a 50×50 pixel source. The results you get will be mediocre at best.

The fastest solution involves "up-rezzing" via the image size command (Image>Image size). Computers are good at duplication, so blow the logo up 200% and choose Nearest Neighbor as the Interpolation method. The resulting image is soft, but may pass quality control. Some adventurous souls attempt to rebuild the text by font matching. If you know the name of the font used, this is a fair approach. If you are hunting, you will need a huge font collection and chances are you will get close, but not exactly right. You do not want to be to blamed when the "logo police" arrive.

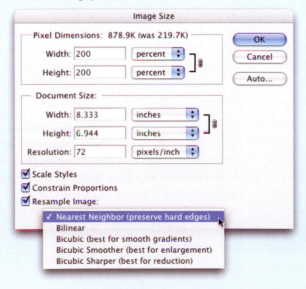

Explore Bit Depth

 If you'd like to examine the following three images, they are in the chapter's folder on the DVD-ROM. Be sure to try various adjustments from the Image menu.

Understanding Bit Depth

The last area that affects the quality of your image is bit depth (also known as pixel depth or color depth). The bit depth measures how much color is available for displaying or printing. Greater bit depths mean more information is available to describe the color (which leads to greater accuracy).

8-Bits/Channel

The most common bit depth is 8-bit. This mode has 256 possible values per color channel (2 to the eight power). This is the most common mode used by video editing applications (although some are starting to offer 10- and even 12-bit editing). For these higher-end systems you will want to build in 16-bit mode.

16-Bits/Channel

The 16-bit mode produces greater color fidelity (though file size tends to double.) Starting with Photoshop CS2, you can build layered files in 16-bit mode. Additionally, many motion graphics and 3D applications can work with 16-bit files. One downside is that not all filters and adjustments will work in 16-bit mode.

32-Bits/Channel

A 32-bit image is often referred to as a high dynamic range (or HDR) image. These images cannot be captured with a single exposure, but are created by merging multiple exposures of an image. Some 3D applications also work with HDR images (for example the Open EXR format from Industrial Light & Magic shows great promise for the special effects industry). Photoshop has limited support for 32-bit processing, but this is an expanding area you should keep an eye on.

Computer and Video Issues

Video traces its history to early pioneers such as John Logie Baird, who managed to record a recognizable human face on video in 1925. The first microcomputer appeared in 1960, developed by Digital Equipment, priced at a mere $120,000 (it did include a keyboard and mouse). These two technologies existed very independently of each other for many years. All computer pixels are square in their native format. Professional video applications often use pixels that are nonsquare.

The National Television Standards Committee, known as the NTSC, has set the standard that television fits to the 4×3 aspect ratio. This is often interpreted by video boards as an image that is 648×486 pixels. Those countries that use the PAL format use boards that work with images that measure 768×576 square pixels. If designing for square systems, it is easy because no conversions are necessary.

Of course, if you offer a standard, it will be broken. In an effort to pack more pixels and increase resolution, the ITU-R BT 601 video standard was developed. It is often called "D1" (after the D1 format invented by Sony in 1986 that was the first component digital format available). In NTSC, the native "board" size of a D1 frame is 720×486 nonsquare pixels. The PAL format uses 720×576 nonsquare pixels.

This format has evolved into the Digital Video (DV) standard, which is employed in the consumer DV format as well as DVCAM and DVCPRO tape and DVD authoring. The native size for DV frames is 720×480 nonsquare pixels for NTSC (six less than the D1 format). The PAL DV format is identical to the standard PAL format and remains unchanged at 720×576 nonsquare pixels. These pixels are played back on analog televisions, which must display them as square pixels at the 4×3 aspect ratio.

Houston, we have a problem.

Discussing pixel aspect ratio is about as much fun as going to a great art museum and spending all your time discussing the doorknobs. Yes, they too are important, but hardly interesting. Please bear with me as I try to resolve this dilemma in a clear and orderly fashion. I will simplify as much as possible without neglecting essential intricacies.

Video Standards

NTSC: The National Television Standards Committee developed the North American broadcast standard in 1953. The group is jokingly referred to as "Never Twice the Same Color."

PAL: Developed in the early 1960s, the Phase Alternate Line format is the standard for most of Europe. The group is sometimes called "Peace At Last."

Go Deeper into Video Pixels

Looking for a more scientific (and mathematical) version? The *Quick Guide to Digital Video Resolution and Aspect Ratio Conversions* takes a much deeper look at the issues. You can find it at http://lipas.uwasa.fi/~f76998/video/conversion/. Be warned though; while it may be quick, it's not easy.

Design versus Production

You will most often have two distinct versions of your Photoshop files; one for design and one for production. Your design files include all of your layers, vector type, blend modes, and layer effects. These are meant to be editable in the future so you can make client changes.

Production files on the other hand are meant to be imported into your NLE/Compositing Application/DVD authoring environment. These often contain flattened layers and must have their layer effects merged as well. Production files are often saved into a portable (easy to move across applications and platforms) format such as PICT or TARGA. By employing the two-format method, you will ensure maximum flexibility *and* compatibility.

Pixel Aspect Ratio

Remember, video is displayed on standard televisions at a 4×3 aspect ratio. Even video that has a different native size must be eventually converted. Natively, an NTSCD1/DV pixel is taller than it is wide, approximately 0.9 to 1. PAL pixels on the other hand are wider than tall, 1.07 to 1.

Many video edit systems, as well as Adobe After Effects, can work with square pixel images, ensuring that they display correctly throughout the editing stage. These video applications must resize square pixel graphics to conform to digital video's nonsquare pixel shape. To avoid this problem, however, many designers choose to manually stretch or interpret their images within Photoshop, which offers powerful interpolation tools that produce exceptional scaling. Before going any further, let me say three things:

- First, there are many conflicting opinions on what size to build graphics and what application to use when resizing them. These opinions are all based on combinations of facts and circumstances, so make sure you understand both before choosing a method.
- Second, *read the manual* that shipped with your editing software because different companies have their own procedures for each editing system. I will attempt to address the most common workflows, but it is a good idea to keep up with changes in your video software.
- Third, if using Photoshop CS or later, you will generally choose to build your graphics with the nonsquare pixel presets. Notable exceptions will be some flavors of HD or if building graphics for use in After Effects 3D space.

Custom Pixel Aspect Ratio...
Delete Pixel Aspect Ratio...
Reset Pixel Aspect Ratios...

Square
D1/DV NTSC (0.9)
D4/D16 Standard (0.95)
✓ D1/DV PAL (1.066)
D1/DV NTSC Widescreen (1.2)
HDV Anamorphic (1.333)
D1/DV PAL Widescreen (1.422)
D4/D16 Anamorphic (1.9)
Anamorphic 2:1 (2)

A standard square and NTSC D1 pixel.

With those three points made, I will present your options for building graphics that will work for most users on most systems.

Step 1: Determine the native size of your video frame

Frame size can be found in your NLE's manual, or you can export out a single frame.

- If you are working with a traditional (switcher-based) analog system, the frame is likely equates to 648×486 for NTSC or 768 × 576 for PAL (using square pixels).
- Most hardware-dependent nonlinear systems that are capturing sources such as Beta SP use the ITU-R BT 601 format (often referred to as D1). The native size is 720×486 nonsquare pixel image for NTSC or 720×576 nonsquare pixel image for PAL.
- In the last few years, many DV solutions have appeared, including DVCPRO and DVCAM. These use a 720×480 nonsquare pixel image for NTSC and 720×576 nonsquare pixel image for PAL.
- HD frame sizes vary greatly and are impacted by both format 720p versus 1080i as well as acquisition formats such as DVCPRO HD and HDV.

The following table sheds some light on the various native sizes you'll encounter.

Video #2 Working with Document Presets

 See the Working with Document Presets video tutorial on the DVD-ROM.

Standard Definition

Format	NTSC Native Size	PAL Native Size
D1	720×486	720×576
DV	720×480	720×576

High Definition

Format	Native Size
HD 720p	1280×720
HD1080i	1920×1080
HDV 1080i	1440×1080
DVCPRO HD 720p	960×720
DVCPRO HD 1080i	1280×1080

(Left) Original image viewed viewed in NTSC D1 editing system such as Avid Media Composer. (Middle) Same image viewed in Photoshop with NTSC standard (with no Pixel Aspect correction). (Right) Same image viewed in Photoshop with PAL standard (with no Pixel Aspect correction).

Step 2: Design your graphics in Photoshop

Depending on your version of Photoshop, your technique will vary. Starting with Photoshop CS, Adobe has offered the monumental change of nonsquare pixel support. Despite this support, not everyone will choose to use nonsquare pixels. Reasons vary but include tradition, resistance to change, or established workflows.

Method #1: Using Photoshop's Nonsquare Pixels

Since Photoshop CS, Adobe supports nonsquare pixels. . . . Life is good!

- Create all new documents using the built-in templates that match your edit system. This can be found in the New Image dialog box File>New or by pressing ⌘+N (ctrl+N). The list of presets has continued to grow and currently stands at 15 for Photoshop CS3.

- If working with square pixel images (such as those from scanners, stock photo collections, or digital cameras) be sure to correctly interpret the pixels. This can be done in three ways:
  - Drag the square pixel images into a nonsquare document. Photoshop will convert the square pixels to match your current document's settings.
  - Open an image and select it by choosing Select>All then press ⌘+C (ctrl+C) to copy it to your clipboard. Paste the square pixel images into a nonsquare document by pressing ⌘+V (ctrl+V).
  - Place square pixel images into a nonsquare document by choosing File>Place. The image will be added as a Smart Object, which can be scaled with greater flexibility.
- If you are working with a frame grab or exported frame from a video editing application that uses nonsquare pixels, you will likely need to identify it to Photoshop. After opening the image, choose Image>Pixel Aspect Ratio and select the right preset for your country and screen shape.

Document Checkup

You can quickly find out the details of a document by ⌥+clicking (alt+click) on the Document Info bar.

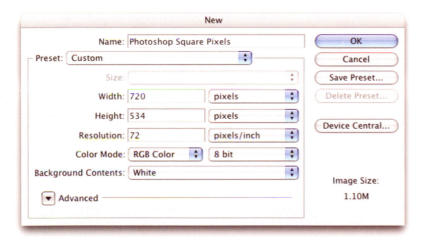

Method #2: Using Photoshop 7 (or Earlier)/Square Pixel Method

If you are designing your graphics in Photoshop 7 (or earlier), you are using square pixels. When a design is finished, you then need to resize your graphic for video usage and force the pixel aspect ratio to change.

There are two major camps: those who recommend stretching horizontally and those who prefer vertically. In the spirit of *The Sneetches* by Dr. Seuss, I'll call them the 'Zontals and the Verts.

The 'Zontals argue that it is best to maintain the same number of scan lines throughout. This is usually done by using an image size such as 648×486 for NTSC D1. This method helps maintain fine details, such as text, by not compressing them. Using this approach, the final image is stretched horizontally to 720×486

No Two Experts Agree

Every edit system and manufacturer has unique requirements. Be sure to see Appendix C for specific suggestions for leading editing and motion graphics applications.

(Image>Image Size, Constrain Proportions unchecked) to fill the video screen. Eventually this image will be squeezed back when playing back on televisions.

The Verts counter that it is always better to shrink raster images than to blow them up. For example, by employing a 720×540 image in Photoshop, the files can be scaled down (as opposed to up). Before saving the file out for video editing, the file must be resized (Image>Image Size, Constrain Proportions unchecked). The 720×540 file is squeezed vertically to 720×486. This vertical stretch will be counteracted by the horizontal stretch when the image is transferred to video.

Square Pixel Graphic Sizes for Standard Definition

Format	4×3 Aspect Ratio (Square Pixels)	16×9 Aspect Ratio (Square Pixels)	Native Size Nonsquare Pixel
NTSC D1	648×486 or 720×540	864×486	720×486
PAL D1	768×576 or 720×540	1024×576	720×576
NTSC DV	648×480 or 720×534	864×480	720×480
PAL DV	768×576 or 720×540	1024×576	720×576

* You will see varying numbers depending on which manufacturer's documentation you look at. For example, Apple recommends for NTSC D1 Widescreen 853 × 486 while Adobe recommends 864 × 486. The differences are very minor (approximately 1%) and will not be visible to the naked eye.

There are strengths to both the Vertical and Horizontal arguments if you need to design with square pixels. Because DV is having such an impact, I recommend designing at 720×540, using a 4×3 aspect ratio if you're stuck in an older version of Photoshop. This size also works for PAL graphics as well. After resizing to the Native Nonsquare size you just need to crop for DV output. Since DV lacks six lines of information (480 versus 486).

Interlaced Displays

Interlacing video is another leftover technology meant to serve as a temporary fix. When television was invented, it was decided that 30 frames per second generated smooth motion. However, it took 60 images per second to reduce flicker. The problem is that the broadcast signal could not hold that much information without significant softening, and the slow speed of phosphors in the tube produced banding.

With NTSC video, the image updates 60 times per second. These fields reduce image flickering by refreshing every other line. To clean up an exported video frame, you will likely need the De-Interlace filter.

In order to maintain a relatively crisp picture, the solution of interlacing was decided upon by the first National Television Standards Committee in 1940. By showing half an image 60 times per second, both goals could be met. The electron beam would scan across the tube, painting every other line. It would then return to the top and paint the remaining lines. These alternating lines are often identified by field dominance, and are referred to as upper (or odd field first) or lower (or even field first). This solution solved the problem between bandwidth, flicker, and smooth motion.

It's important to note that only analog televisions are interlaced. If your video is intended for traditional output, you need to keep this in mind. Standard analog televisions display interlaced video, but newer digital televisions may show progressive scan (or non-interlaced). If you are designing for Web or CD output, you will work with non-interlaced video. Interlacing is not a big issue when you start your graphic in Photoshop, but becomes very important when importing video freeze frames or working in Adobe After Effects. In Photoshop it is important to avoid lines thinner than 3 pixels, or you will definitely introduce flicker to the image. Be sure to choose an anti-aliasing method for fine details such as text as well.

If you import a freeze frame from a source with fast motion, you will likely have visible fields (areas where the two frames of video mixed and a jagged result appears). If this happens, you can choose to run the De-Interlace filter (Filter>Video>De-Interlace). You will have the choice of keeping the odd or even field, as well as creating the replacement through duplication or interpolation. This step is especially important for broadcast designers who are working with freeze frames. If your video contains movement (and you didn't remove interlacing during export from the NLE), you will definitely see the need for this filter. Many lower-cost digital cameras will show a similar problem because they use a similar, image-capture device. It is a good idea to run this filter on video freeze frames every time if the work is to be done in Photoshop.

When animating your graphics in After Effects, interlacing provides smoother movement between frames. The render times are longer, but the quality is worth it. You need to do nothing different inside of Photoshop; just make sure to turn on **Field Rendering** in After Effects' render settings. In fact, make it part of your presets in After Effects by modifying your output module settings.

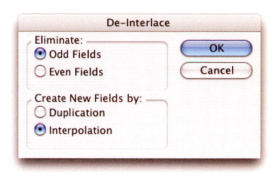

Choose to create new fields by interpolation; field elimination is a subjective choice.

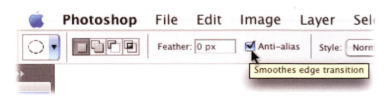

Anti-aliasing

Did you ever play with Lego building blocks as a child? Perhaps you noticed how hard it was to build an arch or a curve. The best you could achieve still had noticeable stair stepping. Guess what, pixels are just like those building blocks. Curved or diagonal lines will not look good at low resolutions, and you must soften the edge.

By choosing to use an anti-aliasing method, Photoshop will generate smoother results—especially when using selection tools (such as the magic wand or lasso tools) or vector-based type. Anti-aliasing works by softening the color transition between edge pixels.

Since only the edge pixels are changed, you lose no detail in the image itself. Anti-aliasing is a useful option for creating text, making selections for filters, or copying and pasting. It will be a recurrent topic throughout this book. You can adjust the anti-aliasing for many tools directly in the Options bar. You must apply this option before a selection is made.

HSB Sliders

Many editors choose to look at HSB sliders (hue, saturation, and brightness). This color model is very compatible with RGB and allows you to examine color information in a more videolike manner.

RGB versus Y, R-Y, B-Y Color

As if the nonsquare pixels, aspect ratios, interlacing, and anti-aliasing weren't enough, let me present our next problem. Photoshop works in the RGB color space. Each pixel you see on your monitor is comprised of light being emitted by a red, a green, and a blue phosphor placed closely together. Our eyes perceive that light as a single-colored dot, or pixel. These red, green, and blue components are referred to as channels. More on channels and channel operations in later chapters.

So what's the problem? Televisions use the same red, green, and blue phosphors, right? Not exactly. Television signals are not transmitted or stored in RGB due to our final leftover problem. Initially, television was black and white. These images were actually a grayscale signal consisting of only one channel that contained the brightness information (known as *luminance or luma*). In an effort to keep consumers happy, color television was made backwards compatible. An RGB broadcast would not work on a black-and-white television, so broadcasters chose (and still use) the Y, R-Y, B-Y color space. The Y is the luminance information, while the two Cs represented the color components (hue and saturation). These three signals would combine to form the composited pixels.

Apple's Final Cut Pro system can warn you when your pixels are not broadcast-safe. Go back to Photoshop and fix the original photo when this happens. Otherwise, you have additional rendering.

How does this affect you? Don't worry too much about the engineering side, but realize that colors will look different on a television screen than they do on a computer monitor. The color shift is minor, but present. There is no setting in Photoshop to correct this. The best solution is to have an NTSC or PAL video monitor connected to your system. If a television monitor is not an option, periodically test your graphics by importing them into your NLE, then outputting to tape or a video monitor.

RGB versus 601 Mapping

Photoshop and video handle luminance values differently. When working in Photoshop, black is an absolute black and white is an absolute white. Photoshop assigns a value of 0 to black and a value of 255 to white. There is no allowance for anything beyond this range. This process is referred to as computer graphics or RGB mapping. Adobe Photoshop and After Effects both work with RGB mapping.

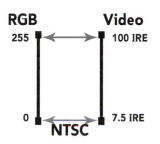
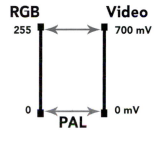

RGB mapping.

RGB mapping assumes that video black (NTSC 7.5 IRE, PAL 0 mV) is assigned a value of 0, and video white (NTSC 100 IRE, PAL 700 mV) a value of 255. If you import or export video from your edit system as RGB, signals above or below this range will be clipped.

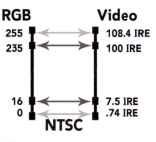

601 mapping.

The ITU-R BT.601 digital video standard (commonly referred to as 601 mapping) does not handle black and white as absolutes. It is allowable to go above "white" and below "black." One reason for this is super-black, which places a darker black in areas that are meant to be luma keyed. Many hardware-based switchers will use a luma key, instead of tying up two channels of a still store to use the fill and alpha matte. This luma key will allow for a real-time downstream key during mobile- and studio-based video production. Video cameras also allow a videographer to shoot beyond 100 IRE, giving the user some overshoot in the captured signal, which can be corrected during editing or playback.

601 mapping specifies that video black (NTSC 7.5 IRE, PAL 0 mV) is assigned a value of 16, and video white (NTSC 100 IRE, PAL 700 mV) a value of 235. This allows for reasonable footroom and headroom in the signal.

When importing or exporting your frames, it is important to use a consistent color mapping method. Most digital nonlinear editing systems now handle RGB levels correctly without any conversion on your part. The default presets will correctly map 100 on the RGB scale to 100 IRE. Each manufacturer calls things by a slightly different name (for example on an Avid you would import with RGB levels, on Final Cut Pro you would use the default setting to process Maximum White as White option). Be sure to see your NLE owner's manual for proper details.

If you are working with 601 levels (such as for an analog video switcher), I suggest you label the files as such. Just add 601 to the file name of graphics prepared with 601 compliant levels. For more on broadcast-safe color, see Chapter 9, "Color Correction: How to Get It Right."

"Print-Worthy" Frame Grabs

One of the most common requests I hear is the desire to take frame grabs from video and format them for use in print. Unfortunately, the mediums just don't mix very well. Remember, in order to capture between 24 to 30 frames per second, a small image is grabbed. Depending on your format, you end up with around 640×480 square pixels of information. If you condense these pixels to a print resolution of say 300 ppi, you get a print size of about 2×1.5 inches—slightly larger than a postage stamp, but not very useful for most printing jobs.

In Photoshop, we can "up-rez" an image through the Image Size command (Image>Image Size). Since this information does not currently exist, the computer will attempt to interpolate the information. I recommend that you switch pixel dimensions to percent, and then up-rez exactly 200% using the nearest neighbor interpolation method. Are the results great? No. But they are acceptable for some uses. You should consider taking the image to a service bureau and getting it outputted on a dye-sublimation printer, which produces photolike output from smaller resolution files.

An excellent Photoshop plug-in called Genuine Fractals uses advanced processing to generate high-quality files from low-quality sources. You can find out more information at http://www.ononesoftware.com.

Superblack (aka, Zero Black)

 A pure luma value of 0 IRE, which falls below the legal limit of 7.5 IRE for NTSC broadcasting. It is often used for luma-keying, a process of transparency generation that would not tie up a second channel of a switcher (for the matte) in order to perform a key.

Luminance and Saturation

Color choice has two issues, broadcast-safe and good taste. Many excellent books are available to assist you with color choice. The principles of a color wheel and selecting harmonious colors are worth your time to study. To get you started, I've included a demo of Color Theory, a Photoshop plug-in, on the disc. Color Theory helps you select color combinations that look good on video. Use this as a starting point to selecting good colors.

Unfortunately, video is a limited medium with a limited color palette. You need to learn which colors look good on video and, even more importantly, which colors look good on DVDs played back on $39 players. It is a good idea to test your graphics often on a vectorscope and waveform monitor, especially for your first few years of working in Photoshop. For more on testing graphics, see Chapter 13, "The Road to the NLE."

To make things simpler, here's a crash course in building your own "big box of crayons." Here are a few color rules to keep in mind:

- Certain colors do not look good on video. Reds have a tendency to bleed on screen; light yellows look like a dog used your TV as a fire hydrant.

Without proper contrast, details may be difficult for your audience to perceive. Combinations such as red and green do not offer sufficient contrast. To test your graphic, use a Saturation Adjustment Layer to desaturate your composition.

- Oversaturated colors will cause problems. Consumer televisions ship with the saturation and red tones turned up too high. You can't tell the customers that they're wrong (even if their TVs are), so turn down the saturation on bright colors. Muted colors will become more vibrant once they make it out to televisions.

- Avoid extremely dark colors. On video, there is very little difference between indigo, charcoal, and slate. Dark tones tend to gravitate towards black in the viewer's eyes.

- Maintain proper contrast. Some viewers will view your work on black-and-white sets; others may be color-blind. Even those with perfect eyes will have a hard time seeing a difference in grayscale contrast between certain color combinations such as blue and purple or red and green. Print your graphics out in grayscale, tape them on the wall, and stand back 15 feet. Can you read it clearly?

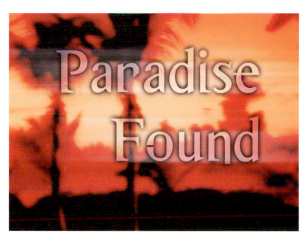

A gradient map is identical to After Effects' Colorama filter. Both provide a great way to map new colors to an image and give it identity.

- Avoid "pure" white. It will bloom on screen, making it difficult to read. Use off-white, especially for text. Also stroke the text with a contrasting color. For more on making readable text, see Chapter 5, "Some Words on Words, Logos, and Symbols."

- Not all graphics need to be full chroma. Using one color—for example, a base blue—with multiple shades, with darker and lighter accents, often looks very good. Duotone effects, where a grayscale image has a new color mapped to it, often look good as well.

- When in doubt, use the NTSC Colors filter (Filter>Video> NTSC Colors) to check your work. But do not rely on the NTSC color filter to fix problems as it produces visible banding. See Chapter 9, "Color Correction: How to Get It Right" for more information.

"Whiter than White"

 Cameras have extra headroom in capturing luminance. These values beyond broadcast white may need to be adjusted in the edit environment to bring the video signal in compliance with broadcast standards.

Online Color Wheel

If you need to try out different color combinations, be sure to try Kuler from Adobe labs (kuler.adobe.com). This flash-based application lets you browse a wide variety of designer created color schemes as well as create your own. It supports all the major rules from Analogous to Shades. The controls are beautifully designed and the entire application really inspires creativity. In order to access it, you will need a live connection to the Internet.

Working with Document Presets

Depending on which version of Photoshop you have, there are presets to use for standard canvas sizes. The newer your version of Photoshop, the more accurate and complete your choices are.

Photoshop CS3's Presets

Photoshop CS3 refines the document-preset system. When you choose the create a new document (File>New. . .) you are presented with a similar window to past versions. However, you now must specify a category in the Preset List (in this case Film & Video). Photoshop then offers 10 standard-definition presets, 5 high-definition presets, and 4 film resolution presets.

These templates include nonsquare pixel support, as well as safe-title overlays. By default they are set to the proper RGB color mode and to the more widely accepted 8 Bits/Channel mode. You can of course change to 16 Bits/Channel mode before clicking OK.

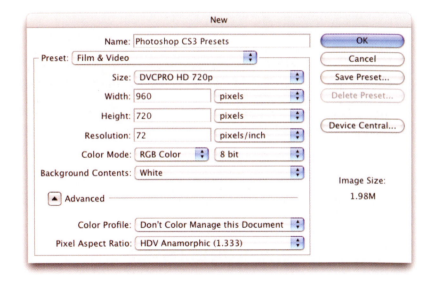

Photoshop CS and CS2's Presets

Video presets with support for nonsquare pixels launched with Photoshop CS. Adobe initially offered 9 presets for both standard and high-definition video. With Photoshop CS2, Adobe expanded support for HD documents and brought the total of presets to 10. These presets can be picked from a dropdown menu when you create a new document ⌘+N (ctrl+N).

You can access templates NTSC and PAL systems, Standard or Widescreen, and 601, DV/DVD, or HDTV. These templates were a well deserved addition to Photoshop (especially since it started its life as a tool for touching up video and film frames).

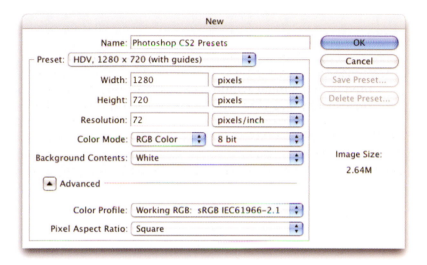

Photoshop 7's Presets

In an effort to make life easier, Photoshop 7 introduced preset document sizes. These can be picked from a dropdown menu when you create a new document ⌘+N (ctrl+N). You have the choice between NTSC and PAL sizes, Standard or Widescreen, and 601, DV/DVD, or HDTV. These presets are useful, but they have a few flaws.

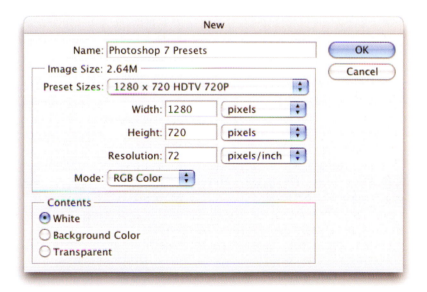

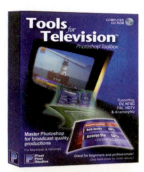

Photoshop Toolbox is a CD with actions, tutorials, royalty-free graphics, and tutorials that teach and assist Photoshop users in designing graphics for video. Tools for Television PRO is a stand-alone application that adds a video-specific palette to Photoshop that provides productivity tools such as template creation, automatic alpha channel creation, frame grabbing from live video, and automated creation of titles and other video-related graphics. Look for a sample of the actions and a demo of both (as well as a special upgrade offer) on this book's DVD-ROM.

First, always check your Image menu. Photoshop presents you with five choices; RGB is the correct one. The second problem: no title- or action-safe guidelines. Action-safe shows the portion of the frame that should show on all TVs. Title-safe is the area in which titles should be created to minimize any text crowding at the edges. If you want to manually add these, the safe-action area is 10% of the original image, and the title-safe area is 20% of the original frame size.

Step 1. Create a new video-sized document.

Step 2. Turn on rulers by pressing ⌘+R (ctrl+R).

Step 3. Right-click on the rulers and change the units to Percent.

Step 4. Add eight guides total—four horizontal and four vertical. Add them at 5%, 10%, 90%, and 95%.

If you are using Photoshop 7 (or earlier) and don't want to create your own safe-title document, then I recommend the Tools for Television Photoshop Toolbox (http://www.toolsfortelevision.com). This solution provides actions for creating safe-title documents (and many other cool things as well). The entire sets add up to only 704 kilobytes, far smaller than even a single template graphic. They work extremely well and are very accurate. You can find a demo for Tools for Television (as well as a discount offer) on the disc.

Advice When Scanning

A common way to get images into Photoshop involves using a scanner. There are scanners for traditional photos as well as specialized scanners or adapters for slides and negatives. The good news is that scanners are almost as common as inkjet printers and the prices have fallen drastically. A video pro can get a perfectly acceptable USB-powered scanner that is cross-platform for $100. Sure, you can spend more and get more, but chances are you scan only a few items per project. Here are a few tips to keep in mind about scanning images.

- Before scanning an image, install the software needed by your scanner provided by the manufacturer.
- The most important thing to remember when scanning is to be consistent. In a multiuser environment, this means posting the scanning guidelines on the scanner lid. A little

consistency goes a long way in speeding up workflow.

- Ensure that the scanner is lying flat, or you may get misregistered scans.

- Use a gentle glass cleaner whenever smudges appear. Spray the cleaner on the soft cloth, and then wipe the scanner bed down.

- Make sure your photos are clean before scanning. Never write on the back of photos; instead write on a Post-It note and then adhere it to the back.

- Align your photos on the scanner. Use the edges to help you maintain parallel edges on your photos. If you get crooked photos, use the automation command File>Automate>Crop and Straighten Photos.

- If your scanner allows you, set the white and black points before scanning. Think of this as a white and black balance that you would do with a video camera. This will produce the best tonal range. You can then use Photoshop's color correction tools to adjust the white and black points as well as make additional color changes.

- If you are scanning in previously printed items such as newspapers, magazines, books, or inkjet prints, you will likely get a moiré pattern. This noise is caused when Photoshop scans the small spaces between the previously printed dots. Most scanners have a de-screen filter in their software. If available, use it when scanning previously printed items. If this is not available, run the Median filter at a low value (Filter>Noise>Median).

- If you are scanning three-dimensional objects, place a piece of clear glass or plastic on top of your scanner's tray to protect it from scratches. You can also remove the scanner's lid and place a shadow box or black cloth on top of large objects.

- Scan at the quality you need. For video, scan so you have approximately 4000 by 3000 pixels. This is generally enough pixel information so you can zoom in for corrections. This will also allow you to crop at a later time, or perform motion control in After Effects or your nonlinear editing system. Remember, you can go down, but you can't go up.

- Save to uncompressed formats such as TIFF, PICT, or Targa for maximum compatibility and disk space usage. The PSD format is great for layered files, but is not as efficient for single layered files. Always use the appropriate file extension for your file type.

- Routinely check your manufacturer's Web site for new drivers. This software improves upon how well your scanner interfaces with Photoshop. The updates are generally free.

- If your scanner malfunctions, power down your system, and check your cable connections. When satisfied, power up the scanner first and restart your computer. If the problem is not fixed, check for new drivers.

Working with Digital Cameras

Digital cameras are generally more expensive than their analog companions. Remember though that you can get by with a camera resolution as low as a 2.1 megapixels. The convenience offered by a digital camera might just help you make a deadline. The elimination (and cost) of developing and scanning makes these a viable choice for video pros. I encourage you to add a digital still camera to your video production equipment; it will come in handy both in the field and back in the office.

Using Raw Files

If you are in the market for very high quality, take a look at cameras that support raw file formats. When digital cameras first launched, manufacturers settled upon JPEG files as a compromise. Storage options were very expensive and JPEGS are very small files. These days though, JPEG is being replaced by raw files.

Newer digital cameras (usually pro models) offer newer formats that capture the raw image data. These new formats offer several benefits over shooting JPEG. Most raw files have a depth of 12 Bits/Channel instead of the 8 used by JPEG. This higher rate allows for a greater tonal range. This gives you better exposure for shadows and highlights.

Camera raw files can be two to six times larger than JPEG files. This extra data is used to hold more image data. This can reduce, or even eliminate, compression artifacts. However, that extra space can take longer for the files to write to the memory card. If you aren't currently acquiring images using a raw file format, I highly encourage you to switch.

Raw Takes More Space

Camera raw files can be two to six times larger than JPEG files; they also require additional processing with the Adobe Camera Raw interface. For more on the Camera Raw.

Importing Digital Photos

There are two major ways of acquiring images from a digital camera. The first involves plugging the camera in with a USB cable. Usually this cable is included with a camera, but a spare is easy to come by at most computer stores. The advantage of this method is that there is no need to purchase additional hardware. The primary disadvantages of this method are that it ties up the camera. It is also easy to damage the delicate ports on the camera by frequently plugging the cable in.

You can purchase stand-alone memory card readers that can read one or multiple formats. Some allow you to read only, which is fine for copying files. Others allow you to read and write, which is helpful for erasing the memory card when you are done copying. A wide variety of manufacturers sell USB card readers priced between $25 to $60; check the packaging for compatibility. Laptop users with a PC slot can purchase an effective card adapter for around $25 for most formats.

Managing Digital Photos

As your digital library continues to grow (and grow) you will need to turn to a digital asset management solution. Depending upon your budget and the volume of photos you have, take a closer look at the following solutions:

- **Adobe Lightroom:** This catalog and imaging solution is provided for both Macs and PCs. It is targeted to towards imaging professionals.

Video #3   An Overview of the Camera Raw Interface

To see the Adobe Camera Raw interface in action, be sure to check out the book's DVD-ROM for a video tutorial.

A Better Bicubic

Newer versions of Photoshop offer two additional versions of Bicubic Sharpening. You can choose Bicubic Sharper for better results when shrinking an image. If you are going to attempt to up-res an image, then be sure to choose Bicubic Smoother.

- **Adobe Photoshop Album:** This catalog solution is targeted towards less savvy or budget-conscious users.
- **Apple Aperture:** This cataloging application is designed to harness the power of modern Macintosh computers. It offers several flexible options for managing and processing digital photos.
- **Apple iPhoto:** This solution works well for the Mac (and it's bundled with new machines as part of the iLife suite). You can also modify iPhoto's preferences so that double-clicking a photo opens it in Photoshop.

Resizing Commands

If you have an existing image, chances are great that it's not sized correctly for video. You will need to take in account pixel aspect ratio as well as canvas size. To change the size of an image, you can use the Image Size or Canvas Size menu commands or use the Crop tool for the adjustment. These three choices can be used individually or in combination to achieve the desired results.

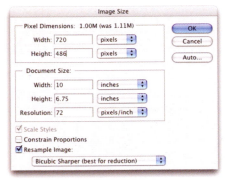

Image Size Command

The Image Size command (Image>Image Size...) lets you permanently reassign the total pixel count, as well as resolution, for a particular image. It is critical to make sure the Resample Image box is checked; otherwise you will not be able to change the document size. It is best to use bicubic interpolation for resizing most images.

Leave the Constrain Proportions box checked, or you will introduce additional squeezing. You are concerned with the pixel dimensions, so look at the total pixel count in the top boxes. Many editors choose to specify the resolution as 72 pixels per inch, although this is not necessary.

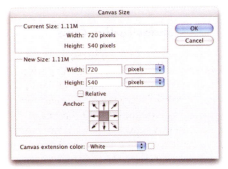

Canvas Size Command

The canvas size is your work area. Canvas size adjustments are a way to crop or extend the canvas of the work area. When you first launch the Canvas Size command, you are likely to see measurements in inches. The key is to change the units of measurement to pixels. You can temporarily change the units of measurement to pixels (with the drop-down lists) or permanently change your units of measure in Units and Rulers in the Preferences area (see Chapter 1).

Once you are measuring in pixels, type in the desired size and specify an anchor point. The anchor point tells Photoshop whether you want to keep the image centered or expand/crop from a particular edge. Photoshop will either contract or expand based upon the input values. It is possible to extend the border of an image, particularly on a source with portrait aspect ratio. In this case, the empty space surrounding the image would be filled by the background color.

Pixels are All that Matters

Pay close attention to the pixel dimensions when sizing an image. The document size does not matter for video purposes.

Crop Tool

The Crop tool is the fastest way to size an image for video. Cropping is a way to remove parts of an image permanently in order to create a focal point. Additionally you can use the Crop tool to resize an image.

You can perform a crop two ways. The first is to make a selection with one of the selection tools (such as the Rectangular Marquee). You then choose Image>Crop. Most users find that the Crop tool provides better control. You can select it by pressing the letter C on your keyboard. Draw to make a selection then click the commit check mark in the options bar (or press the ` Return `/` Enter ` key).

Resizing an Existing Image

Let's get some hands-on practice using two techniques. The first technique, the Power Crop, works for all versions of Photoshop. The second technique, the Nonsquare Place, requires Photoshop CS or later.

Video #4   Resizing in Action

See the Image Resizing video tutorial on the DVD-ROM.

Power Crop

It's very easy to size a graphic using the Crop Tool. The Power Crop technique will let you crop and size in one step. Let's give it a try; open up a photo of your own or use the photo `Ch2_Size1.tif` in the chapter's folder on the DVD-ROM. If working with a square pixel source (even if working in Photoshop CS), be sure to crop with one of the square pixel presets.

Step 1. Select the Crop tool in the Tool Box or press C.

Step 2. In the options bar, type in the square pixel size for your video editing system. For this sample project use 720 px × 540 px. Be sure to enter px after each number so Photoshop knows you are measuring in pixels.

Nondestructive Crop

Did you know that you can crop without permanently discarding image data? Simply double-click on the Background Layer and name it before you initiate the Crop. Then, after marking the crop, click the Hide radio button in the Options Bar and click Apply.

Step 3. Click and drag in the upper left corner of the image and drag diagonally towards to lower right corner. Highlight the area of the image you'd like to keep. When you drag to crop the image, your box will constrain to the proper aspect ratio. This allows you to resize and crop in one step. The shielded (darkened) areas will be cropped when you press `Return`/ `Enter` or click on the Commit button in the Options bar. To toggle the shielded area off, press the forward slash (`/`).

Step 4. To convert to nonsquare pixels, you can choose Image> Image Size. . . . Uncheck the Constrain Proportions box and enter the correct height in nonsquare pixels (in this case 486 px). If you are unsure of the correct heights, see page 34.

Nonsquare Place

If you are working with Photoshop CS (or newer), you can use the Place command and a nonsquare preset to create video graphics. This method takes as much time, but doesn't require you to remember document sizes.

Step 1. Create a new document using a video preset. For this example use the NTSC D1 document sized 720×486.

Step 2. Choose File>Place . . . in the dialog box to navigate to an image you'd like to use. If you need an image, use the file `Ch2_Size2.tif` on the DVD-ROM. Select the image and click Place.

Step 3. The image is added to the canvas with control handles for sizing. Hold down the `Shift` key to constrain proportions and the `⌥`/`alt` key to scale from the center. You can drag the image around to reposition it on the screen.

Step 4. Press the `Return`/`Enter` key or click the Commit button in the Options Bar. The image is sized and its pixel aspect ratio is converted to match the open document.

Final Advice

I have sat in workshops where the entire time has been eaten up by conversations on frame size and pixel aspect ratio. We seem to accept our frame rates of 29.97 fps (or 25 fps) with little question. But the mixing of square and nonsquare pixels is often mind-boggling. Pixel aspect ratio is the most boring and inflexible aspect of designing graphics for video. You can choose to fully understand it, use templates, or keep a list of presets and notes next to your computer. Whatever it takes, accept it, embrace it, use one of the aforementioned techniques consistently, and move on. On behalf of you, the reader, let's get to the fun stuff!

Speed Up Cropping

 To make things even easier, harness the power of Photoshop's Preset Manager. You can create tool presets that already have the values for a tool loaded. In fact, on the DVD-ROM you'll find a file called VideoCrop.tpl in the chapter's folder. Locate your Tool Presets folder (Adobe Photoshop CS3>Presets >Tools) and copy in the file. The next time you launch Photoshop, the different aspect ratios required for video will be available from the Tool Presets tab or a drop-down menu in the Options bar.

Hands On | 02

Creating Custom Backgrounds—*with Glen Stephens*

By combining multiple grayscale textures using blend modes, new textures can be generated. Using blending modes ensures several different looks based upon the randomness of mixing your textures together. These looks can then be colorized or further modified to create entirely new backgrounds that are well-suited for video. In fact a texture library can be used to quickly create DVD menus, lower-thirds, or full-screen graphics.

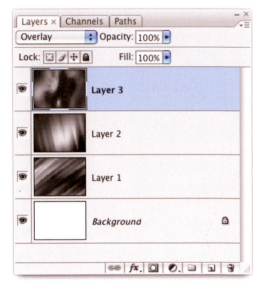

You'll find several textures on the DVD-ROM that can be used to create all new backgrounds. Be sure to complete this tutorial, then utilize the many textures to create our own backdrops.

You'll find Exercise 02 on the DVD-ROM.

PRO*file*: Angie Taylor

Angie Taylor's animations, visual effects and motion graphics have been a regular fixture on European screens for many years. She's produced work for a broad range of clients including the BBC and Channel 4 in the UK. She has worked alongside some of the most innovative directors in the UK including John Williams and Chris Cunningham. Last year she created visual effects for John Williams' ground-breaking short film, "Hibernation" which picked up awards at the Edinburgh International Film Festival and the Rhode Island Film Festival, among others.

Angie is currently taking a year out from production work and writing to focus on a personal project. She has written and designed characters and plots for an animated series and is in the process of art direction and storyboarding with an aim to getting it commissioned.

Angie works from her home-based studio in Brighton, a vibrant seaside city on the south coast of England well known for its population of creative businesses and individuals. She also commutes into central London to work on a freelance basis for other production companies.

"Most of the work I've undertaken has been for television although I am now getting into film work," said Angie. "I use a Mac desktop system to design and produce my animations, although most of my work is done on my MacBook Pro. Brighton has the first wireless seafront in the UK so I can work in any bar or café on the beach whilst sipping coffee and watching the world go by."

"I try to provide plenty of variety in terms of graphic style. You need to always push forward and endeavor to improve on what you've already done, exploring new methods and techniques constantly. For example, I've just recently been trying out a Cintique from Wacom to draw my characters with. It's introduced a whole new perspective to my work, although it's not quite portable enough to take to the beach!"

The flexibility of desktop systems has allowed Angie's business to grow and adjust to economic change. "Working on desktop systems opens up a lot in terms of being able to have more than one designer working on some of the bigger projects. Rather than having one person working on a Henry or Flame, I can sub-contract other freelancers and have two or three people working on their own desktop systems."

Despite her mastery of everything desktop video has to offer, Angie Taylor took a roundabout path to the video industry. After earning an honors degree in sculpture and drawing, she set off for London to be a prop maker for the television and theatre industry.

"As a result I visited various special effects departments and was fascinated by them. At that time computers in that field were still in the very early stages."

"One thing led to another and, for a time, I became involved in producing original artwork for the music industry as well as deejaying in the London club scene. Then one day, one of the record companies sent me to a graphic design studio. From

across a crowded room I saw a guy using Photoshop on a Mac to composite my images together. It was love at first byte!"

"I'd used music sequencers when I was deejaying, which led me to think that surely you could sequence images in the same way? A friend then acquainted me with Photoshop and After Effects on a Mac and I've worked with them ever since."

Angie is an expert at combining Photoshop and After Effects together to produce unique results. Angie has written a successful book entitled "Creative After Effects 7" which contains several interactive tutorials that teach the techniques she uses in her everyday work.

Angie is also a regular demo artist for Adobe and Apple, as well as a popular presenter of After Effects and Photoshop in Europe and the United States. If you ever get a chance to see Angie present, her creativity and expertise burst through.

Angie says that dreaming about possibilities really opens up her video work. "I like to learn the software inside out so that I really know what its capable of," said Taylor. "I have a natural inquisitiveness about how things work and this takes me beyond the everyday functions of an application and into the nitty-gritty."

Angie puts Photoshop through its paces. She uses it to prepare images for TV broadcast as well as to draw her characters for her layer-based animations. She also employs its powerful Vanishing Point tool, Healing Brush, and Photomerge features to create background and scenes for her animations. Angie is quite adept at designing multi-layered templates, creating backgrounds and textures which are used on-screen by clients requiring professional graphics to give their edits a more polished finish. She regularly uses Photoshop to design menus and graphics for DVDs as well as for her own Web sites.

When asked to define a Photoshop Power user, she replied: "It's somebody who really understands fundamentals like channels and paths; and who knows how to control and manipulate images without losing vital information. They would constantly push the tools to do new and interesting things, discovering original techniques and driving the software forward.

"I have an obsession for knowing what every single menu item does in a software application," said Taylor. "If I find an item that I don't understand, I delve into the Help files to find out; if that doesn't help I get onto the user forums. It's amazing how quickly you learn the software if you develop an obsession like mine!"

Angie also offered a few of her favorite keyboard shortcuts to speed up your Photoshop work:

- Use **D** to load default colors of black and white for masking
- Use the **X** button to toggle between black and white when in Quick Mask mode.
- Hold down the **spacebar** when making a selection to move the selection.
- **⌘** / **ctrl** – **J** to place a selection onto a new layer

Taylor stressed that the key to success in this field is to "Work bloody hard and love what you do." She also said that being flexible, comfortable and knowledgeable with your tools would keep your clients coming back for more.

"Clients are encouraged to sit with me in the preliminary stages, experimenting and interjecting ideas here and there," said Taylor. "I think it's important to deliver on time, especially when you're a one-stop-shop or a freelancer. People need to depend on you and you need to prove yourself a little more than the big production companies do."

To see more of Angie's work, visit:

http://www.creativeaftereffects.com/author.html
http://www.adobe.co.uk/motion/gallery/taylor/main.html

WHY LAYERS?

When Photoshop was created, it did not have layers. It was an application that worked extremely well for touching up photos, frames of film, or video stills. The introduction of layers moved Photoshop from image touch-up program to robust graphic tool. The key to being fast in Photoshop is understanding the Layers palette.

Think of layers as tracks from a video timeline. The way you build and organize the show affects your end results. With proper organization, you can come back later and quickly make changes. Clear labels make it easier to move the project into After Effects or your nonlinear edit system. Mastering layers is your first step to becoming a Photoshop power user.

What Are Layers?

One view of layers is that they are like traditional animation cels. You place objects on clear pieces of acetate and begin to stack them up. These sheets typically contain a single character or element. Layers can contain photos, text, logos, shapes, and even textures. As you build your composition, the stacking order affects depth perception.

There are lots of ways to create and manage a layered document, but it all comes back to an organized design. Video folks usually find the basic interface of the Layers palette similar to most NLEs. Not taking sides on who's copied whom, it's safe to say that Photoshop and most popular video applications share a similar interface. Just as it's hard to edit video with your Timeline window closed, you really should leave the Layers palette open at all times. If you need to hide it temporarily, press the Tab key.

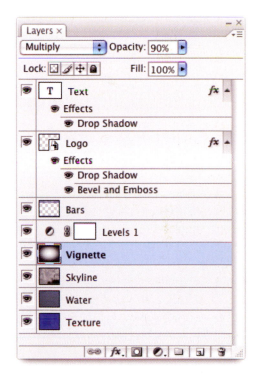

Layers can contain objects, text, effects, or image adjustments. Good naming and organization is crucial in a fast-paced production environment.

Creating Layers

It is very easy to create a new layer. You can click the Create New Layer icon (which looks like a note pad) at the bottom of the Layers palette. Additionally, you can choose Layer>New>Layer or press *Shift*+*⌘*+*N* (*Shift*+*ctrl*+*N*). Layers can also be copied or dragged from one document to another.

Duplicating Layers

Sometimes you will want to duplicate a layer to use multiple instances of an object (such as a logo). You can choose Layer> Duplicate Layer or contextual-click on a layer's name in the Layers palette. The fastest way though is to press *⌘*+*J* (*ctrl*+*J*) (think jump) to create a copy of a layer immediately above itself. Additionally, if you have an active selection, only the selected part will copy to the new layer.

Deleting Layers

If you know that a layer is definitely no longer needed, you should throw it away. This will reduce the size of your file, so it will take up less disk space and less memory. Layers can be thrown away by dragging them into the trashcan at the bottom of the Layers palette. You can also contextual-click on a layer's name to throw it away or choose Layer>Delete>Layer.

Under Control

There are many controls tied to the Layers palette. This chapter will cover layer creation, navigation, blending, and organization.

- For Layer Styles, see Chapter 6.
- For Layer Masks, see Chapter 4.
- For Adjustment Layers, see Chapter 9.

Fill Layers

In addition to layers that you create or import (via the Copy & Paste or Place… commands), Photoshop allows for the creation of specialty Fill Layers. You access these by choosing Layer>New Fill Layer and the choosing Solid Color… Gradient… or Pattern… You can also access these by clicking the black and white half-circle on the bottom of the Layers palette.

- **Solid Color.** Any color can be used to create a Solid Color layer. To edit the color layer, just double-click its thumbnail in the Layers palette.
- **Gradient.** A gradient is a gradual blend between two or more colors. For more on gradients, be sure to read Chapter 11.
- **Pattern.** Photoshop can use its library of seamless patterns to create a new layer filled with a pattern.

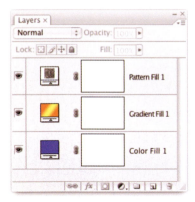

How Layers Work:
Understanding Composite Images

Layers are much more than a storage bin. They can contain text, image adjustments, special effects, and annotations about your work. After Effects users will feel right at home; Photoshop's Layers palette is a close sibling to AE's timeline. From the Layers palette, you can control visibility, opacity, blending modes, naming, and stacking order.

With most NLEs offering at least partial support for Photoshop layered files, you can keep similar elements for one show, such as all the lower thirds, in a single document. By consolidating, you have fewer files to keep track of. Updates are easier too; change the color of the bar in one document, and you can quickly update in your timeline. By turning layers off and on, you can generate all of your namebars. You also won't need to worry about small shifts in the bar or logo, a common problem with multiple versions.

I use Photoshop to complete 75% of my After Effects and DVD menu work. The superb alignment tools, text controls, and quick-rendering filters allow me to prebuild my work. I can then import layered documents into Adobe After Effects and Encore or Apple's DVD Studio Pro. It is then easy to swap in some moving elements. It is far faster to render text and shadows in Photoshop whenever possible. I also find it far easier to do on-screen layout in Adobe Photoshop. Be sure to look at the great tutorials on the DVD about using Photoshop for Motion Graphics and DVD work.

Delete Many at Once

Starting with Photoshop CS2, you don't have to throw layers away one at a time. By using a ⌘+Click (`ctrl`+click on multiple layers, then delete, you can then use any of the delete methods to remove all at once.

Working with the Layers Palette

As a common starting point, open up the file `Ch03_Layered_DVD.psd` from the book's disc. This 10-layer document is a good example of using the general features of the Layers palette. To start, all layers are turned off; don't be surprised to see an empty screen or checkerboard pattern. (The checkerboard is Photoshop's default way of showing transparency.)

Step 1. Begin turning layers on from the bottom up, starting with Texture.

The bottommost layer is a simple pattern that adds a sense of depth to the piece. This pattern was made by painting a physical canvas with traditional media. A digital photo was taken and tinted using Photoshop. You'll find a sample folder of textures on the book's DVD-ROM.

Step 2. Turn on the next layer, Water, and click its name to select the layer.

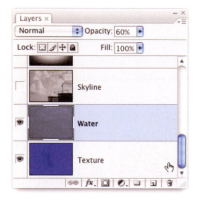

At the top of the Layers palette, you should notice that the layer is set to 60% opacity. Opacity is the opposite of transparency. Something that is 60% opaque is 40% transparent.

There's a great shortcut for changing opacity of a layer, but you must have a tool selected that does not have its own transparency settings (such as the Move or Marquee Tools). To change the opacity of a layer, type the corresponding number on the numeric keypad. For example, press the 2 key for 20%, the 5 key for 50%, and so on. If you want to be really specific, you can quickly type a number such as 23 for 23%, and Photoshop will adjust the layer accordingly. This only works when you have a tool selected without its own transparency settings.

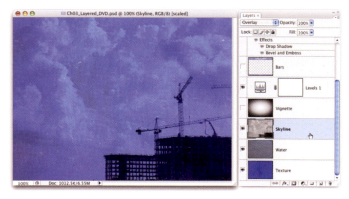

Step 3. Turn on and select the third layer, Skyline. This introduces another layer feature: blending modes.

If you look in the top left corner of the Layers palette, you'll see this layer is set to Overlay. Here I'm using a grayscale image to add a silhouette of a building. Blending modes are the most underused, least understood part of Photoshop. They are the foundation of my design work and a useful tool in digital video (see "Blending Modes" on page 65 for more info).

Step 4. Turn on and select the fourth layer, Vignette, and you'll see a similar technique employed to add an area of focus to the image. A good technique is to try changing the blending mode before you make an opacity change. This subtle change to your working style will give you dramatic results.

Step 5. Turn on and select the fifth layer, which looks different than the rest. It is an adjustment layer.

Here I have applied a Levels adjustment to multiple layers simultaneously. A Levels adjustment affects the overall balance of lights and darks in an image. It is similar to a gamma adjustment in video. The key benefit of the adjustment layer is that it is nondestructive; the effect is "live," in that you can alter or disable it at any time.

Now, double-click on the Levels Adjustment Layer's circular icon, and the controls pop up. Try adjusting the middle slider and see the resulting changes.

You will likely make a Levels adjustment on every composition; it is the key to maintaining video-safe levels and attaining proper lighting and contrast. Levels adjustments are covered in greater detail in Chapter 9, "Color Correction: How to Get It Right."

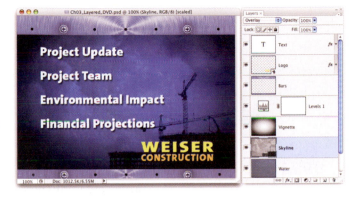

Step 6. Turn on the next layer, Bars.

These borders will be used to create an edge effect. The empty area between the bars is transparent and allows other layers to show through.

Step 7. Turn on and select the Logo layer.

This logo is a Smart Object as indicated by its special icon. Smart objects can add flexibility to the design process, as they allow for the ability to scale and transform a vector object repeatedly without losing quality. This layer also has layer effects applied to create a slight beveled edge with a drop shadow.

Step 8. Turn on the final layer, Text.

Photoshop has a robust text engine that is useful for creating screen-ready text. We will fully explore the robust text capabilities of Photoshop in Chapter 5.

⌘ + [(ctrl + [ )	Move current layer down one spot
⌘ +] (ctrl +])	Move current layer up one spot
Shift + ⌘ + [(Shift + ctrl + [ )	Move current layer to the bottom of Layers palette
Shift + ⌘ +] (Shift + ctrl +])	Move current layer to the top of Layers palette

By employing proper use of layers, I have generated a professional-looking DVD menu that I can use as is or import the layers into another application to animate. Proper naming makes it easy to find each layer. To name a layer, double-click on the name in the Layers palette. Note that old versions of Photoshop require you to ⌥ +double-click (alt +double-click) on the name.

Layer Organization Techniques

Layer organization starts with naming, but does not end there. A lot of effort has gone into developing technology for improved layer management. Intermediate steps include linking, aligning, distributing, locking, merging, and flattening layers. Advanced options include grouping, color-coding, and use of Layer Sets. For this lesson, open `Ch03_Organization.psd`.

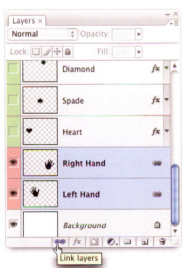

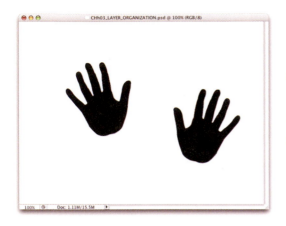

Linking

Multiple layers can be linked together. Linking enables you to move multiple objects together.

Step 1. Make the Right Hand and Left Hand layers visible.

Step 2. Select the Move tool by pressing the letter V.

Step 3. Now click on one of the red layers, and *Shift* click to select the second layer. Multiple layers can be selected by holding down the *Shift* key to select a range of contiguous layers (adjacent). Alternately, you can select discontiguous layers by holding down the ⌘ (*ctrl*) key and clicking to select them.

Step 4. Click the Link layers button at the bottom of the Layers palette.

You can now move the two layers as one. With the Move tool selected, you can click and drag. You can also use the arrow keys to move the image one pixel. Add the *Shift* key and you can super-shift 10 pixels at a time.

Align and Distribute

It is possible to have precise alignment in Photoshop. You can align or distribute objects in relationship to one another.

Step 1. Hide the Hand layers by clicking on their visibility switches.

Step 2. Now turn the green layers on. You should see the four playing card symbols randomly arranged on the screen.

Step 3. Select the heart symbol, then use the Move tool to position it where you'd like it to fall on the screen.

Step 4. The first step to aligning or distributing is to link the objects together. Link the other three symbols to the heart.

The Alignment tools are tied to the Move tool. If you have the layers linked together and the Move tool selected, you should see them at the top of the Options bar. It takes two or more objects to perform an alignment. The alignment is based upon the object you have selected.

Step 5. In this example, click the Align Bottom button in the bar. The other three will move while the heart remains stationary.

The misalignment problem is solved, but things still aren't right. The viewer's eye expects these objects to be evenly spaced; this is called distribution. You must have at least three items to perform a distribution. In this case, four is more than enough. The second set of boxes in the Options bar is for distribution.

Smart Guides Save Time

Smart Guides were first added to Photoshop CS2, but are similar to what you'll find in Illustrator or DVD Studio Pro and Motion. When you start to drag an object, Smart Guides will highlight the edges or center to show alignment. If they aren't visible, be sure to turn on Smart Guides under the View menu.

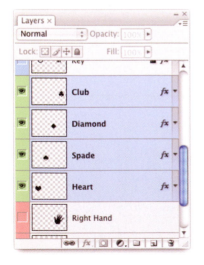

Align bottom edges   Distribute horizontal centers

Step 6. Choose the second-to-last box to distribute horizontal centers. Notice how the objects snap to place perfectly.

Locking

Photoshop offers great flexibility in locking layers. It is possible to lock the transparent areas of an image, lock the pixels to avoid changing color, lock position to prevent accidental shifting, or any combination of the three. These features are enabled by highlighting the layer and then picking from the Lock icons at the top of the palette.

This is a good way to avoid accidental changes. If you do need to make a change, unlock the layer. Take a look at the key layer; you should see a Lock icon. If you try to use the Move tool, Photoshop will warn you that the layer is locked.

The Key is to Lock

Locking a layer only does so in Photoshop. This is a useful way to avoid accidental edits or movement on a layer.

Merging and Flattening Layers

Sometimes, you know that you'd like to permanently join two objects together. This is called merging; it is the Photoshop equivalent of a video mixdown or render.

Step 1. Turn off all layers except the yellow Base and People layers.

Step 2. Highlight the Base layer and link these two layers together.

Step 3. From the Layers palette submenu (the triangle in the right corner), pick Merge Linked. The two layers are now permanently joined. This is a useful way to cut down on layers and simplify your project. For now, choose Edit>Undo.

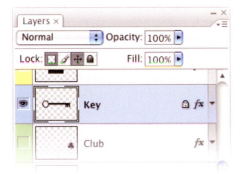

Another technique is to merge linked layers to an empty target layer. Think of this as a selective merge. Highlight the Sign Target Layer and link the other yellow layers to it. Now hold down the ⌥ (*alt*) key and select Merge Linked. Notice how a flattened copy appears on the new target layer, while the originals are left behind. This is a useful technique for simplifying your project while still preserving source layers.

There are times when you want to merge all of the visible layers in the document. Simply choose Merge Visible. One step further is to Flatten your composition. This discards all nonvisible layers and merges all visible layers

into a single background layer. It is very rare that you will need to perform this step. There is a myth that you must flatten your artwork before sending it to some NLEs. This is inaccurate; you should choose Save a Copy in a format that does not support layers (such as PICT or TARGA) in order to import into some NLEs. This saves an additional flattened copy to the specified location. It does not get rid of your layers in the .psd file. Layers are key to future changes; preserve them or regret it later.

Targeted Flattening

You can merge multiple layers into one layer to make it easier to manipulate. This is also a necessary step for creating alpha channels from layer styles.

Step 1. Link the source layers to a blank target layer. Make sure that none of the layers are a locked *Background* layer. Otherwise, double-click on the Background layer and name it.

Step 2. Highlight the target layer.

Step 3. Hold down the ⌥ (*alt*) key.

Step 4. Choose Merged Linked from the Layers palette submenu.

This flattened copy will now import cleanly into your NLE, Compositing application, or DVD authoring application. The editable version is left as well for future changes. For more on Layer Styles, see page 141.

Clipping Mask

Using a Clipping Mask (previously called Grouping) will allow you to take one layer and apply its pixels to the opaque areas of the layer below. This is very similar to using a track matte in After Effects.

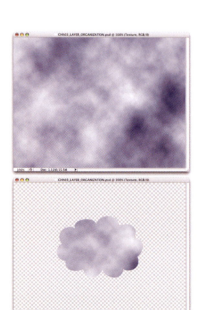

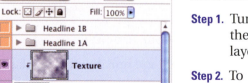

Step 1. Turn off all layers except the Cloud and Texture layers.

Step 2. To map the Texture layer, highlight and Layer> Create Clipping Mask. You should notice that the layer indents. Another way to perform the same task is ⌥-clicking (*alt*-clicking) between two layers in the Layers palette.

A Clipping Mask is a great replacement for Paste Into because it takes one step instead of five.

Color-Coding

Throughout this lesson, the layers have been color-coded. This is a great way to identify items, and helps to mentally organize a complex composition. These colors only appear in the Layers palette and do not affect your final output. To assign a color to a layer, you must access the Layer Properties command. With a two-button mouse, you can right-click on the desired layer. One-button mouse users should hold down the `ctrl` key when clicking. Alternately, you can `⌥`+double-click (`alt`+double-click) the layer's name.

Layer Groups

An incredibly useful feature is Layer Groups (previously called sets). Think of these as folders in a file cabinet. Instead of throwing everything in a drawer, you can make life easier and put similar things together. This makes it easier to work with layers, and is also a great way to prepare options to show the client. For example, you can prepare the same headline two different ways. Headline 1A has a serif font, while Headline 1B uses a sans-serif typeface. It is easy to turn entire sets off and on as a group. Layer Groups can also have their blending modes and opacity changes as a group.

Use of Layer Groups and color-coding is an essential part of gaining speed.

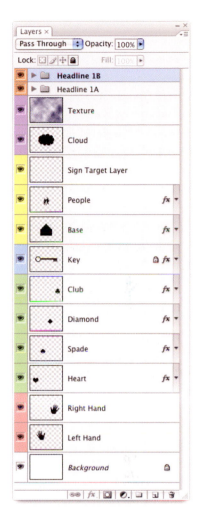

There are several ways to create a set. You can click on the New Set icon and drag the layer into the set. An easier method involves linking.

Step 1. Go back to the Heart layer; and select all four symbol layers.

Step 2. Now choose New Group from Layers from the Layers palette submenu and name the set "Poker." By employing a Layer Group, you can align a group of objects.

Step 3. Highlight the Background layer and link it to the new Layer Group Poker.

Step 4. Select the Move tool.

You now have the Align tools available and can choose to center the symbols as a single unit. Centering objects on a page is as simple as linking the layers or Layer Groups to the highlighted Background layer and using the Align tools.

Starting with Photoshop CS, Layer Groups have gotten even better. It is now possible to have up to five levels of nested groups. While five Layer Groups are likely more than you need, the flexibility is empowering. You can now drag Layer Groups inside other

Video #5   Organizing Layers

You can see these layer organization techniques by watching the video tutorial on the DVD-ROM.

Groups, allowing for complex organization. Be aware that most NLEs will improperly interpret Layer Groups. Some will import the contents as a flattened layer while others will improperly try to interpret the layer data. Fortunately, Adobe After Effects and Apple Motion handle Layer Groups fairly well.

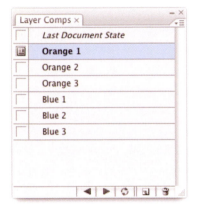

Storing Alternate Designs with Layer Comps

During the normal design process, you will often create several variations upon your design. For example when designing a lower-third graphic you might try positioning the logo in different positions as well as using a drop shadow or glow to help offset it. Instead of having a separate document for each variation, you can harness the power of Layer Comps.

Layer Comps were first introduced with Photoshop CS. When properly used, Layer Comps can significantly extend design flexibility. Essentially, a layer comp is a snapshot of your Layers palette, which allows you to memorize different combinations of layers. A layer comp can record three types of layer options:

- Layer visibility
- Layer position within the .psd file
- Layer appearance (use of Layer Styles)

How to Create Layer Comps

In order to practice with Layer Comps, open the file `Ch03_Layer_Comps.psd` from the DVD-ROM. Then make sure the Layer Comp window is visible (if not, choose Window>Layer Comps).

This document already has six layer comps added to it. If you click the forward or backward triangles at the bottom of the Layer Comps palette, you can apply each Layer Comp. These six options showcase variations in color, font, and logo position. There are three additional options to create.

Step 1. Select the first Layer Comp called Orange 1 and make it active by clicking in the column next to its name.

Step 2. Disable the visibility for the Orange layer by clicking its eyeball icon. Then enable visibility for the Red layer.

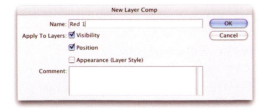

Step 3. Click the Create New Layer Comp button at the bottom of the Layer Comp palette. Name the Comp Red 1 and choose to memorize both Visibility and Position. Click OK to store the Layer Comp.

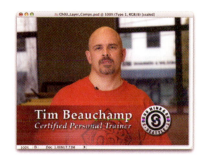

Step 4. Turn off the visibility icon for Font 1 and enable the visibility for Font 2.

Step 5. Click the Create New Layer Comp button at the bottom of the Layer Comp palette. Name the Comp Red 2 and choose to memorize both Visibility and Position. Click OK to store the Layer Comp.

Step 6. The final Layer Comp involves a position move. Since it is most similar to a previous state, select and activate Orange 3.

Step 7. Duplicate the Orange 3 state by contextual-clicking and choosing Duplicate Layer Comp.

Step 8. Disable the visibility for the Orange layer by clicking its eyeball icon. Then enable visibility for the Red layer.

Step 9. Click the Update Layer Comp button at the bottom of the Layer Comp palette.

Step 10. Double-click on the Orange 3 copy layer and rename it Red 3. Drag it to its proper position at the bottom of the Layer Comp window.

Step 11. Press ⌘ + S (ctrl + S) to save your work.

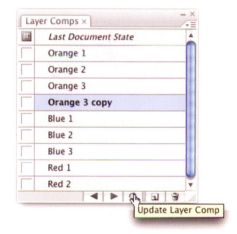

How to Update Layer Comps

If you delete or merge layers, you can create an invalid state where a Layer Comp can no longer be used. You'll be alerted by an exclamation point when this happens. At this point, you have three options:

- Choose Edit>Step Backwards or press ⌥+⌘+Z (alt+ctrl+Z) until the warning is removed.
- Ignore the warning and accept that some (or all) of the layers in the comp may be lost.
- Update the Layer Comp by clicking the Update Layer Comp button.

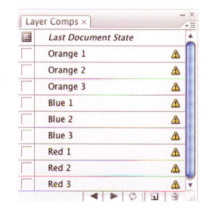

How to Use Layer Comps

You can now toggle between the comps to see the different states of the image. Layer comps can't remember font changes to text layers or the color of pixel on a layer. If you want to change color, try using layer styles to color your layers, and not actually

Video #6   Layer Comps in Action

You'll find a video tutorial on the DVD-ROM that will help illustrate how Layer Comps can be used.

fill the pixels. Layer Comps have several ways that they can be used to streamline a project:

- Layer comps are useful for storing alternate designs with one document.
- Layer comps allow you to have several options ready to quickly show to your client.
- You can also save all Layer Comps out as separate PSD files by choosing File>Script>Layer Comps to Files.
- You can create a PDF file to send your client via e-mail to get feedback. Choose File>Script>Layer Comps to PDF.

You may find that Layer Comps are a helpful addition to your workflow… or not. Layer comps cannot store all design choices you may need, but their flexibility can prove useful. Like all features, give them a thorough workout and see what you think.

Working with Smart Objects

Adobe launched a new technology starting with Photoshop CS2 called Smart Objects. This powerful option allows you to embed raster or vector data into a layer. The layer can then be transformed indefinitely, as the embedded data remains editable and scalable (up to its original size). Additionally, you can combine one or more layers in a document into a Smart Object as well.

Unlike After Effects or an NLE that may link to a source file, Photoshop will actually embed the data. A Smart Object is simply one file embedded inside another. This can be very useful as Smart Objects allow greater flexibility. You can perform most transform commands on the object, and never experience a loss in image quality (provided you do not scale a raster file larger than its original size).

Using the Place Command

One way to create a Smart Object is to use the Place command to add the file into your current Photoshop document. Placed objects remain as Smart Objects, giving you the ability to access all of the original raster data. This essentially allows you to size and resize an object repeatedly without quality loss. Let's try Smart Objects out.

Step 1. Open the file `Ch03_Background.psd` from the chapter's folder on the DVD-ROM.

Step 2. Choose File>Place… and a navigation services dialog box opens.

Step 3. Navigate to the file `Ch03_see_the_difference.eps` in the chapter's folder and click Place.

Export a Smart Object for Additional Use

The good news is you can also export Smart Object layers as individual files in order to work with them. Just choose Layer>Smart Object>Export Contents. Raster layers will create a Photoshop document and Vector files will create an Illustrator file.

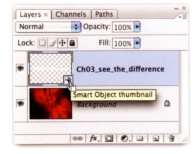

Step 4. Adjust the scaling of the placed object using your mouse or the Options Bar. Hold down the **Shift** key to constrain the Scale equally in all directions; hold down the **⌥** (**alt**) key to scale from center. Scale the object very small and position it in the lower-right corner.

Step 5. Click the Apply checkbox in the Options bar or press **Enter** twice. The object is rasterized and is flagged as a Smart Object in the Layers palette with a special icon.

Step 6. To illustrate the scaling abilities of Smart Objects, you will now scale the object larger. Press **⌘**+**T** (**ctrl**+**T**) to invoke the Free Transform Command.

Step 7. Hold down the **Shift** key and scale the logo larger by dragging its left corner away from the logo.

Step 8. Apply the transformation and examine how the logo redraws with perfect clarity.

The primary advantage of placing files is scale and transform. Be sure to examine the Layer>Smart Object menu to explore other options. A raster object can be scaled up to its original raster size or infinitely if it was a vector object. You can also edit the original object by double-clicking the smart object thumbnail in the Layers palette. Additionally, you can replace the content of a Smart Object by selecting the Smart Object layer, and choose Layer> Smart Object>Replace Content.

Blending Modes

Photoshop's least-used feature is also its most powerful. Nothing is as mysterious as Photoshop's blending modes. I have read many convoluted attempts at explaining these 25 different options, but there are few absolutes when it comes to blending modes. Ask 10 knowledgeable users what they do and you'll get at least 10 answers. When pressed for more explanation as to what blending modes actually do, the common answer is "It depends. "

Your next logical question is likely "Depends on what? " Simply put, the effect achieved by blending two layers varies with the contents of those two layers. A blending mode compares the content of two layers and enacts changes based on the contents of both layers. In real-world terms, you can put milk, strawberries, and vanilla ice cream in a blender and get a great milkshake. Use the same blender with other ingredients—say, tomatoes, onions, jalapeños, and cilantro—and you've got salsa. The same appliance gives different results depending on the ingredients.

Explore Blending Modes

Blending modes appear in virtually every tool, can be combined with every filter, and show up at every turn. Blending modes are the final exam on the Photoshop Guru test. So please, read on, and I promise to let you in on all the secrets.

Step 1. Open the file named `Ch03_Blend_Modes_Demo.psd.` In this five-layered document, I have used four different blending modes. I have applied these modes for artistic effect, although there are *many* postproduction-oriented uses as well. Let's dissect this document and see how modes are used.

Step 2. Turn each layer off, starting at the top, and notice how things change.

Step 3. Turn off all but the two bottommost layers in our test file. Select the layer Globes; then pick the Move tool.

Step 4. You can cycle forward using *Shift*+=; you can cycle backwards with *Shift*+−. This shortcut works as long as you have a tool selected that does not have its own blending modes (such as the Move or Marquee tools). Cycle through until you find a look that you like.

Step 5. Switch to the remaining layers and repeat. It is possible to generate many different looks by changing the blending modes on multiple layers.

The Secret of Blending Modes

Layer blending modes offer a lot of variety. In your quest to understand them, don't rush to judgment.

The *first* secret is "Don't try to memorize what they all do. " The good news is that they are grouped by similar traits. As you make your way through the list, you will notice a gradual progression through styles. The first group darkens your underlying image, while the second will lighten it. The third set adds contrast, while the last two generate dramatic results by comparing or mapping values. Depending on your sources, some blending modes will generate little or no results. Sound confusing? Keep reading.

The *second* secret is "Experiment. " The best way to use blending modes is to try them out. Clicking through a long drop-down menu is boring. A much better alternative is to use keyboard shortcuts *Shift*+= and *Shift*+−.

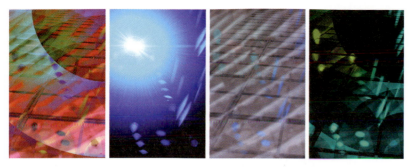

These are four of the many combinations made possible by employing blending modes. Most users never explore the flexibility offered by these great layer options.

The *third* secret is "Exploit them. " Need a quick visual pop? Try blending a blurred image on top of itself. Need to tint something? Place a solid or gradient on top and change to hue or color mode. Need to quickly luma key an item? Multiply knocks out whites; Screen knocks out the blacks. You'll find blending modes in virtually every filter (choose Fade Filter from the Edit menu) and all of your brush tools. Blending modes rock, and they can be *our* little secret.

Blending Modes Across Applications

Many nonlinear editing applications and all motion graphics tools support blending modes. Applications vary by manufacturer and they may not have the exact number of blending modes that Photoshop has. If an application has the same modes as Photoshop, it will generally be a clean exchange across programs. If modes differ, then the transfer process may produce unexpected results. Be sure to read the documentation that comes with your editing and motion graphics tools regarding blending (or transfer) modes.

Blending Modes

Original

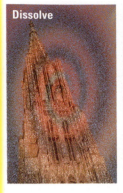

Overlay

Dissolve

Random replacement of the pixels with the base or blend color.

Darken

Pixels lighter than blend are replaced; darker ones are not.

Multiply

Similar to drawing strokes on the image with magic markers.

Color Burn

Evaluates each channel; darkens base by increasing contrast.

Linear Burn

Evaluates each channel; darkens base by decreasing brightness.

Lighten

Evaluates each channel; uses base or blend color (whichever is lighter).

Screen

Results in a lighter color. Useful for "knocking" black out of a layer.

Color Dodge

Evaluates color information and brightens base by decreasing contrast.

Linear Dodge

Evaluates color information and brightens base by increasing brightness.

Overlay

Overlays existing pixels while preserving highlights and shadows of base

Soft Light

The effect is similar to shining a diffused spotlight on the image.

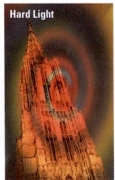

Hard Light

The effect is similar to shining a harsh spotlight on the image.

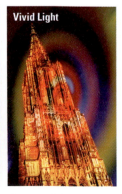

Vivid Light

Burns or dodges by increasing or decreasing the contrast.

Blending Modes continued

Linear Light

Burns or dodges by decreasing or increasing the brightness.

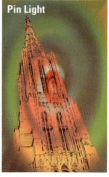

Pin Light

Useful for adding special effects to an image.

Hard Mix

Enhances the contrast of the underlying layers.

Difference

Evaluates each channel and subtracts depending on greater brightness.

Exclusion

Similar to, but lower in contrast than the Difference mode.

Hue

Uses luminance and saturation of the base and the hue of the blend.

Saturation

Creates color with luminance and hue of the base and saturation of the blend.

Color

Preserves gray levels. Useful for coloring and tinting.

Luminosity

Inverse effect from that of the Color mode.

Lighter Color

When blending two colors using this mode, only the lighter color will be visible.

Darker Color

When blending two colors using this mode, only the darker color will be visible.

Blending Modes—Blending a Blurred Copy of an Image

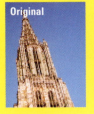 Original

 Blurred

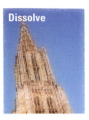 Dissolve

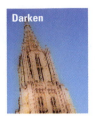 Darken

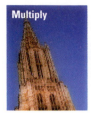 Multiply

 Color Burn

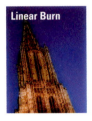 Linear Burn

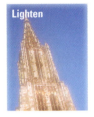 Lighten

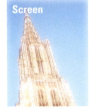 Screen

 Color Dodge

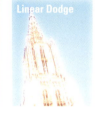 Linear Dodge

 Overlay

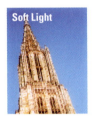 Soft Light

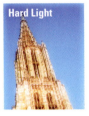 Hard Light

 Vivid Light

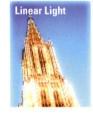 Linear Light

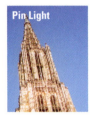 Pin Light

 Hard Mix

 Difference

 Exclusion

 Hue

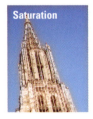 Saturation

 Color

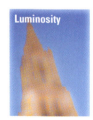 Luminosity

 Lighter Color

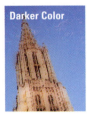 Darker Color

Export Issues with Layers

While motion graphics applications and NLEs often recognize Photoshop layers, it's often not a seamless exchange. The best advice is to have things clearly labeled. The default naming scheme of Layer 1, Layer 2, Layer 3 will not help you make your deadline. Use descriptive, *unique* names per layer. Photoshop will allow you to have identical names, but your editing application will become confused by the duplication. Here are some other points to consider.

Saving a Flattened Copy for Your NLE

It is common to need to save a flattened version for your editing system. If this is the case, *do not* flatten your .psd file. Choose Save As or use `Shift` + `⌘` + `S` (`Shift` + `ctrl` + `S`). Select a flat file format that your edit system recognizes. The two most common formats will be a PICT or Targa file. When you pick these formats, the Layers box will automatically gray out and the As a Copy box is checked, but grayed out. If you want to save a flattened file, Photoshop will make it easy and preserve your layers at the same time. You worked hard for those layers. Keep them.

Exporting with Layers for Animation

If you want to send a layered Photoshop file to another program in order to animate your layers, you may choose to optimize the file. Depending on which application you'll be importing the PSD file into, different steps will be needed (be sure to see Appendix C at the end of the book).

Some important general consideration to keep in mind. Be sure your layers have unique names. If a file doesn't import cleanly, you may want to rasterize it (Layer>Rasterize>All Layers). This is a good extra precaution, but it may only be needed if you intended to import the *layered* file into a Nonlinear Editing System. Flattened files (such as PICT or Targa) already rasterize type and objects when you save. If you are going to rasterize, make sure to make the changes to a *copy* of the original. This way, you can go back and make future changes.

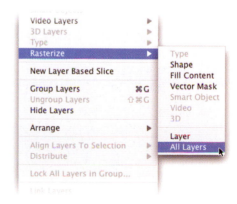

Blending Mode Shortcuts

by Adobe Evangelists (http://www.adobeevangelists.com)

Blend Mode	Macintosh	Windows	
Normal	Shift + ⏎ + N	Shift + alt + N	(N)ormal
Dissolve	Shift + ⏎ + I	Shift + alt + I	D(I)ssolve
Behind	Shift + ⏎ + Q	Shift + alt + Q	(Q)uick! Hide behind that layer!
Clear	Shift + ⏎ + R	Shift + alt + R	Clea(R)
Darken	Shift + ⏎ + K	Shift + alt + K	Dar(K)en
Multiply	Shift + ⏎ + M	Shift + alt + M	(M)ultiply
Color Burn	Shift + ⏎ + B	Shift + alt + B	Color (B)urn
Linear Burn	Shift + ⏎ + A	Shift + alt + A	Line(A)r Burn
Lighten	Shift + ⏎ + G	Shift + alt + G	Li(G)hten
Screen	Shift + ⏎ + S	Shift + alt + S	(S)creen
Color Dodge	Shift + ⏎ + D	Shift + alt + D	Color (D)odge
Linear Dodge	Shift + ⏎ + W	Shift + alt + W	W has many LINES to DODGE
Overlay	Shift + ⏎ + O	Shift + alt + O	(O)verlay
Soft Light	Shift + ⏎ + F	Shift + alt + F	So(F)t Light
Hard Light	Shift + ⏎ + H	Shift + alt + H	(H)ard Light
Vivid Light	Shift + ⏎ + V	Shift + alt + V	(V)ivid Light
Linear Light	Shift + ⏎ + J	Shift + alt + J	Javelins are linear and Light
Pin Light	Shift + ⏎ + Z	Shift + alt + Z	Zero connection to Pin Light
Hard Mix	Shift + ⏎ + L	Shift + alt + L	Learning blend modes is hard
Difference	Shift + ⏎ + E	Shift + alt + E	Diff(E)r(E)nc(E)
Exclusion	Shift + ⏎ + X	Shift + alt + X	E(X)clusion
Hue	Shift + ⏎ + U	Shift + alt + U	H(U)e
Saturation	Shift + ⏎ + T	Shift + alt + T	Sa(T)uration
Color	Shift + ⏎ + C	Shift + alt + C	(C)olor
Luminosity	Shift + ⏎ + Y	Shift + alt + Y	Luminosit(Y)
Lighter Color	No Shortcut	No Shortcut	
Darker Color	No Shortcut	No Shortcut	

Making Textures—*with Robert Lawson*

Need a little photo-realism? Photoshop excels at allowing you to incorporate photographic sources into your projects. But what happens if you need some texture, but lack the photos? Don't worry about it.

By harnessing the power of layers and filters, photo-realistic textures can be created. This tutorial shows you how to create two common textures: scratched metal and glass. You can utilize these textures for text or design elements as part of your television graphics.

You'll find Exercise 03 on the DVD-ROM.

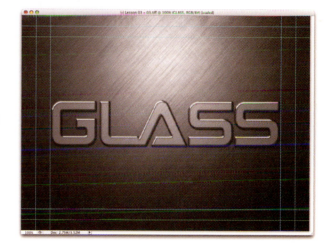

PRO*file*: Neil Rubino

Rubino has spent his entire professional career working in video. But he frequently goes beyond the editing and gets involved with all aspects of a project.

"My jobs have always required me to shoot and edit the video projects I am assigned. So I have evolved from a shooter/ editor to a producer and director of my own projects. I started in the television news media as a videographer," said Rubino. "I moved from news programming into shooting and editing cable TV programs for a number of years. I now work on corporate and educational videos that vary from two to forty minutes in length."

Rubino quickly discovered that he needed to be confident in making his own graphics for use in video. Photoshop has filled that role nicely.

"I use Photoshop at this point to prepare almost all of the graphics for a video project, no matter what the type. Lower third ID titles and full screen titles, logo treatments, charts and graphs, newspaper clippings, site plan maps and even custom mask shapes are all created first with Photoshop and then imported into my video projects. I also use still photographs in my videos from time to time, and I prepare and perfect them first in Photoshop."

Integrating Photoshop as a key skill has been helpful in Rubino's career. He frequently delivers completed projects for

broadcast including television commercials, public service announcements and cable programming. To meet tough deadlines, Rubino says one has to be knowledgeable about approaching production challenges.

"I think that knowing how to get a job done quickly is one measure of a power user. Knowing the shortcuts the program provides really helps in this area," said Rubino. "But beyond the keyboard short-cuts, knowing the ways to attack a task really makes someone a Photoshop power user. Some projects can be approached in Photoshop in a number of ways. Knowing which method will deliver the desired effect with the highest quality result in the least time is the mark of a power user."

Rubino says a thorough knowledge of Photoshop is essential for video editors these days. If you're thinking about freelancing or changing jobs, make sure your skills are in line first.

"I think that it is extremely important for anyone in the profession of media creation for broadcast to know Photoshop," said Rubino. "Photoshop is very helpful for video editors as well as writer/producers. So I would suggest that anyone entering the job market concentrate on learning Photoshop before embarking on a job search in television production."

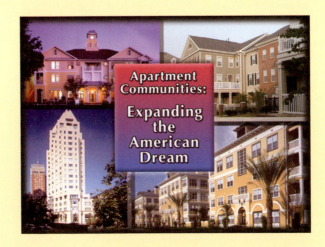

4

WHAT ABOUT TRANSPARENCY?

One of Photoshop's greatest powers lies in its ability to preserve complex transparency. It is possible to have several different of levels of transparency within a Photoshop document, which leads to greater flexibility in compositing multiple layers together. For example, in an image set to 8-bit mode, Photoshop supports 256 levels of transparency. Switch to 16-bit mode and that number jumps dramatically to 65,536 levels. By employing masks, both in layers and embedded into the saved files as alpha channels, this transparency data can travel seamlessly into the nonlinear editing or motion graphics environment.

Essential Terminology

Before we begin exploring transparency in depth, it is necessary to establish essential terminology:

> **Foreground element.** A foreground element is any layer that contains objects to be composited over the background layer or plate.

> **Matte.** The matte determines the opacity of the foreground elements, as well as defining the edges of the foreground element. It is important to keep your background in mind when developing independent foreground elements (and their mattes/masks/alpha channels) inside of Photoshop. Know what you intend to key and where you intend to key it.

Understanding Bit-Depth

Photoshop is most often used an 8-bit image editor. That is to say, each channel contains 8 bits of information. Eight bits is another way of saying two to the eighth power, or

Each channel normally contains 8 bits of information. It is best to view channels in grayscale to see contrast and detail.

The left screen shows a layered Photoshop file with transparency information stored in layers. The center screen has an added alpha channel, which also includes a drop shadow. This allows the image to be keyed or composited over other layers or video during the edit.

2×2×2×2×2×2×2×2, which equals 256. These 256 different shades of gray combine to form a complex image.

RGB images contain 24 bits of information, 8 bits per channel. If you add an alpha channel, you have added another 8 bits of information. A grayscale image contains 8 bits. It is a good idea to stick with RGB or grayscale images for video purposes, as CMYK and other formats are mostly unsupported.

Depending on your version of Photoshop, 16-bit images are supported to varying degrees. The 16-bit images can be scanned by higher-end scanners as well as captured by most digital cameras that are shooting raw formats. This extra data can be useful if you are doing a lot of color correction or compositing. Photoshop CS introduced the ability to have layered 16-bit images, which is a nice boost in quality (especially for glows and gradients). It is important to note that working with 16-bit images limits your options. For example not all of Photoshop's built-in filters work. Because they are higher quality, 16-bit images occupy nearly twice as much disk space. In general, you will work with RGB images with 8 bits per channel, for a total of 24 bits. If you add an alpha channel, you will have 32 bits. Be sure to check with your NLE manufacturer for support of 16-bit images as well as in Appendix C.

Selecting and Extracting Images

In order to work with something in Photoshop, it must be selected. While the human eye can differentiate between objects in a photo, software is not as advanced. Photoshop must be told what you want selected and what should happen to those selected pixels.

This process involves making a selection and is often done using the Marquee, Magic Wand, or Lasso tools. These tools are fairly intuitive and can often produce acceptable results with little work. A disadvantage of these tools is that once you deselect something, the selection data is not permanently saved with the document.

In order to facilitate a smoother workflow, many people isolate individual pieces of a composition to their own layer. It is possible to place only what you want on an isolated layer. The empty space, often represented by a checkerboard pattern inside of Photoshop, is called transparency. An advantage to isolating elements to their own layers is that you can quickly load them as a selection and make further changes.

There are many approaches to extracting images. Some are obvious, such as using an eraser or selecting and deleting. Word processor-like functions of copy, cut, and paste also exist. Photoshop has a built-in "dummy" tool called Extract, which is very tempting, but proves lacking. Intermediate techniques include layer masking. Of course, this transparency needs to travel out to the NLE or motion graphics environment, so you'll need to look at alpha channels and support for the .psd file format. Transparency is the foundation of compositing, and since there are many different situations, there are also many different tools.

Tool	Command
Rectangular Marquee tool	M
Elliptical Marquee tool	M
Lasso tool	L
Magnetic Lasso tool	L
Polygonal Lasso tool	L
Quick Selection tool	W
Magic Wand tool	W

The Easy Ways

There is an assortment of tools that you can learn quickly. With a little bit of practice, the Lasso, Magic Wand, and Quick Selection tools can generate acceptable results. Once you have a selection, tools can copy it to a new layer, inverse the selection and delete the rest, or use the selection to generate a layer mask or alpha channel. Some new users are attracted to the Eraser tools, but these tools are very inaccurate. They make a selection and delete in one step. The Eraser tools produce destructive editing and should be avoided.

Feather from the Start

You can feather your selections first by selecting a feathering width in the Options bar. Feathering produces a gradual edge, which is often desirable.

Modifying tools can be accomplished by accessing the Options bar. Select the tool you want to use, then press *Return* (*Enter*) to access the Feather or Tolerance field. Type in the number you want, and then press *Return* (*Enter*) again to apply it. If there are multiple fields, you can tab between them.

Lasso Tool

The Lasso is a freehand selection tool. Draw around the area you want, and it is selected. This is much like a football sportscaster drawing on the screen with a telestrator. The better you are with the mouse or pen and tablet, the better you will be at making a selection. The regular Lasso tool has only two options: Feathering and Anti-alias. A feathered edge will generate a soft edge. You can feather up to 250 pixels, but you'll rarely need to use that much on a low-resolution source. The Anti-alias option will smooth out your line to cut down on jaggies that will produce poor results on screen.

Polygonal Lasso Tool

This tool is a favorite among broadcast designers. It is frequently employed as the quick way to extract a headshot for producing on-air graphics. The advantage of the Polygonal Lasso is that you can release the mouse button as you draw. You simply click to add the first anchor point, then move the mouse to the next anchor and click again. Proceed to draw around the subject until you return to your starting point. If you make a mistake, press the Delete (Backspace) key to delete one point back (you can delete multiple points). At any time, you can double-click, and Photoshop will close the loop for you. The Polygonal Lasso tool works well for areas with large amounts of straight lines. Smoothing and feathering are particularly useful in avoiding an X-Acto-blade look.

Lasso Practice

You can open the file `Ch04_Lasso_Tools. tif` in order to try out the Lasso tools.

Combo Lasso

Want to use both the Standard and Polygonal Lasso tools? You can toggle Lasso tools in midselection. Hold down the ⌥ (alt) key and drag.

Magnetic Lasso Tool

The Magnetic Lasso tool contains many options. By adjusting parameters based on your source image, Photoshop can use edge detection to help you in making a selection. To preview the brush size of the Magnetic Lasso, depress the Caps Lock key. (Note that this is directly opposite of what you would do with any other tool.)

- To start, specify the width that Photoshop will look for edges. The Magnetic Lasso will detect edges only a specified distance from the pointer. You can adjust the size of the brush by using the [and] keys ([for smaller,] for larger).
- Next, specify the Edge Contrast to determine sensitivity to edges in the composition. You can choose a value between 1% and 100%. High values sense sharply contrasting edges; low values detect lower-contrast edges.
- The final option is Frequency, which specifies how often Photoshop sets fastening points. You can enter

a value between 0 and 100. Higher values draw the selection quicker, with greater accuracy, but may cause aliasing problems (because the tool is now acting more like the Magic Wand). Make sure to smooth or feather your edge before using the selection.

For images with soft edges, use a lower width and edge contrast, and take your time when tracing the border. Images with well-defined borders can be traced more quickly. You can use higher width and edge contrast settings to generate good results. For pen and tablet users, you may choose to use the Stylus Pressure option to dynamically adjust the edge width based on pen pressure.

Greater Averaging in Photoshop CS3

Photoshop has offered several different sampling methods. Photoshop CS3 offers more options to deal with higher-resolution photos. You can now use 11×11, 31×31, 51×51, and 101×101 averaging to sample the average color of a larger region.

Magic Wand

The Magic Wand can be used to select areas of color. The sensitivity is driven by the Tolerance control. The larger the number, the more Photoshop will accept similar pixels (based on brightness and color level). The sample size setting in the Eyedropper tool. You can choose various averaging settings including Point Sample, 3×3 average or 5×5 average. If the wand is acting oddly, adjust the tolerance settings in the Eyedropper options.

For more accurate control, most users select the contiguous option from the Options bar. This forces the Magic Wand to only make selections of adjacent pixels. This is particularly useful when trying to select background objects, such as the sky. This way, only adjacent pixels are chosen, not similar blues in the clothes or foreground. With this option deselected, Photoshop chooses all of the similar pixels throughout the entire document.

The lower third for this commercial harnesses Photoshop's alpha channel capabilities. It is possible to build complex effects that are impossible or time consuming in an NLE title tool. (Courtesy American Red Cross.)

Another option is Use All Layers. This will ignore which layer you are currently using. Instead, all visible layers become part of the selection. You still must switch layers to manipulate data not on your current layer. However, you can make a selection based on several layers using this method.

Magic Wand selections tend to be very fragmented with rough edges. This happens because selections are based on pixels and tolerance settings. Essentially, the Magic Wand is a bitmap tool; pixels are either on or off. This is the primary disadvantage of this tool: it leads to pixelated edges. To minimize this, choose the Anti-aliased option. It is possible to further smooth out the selection's edges to generate a usable selection. The first step is to grow the selection to fill in gaps. You can choose to add to the selection by *Shift* +clicking in adjacent areas. This will add to the primary selection based on the Magic Wand's setting. It is better to use a

It is often easier to select what you don't want, such as the sky, first. You can then inverse your selection.

Wand Practice

You can open the file `Ch04_Magic_Wand.tif` in order to try out the Magic Wand tool. Truth be told, this is the least-useful selection tool.

Practice Quick Selections

You can practice using the Quick Selection tool by opening `Ch04_Quick_Selection.jpg`. You must have Photoshop CS3 installed to access this tool.

Tame Those Edges

Rough edges? If you have the jaggies, try running the median filter on your Quick Mask (Filter>Noise>Median). This will allow you to smooth over selections made with the Lasso or Wand tools.

lower tolerance and click multiple times than it is to use a high-tolerance setting. This is because more control is possible. Think of it as the difference between a hatchet and a pocketknife. If you want detail, it's better to take several shorter strokes and maintain finer control.

Quick Selection

The Quick Selection tool is a new and welcome addition to Photoshop CS3. It builds upon the functionality of the Magic Wand and produces better results with fewer clicks. In fact, the Quick Selection tool takes priority over the Magic Wand and it is a suitable replacement. Click and drag in the image to make an initial selection. To make another selection, click and drag again. If you get too much of a selection, hold down the ⌥ (*alt*) key to subtract from the selection.

Refining Basic Selections

When you have most of your desired pixels, you can pick up little stray pockets by using the Select menu. There are seven additional options available in all versions of Photoshop that are useful. They are available for all selection tools and methods.

Grow. Expands your selection by choosing pixels that are both adjacent to the current selection and resemble the colors in the current selection. The selection will grow based on the tolerance setting you have in the Options bar for the Magic Wand.

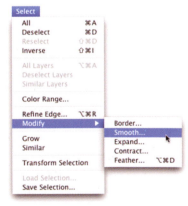

Similar. This command works like Grow, except pixels need not be adjacent to the current selection.

Contract. This pulls the active selection inward a specified number of pixels.

Expand. This pushes the active selection outward a specified number of pixels.

Smooth. This useful command rounds out selections and gets rid of sharp corners. Specify an amount as a Sample Radius (larger numbers mean smoother edges).

Border. This command uses the current selection to create a new area of a user-specified thickness that borders the previous selection. It is limited in its practical applications, but can be useful for video pros to "defringe" an object. If your object has rough edges, you can load the object, and then use the border selection to specify a thin 2- or 3-pixel border. This area can then be deleted or blurred. (Think of this as "choking the matte.")

Feather. The final step of most selections is feathering. This generates a graduated edge. Think of feathering as the difference between a ballpoint and felt-tip pen.

Refine Edge Command

While the Select menu offers several options, there is always room for improvement. Photoshop CS3 offers a powerful option for refining a selection. The Refine Edge command can be accessed two ways. It is available in the Options bar for all selection tools, and can also be chosen from the menus by choosing Select>Refine Edge. This command is very intuitive and its sliders provide quick feedback as you refine a selection.

Step 1. Open the file `Ch04_Quick_Selection.jpg` from the DVD-ROM.

Step 2. Make an initial selection using a tool of your choice (the Quick Selection tool works well).

Step 3. Click the Refine Edges button in the Options bar.

Step 4. Click the triangle next to the word Description to see a more detailed description of the options for selection refinement.

Step 5. Adjust the different sliders to tweak the selection.
- **Radius**. Refines the selection edge.
- **Contrast**. Increase the contrast of a selection's edge.
- **Smooth**. Removes any jagged edges.
- **Feather**. Softens the edge of the selection
- **Contract/Expand.** This will grow or shrink a selection.

Step 6. Click one of the preview icons to change how the selection is displayed. There are five options to choose from; experiment with the different choices to see which one you prefer.

Step 7. Click OK to create the selection.

Extract Filter

The Extract filter is very labor-intensive, requiring you to draw around the edges and fill the areas you want to keep. This command takes as much (or more!) time than layer masking. It also

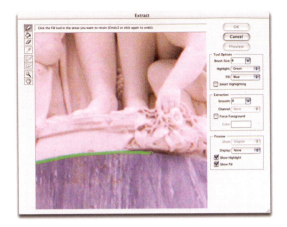

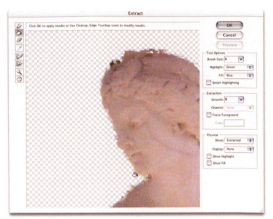

uses destructive editing techniques that permanently discard pixel data. I'd recommend skipping ahead to layer masking. However, many users like to try all the tools, so I will attempt to make this command useable.

The Extract filter can be found under the Filter menu. It requires you to paint around the edges of your subject with a "highlighter." It is a good idea to zoom in when drawing your edge, and then use the Hand tool to pan around. Use the common keyboard short-cuts ⌘+➕ or ➖ (*ctrl*+➕ or ➖) to zoom and the `Spacebar` to temporarily access the Hand tool. After drawing your edge, you fill in the areas you want to keep, with the Paint Bucket tool. You can adjust smoothing controls to get better edges.

The Extract filter will provide good results when used with a subject that has a high-contrast background. However, it is prone to eating away at the edges of your subject if there is a similar luminance or color in the foreground and background. When you can accept the preview, click OK. Again, the primary disadvantages are that the Extract filter is destructive and that it does not offer the flexibility of layer masking.

Layer Masking

Layer masking is the best way to extract an image. It is extremely flexible in that it supports multiple levels of transparency. Also, you can continue to touch up your mask throughout the postproduction process. Change your mind, and you can restore any part or even all of the background.

To encapsulate the technology, a grayscale image is attached to the layer, which then masks part of the layer. The term *mask* is very appropriate because parts of the layer are *hidden*, not erased. You can add or subtract to a layer mask by simply painting on the mask. Masks are stored with the document when you save it and can be modified at any point.

Create the Layer Mask

The best way to learn masks is to create one. This process is fairly in-depth, but the payoff is big. With practice, layer masking becomes significantly easier. Let's explore layer masks by building one.

Step 1. Open up `Ch04_Layer_Mask.tif` from the chapter folder. This document contains no layers.

Step 2. You cannot mask the background of an image because it is not a layer. You must convert it to a layer by double-clicking and naming the layer. You can also use +double-click (*alt*+double-click) to float the layer without naming it.

Step 3. It is best to start a layer mask with a rough selection. Once you have the Background layer unlocked (floating), make a rough selection with the Polygonal Lasso tool.

Step 4. With the selection active, click on the Add Layer Mask button at the bottom of the Layers palette. A black-and-white matte is now added to the layer. Black areas are 100% transparent; white areas are 100% opaque. These layer masks can also be blurred for soft edges or contain gray values for partial transparency.

Step 5. When you are ready to clean up the layer mask, select your Paintbrush tool and load the default colors by pressing the *D* key. White will be used for areas that are opaque (solid), and black will be used for areas that are transparent. You can now toggle between black and white by pressing the *X* key. A good mnemonic for this shortcut is Devil's Xylophone. For large areas, use a large brush. You can quickly change brush size by using the *[* and *]* keys. You can change brush softness with *Shift*+*[* or *]*.

Step 6. Zoom into the document so that you can easily see what you are working on. Start to paint, using a soft-edge brush. Make sure you are working on the mask. Look for a thin border around the mask thumbnail, which is to the right of the layer thumbnail. If you are working on a tough area, you may want to switch to a smaller brush or reduce the opacity of your working brush. Less opacity will require more strokes to build your mask. (Think of them as coats of paint.)

Resolution Matters when Masking

 If possible, work with a higher dpi source image. This way you can zoom in farther without pixelization. This is helpful when building the layer mask. You can always downsample later.

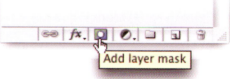

Add layer mask

Video #8 Effective Layer Masks

Want to see layer masking in action? Be sure to view the Masking movie on the Chapter's DVD-ROM.

Step 7. You can use the Paintbrush tool to draw straight lines. Click for the starting point, and hold down the `Shift` key and click for the second point. Photoshop will draw the straight line.

Step 8. Don't worry about "perfect"; you can clean things up later.

Refining the Layer Mask

Chances are the layer mask is pretty good, but like most things it can always be better. There are a couple of special tricks you can use to make a "perfect" layer mask:

Contrasting. First, place a high-contrast, solid color directly behind the masked layer. This is a temporary step, but it makes it easier to see stray pixels. In our case, go to the Create New Fill Or Adjustment Layer icon at the bottom of the Layers palette and choose Solid Color. At any time, you can change the solid's color by double-clicking on the Layer icon.

Smudging. By using blending modes, the Smudge tool becomes a great way to touch up your layer mask. There are two additional modes available to the Smudge tool when in the Mask mode—Lighten and Darken. You can quickly shift between these modes by using the `Shift`+`=` and `Shift`+`−` key combo. Use the Darken mode to push the dark edges of the mask in; use the Lighten mode to push the white pixels out. Set the Smudge tool to a low-pressure setting, and use short strokes to push the pixels around and fill up your layer mask. As always, the `[` and `]` keys change brush size, and the `Spacebar` will give you the Hand tool to pan around.

Blurring. You can use the Blur tool to control the blurring directly or use a filter. Remember, you are blurring the layer mask only, not the image. The more blur you use, the more the edges will feather. Experiment with blurring until you get a realistic edge. If you ever go too far, you can always paint detail back in by painting with white.

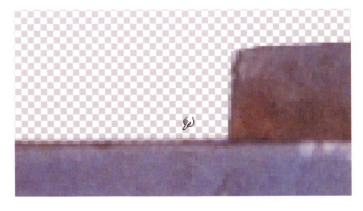

Once you have the perfect layer mask, you can use it in different ways. If you keep it inside of Photoshop, the transparency is preserved. To use it in applications that do not recognize .psd layers, you must create an alpha channel (more on that beginning on page 96). At any time, you can choose to enable, disable, or permanently apply the layer mask. You access these advanced options by right-clicking on the Mask icon.

Color Range

A very powerful but overlooked tool can be found under the Select menu. Color Range makes it easy to select large areas of color (or color ranges). To begin, use the Eyedropper on the desired color or area. To add to the selection, use the Plus Eyedropper; to subtract, the Minus Eyedropper. The Fuzziness control will soften your selection by increasing tolerance for stray pixels. It is also possible to preview the selection as a mask by using the Selection Preview pull-down menu. The Color Range command can also be accessed with the contextual menu when a selection tool is active.

Step 1. Open the file `Ch04_Color_Range.tif` from the chapter's folder on the DVD-ROM.

Step 2. Choose Select>Color Range to launch to launch the Color Range command.

Step 3. With the eyedropper, click on the blue sky. You'll see an initial selection created in the dialog window.

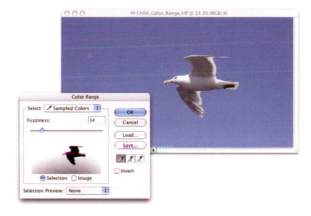

Step 4. Hold down the _Shift_ key and click on more of the blue sky to build a larger selection.

Step 5. Adjust the Fuzziness slider to taste.

Step 6. If you have selected too much, you can hold down the ⌥ (_alt_) key to subtract from the selection.

Step 7. When satisfied, click OK.

Step 8. Let's use the selection to make an isolated image adjustment. Choose Layer>New Adjustment Layer>Hue/Saturation.

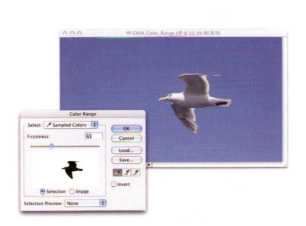

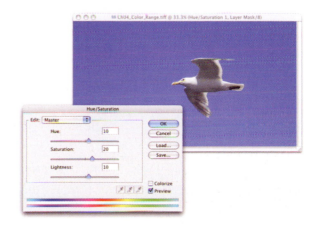

Step 9. Adjust the sliders to enhance the sky color — Hue: +10, Saturation: +20, and Lighten: +10.

Step 10. Click OK.

Move a Selection

There are a few ways to reposition a selection:

- While drawing a selection (with the mouse button still depressed), you can hold the `Spacebar` down and move the selection.
- With an active selection, choose a marquee tool and move the cursor inside the selection border (marching ants). The icon will change to a triangle with a marquee border; you can now click inside and drag the selection to move it.
- To modify a selection with controls similar to the Free Transform command, choose Select>Transform Selection. All of the options available to the Free Transform command can be applied to the selection border.

Important Keyboard Commands for Selections

There are three standard modifier key combos used when building selections:

- Holding down the `Shift` key before making a second selection, adds to the initial selection.
- The (`alt`) key lets you subtract from an item.
- Holding down `Shift` + (`alt`) creates the intersection of the two selections.

By employing these three modifiers, it is possible to use the basic tools and build up a selection. But don't try and build your selection all at once.

- You can add the `Shift` key after you have begun drawing with the Marquee tool to constrain the selection to a perfect square or circle.
- Holding down the (`alt`) key will enable you to draw from the center with the Selection tool. This is particularly useful when selecting a circular area.
- It is possible to combine the two key combinations.

Get Better with Brushes

Masks are very dependent on your paintbrush skills. Remember to practice free-drawing with the mouse or tablet to improve your ability to create brushstrokes.

Complex Selections with the Quick Mask Mode

The Quick Mask mode is another one of those overlooked features that really should make its way into your skill set. In Quick Mask mode, you can use Paintbrush tools and the Smudge and Blur tools to generate an accurate selection. Enter this mode from a button near the bottom of the toolbox. It is a good idea to build a rough selection first.

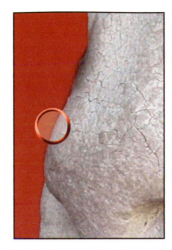

Don't like red? The mask color and transparency can be changed. Just double-click on the Quick Mask icon.

Use the Smudge tool or Blur tool to touch up your mask; at low-pressure settings, it is easy to feather your edges.

The Navigator serves two purposes: it's a great way to quickly zoom and pan around a large image and it gives you a large reference image when you are zoomed in making small corrections.

Open up the image `Ch04_Quick_Mask.tif` from the chapter folder. Use your selection tools to build a rough selection. When you are satisfied, click on the Quick Mask icon or press **Q**. Depending on user preference, either the masked or selected areas will be covered with a color overlay signifying the masked areas. By default, this is a 50% rubylith mask. This is customizable: just double-click on the Quick Mask icon. You may find it helpful to pick another color that is higher contrast or to make the mask more opaque.

As you work your way in to the finer parts of the mask, particularly soft edges, it is a good idea to zoom in. If you are scanning your own images, scan at a higher ppi so that you can zoom in farther before the image begins to degrade. You can always resize the image after you perform the extraction or mask. While painting, holding down the **Spacebar** will temporarily switch you to the Hand tool. This makes it easier to move around the work area without having to slow down. Some people will also place the Navigator palette in plain view. The red box signifies the current view area and can be dragged around easily. The Navigator gives you a visual interface to the work area.

Now you need to clean up the quick mask. To start, press the **D** key to load the default colors, pure black and white. When you create the quick mask (or any mask), using black will add to the mask; white will subtract. If you use the brush at less than 100% opacity, you will generate feathered edges. It is a good idea to paint as close as you can with a large, soft brush. You can make your active brush larger by pressing the **]** key; the **[** will reduce the

Better Edges through Feathering

 Feathered edges are important for creating believable composites. A feathered edge uses graduated steps to go between selected and unselected. Think of it as the difference between a ballpoint pen and a felt-tip marker. You can feather after making a selection by going to the Select menu and choosing Feather. You can feather up to 250 pixels, but the amount needed will vary based upon the resolution of the source image. You can also modify the Marquee tools to have feathered edges. Experiment with feathering to improve your selections.

brush size. To soften the edges of your brush, use the Shift and [or] keys.

The final touches to a quick mask come from the Smudge and Blur tools. Adjust the pressure setting to a low value. Zoom in so you can clearly see your edges. By employing a series of short strokes, you can touch up the soft edges of your mask. When you are satisfied with the Quick Mask, click on the icon or press Q to turn the Quick Mask into a selection. It is a good idea to save the mask in a format that other programs can recognize. You can convert it to a Layer Mask or save it an alpha channel.

Masking versus Erasing

Once you have built a good selection, you have an important decision to make. You can add transparency in a destructive or nondestructive way. Many users will choose to cut and paste the selected object—or invert their selection and press the Delete key.

A better choice is the layer mask. First, make sure that the layer you want to mask is not a locked *Background* layer, if it is, double-click and name the layer. Once you have made a selection, click on the Add Layer Mask button at the bottom of the Layers palette. This will generate a grayscale matte attached to the layer.

Editing the mask is easy and allows plenty of fine adjustments. First, click on the Layer Mask icon. A border now appears around the mask icon. The process is now identical to editing a Quick Mask. Use your Paintbrush tools and touch up your edges with the Blur and Smudge tools.

When finished, you can click on the layer thumbnail and edit the picture. It may be helpful to place a blank layer behind your masked layer and fill it with a high-contrast color. This will let you see any stray pixels. By Shift +clicking on the layer's mask, you can temporarily disable masks.

Look for Paths in Stock Photos

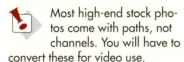

Most high-end stock photos come with paths, not channels. You will have to convert these for video use.

⌘+click (ctrl+click) on the path's name in the Paths palette.

(Optional) You can choose to feather the selection.

Then switch to the Channels palette and click on the Save Selection as Channel icon at the bottom.

Saving Selections as Paths

Paths do not allow soft edges, and generally find the most use in print applications. However, creating a path from an existing mask or channel is easy.

Step 1. Make an active selection. If you are in Quick Mask mode, exit. If you have an alpha channel or layer mask, hold down the ⌘ (ctrl) key and click on the layer's thumbnail.

Step 2. Switch over to the Paths palette, which is usually docked with the Layers palette.

Step 3. Click on the Make Work Path from Selection button at the bottom of the palette. You should see a path appear with the title Work Path.

Step 4. Italicized paths or masks are temporary. It is necessary to double-click on these and assign a name.

Step 5. The path can now be exported out to Adobe Illustrator, where it can be cleaned up or sized. This can be useful for creating a silhouette image. Vector graphics have the advantage of unlimited scaling, with no quality loss.

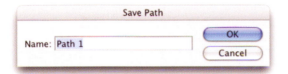

You may need to go the other direction when using stock images. Because paths are vector-based, they take up much less room in file size. These savings make it much more likely to find clipping paths with stock photos collections on CD-ROM. You can ⌘+click (*ctrl*+click) on the path's icon, and then switch over to the Channels palette. Click on the Save Selection as Channel icon, and you are set.

Creating a Path with the Pen Tool

The Pen tool can be used to create paths from scratch, and is well suited for images that contain curved shapes. While many users swear by the Pen tool, keep in mind that it's not the easiest tool to use. The Pen tool creates a path when you click around the image and add anchor points. Photoshop connects those points with vector lines, which can be adjusted or repositioned. If you use Adobe Illustrator or After Effects, you may find the Pen Tool relatively easy to use. Let's give the Pen Tool a try:

Gray is Not Boring

It is best to view channels in grayscale to see contrast and detail.

Step 1. Open the file `Ch04_Pen_Tool.tif` from the chapter's folder on the DVD-ROM.

Step 2. Choose the Pen tool from the Toolbox or press the keyboard shortcut Ⓟ.

Step 3. Choose the following options from the Options Bar:
- Choose Paths from the first three buttons. This will create a new path in the Paths palette.
- Select Auto Add/Delete so anchor points will automatically be added when you click a line segment. Likewise, Photoshop will automatically delete an anchor point when you click on it with the Pen tool.

- Click the inverted arrow next to the shape buttons in the Options Bar to access the submenu. Choose the Rubber Band option, which will make it easier to preview path segments while drawing.

Step 4. Position the Pen tool in the top-left corner of the cockpit and click. An initial anchor point is added.

Step 5. You'll now need to draw curved paths. When you click to add a new point, keep the mouse button depressed. You can drag to create the curve.

- Drag towards the curve for the first point. Drag the opposite direction for the second point.
- Hold down the Command (ctrl) key to modify handles while drawing.
- Hold down the ⌥ (alt) key to change a handle's direction while drawing.
- Dragging both direction points in the same direction will create an S-shaped curve.
- Try to minimize the number of anchor points added…move forward along the object and pull to form the curve.

Step 6. When you reach the end of your path, you can click to close the shape. Just like the Polygonal Lasso tool, you must click on your starting point to close the path.

Step 7. To end an open path, ⌘+Click (ctrl+Click) away from the path.

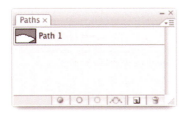

Step 8. The path can be adjusted by using the Direct Selection tool (A). This will allow you to click on an anchor point or handle, and adjust the position or shape.

Step 9. When satisfied, you can ⌘+Click (ctrl+Click) on the path's thumbnail in the Layers palette. You will see the "marching ants," which indicate an active selection has been made.

Keep in mind, the Pen tool and Paths are not for the meek. You will likely have strong feelings that will either draw you to the Pen tool all of the time or send you seeking alternatives. With practice, the Pen tool can become easier to the less initiated.

Converting Channels into Masks

Sculptors often say that the figures are already in the stone; they just release them. The same is often true with alpha channels. Look at each channel independently until you find the ones with highest contrast. You can use one or more color channels as the basis for creating an alpha channel.

Converting a Single Channel into a Mask

Oftentimes you can use a single channel as the basis for an alpha channel or layer mask. This is especially true for scanned or flattened logos.

Step 1. Open the file `Ch04_Channel_Extract.psd` from the book's DVD-ROM.

Step 2. Switch to the Channels palette or choose Windows> Channel if it is not visible.

Step 3. Duplicate the Gray channel by right-clicking and choosing Duplicate Channel… Name the Channel Alpha, and click OK.

Step 4. The new channel needs to be cleaned up. The "white" paper has some discoloration. Turn the alpha channel's visibility icon on (the eyeball icon) and disable visibility for the gray channel. With the new channel selected, press ⌘+L (ctrl+L) to open the Levels dialog box. Drag the black point and white point sliders towards the center until you move beyond the histogram data. This makes the black and white in the channel perfectly "clean."

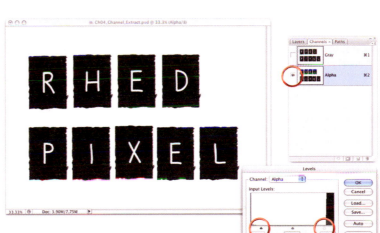

Step 5. The "holes" in the channel must be filled in to create clean transparency. Press B to select your Brush tool then press D to load the default colors of black and white and X to switch black to the Foreground color. Paint out the white letters in the center of the box. This will ensure that the white part of the logo is not interpreted as transparent.

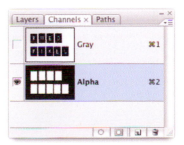

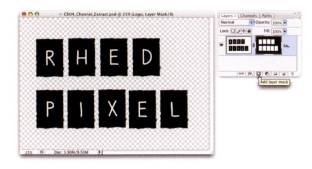

Step 6. The alpha channel must be reversed to "cut the matte." With the alpha channel selected press ⌘+I (ctrl+I) to Invert the channel.

Step 7. To load the alpha channel, ⌘+Click (ctrl+Click) on its thumbnail in the Channels palette. Once you have an active selection, you can turn on the visibility icon for the Gray channel then turn off the visibility icon for the alpha channel.

Step 8. Switch to the Layers palette. The logo layer is locked as it is a flattened document. Double-click on the layer's name and call it Logo.

Step 9. Click the Add Layer Mask button at the bottom of the Layers palette to store the transparency selection with the layer. You can now save the file as a PSD document to store the transparency.

Converting Multiple Channels into a Mask with Calculations

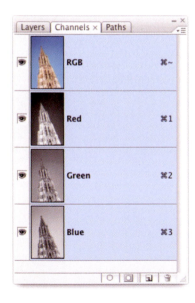

We will use an advanced procedure called Calculations to combine two channels into a new channel, which will function as the alpha. Depending on the source photo, you will generate anything from a perfect mask to a great start.

Step 1. Open the document Ch04_Calculations.tif from the chapter's folder.

Step 2. Call up the Channels palette and look for the highest contrasting channels. Because you want to remove the background, look for the highest contrast between foreground and background. The red channel should stand out the most.

We will now use an advanced command to merge channels together. Before Photoshop had layers, it had Calculations. The name scares most people off—math is not a favorite course at most journalism and art schools. Relax. The computer does the math. All you have to do is enable the Preview function and tweak a few drop-down menus. This feature is designed to combine channels from the same document or documents of an identical size.

Step 3. Call up the Calculations command from the Image menu. Make sure the Preview box is active.

Step 4. You can now combine the Red, Blue, Green, or Grayscale composite channels to form a new channel. With this image, use the Red channel as your first source.

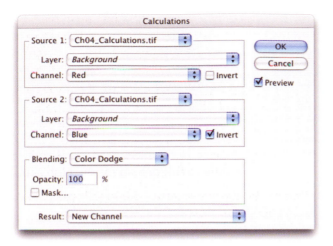

Step 5. Combine it with the blue channel. Click the invert box for the blue channel and try the Color Dodge blending mode. The resulting image should show a high-contrast image, a white shape for the church tower, and a gray image for the sky.

Step 6. Click OK and generate the new alpha channel.

Step 7. Now make a Levels adjustment to clean up the matte. You want a high-contrast black-and-white matte. Adjust the midpoint and black point until a clean matte is generated.

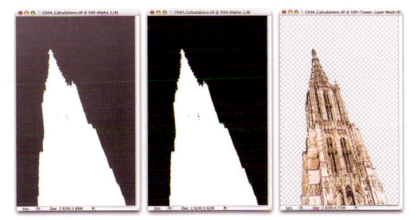

The left image shows the matte generated by the Calculations command. The center image has been touched up with the Levels command. The right shows the effect of loading the selection and applying it as a layer mask.

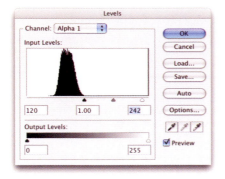

With a little bit of experimentation, a perfect matte can be generated. This alpha channel can be kept and used in a video application, or it can be loaded and turned into a layer mask. Calculations aren't a solution all the time, but they are worth a try when you have high-contrast channels.

Advice on Selections

There is no single technique that is perfect for making the ultimate selection. It is the situation that dictates the technique, not your comfort level. It is important to get comfortable with all of the methods discussed in this book so you can begin to unlock Photoshop's power.

Garbage Mattes

Garbage matte is a compositing term. It means using a simple matte to block out the complex noise or garbage in the image that would otherwise interfere with a more elaborate matte. In other words, we chop the object out and then refine it.

When making selections, move quickly but effectively. I don't imagine you have time to spend 30 minutes generating the perfect selection. By making a broad selection with the Lasso, Quick Selection, or Color Range method, you have less to worry about. Then start to refine things down inside the Quick Mask mode. Finish it off with some touchups and feathering using the Blur and Smudge tools or the Median and Gaussian Blur filters. You also may find the Minimum and Maximum filters useful for "choking" the matte.

Along the way, you can employ intermediate alpha channels so that you can save your selection. If you mess up, some quick painting of the matte will get you back on track. Most intermediate users try to make the entire selection in one step, but they soon realize that a good selection involves several short (and quick) steps. Don't try to do too much with one click. Use all the methods as needs arise, and you will be fine.

Paths and Channels

If a photo comes with a path or channel, use it. Many editors are so deadline-driven that they forget to check if someone has already created a channel or path. There are a few ways to handle embedded data; all of them are far quicker than starting from scratch. As they say, there's no need to reinvent the wheel. Always check your Channels palette for an included alpha channel and the Paths palette for an included path or clipping path.

Look First

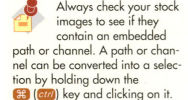

Always check your stock images to see if they contain an embedded path or channel. A path or channel can be converted into a selection by holding down the ⌘ (*ctrl*) key and clicking on it.

If you have a path or clipping path, simply ⌘+click (*ctrl*+click) on the path thumbnail in the Paths palette. Then switch over to the Channels palette and click on the Save Selection as Channel icon. If you'd like a softer edge, run a Gaussian Blur filter on the alpha channel.

If you have multiple paths or channels that you'd like to combine, load the first one by ⌘+clicking (*ctrl*+clicking) on the path/channel thumbnail. To load additional items, use the same key combo, but add the *Shift* key. When you have loaded all the selections, click on the Save Selection as Channel icon. It is a good idea to throw away any unused alpha channels before saving for your NLE. Most systems do not correctly interpret multiple alpha channels.

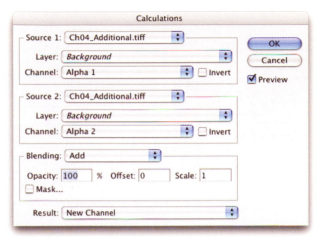

Unlike layers, you cannot merge channels, but Photoshop does have two helpful techniques for this situation. The Load Selection command (Select>Load Selection) allows you to load the first channel, and then add the second one. This creates a new selection, which then must be saved as a channel.

Let's try merging two alpha channels:

Step 1. Open the file `Ch04_Additional.tif` from the book's DVD-ROM.

Step 2. Open the Channels palette and view the two existing alpha channels.

Step 3. Choose Image>Calculations to launch the Calculations dialog.

Step 4. Set the Source 1 Channel to Alpha 1 and the Source 2 Channel to Alpha 2.

Step 5. Set the Blending mode Add, which will combine them together.

Step 6. Specify that you want the result to be a New Channel and click OK. The new "merged" alpha channel is created.

While many nonlinear editing systems support Photoshop layers, it is still a good idea to save flattened files with alpha channels. A PICT or TARGA file with an embedded alpha channel gives predictable, consistent results. (Courtesy of the American Red Cross.)

The Best of Both Worlds

By saving your document as a layered TIFF file, most NLEs and compositing applications will read the file as "flat." However, you can open the file and make edits to layers and transparency, which will then update after you close and save.

Video #9   Perfect Alpha Channels

For more on alpha channels, don't miss the video tutorial on the DVD-ROM.

Creating Perfect Alpha Channels

When do you make an alpha channel? Whenever you want to embed the transparency data into the flattened file. You worked hard for that transparency. Why throw it away? Think of an alpha channel as a stencil or mask. Most nonlinear editing systems support some form of real-time alpha keying. It's a good idea to use it.

Now you're probably thinking, "My NLE supports Photoshop layers and transparency. I don't need an alpha channel." Wrong. Support for layers and transparency is great, but you will not get a perfect import. Even if your layer effects, grouping, and blend modes make it in (they won't, by the way), do you really want a five-layer lower third? Talk about hogging tracks in the timeline. I'm happy to have layer support, but I still pick a single, streamlined file 90% of the time. Sometimes you will want to animate or manipulate layers within the NLE, but that's why you always keep a layered design file to go back to. Proper use of alpha channels lets you change part of a composition without having to redo all of your work.

What are Alpha Channels?

Alpha channels grew out of work done at the New York Institute of Technology back in 1977. The goal was to embed transparency data directly into each file to cut down on rendering. The name alpha was chosen because it is the part of a mathematical equation that represents blending between composited images. The embedded alpha channel eliminated the need for a separate traveling matte. After Effects users should consider embedding alpha channels like Photoshop users do. Embedded mattes reduce the need for two-step rendering and eliminate the possibility of a misaligned matte.

Creating a "Perfect" Alpha Channel

Making a perfect alpha channel starts with having an active selection loaded. One easy way to create a perfect selection is to use a "targeted merge" approach. If you have not already extracted objects to their own layers, use the techniques described earlier in the chapter. Once everything is on extracted layers, you need to create a composite layer to generate the selection.

Step 1. Open the file `Ch04_Lower_Third.psd` from the chapter folder on the DVD-ROM.

Step 2. Turn visibility icons off (eyeballs) for all layers that should not be part of the alpha channel.

Step 3. Create a new layer by clicking on the new layer icon at the bottom of the Layers palette and highlight it.

Step 4. Hold down the ⌥ (alt) and choose Merge Visible from the Layers palette submenu.

Step 5. Now you have only one layer to load. ⌘+click (ctrl+click) on the composite layer's thumbnail to create the marching ants. You can now throw this layer away.

Step 6. Switch to the Channels palette and click the Save Selection as Channel icon (second from left). Make sure you have only one alpha channel for your document (if you have more than four channels in an RGB+Alpha image, you have more than one alpha channel).

Step 7. Save your native .psd file.

Step 8. Choose File>Save As..., and choose a format supported by your NLE. The most common formats are PICT and Targa. Make sure the Alpha Channels and As a Copy boxes are checked.

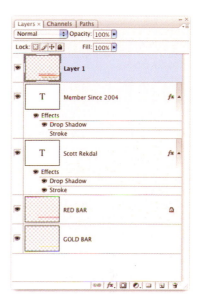

Photoshop used to have the Save a Copy menu option. This is actually the preferred method for saving a flattened file, and still saving and preserving your .psd file. The keyboard command still works. Choose ⌘+⌥+S (ctrl+alt+S) and you will automatically be in Save a Copy mode. Save a Copy is the preferred method because it allows you to save any changes you make, first into the flattened production file, and then in the layered .psd design file (upon closing the document). Save the flattened file to the appropriate location. Then, when you close your layered .psd file, tell it to save changes. That's it; no voodoo magic. Have a selection made, switch to the Channels palette, and save it.

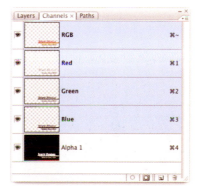

A good alpha channel starts with a good selection. With the selection active, click on the Save Selection as Channel button in the Channels palette. Save your flattened file with the alpha channel attached and you're done!

Premultiplied versus Straight Alpha Channels

You have to make some choices in Photoshop if you are saving out flattened files with alpha channels. It's important to decide between premultiplied or straight alpha channels. This becomes an issue when you have soft edge effects, especially drop shadows and glows.

The alpha channel stored the transparency information as an 8-bit or 16-bit file. This grayscale file contains levels of opacity. The stars in the accompanying figure have a yellow glow applied to them. The star on the left is over black, a common background color used by video pros when building graphics. The star on the right (it's really there) has been placed over a background that is the same color as the glow.

The star on the left is premultiplied; the glow is composited over black. The star on the right cannot be seen without enabling the alpha channel. The right star will generate better results when keyed over a video source.

Even Faster with Actions

If you load the Video Actions that come with the built-in presets, you'll find the alpha channel action saved for you. I created this for Adobe and it automates the above steps. Just open the Actions palette and click on the palette submenu to load them. The instructions are built in when you run the action.

When we create an alpha channel for these files, the shape is identical. The star over black, however, is considered premultiplied, a benefit when working in Photoshop so that we can see our work. The star on the right contains a straight alpha—that is, the alpha contains the glow info, but the background is a solid color that will become the glow when the image is keyed.

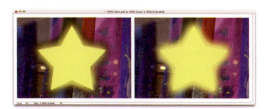

Premultiplied alpha channels will often pick up noise from the background layer. This is evident in the left star by the black fringe in the outer glow.

Notice how the premultiplied alpha picks up black around the edges. This is a subtle but nasty problem. It will show up when you have light-colored glows or drop shadows. The second star, with a straight alpha, keys perfectly with no color contamination. To create a straight alpha channel you must do one of the following:

- Place a solid color behind the objects that matches your glow or shadow.
- Place a copy of the photo behind the masked layer. This will allow the soft edges of the image to blend with the colors in the photo.

It is a limitation that Photoshop cannot generate a straight alpha channel when saving. While some programs such as Adobe After Effects and Apple Final Cut Pro will try to automatically compensate for a premultiplied alpha channel over a black or white background, it is not a perfect process. While it is an extra step to create a straight alpha, it's worth doing before saving your flattened files for video.

For Best Results with Alpha Channels

- Have only one alpha channel per document; delete unused channels before saving.
- Choose a 32-bits-per-pixel alpha channel.
- Do not use any compression when saving your file.
- Do not check the Save Transparency box in the TIFF dialog box as it cancels out your Embedded Alpha channel.

Hands On | 04

Case Study: Making a Matte Painting—*with Frank Rogers,*
Interface Media Group

Years ago it took a really big sheet of glass and really good painting talent to do a believable matte painting. I saw the death of that skill and wasn't even aware of it. On the "New York City" set (in North Carolina) of *Young Indy* I noticed a guy on an apple box with a laptop. Looking over his shoulder I saw he was sketching some roof extensions and skyline over a frame grab. Asking if this was a sketch that would be painted at ILM later, I was told this was the painting.

Now, with Photoshop, pieces of the set can be repeated, elements flipped or re-colored. Additionally, perspectives can be changed, and models or actual location photos can be inserted and blended. All without a hint of oil paint.

You'll find Exercise 04 on the DVD-ROM.

PRO*file*: Jayse Hansen

Jayse Hansen started his career with a Bell and Howell Super-8 camera when he was nine years old. This hobby was short lived, because $18 for three minutes of silent film is hard to come by on an allowance.

"I started in photography, migrated to print and Web design, and now combine all of that background into my motion design and visual effects," said Jayse. "I knew from age 10, when I fell in love with *Return of the Jedi*, that I wanted to work in film and video. So in a way, I'm fulfilling my lifelong dream."

Jayse makes a living in Las Vegas designing show intros, bumpers, special effects, Web pages, and print work. Jayse's work is known internationally, and he works with clients in Europe, South Africa, and Canada. He is a master at combining After Effects and Combustion with Flash, Illustrator, Photoshop, and anything else that works. Visitors to Creative Cow's forums and tutorial pages appreciate his motion graphics work. He is also the creator of VTC's Adobe After Effects Essentials and Adobe Photoshop Advanced Artistry video training, available at www.xeler8r.com.

"In motion, I like to do stuff that's like my digital still art. I create emotional imagery. I usually use tons of layers, duplicates, blending/transfer modes, and strong typography to create a final piece that I hope provokes the audience to feel something powerful."

At its core, motion graphics are a series of still images. To support his motion habit, Jayse relies on a still program, Photoshop.

"Photoshop is my number-one program. For video work, I find it much more efficient to work with layer masks and layer styles than to try to recreate that (and render each frame) in After Effects. Even if I need to recreate the text in AE, I'll often design in Photoshop because of its superior capabilities and layout finesse."

After a short conversation with Jayse, it is clear that he is all about digital. His work is on the cutting edge, and he helps develop tutorials for leading plug-ins. Despite this love for digital, he warns against the fast-and-cheap aspect often associated with modern video production.

"Most video editing software has a very distinct look to its graphics. I call it the 'DV' look. It's downright cheap looking. If you surf through local TV ads, you'll see evidence of this all too often. Buzzing-Awkward-Text that just looks thrown on last minute. For backgrounds and titles, Photoshop is invaluable," said Jayse. "If someone's still using marble or gradient backgrounds in pink or blue with big beveled boxes just because that's what comes built into their video editing program, they need to invest in Photoshop and create something a bit more modern and different. Respect yourself and your work enough to take it up a notch."

Many editors and motion graphic artists find it difficult to master all of Photoshop. This is not because they are incapable; time is just in such short supply.

"In my opinion, there is absolutely no substitute for learning Photoshop. Even advocates of competing art and photo programs are very well versed in Photoshop. If you want to have that extra edge, gain that extra respect, and free your creative genius, learning Photoshop is an absolute must."

To get you started, Jayse stresses that the key to his successful designs is the combination of layer masks, adjustment layers, and transfer modes.

"For most of my work," said Jayse, "I find myself using Gaussian Blur, Motion Blur, or Radial Blur (zoom) on layers—or on duplicated layers with their transfer modes set to Lighten, Soft Light, or Overlay. Sometimes I'll also use Filter>Texture>Grain to blend things or add depth. That's about it for filters."

The key is not how many filters you have, but how fast you can move through Photoshop. Learning the keyboard shortcuts will allow you more time to be creative.

"If you focus on learning shortcuts, you can really master a program—and people

who watch you work will know you know the program. These are my all-time superfaves:

- `⌘` + `Spacebar` (`ctrl` + `Spacebar`) while dragging a marquee box to zoom in on a very specific area of my image. Clients' mouths drop open whenever I do that. Add `⌥` (`alt`) and click to zoom out. Then I keep the `Spacebar` held down and click and drag to move my image to just where I want it.

- `[` and `]` while using a brush to enlarge and decrease its size.

- `⌘` + `Shift` + `<` or `>` (`ctrl` + `Shift` + `<` or `>`) to increase or decrease the font size of seleced text. Love that. Add `⌥` (`alt`) to supercharge it!

- `⌘` + `T` (`ctrl` + `T`) for Free Transform—access to all your transformation needs!

Jayse admits that creating graphics in front of a client can be intimidating. "Know that, whatever a client asks of you, anything can be done in Photoshop. I've proved it many times, when even I questioned it at first."

Jayse also said that Photoshop can set you apart from others in the digital video world. "Wherever your work—make it your goal to be indispensable, and you'll be set—take the extra step of learning or even mastering Photoshop."

Jayse has several great tutorials and tips, as well as an impressive portfolio, which you can browse for inspiration. Be sure to drop in for a visit at http://www.jayse.us.

SOME WORDS ON WORDS, LOGOS, AND SYMBOLS

Proper use of type is crucial in designing effective graphics for video. Designing motion graphics (or even graphics that must be keyed over a moving source) is an extremely challenging task. It becomes necessary to balance legibility with style, fitting enough information on the screen, but not crowding it. Despite the importance of good typography, this is one of the weakest areas of the video industry. Chances are you've never taken a class just on typography; this chapter will give you a crash course.

Vector Type

The key to Photoshop's flexibility is its use of vector-based type. Vectors are mathematically defined shapes that describe all of the characters in a typeface. These fonts can then be scaled to whatever size is needed, producing clean results at almost any size. Fonts are often available in multiple formats including Type 1 (PostScript), TrueType, and the newer OpenType. OpenType offers the advantage that the same font can be read by both Mac and PCs. You will need to check the manuals of your operating system and other video software to see which font formats are supported. Nearly all font foundries provide you with multiple formats, but some of the cheapie packages ($29 for 1,000 fonts) often provide only PC-compatible TrueType. I am not saying that fonts need to be expensive—many of my favorite foundries give away freebies— but make sure that you buy compatible fonts.

When you add a type layer to Photoshop, it adds it as pixels, or *raster information*. The rendered type layer is written at the resolution of the composition. However, the link to the original font is preserved, and you can modify the type layer (provided the font is loaded on the system) at any point in time. This is extremely helpful for fixing spelling problems or for scaling the size of text. You must save your design files as Photoshop, Photoshop PDF, or layered TIFF to preserve this flexibility. If the font is not loaded on

The right font helps set the mood for your piece. The Bawdy font family was chosen for its energy.

Vector Type

Type in Photoshop is vector-based. This allows you to easily resize or edit it at any time (as long as the correct font is loaded). "Old timers" will remember the pains suffered with the old Type tool.

103

Font Management Made Easy

Extensis Suitcase helps you track all the fonts on your system. You can create sets by client and also preview fonts before loading them. For more information, visit www.extensis.com.

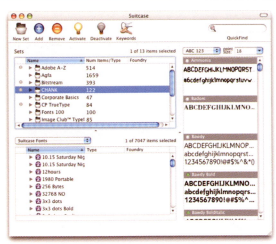

SERIF vs. SANS-SERIF

The clearest distinction between fonts is serif and sans serif. Featured are two faces from the Chank Company: BrainGelt and Mingler.

the system, the font layers will be marked with an exclamation point (!) icon. The font will display correctly, unless you attempt to edit the type layer.

Selecting the Right Font

Whenever I visit a post-production facility or television station, I am amazed at how many fonts are loaded on the system. I often carry 2,000 fonts or so on my system, but rarely have more than 75 active at any time. If you have hundreds (or even thousands!) of fonts active on your system, you could have an unmanageable mess on your hands. Too many fonts loaded may make it difficult to find the right font. It also can lead to serious performance issues such as an unstable operating system and slow launch times.

Here's a common scenario that I see repeated far too often. The editor will randomly pick a font and ask the client if they like it. If the answer is "no," they go to the next one on the list. Eventually, out of exasperation, all parties decide on a font, usually somewhere in the Hs of the list. Instead of scrolling all day long, interview your client about the style and mood they want to invoke. If they suggest a boring font, steer them towards an alternative that looks similar, but may be better optimized for video.

Serif versus Sans Serif

There are two major distinctions when dealing with fonts: *serif* or *sans serif.* For instant clarity, serif fonts (such as Times, Garamond, or Concorde, the text font of this book), have small strokes at the end of the larger strokes of the text. The alternative is sans serif fonts (such as Helvetica, Arial, or Univers, used for this book's chapter headings), which have a cleaner style comprised of generally even-weighted lines.

When working with serif fonts, be careful with the thickness of each character. Because serifs often come to small points, it is essential that the type is thick enough, or you will get shimmer. Serif fonts are much more likely to vibrate on video, especially at light weights and small sizes. Many clients prefer serif fonts because they are more traditional and are considered by many as easier to read in print. There are often more serif fonts to pick from because serif type has a long history. Serif fonts are modeled after many handwritten texts as well as the initial type used in printing presses.

Sans serif fonts are a more modern development. It is often possible to compress more text into a smaller space by using a sans serif font. These fonts are also more likely to be optimized for on-screen viewing. For video purposes, sans serif fonts are often easier for an audience to quickly comprehend, and they read better in smaller point sizes.

	PROS	CONS
Serif	• Increased readability • More traditional • More options available due to longer history	• Thin lines can cause problems for low-resolution printing or applications like video and Internet
Sans Serif	• More modern • Can compress more information into a smaller space • Optimized for screen usage	• Letter shapes not often as unique • Can be harder to read if too stylized

X-Height

The x-height is the distance from the top to bottom of a lower-case x. The x is measured because it is a clean letter with a distinct top and bottom. The height of the x does a lot to define the character of a font. The visual distinctiveness of a font is a combination of its x-height and the ascenders and descenders that grow from that center space. This height is perhaps the second most distinctive aspect when comparing two fonts.

Font Weight

The most useful fonts are those that have multiple weights. A font will generally have a book (or roman) weight. A font family may also include Light, Medium, Bold, Black, Italic, and more alternates. These alternates are helpful in designing effective screen graphics because you can cut down on the number of fonts used and stick with one font family.

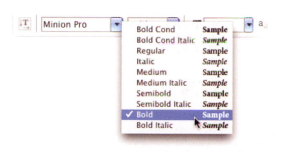

Appearance on Screen

Some fonts are meant for printing only. This fact is easier to accept if you remember that the print industry has been around a heck of a lot longer than the television industry. Test your fonts. If they are too busy or have too many elaborate serifs, make them inactive or remove them from your system.

Text Tool Presets

If you have a specific type of text combo that you use a lot (say Bookman Bold at 45 points with a tracking value of 50) you can save it. Just enter all of your text settings as you need into the Character and Paragraph palettes. Then, in the upper left corner of the Options bar, click on the drop-down menu. You can add new Tool Presets (just click the pad of paper icon).

Select Text without a Highlight

When you double-click on a text layer to select it, Photoshop inverses the text with a black highlight to indicate a selection. This can be distracting. Once you have an active selection, press ⌘+**H** (*ctrl*+**H**) to hide it.

Many modern fonts look particularly good on screen. Some recent additions include Georgia, Verdana, Myriad, Impact, Trebuchet, Gill Sans, Helvetica Neue, and Futura. These are just a few of the fonts that have been optimized for viewing on computer displays. Any font marked as optimized for Web output is also well suited for video work.

Style

Ask your client to describe the video. I generally ask for 10 to 20 adjectives that describe the company or product being featured. I then dig deeper and ask what the new video is supposed to accomplish. With this knowledge, you can make sound aesthetic decisions and impress your client with your good taste. Remember to use a distinctive display font for titles or headlines. Text or body fonts should be used for bullets or smaller copy.

Check out the interview with Chank Diesel at the end of this chapter (page 136) for great advice on how to make style decisions, as well as to get a better perspective on what goes into making a font. Different goals need different fonts to communicate.

Using the Character Palette

The Character palette provides you with total control over the appearance of text in your graphics. To get started, call up the Character palette by selecting it from the Windows menu or by clicking on the palette's button in the Options bar when you have the Text tool selected. Next, select the Type tool and click in your document to add a type layer. Single-clicking will enable point type, or you can click and drag to define a block for paragraph type.

There are many fields in the Character palette. The easiest way to understand them is to quickly run through each field's function. Feel free to jump ahead if you are comfortable with a particular area. I will mention shortcuts wherever possible.

Field 1: Set the Font Family

Here's where you pick the font to use. You can quickly cycle through fonts by clicking in this field and using the up and down arrows. Add the **Shift** key and you will jump to the top or bottom of your font list. Press the Tab key to move to the next (and subsequent) fields. If your preferences are set correctly you can click to see the font list in their actual typeface.

Field 2: Set the Font Style

If a font has multiple styles, such as a bold, italic, or black version available, this will make it quickly available. These too can be cycled with the arrow keys. It is *always* more desirable to use the actual bold or italic version of a font rather than the Faux Bold or Faux Italic buttons.

Field 3: Set the Font Size

It is possible to set the font size to any unit of measure. The standard is points, but you can type in a number followed by *px* (for pixels) if that is easier for you. The up and down arrow keys will increase 1 point each; add the Shift key and you will jump 10 points. For an additional shortcut, press ⌘+Shift+< or > (ctrl+Shift+< or >) to decrease or increase font size.

You can click on this toggle button to open and close the Character and Paragraph palettes.

Field 4: Set the Leading

Leading (pronounced "ledding") is a term derived from the days of a printing press when the printers inserted actual pieces of lead between the typeset characters. It refers to the space between the two lines of type measured in points. It is measured from the baseline, which is where the lowercase x sits in a line of type (see the previously mentioned x-height).

You can generally trust the auto setting for standard leading. Type is usually set with leading being 120% of the point size. For example, 24-point type would have 28.8 point leading. You can choose to adjust this manually, or pick from a drop-down pre-set list. If you haven't noticed the pattern, the arrow and Tab keys work here, too. A problem often arises with setting the leading for lines of text at different point sizes. Often descenders from the top line will cross ascenders from the lower line. These occurrences are called *tangents*. They are usually undesirable if they form accidentally. A tangent will draw your viewer's eye to the intersection. Since video graphics are often visible for only a short time, you don't want your viewer getting stuck. Adjust the leading or kerning to avoid tangents.

Field 5: Set the Kerning Between Two Characters

The space between two letters is called kerning. This is the most subjective area of typography. You'll need to develop a sense of visual balance. The goal is to have the text appear evenly weighted. Proper kerning allows the reader to easily recognize word shapes and lets them keep reading without having to pause on a word.

While you can edit kerning from the field, it is far easier to use the keyboard. Move your cursor using the arrow keys. When the blinking I-bar is between the two letters in question, hold down the ⌥ (alt) key and use your arrow keys. The left arrow will pull the text closer; the right arrow will push it further apart.

The space between two lines of type is the leading. This term dates back to the traditional printing press days, when strips of lead were inserted between lines for proper spacing.

Faux Bold?

That's just another way of saying Fake Bold. Always choose a true bold or italic typeface from the font menu before invoking the faux options of the Character palette. The true bold and italic versions created by the font's designer will always look better.

improper kerning

proper kerning

loose tracking

tight tracking

H_2O

negative baseline shift

Faux Bold

Faux Italic

ALL CAPS

Sᴍᴀʟʟ Cᴀᴘs

Superscript²

Subscript₃

Underline

~~Strikethrough~~

The most common complaint is that this is a time-consuming process. It is, but it is critical that you kern your text. People always ask why they don't have to kern in a word-processing program. The difference is that the gaps don't stand out at 12-point. However, when the text blows up significantly larger in Photoshop, minor flaws become gaping holes. If you skip this step, it's the equivalent to forgoing scene-to-scene color correction or a final audio mix. This is the professional polishing of graphics.

If you have worked on Avid editing systems, the Title Tool incorrectly identifies kerning as the space between all characters on a line. That is called *tracking*, which is our next field.

Field 6: Set the Tracking for Selected Characters

Tracking refers to the looseness or tightness of text, the space between the letters. Photoshop provides a handy list of drop-down presets. Tracking is how you can get that pesky Executive Vice-President of External Communications and Community Affairs title to fit on one line. You can also adjust the tracking by highlighting the desired words, holding down the ⌥ (*alt*) key, and using your left and right arrow keys.

Fields 7 and 8: Vertically and Horizontally Scale

These two fields enable you to stretch your text to force it to fit. Horizontal scaling set at 75% to 95% is another useful way to compress a line of text that cannot wrap to another line. Use Scaling as a last resort, but don't forget that it's there to help you out of a jam.

Field 9: Set the Baseline Shift

If you write out scientific expressions or mathematical notations, you'll need to shift the baseline. Highlight the text in question; enter a positive number to shift it up and a negative number to shift it down.

Field 10: Set the Text Color

Click and you're in the standard color picker. No surprises here.

Area 11: Type Enhancement Buttons

These buttons pull out type modifications that used to be buried in menus. You do not want to overuse these effects.

- **Faux Bold.** Faux is French for fake. Do not use a faux bold if a true bold is available. This option makes the text thicker (and harder to read).
- **Faux Italic.** Same deal here…this option skews the text to the right (it does not make it italic). Always choose an italic version from the Font Style field.
- **All Caps.** If you want the text in all uppercase, just click this button instead of retyping.

- **Small Caps.** This effect works well with titles and in certain layouts. It replaces all lowercase text with a smaller version of the capital letter.
- **Subscript.** This is used for scientific notation and other specialty purposes where a character is reduced in size and moved below the baseline.
- **Superscript.** This is used for specialty purposes such as showing mathematical power. This reduces the character and moves it above the baseline.
- **Underline.** This places a line below the text. You may want to manually add a line on another layer for better control.
- **Strikethrough.** Places a line through the characters.

Menu 12: Language Selection Menu

To harness the power of Photoshop's spell-checker, you must set the language on the selected characters. This also drives the automatic hyphenation.

Menu 13: Anti-alias Menu

These are the same controls available from the Options bar. Photoshop 7 added additional anti-aliasing options. Very small text (under 16 points) should not be anti-aliased. To improve anti-aliasing on small type, deselect the Fractional Width option in the Character palette menu. This will improve the spacing between letters at small sizes.

Larger font sizes often benefit from anti-aliasing; however, it gently blurs the edges of the type, making it appear smoothly composited with the background layers. You will need to experiment with anti-aliasing because it will vary with fonts chosen and the user's taste.

There are five levels of anti-aliasing to choose from:
- **None** applies zero anti-aliasing.
- **Sharp** makes type appear the sharpest.
- **Crisp** makes type appear somewhat sharp.
- **Strong** makes type appear heavier.
- **Smooth** makes type appear smoother.

Photoshop provides support for several languages in its spell-checker.

Using the Paragraph Palette

The Paragraph palette is generally docked with the Character Palette. You can call it up individually, or tear it free from the Character tab. The Paragraph palette works on a limited basis for point text. To access full control over type, you must add a text box. Paragraph Text constrains the text to the edge of that box, and will wrap when it hits the edge. To create a paragraph text block, click and drag using the Horizontal Type tool to define the paragraph area first.

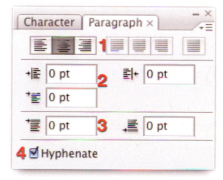

	PROS	**CONS**
Point Text	• Instant results • Good for small amounts of text • Greater flexibility with Warped Text	• May lead to manual reformatting including inserting hard returns
Paragraph Text	• Adds column-like behavior to layout • Allows for use of hyphenation and Adobe Every-line Composer for smoother layout	• If point size is too large at start, the entire text entry may not be seen. • Can require designer to resize text block to accommodate copy or font changes

Field 1: Alignment Buttons

You can specify alignment, as well as justification. Left justification is the easiest alignment to read. However, you may choose other alignment options for style reasons.

Field 2: Indent Fields

You can specify how much to indent a particular paragraph or the first line of a paragraph. These controls will enable you to have fewer text blocks by giving you better control.

Field 3: Spacing Fields

Tell Photoshop how much space you want after each hard return. This will enable you to space paragraphs out without needing to insert blank lines.

Field 4: Enable Hyphenation

In order to fill more horizontal space, words are often broken across lines at a suitable point within the word. If you want it, check it. Photoshop will use the installed dictionary for the language you specify in the Character palette. This will ensure that words are properly hyphenated.

Working with Type Color

Broadcast Safe Colors

While they get boring quickly, only a few colors look good for text and remain clear to the viewer. The most popular color for text in video is white. Depending upon how your video software interprets white, this may be set to a value of 235 or 255 for an 8-bit image. The second most popular color is video black (again,

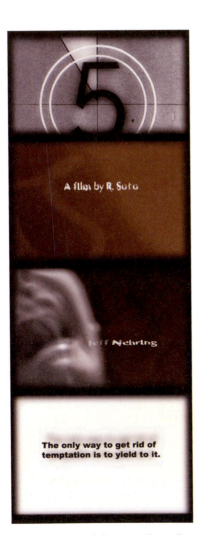

Type sets the mood. An aggressive trailer needs a matching typeface. (Trailer by Raymond Soto.)

depending on software this can be 16 or 0 on the RGB scale). Not happy with these two colors? Then feel free to pick another hue, but make sure to use very light or very dark shades. Lighter colors that work well include light blue, yellow, and tan. Darker colors that hold up include navy and forest green. You will want to keep your text towards the very dark or very light range, or readability will become an issue when the text is placed over a motion background.

Pantone Colors

Coca-Cola Red, AT&T Blue, the Golden Arches. The colors are distinct. Companies keep consistent colors by specifying Pantone colors. The Pantone Matching System (PMS) is the mostly widely accepted color standard in the printing industry (http://www. pantone.com). Each color is assigned a PMS number, which corresponds to specific ink or mixing standard, thus ensuring that a client will get consistent printing results.

So what does this aspect of printing technology mean to you? Everything. Clients will expect consistent colors through all media outlets, print, Web, and video. Each TV is set up differently, though they all probably have the reds overcranked (hence the Never Twice the Same Color concept). But if you stay consistent at least during the creation stage, you have ground to stand on if the client ever questions the colors you've used.

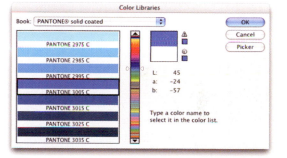

Accessing Pantone colors within Photoshop is easy.

Step 1. Double-click on the foreground or background color swatch.

Step 2. In the Adobe Color Picker click the Custom button.

Step 3. From the Book menu, you must choose between several options. Always ask your clients if they are using coated or uncoated printing. Also check which library they used—solid is the most common, but you will find separate libraries for metallic and pastels.

Step 4. To speed up your search, type the number of the color.

Step 5. Double-check yourself. Show the client your Pantone book and what comes on screen. You can also save off a square and e-mail it. An uncompressed format such as TIFF works best.

Step 6. Click in your Swatches palette and add the color so it's readily available. Be sure to name it with the PMS Color name or number.

What's My Name Again?

Need to find out the PMS color of a physical object? The Pantone Color Cue is a small (and affordable) device that can measure the color value of any surface. It can also read RGB values as well, which can make it very useful for color correcting to a reference object (www.pantone.com).

Do You Work in Web or Print?

If you're primarily a print or Web designer, video text will feel uncomfortably large. But yes, it really does need to be that big. Start testing your graphics on a video monitor right away and be sure to step away from the screen so you are at a "real-world" viewing distance.

Testing and Improving Readability

The most common problem with video graphics is that small type is used without any visual assists for contrast. When we are building our graphics, we are likely 1 to 4 feet away from the computer monitor. Virtually no one in your audience is sitting that close to the television set (and if they were, their mothers would be aghast.)

Readability is best tested on a true video monitor, but you can make a reasonably informed decision on your computer's monitor. To check your graphics, you need to put some distance between you and the computer. I recommend putting the graphic into full screen mode. Press the `Tab` key to hide your palettes, and then press the letter F to go to full-screen mode. If you need to, use the keyboard to zoom in with `⌘`+`=` (`ctrl`+`=`). Your computer monitor should now resemble a television set. Stand up, pry your hands off of the mouse and keyboard, and walk to the opposite side of your office or edit suite. When you are at least 10 feet away, look back at your monitor. Can you still read everything?

You have been viewing graphics on a relatively high-resolution device at short focal distances. Imagine how much different those graphics will look on low-resolution televisions, dubbed to VHS tape (or compressed to DVD), and viewed from 10 to 30 feet? Repeat after me: "I will design for the back of the room. "

Special Typographic Effects

Photoshop has a number of ways to specially set off text. By employing layer styles, it is possible to quickly generate impressive type effects. All of these techniques were created using layer styles. The two primary advantages of using styles are no render times and editability. By using photos for texture maps, extremely unique type effects are possible.

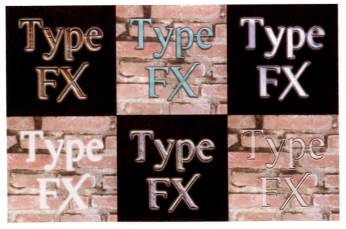

For more on layer styles, see Chapter 6, "Bugs, Bevels, Glows, and More" on page 141. Also check the Chapter 5 folder, where many styles can be found. You'll also find a sample document called `Ch05_TypeFX.psd.` Use these as starting points for your own text effects. All of these can be easily modified by changing the individual layer styles. Reserve heavily stylized effects such as these for titles and header graphics. For body text, use simpler drop shadows to help counteract the type on pattern problems associated with video and text.

Free Transform Command

One of the quickest ways to resize and reposition text is the Free Transform command. Because text is vector, you can modify it indefinitely, and it will link back to the installed font and redraw. Your text layer must be in a committed (nonediting) state before accessing the transformation commands. If you have been modifying text (or adding it for the first time), you must click the Commit button in the Options bar, or press *Enter* on the numeric keyboard.

When you are ready to resize or reposition the text, press ⌘+*T* (*ctrl*+*T*) to access the Free Transform command most quickly. Free Transform lets you rotate, scale, skew, distort, and change perspective in one continuous adjustment. Instead of choosing many different commands, you hold down modifier keys to switch transformation types.

- To scale, grab a handle and pull.
- Add the *Shift* key while pulling to constrain proportions.
- Hold down the ⌥ key (*alt*) to scale from the center point.
- Combine the *Shift*+⌥ (*alt*) keys for quick text sizing.
- To rotate, place your cursor arrow outside one of the corners. When the cursor changes to a curved arrow, you can drag the item to rotate. Add the *Shift* key to constrain rotation to 15° increments.
- For free distortion, press ⌘ key (*ctrl*), and drag a handle.
- For skewing, press ⌘+*Shift* (*ctrl*+*Shift*), and drag a side handle.
- When positioned by a side handle, the pointer becomes a white arrowhead with a double arrow. To apply a perspective change, press ⌘+⌥+*Shift* (*ctrl*+*alt*+*Shift*), and drag a corner handle.

All of these options can also be accessed with precise numerical controls from the Options bar. To constrain proportions numerically, click on the Link icon. The reference (or anchor) point can be modified from the Options bar by clicking on the miniature grid in the upper left corner. It is possible to drag the anchor point manually as well. To move an item, enter new values into the x- and y-axis boxes. You can also choose to move the item manually, adding the *Shift* key to constrain movement to one direction.

To apply the transformations, press the *Return* (*Enter*) key, click the Commit button, or double-click inside the transformation marquee. To cancel, press Esc or click the Cancel button in the Options bar. Before committing or escaping, you can go back one transformation by pressing your Undo key ⌘+*Z* (*ctrl*+*Z*) or selecting Undo from the Edit menu.

You can *ctrl*+click (right-click) to access specific transformations when you are in the Free Transform mode.

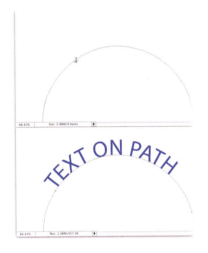

Just a few possibilities using the Distort Text feature. You can continue to modify the text with no quality loss, as it stays vector throughout the process.

Warped Text

Warped text is one of those cool features that you should reserve for special occasions like show or segment titles. The Warped Text command allows you to distort text to a variety of shapes, including Arc, Bulge, Flag, Fisheye, Squeeze, and Twist.

Step 1. To access Warped Text, select your type layer and choose the Horizontal Type tool.

Step 2. Click on the Create Warped Text button (a T above an arc) in the Options bar.

Step 3. Choose a style from the drop-down menu, and then adjust the options for a more precise effect.

Step 4. To apply, click the OK button.

To remove a warp, double-click on the type layer; then click on the Create Warped Text button, and choose None from the Style menu. Note that you cannot warp text that has the Faux Bold formatting applied or if the font is only a bitmap font.

Text on a Path

Have you ever needed to wrap type around a logo? Or maybe you want text to bend around an object? In the past, you had to jump over to Illustrator for this popular effect. No more! Photoshop CS added the long requested Type on a Path command.

Step 1. Create a path with the Pen tool *or* load a selection, switch to Path palette, and click Make Work Path from Selection.

Step 2. Make sure the path is active in the Path palette.

Step 3. Select the regular Horizontal Type tool and click on the path. The tool will automatically switch to the Path Text tool.

Step 4. Add your type.

Step 5. Press _Enter_ or the Commit button to apply the text.

Moving Type Along the Path

Step 1. Choose the Direct Selection tool or Path Selection tool and position it over the type. The pointer will change into an I-beam with an arrow.

Step 2. Click and drag to move the type along the path. Do not drag across the path.

Flipping Type to the Other Side of a Path

Step 1. Choose the Direct Selection tool or Path Selection tool and position it over the type. The pointer will change into an I-beam with an arrow.

Step 2. Click and drag the type across the path, which will flip the type to the other side.

Video Type Details

Help, I Have Diffikultie Speling

This may sound obvious, but the best way to avoid mistakes is to copy and paste text directly from the script. Ask your client or producer to provide you a .txt or .rtf file, and open it with your computer's text editor. You can now copy and paste titles directly. While this is not a foolproof solution, it does make it easy to figure out where the error occurred (and it usually will not be with you).

Spell-checker

Photoshop has become a freestanding graphic creation tool. It is now possible to proof your text in a number of different languages. If you are familiar with a word processor's spell-checker, Photoshop's will seem completely standard. Remember, you must set the language for a text field by using the drop-down menu in the Character palette. To launch the spell-checker, choose it from the Edit menu (Edit>Check Spelling). If it flags a word that you know is right, you can choose to ignore it or add it to your dictionary. There's no earth-shattering technology here, but the cries of Web and video designers have been answered.

Related to the spell-checker is a Find-and-Replace command. This allows you to go through all of your text layers and swap out words. Say that you've listed Williamstown Resort throughout your full-screen graphics. A few days later, the client calls and says it's actually Williamsburg Resort. You can have Photoshop scan through and replace all instances of the improper name throughout your composition. Again, the technology is standard, but it can be a time-saver.

Spell-check? Ewe Betcha

Photoshop 7 added a spell-check feature to the Edit menu.

Safe-Title Area

If you put a computer screen next to a television screen, one distinction should stand out: Computer monitors have black borders around the viewable areas, while televisions provide edge-to-edge viewing. On any given television set, up to 10% of the viewable signal is lost because the tube is recessed into a case. This viewable area is called the action-safe area.

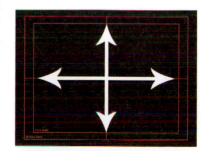

All type must fall within the inside box (safe-title area) for traditional video. This region is approximately 80% of the full-screen size. *(Original template from Tools for Television.)*

We must move all text elements in an additional 10% (or 20% total from the outer edge.) By placing text within the safe-title area, we ensure that it is readable. If you are using Photoshop CS (or newer), then you have new safe-title area templates built into the application. If you are using an earlier version of Photoshop or would like to make your guides a little more robust, you'll want to manually create a safe-title area overlay. If you are in a hurry, these steps are recorded in the Video Actions set that you can load in the Actions palette; otherwise keep reading for a more thorough understanding.

Several alternatives to creating a safe-title area were discussed in Chapter 2, "Pixels: Time for Tech." Here is one additional method using Photoshop's built-in features: create an action for this item so that you can recall it for later use. There are several steps involved, so if you have a good template, use that. I present this so that if you are ever in a jam, you can build your own safe area overlay document. We are going to build a safe-title document for a D1 system, sized 720×486.

Step 1. Create a new document, and pick the NTSC D1 720×486 preset from the drop-down menu. Set the document to RGB mode. By default, Photoshop CS (or later) will add guides for the safe-title area. Let's make these a little more robust with an actual overlay.

Step 2. Choose Select All by pressing ⌘+A (ctrl+A). Then, choose Edit>Fill and fill with black.

Step 3. Create a new (empty) layer by pressing Shift+⌘+N (Shift+ctrl+N). Name the layer Safe Area Overlay. You should still have an active selection.

Step 4. Scale the active selection to 90% by choosing Select> Transform Selection, and then typing in 90% in the Options bar for width and height. Press Return (Enter).

Step 5. Load a red swatch as the foreground color. Then choose Edit>Stroke and specify four pixels centered. This is the action-safe area.

Step 6. Choose Select All by pressing ⌘+A (ctrl+A), and scale the active selection to 80% by choosing Select>Transform Selection. Type in 80% in the Options bar for width and height. Press Return (Enter).

Step 7. Choose Edit>Stroke and specify 4 pixels centered. This is the safe-title area.

Step 8. Lock the Safe Area Overlay layer by clicking on the Lock icon in the layer's palette.

Step 9. Save your work.

Even though the first image looks too loose, you must still follow safe-title area. When the video is viewed on a television, the outermost edges are lost.

Anti-aliasing Revisited

In the case of type, anti-aliasing is the process of blending the edges to produce a smoother image. Anti-aliased text is less likely to "buzz" or "shake" on screen. You have five choices in Photoshop. These can be accessed easily through the Options bar or Character palette. You can change the anti-aliasing at any point in time, provided the fonts used in your composition are loaded on your computer.

You can access anti-aliasing from the Options bar or Character Palette.

Larger font sizes generally benefit from anti-aliasing because it gently blurs the edges of the type, making it appear smoothly composited with the background layers. You will need to experiment with anti-aliasing because it will vary with fonts chosen and user's taste. Remember, many serif fonts will produce unsatisfactory results with or without anti-aliasing. There are five levels of antialiasing to choose from:

- **None** applies zero anti-aliasing.
- **Sharp** makes type appear the sharpest.
- **Crisp** makes type appear somewhat sharp.
- **Strong** makes type appear heavier.
- **Smooth** makes type appear smoother.

If you look closely at the smooth version, it is possible to see the impact of anti-aliasing. Anti-aliasing dramatically cuts down on "flicker" in video work.

Type on Pattern

Unlike most print designers, video artists must design type over diverse canvases. Often this background contains a full spectrum of color. Achieving sufficient contrast is the key to preserving legibility. When using light-colored type, it is essential to make it larger than if it were dark type. Don't be tempted to use all uppercase to make the letters stand out. Unfortunately, uppercase letters take more time for the viewer to recognize word shapes and process what they are seeing. This is generally time they don't have.

Applying a stroke, outer glow, or tight drop shadow is an effective way to getting a contrasting edge. The biggest problem with type and video is that there will always be light and dark elements in your scene. It is crucial to add a contrasting edge to any type that is going to be keyed over a full-chroma, moving background.

One way to test your contrast is to convert the file to grayscale. This can be achieved with several methods:

- You can print it out in Grayscale.
- Add a saturation adjustment layer, and desaturate (set to 0% Saturation).
- You can use the History palette to create a duplicate document that you flatten and desaturate.

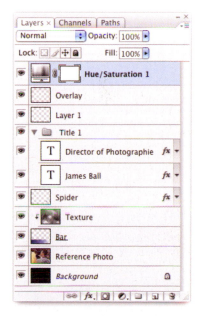

A Hue/Saturation adjustment layer offers a nondestructive way to check contrast of type over a patterned background.

Adequate separation between foreground and background elements will make for better viewing for your audience. Think of color as tonal value. Some combinations show very low contrast when desaturated.

Composition, Space, and Alignment

Give careful attention to how your text fills up the page. The screen is not a box that must be packed edge to edge with as many words as possible. White space is the empty area around the text, and it helps focus the viewer's eyes on the text. Think of white space in terms of the printed page. Don't cram, or you will cause information overload. Think of white space as visual breathing room for your composition.

In terms of alignment, Western civilizations are most used to left-justified text. Look at the proliferation of newspapers, magazines, and books that follow this practice. It is okay to rock the boat, but be prepared to allow more time for your audience to read and comprehend the information.

Pay close attention to your first, second, and third read points. Where is the viewer's eye attracted to first? Then what brings them to the second point, followed by what motivates them to go to the next focal point? These read points are primarily formed due to scaling, composition, and color. Remember: design first, and add effects later.

Be careful with tangents, the places where ascenders and descenders overlap. A tangent adds a focal point to your text, but accidental tangents are undesirable because they make the viewer's eyes work harder. Tangents are an unintentional effect when different point-size lines are mixed together. A good way to check for tangents is to take a flattened copy of your composition and apply a 30-pixel Gaussian Blur. Look for dark areas that signify high density, and adjust leading and kerning to correct them.

By blurring the text, it is easier to see the tangent. Unintentional tangents will likely distract from your layout and impact your viewer's focus.

Keep It Vector

An Adobe Illustrator or Vector EPS file is the best format to get a logo in.

Keep It Legal (the Other Way)

Often a scanned logo will have its legal symbol become illegible. You may choose to insert these special characters using the Key Caps on a Mac or the Character Map on a PC. The following keyboard shortcuts are also available on a Mac:

- ™ (⌥+2)
- © (⌥+G)
- ® (⌥+R)

Logo Standards

Despite your personal experience, logo standards do not exist to make your life difficult. A company places a lot on that little piece of art. A logo helps a company stand out; it stands for quality and uniqueness. For large companies, a fortune is invested in developing that logo and promoting it to the world. Companies want to have that logo and brand identity moving in the same direction.

Of course, problems do arise. Logos may contain serifs or fine design elements that don't hold up at low resolutions. Often arguments will pop up in the edit suite about drop shadows or glows. Other times it will be over the need to keep the ®, ©, or ™ symbols, which turn to little blobs on the television monitor. A great place to start is the company's Web site. Look at how the logo has been simplified to work on the "little" screen. You'll find that several of your battles will have already been decided.

Every company that takes its brand seriously will have a style guide. Here you will find precise details on fonts, colors, size, and placement. You *must* get a copy of this. Ask your clients. If they are unsure, start making phone calls. Try the in-house graphics department, the marketing group, the creative department, or the company's ad agency. If the group is small, you might even ask who created the logo and follow up with the designer.

Creating Lower Thirds

Most video editors choose to build their title graphics (or lower thirds) within the title tool of their nonlinear edit system. These built-in character generators are *very* limited and do not give the precise control over text and graphical elements that Photoshop provides. I recommend that you use Photoshop as a supporting player or let it assume the role of character generator entirely. As a supporting player, Photoshop is quite effective at making complex gradients for use in bars. Let's create a lower third bar from scratch.

Engaging Lower Thirds

Looking to make your lower thirds more stunning? Be sure to try adding texture to a bar. There are several texture images on the DVD; you can also use them slightly out of focus by running a blur filter.

Designing Custom Lower Thirds

Step 1. Open a safe-title document. Use the one created earlier in this chapter, Photoshop's built-in template, or try out the Tools for Television Safe Grid Action found on the DVD.

Step 2. Grab the corner and expand the document so that you can see some of the empty space around the canvas. It is a good idea to place a photo or freeze frame in the background for reference purposes.

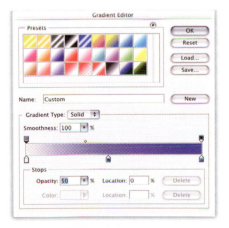

Photoshop's Gradient Editor outperforms all other gradient tools (even those in other Adobe applications). Choose from complex shapes, multiple color or hues, and advanced blending options for superior results.

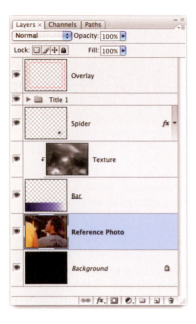

Step 3. With the Rectangular Marquee tool, draw a box across the lower fifth (you thought I'd say lower third?) of the screen. You may choose to have the box extend to the bottom or have it stop around the action-safe area.

Step 4. Select the Gradient tool. Click on the gradient in the Options bar to edit the gradient to your choice. You may load gradients from the submenu or create your own from scratch. You may want to adjust the opacity stops for a ramp effect.

Step 5. Draw the gradient within the selection. Experiment with different gradient shapes, as well as point of origin and length of gradient.

Step 6. Deselect the gradient, and apply a Gaussian Blur filter on the layer to soften the edge.

Step 7. If you'd like to introduce some texture, place a grayscale photo or pattern directly above the layer and group it with the bar with the Create Clipping Mask Command (Layer> Create Clipping Mask). You may also choose to adjust the blend mode (Luminosity works well) and the opacity to achieve the desired effect. You will find some texture files in the chapter folder that you can use.

Step 8. Add the logo. If the file is an Adobe Illustrator file, choose Place from the File menu. Otherwise, you can open the document and copy and paste the logo. You may want to use layer styles, such as a drop shadow or glow to offset the logo from the bar. See Chapter 6, "Bugs, Bevels, Glows, and More" for more details on layer styles.

Step 9. Draw the text block for the name. I recommend using Paragraph text so you have better control over the characters.

Step 10. Duplicate the text layer, shift it down, and modify the text and font. Choose a smaller point size and different font or style for the title, which is generally longer than the name.

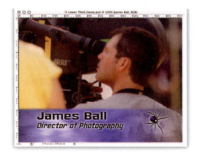

Step 11. Apply a contrasting edge effect such as a glow, drop shadow, or stroke.

Video #10 Exploring Gradients

Video #11 Designing Lower-Third Graphics

Looking for more details? See the video tutorials on the DVD-ROM.

Step 12. Select or link the two text layers together and choose new set from the submenu of the layer's palette. You can now duplicate this set by choosing Duplicate Layer Set from the Layer menu (or drag its layer onto the Layer Set icon in the layer's palette) as many times as needed. Turn off the Visibility icons and work with one copy at a time for each title. In this way, you can use a layer set for each "talking head" in your video.

Targeted Flattening Revisited

When you are ready to save for the graphic for your video editing software, you will usually save the composition out as a flattened file (most often PICT or TARGA) with an alpha channel. There are several approaches to flattening a file. Targeted flattening, introduced in Chapter 3, is one technique that works well.

Step 1. Turn off all elements you do not want flattened (including the background or reference image).

Step 2. Create a new (empty layer) and highlight it.

Step 3. While holding down the (*alt*) key, choose Merge Visible. All layers are now flattened to the single, selected layer.

Step 4. Turn this layer off by clicking on its visibility (eyeball) icon.

Step 5. Hold down the ⌘ (*ctrl*) key and click on the merged layer's name in the layer's palette. The selection border (aka marching ants) should encircle the layer.

Step 6. Switch to the Channels palette and click on the Save Selection as Channel button.

Step 7. Choose Save As from the File menu and use the Save A Copy option to create a PICT or TARGA file with an alpha channel included.

Step 8. If you have multiple titles, discard the alpha channel (NLEs get confused if there are multiple alpha channels) and repeat for each lower third. Simply turn off the current group of titles and activate your next set. Then repeat steps 1–7.

While this process may seem time consuming, you'll become quick at it with a little practice. The quality you can achieve is superior to any stand-alone character generator or built-in title tool. The time savings really add up for multiple titles. Remember to always save a layered file so that you can make changes.

Title Tools versus Photoshop

There are still a few reasons to use the title tool that came with your editing application:

- Rolls
- Crawls
- Animated Character Effects
- Embedding titles in Sequence file

Photoshop, however, has its own benefits that push it over for standard titles and lower thirds work.

- Layer Styles
- Speed
- Spell-checker
- Advanced Character Control
- Advanced Paragraph Control
- Texture Mapping and Fill Effects

Prepping a Logo for Animation

By using Adobe Illustrator, an Illustrator or vector EPS file can be split into layers. This layered file can then be imported into Adobe After Effects as is or these layers can be saved as a layered Photoshop file. This file can be tweaked in Photoshop and easily imported into After Effects or your NLE. Once there, you can animate and render. See? That's only six degrees of separation. Let's try it out.

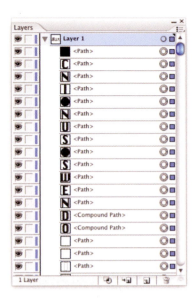

Drag the layers to "un-nest" them.

Step 1. Open the file **Ch5NSI.ai** or another vector logo in Adobe Illustrator.

Step 2. Call up the layer's palette and flip down the twirl-down menu. You should see every item in the logo listed separately.

Step 3. It is necessary to consolidate items a bit to make them more manageable. Press A to activate the Direct Selection tool.

Step 4. Lasso around the newspaper, and choose Object>Group or press ⌘+G (ctrl+G).

Step 5. Repeat for the microphone, copyright symbol, and corporate name, grouping each one individually. Your layer's palette should be much cleaner.

Step 6. Highlight layer #1. Go to the palette's submenu and choose Release to Layers (Sequence). This will put each group on a new layer. The Build option would do a progressive build where each layer would contain all of the previous items, plus one additional item.

Step 7. If you would like to name a layer, double-click on its name. You can also drag the layers to change their stacking order. For predictable results, it is a good idea to "un-nest" the layers by dragging them out of the layer set.

Step 8. Choose File>Export; then name the file and select Photoshop (.psd) as the format.

Step 9. Specify resolution, and choose to write layers. Do not change the color model during export. It may affect the onscreen appearance (especially with gradients and transparency). Allow Photoshop to do your color conversions instead. It is generally a good idea to write the file at 150 to 450 ppi depending upon the size of the source file. You can always resample the image in Photoshop.

Step 10. Open up the file in Photoshop. All your layers should be intact. Feel free to filter or process the image with layer styles (if you use styles, be sure to flatten them).

Step 11. Import into your editing or compositing application. You can now animate the individual pieces so they scale, move, or fade as they move into place. It is a good idea to add the end keyframes first before moving layers. This way, all of the elements will return into proper registration.

Design Ideas

The two most common techniques to help a logo stand out are a glowing edge or a drop shadow. This is based on the principle of type on pattern, which says that a contrasting edge makes it far easier to see something when it is positioned over a busy or moving background. Use `Ch05_Logos_Start.psd` to get started, or grab a copy of your own logo.

Reflections

By employing the Free Transform command, we can cause a logo to reflect off a flat surface. This effect can be keyed, but looks particularly effective when positioned over a background created with a reflected gradient.

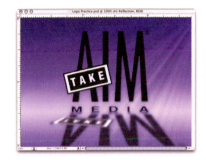

Step 1. Scale the logo to about 60% screen size, positioning it near the top of the safe title area.

Step 2. Duplicate the logo layer by pressing ⌘+J (ctrl+J).

Step 3. Use the Free Transform command on the duplicated layer. Flip vertically by right-clicking and selecting Flip Vertical. Nudge the logo down using the arrow keys so that the bottom edges line up. You can add the Shift key for a power nudge.

Step 4. Scale the logo to make it shorter by grabbing the bottom edge and pulling up towards the top of the screen.

Step 5. Access the perspective distortion by right-clicking. Spread the logo out to simulate a cast reflection. Click the Apply Transformations box, or press Return (Enter).

Step 6. Reduce the opacity and blur the layer to achieve the desired look.

Step 7. You may choose to add some lighting effects for an additional effect. Make a new empty layer, select all and choose Copy Merged (Edit>Copy Merged), or press Shift+⌘+C (Shift+ctrl+C). You can render out the lighting effects using the excellent plug-in from Digital Film Tools called Light! (You'll find a demo on this book's DVD.)

Light! from Digital Film Tools has many possibilities for both design and production.

Step 8. It is likely that the © symbol will need to be replaced. Add a new type layer and insert the needed symbol.

3D Perspective

Sometimes you will want your shadow to have a little depth. This effect is simple but extremely popular because it dramatically improves readability.

Step 1. Position your logo on the screen.

Step 2. Make a copy of the logo by duplicating the layer. The fastest way is ⌘+J (ctrl+J).

Step 3. Place the copy behind the original by dragging it in the Layers palette.

Step 4. Load your default colors by pressing the D key. Black should now be loaded as the foreground color.

Step 5. Load the duplicate layer by holding down the ⌘ key (ctrl key) and clicking on the layer's thumbnail. Press ⌥+Delete (alt+Delete) to fill with the black foreground color.

Step 6. Leave the layer active, and select the Move tool by pressing V.

Step 7. You are now going to nudge a copy. Hold down the ⌥ key (alt key) and quickly tap the down and right arrow back to back. Repeat until the desired edge appears.

Step 8. To further enhance the effect, you can apply a beveled edge to the original logo on top.

Step 9. It is likely that the © symbol will need to be replaced. Add a new type layer and insert the needed symbol.

Distressed Type or Logo in Photoshop

Want to make editable vector type with distressed edges? You can by harnessing a photo texture and layer masks.

Step 1. Typeset your words over your background layer or add a logo.

Step 2. Add a photo with a lot of texture to your document (in this case a photo of a wooden fence). You'll find a usable sample in the chapter's folder on the DVD-ROM. You can also use the items contained in the distressed layer set to create this look. Place the photo above the logo in the Layers palette.

Step 3. Desaturate the photo by pressing Shift+⌘+U (Shift+ctrl+U).

Step 4. Increase contrast in your photo through a combination of Levels adjustments and Artistic filters such as Film Grain.

Be sure to achieve a high contrast, yet allow gradual transitions. A gentle Gaussian Blur filter can help soften the image a bit.

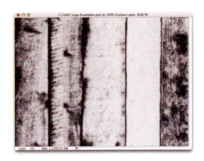

Step 5. Switch to the Channels palette and ⌘+Click (*ctrl*+Click) on the RGB composite channel to load a selection. This will create a ragged selection based on the details in the photo.

Step 6. Switch back to your Layers palette and turn off the texture layer's visibility icon.

Step 7. Select your text or logo layer and add a Layer mask by click on the Add layer mask button at the bottom of the Layers palette.

Step 8. You may want to add a drop shadow or slight emboss to your text or logo using layer styles. Experiment with blending modes as well.

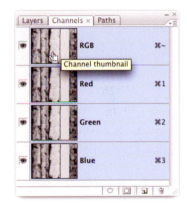

Step 9. If you want to distress the type further, you can keep going. Load the text or logo layer by ⌘+Clicking (*ctrl*+Clicking) on its layer thumbnail.

Step 10. Create a new empty layer and fill the selection in with Black. Then deselect the layer by pressing ⌘+*D* (*ctrl*+*D*).

Step 11. Choose Filter>Artistic>Cutout… to process the image further. Turn of all layers except the filtered layer.

Step 12. Switch to the Channels palette and ⌘+click (*ctrl*+click) on the RGB composite channel to load a selection.

Step 13. Switch back to the Layers palette and disable to the Cutout layer. Reenable the text layer and background.

Step 14. Select your layer mask on your text layer and choose to Edit>Fill… and use Black. Your edges should erode more (if not, you can inverse the selection and fill again).

Step 15. You can run a Levels adjustment on the layer mask to refine its transparency.

Fill with a Pattern (Create Clipping Mask)

You will often be asked to place a pattern or image inside the letters. In the past, I would have suggested the Paste Into command. However, now a much more flexible solution called grouping exists. This effect is similar to a track matte. To make this effect easier to show, use the items in the layer set called #3 Group. The font used is Mingler Snowy by Chank.

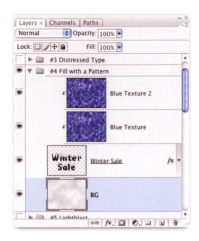

Step 1. Position the logo where you want it.

Step 2. Add a texture layer above.

Step 3. Select the texture layer and create a clipping mask by pressing ⌘+⌥+G (ctrl+alt+G).

Step 4. Adjust the blending mode and opacity to isolate the effect.

Step 5. You may choose to add an outer glow or drop shadow to the logo layer to help it stand out more.

Step 6. Any changes to the logo layer will automatically update with the new texture.

Lightblast

One technique to offset a logo is to "light" it from behind. This technique is easy to accomplish. The background in this example was made with Glitterato from Flaming Pear.

Step 1. Position the logo where you want it.

Step 2. Make a copy of the logo by duplicating the layer. The fastest way is ⌘+J (ctrl+J).

Step 3. Run the Radial Blur on the duplicate layer. Choose the Zoom option, set to Maximum Blur, and use the Good option. (Best takes a very long time to render.)

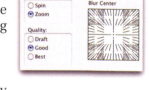

Step 4. Press D to load the default colors.

Step 5. Load the duplicate layer by ⌘+clicking (ctrl+click) on it. Fill the selection by pressing ⌥+Delete (alt+Delete). Deselect the layer by pressing ⌘+D (ctrl+D).

Step 6. Repeat the blur, load, and fill cycle until your rays are the desired length.

Step 7. On the blurred layer, apply the color overlay layer style. Select the desired color and adjust opacity to taste. You should get a real-time preview of your work if the Preview box is checked. Click OK.

Step 8. Place the glow layer behind the logo so the beams shoot past.

Step 9. Optionally, you may also choose to place an additional copy of the beam layer on top. Adjust the opacity to make the color look like it has wrapped around the logo.

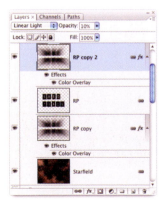

Cast Shadows

This technique is similar to the reflected type treatment. It allows you to cast a shadow in any direction.

Step 1. Position the logo where you want it on the screen.

Step 2. Make a copy of the logo by duplicating the layer. The fastest way is ⌘+J (ctrl+J).

Step 3. Press D to load the default colors.

Step 4. Load the duplicate layer by ⌘+clicking on it (ctrl+click). Fill the selection by pressing ⌥+Delete (alt+Delete).

Step 5. Apply Free Transform to the layer and select the Perspective Transformation. Access the perspective distortion by ctrl+clicking or right-clicking. Be sure to grab the transform handle in the middle of the top edge. Put it to the right or left, depending on your "light" source.

Step 6. Next, access the scale command by right-clicking. Adjust the length of the shadow to taste. Click the Apply Transformations box, or press Return (Enter).

Step 7. Blur the shadow and change its blending mode to Multiply.

Step 8. You may want to add a contrasting edge depending upon your background layer.

Step 9. It is likely that the ® symbol will need to be replaced. Add a new type layer and insert the needed symbol.

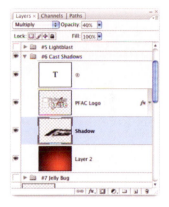

Access distortion controls by ctrl+clicking with a one-button mouse or right-clicking.

Glass Bug

Do you need to create a network-style jelly bug—those semi-transparent logos that sit in the corner and look like they are made of glass? The technique works well for simple logos or station numbers.

Step 1. Split your logo or bug up into as many layers as you need so the pieces are clearly separated.

Step 2. Be sure you have transparency surrounding the objects. This will likely be the case if you have masked each object or started with a vector logo.

Step 3. Place a reference photo or frame grab below the logo so you can judge the effect.

Step 4. Apply a Bevel and Emboss layer style as well as a slight white drop shadow. Keep the bevel thin and crisp.

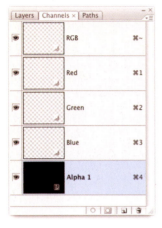

Step 5. Adjust the Fill command for the layer, which will lower the original fill, but preserve the opacity of the effects. You can do this from the Blending options, the Custom area of the Styles dialog box, or from the top of the Layers palette.

Step 6. Turn off all layers except the bug.

Step 7. Make a new (empty layer) and select it.

Step 8. Choose Layer>Merge Visible while holding down the ⌥ (*alt*) key. You will get a merged copy that is perfectly registered with the layers below.

Step 9. ⌘+Click (*ctrl*+Click) the new layer's thumbnail in the Layers palette to load the selection.

Step 10. Switch to the Channels palette and click the Save Selection as Channel button to create an alpha channel.

Step 11. Save the file as PICT, Targa, or PNG-24.

Step 12. Import into After Effects or your NLE. You should tell it that the graphic is premultiplied with White to get the cleanest edge.

Those Other Programs

Sometimes there's no way around it: you have to work with programs other than Photoshop—or at least you have to know how to make another program's output cooperate with Photoshop. Here are a few tips from the trenches on handling the usual suspects.

PowerPoint

While in business school, I finally worked closely with those "other" people who make all of the awful speaker support slides we get. You know, the "I need to use this PowerPoint presentation in my video" kind of folks. I was amazed at the decisions (or lack thereof) that went into making a presentation.

In response, I developed a list of "deadly sins." I've shared this list with lots or presenters through the years. Now I'd like to bring a concentrated version to you. Use this advice when building new graphics for clients or reformatting existing presentations for the screen.

Need to Go Deeper with PowerPoint?

I invite you to pick up *How to Wow with PowerPoint*, a book I co-authored that offers advice on harnessing the power of PowerPoint 2007. If you work in internal communications or corporate video, PowerPoint knowledge can go a long way.

Seven Deadly Sins

1. **Too few slides/screens.** There is no per-screen charge.
2. **Too many words.** You are not creating "open captions for the thinking impaired." Just a key phrase or few words to reinforce the current point.
3. **No road signs (Where are you going?).** Use several titles slides for each section so that it is clear where you are. Make it clear where you are in the video.
4. **Reliance on gimmicks.** If you have to use a Kiki wipe to keep your audience's attention, your full-screen graphics aren't working.
5. **Ignoring design.** Just because the client says it all has to fit on one slide doesn't mean you shouldn't suggest alternatives. You are being hired because of your good taste and technical skill. Use them.
6. **Not proofing.** Many little mistakes sneak in. Changing tenses for verbs, first or third person writing, small spelling errors such as *your* versus *you're*. Don't assume that any presentation you are given has actually been proofread.
7. **Forgetting your audience.** Remember, you want the audience to actually be able to read the slides *and* comprehend them. Keep them uncluttered and the point size readable.

Rules of Good Presentation Design

1. **Limit fonts used.** No more than three; aim for two. Stick with a font family, if possible, to keep it looking clean.
2. **Use a heavy font.** Make sure it is readable on screen. Use a medium-to-black weight if possible.
3. **Avoid stock templates.** Do you want an engineer in Redmond, Washington designing graphics for your video? Build new backgrounds that complement your client's message; then offer them JPEGs of the Background so they can use them in their presentations in the future.
4. **Use three to seven bullets per page.** Any more is "death by bullets."
5. **A bullet is one to five words.** You are giving the audience a key word or phrase to help them encode the information. You are not placing the script on the screen. That's what closed captioning is for.
6. **Readability test (design for the back of the room).** It may look big from your chair, but stand back and test it.
7. **Use builds or simple animations to bring bullets on line by line.** Reveal the information to keep your audience's attention. Every time something moves, your viewer is likely to look at the screen.

8. **Be consistent with justification and capitalization.** This one is tough. Decide in advance. Are you going for sentence case or title case? Establish a style guide per project and follow it. Share it with others working on the project as well.

9. **Use transparency.** Ramp effects, partial transparency, and soft drop shadows/glows help to make the presentation seem more "organic."

10. **Easy to change.** Create a template and use it. Always keep layered files around, even after the project is done. If you have full-screen graphics in your video, they are the most likely things to be changed in the future.

Exporting PowerPoint Slides

You may often find yourself needing to edit slides into a talk by a speaker. Fortunately, PowerPoint makes is relatively easy to export slides into graphics that can be read by Photoshop or video software.

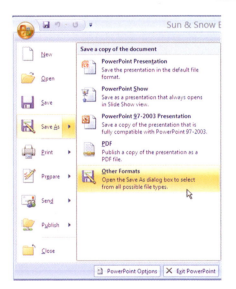

Step 1. Open up the PowerPoint presentation file using Microsoft PowerPoint.

Step 2. Remove any unnecessary slides in the Slide Sorter view. Select unwanted slides and press *Delete*.

Step 3. Saving slides out will vary depending which version of PowerPoint you are using. For most versions, choose File>Save As. In PowerPoint 2007, you will want to click on the Office button and choose Save As>Other Formats.

Step 4. Pick a file format such as TIFF. Click the options buttons and choose to resize. Specify a square pixel size such as 720×540; this can easily be converted to other video sizes within Photoshop.

Step 5. Specify a destination folder to hold the slides.

Step 6. Click Save. An image for each slide will be saved, but they will be flattened files.

Be sure to also save any background and logo files out for use in your video. If you do not own PowerPoint (and run Mac OSX), Keynote is an affordable alternative that can read PowerPoint files with relative accuracy. Be warned; there are several Windows-only third-party plug-ins for PowerPoint.

Exporting Apple Keynote Slides

Apple's Keynote presentation software has proven to be a strong entry into the speaker support software market. In fact, many of my own clients have switched to it due to its excellent support for graphics, full-motion video, and anti-aliased text. You can even export a full-screen QuickTime movie if you need to bring a Keynote animation into your video edit. In our situation though, let's assume you want stills.

Step 1. Open up the Keynote or PowerPoint Presentation using Keynote.

Step 2. Remove any unnecessary slides.

Step 3. Choose File>Export…

Step 4. Specify that you want to export Images, use the TIFF format, and click Next…

Step 5. Specify a destination and click Export to save your files.

Step 6. Open the graphics in Photoshop where you can crop and size for your video needs.

Sending Photoshop Text to After Effects

If you need to animate your Photoshop text in After Effects, the process has gotten much easier. After Effects can now convert Photoshop text layers back to editable vector text. This will make it easier to complete credit rolls or title animations.

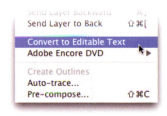

Step 1. Import your PSD file as a layered comp into After Effects

Step 2. Open the comp by double-clicking its icon in the project window.

Step 3. Select a text layer in the After Effects timeline (you can only do one at a time).

Step 4. Choose Layer>Convert to Editable text. After Effects converts the Photoshop text layer to an AE text layer that can be animated or scaled while harnessing the full power of vector text.

EPS and Illustrator Files

Earlier we solved the color problems with client files, but we're not done yet. If you are ever asked how you want a client's logo, answer, "An Encapsulated PostScript or Adobe Illustrator file would be best, please." Even though we are working in a primarily raster program, the flexibility in scaling a vector file will prove invaluable.

RasterVector.ai   see_the_difference.ai   TAM LOGO.eps

An Adobe Illustrator or Vector EPS file is the best format to get a logo in.

Be careful, however. Not all EPS files are vector. Always ask for a vector file. If the client tells you to get it from their Web site, it is likely that they didn't understand what you were asking for. It's worth the extra effort to get the right file from the get-go. If a raster file is the only available option, then you can try to use LiveTrace in Adobe Illustrator, which proves invaluable when converting between raster and vector.

One important gotcha: you don't open a vector file in Photoshop, you place it (File>Place…). You will be presented with a bounding box identical to the Free Transform command. Remember, holding down the ⌥ (*alt*) key will scale from the center. The *Shift* key constrains the width and height scaling. You can also rotate the image by moving your cursor to the outside edge.

WordArt

I bring this up only because I have to. Every once in a while, you will come across a logo created in Microsoft Word. Microsoft pushes its Office Suite as an all-in-one solution to business owners. Don't be surprised to find simple logos being created inside the word processor. Your clients may be telling you the truth when they say that a Word document is the only version they know of.

Generally speaking, these logos are vector. Your first reaction would be to take it into Adobe Illustrator. While this preserves the vector data, the image's appearance will likely be distorted because it does not copy and paste cleanly into Illustrator. The trick is to size the logo inside Word.

Step 1. If you have Microsoft Word, open the file `Ch05_WordArt-Demo.doc.`

Step 2. Copy the logo to your clipboard.

Step 3. Create a New document in Word.

Step 4. Paste the logo.

Step 5. Click on the logo. The WordArt formatting palette should appear.

Step 6. Click on the Format WordArt button to access scale controls. You should be able to enlarge the logo to the required size. Be sure to click the Lock Aspect Ratio check box.

Step 7. Copy the item to your clipboard. Word works at 300 dpi, so this should provide plenty of pixels to work with.

Step 8. Create a new document in Photoshop. The new document will automatically be sized to the clipboard's contents.

Step 9. Paste, save, and start working.

In the Know

Need to know more about type? If you feel like searching the Web, here are some great starting points:

- Chank   www.chank.com
- Fonthead   www.fonthead.com
- DincType   www.GirlsWhoWearGlasses.com
- Fontalicious   www.fontalicious.com
- Acid Fonts   www.AcidFonts.com
- My Fonts   www.myfonts.com
- Microsoft   www.microsoft.com/typography/
- Adobe   www.adobe.com/type/main.html
- Font Lab   www.fontlab.com/

Use an AE Plug-In

I am embarrassed to admit how long it took me to figure out that you could use After Effects plug-ins on Photoshop files. How, you ask? It just involves a slight "road trip." You may know that importing a layered Photoshop file into After Effects is easy. You might not have realized that you can make changes and save them back out. I've included a simple, two-layer file called `Ch05_For AE.psd` in the chapter folder. We're going to take it into After Effects to use a third-party effect created by Trapcode called Shine. If you don't have Shine loaded, you can load a demo from the book's DVD-ROM.

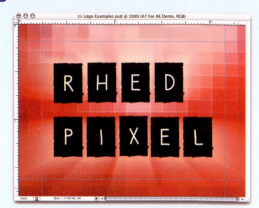

Step 1. Launch After Effects.

Step 2. Import the file `Ch05_For AE.psd` as a composition.

Step 3. To avoid cutting of the edges of our effect, we must precompose the logo layer. Highlight RP and choose Layer>Pre-Compose and leave all attributes.

Step 4. Click the Collapse Transformations switch for the precomposed layer.

Step 5. Highlight layer 1, the precomp, and duplicate it by pressing  (ctrl + D).

Step 6. Select layer 2 and apply the desired AE Effect, in this case Effect> Trapcode>Shine. You may want to turn off layer 1 so it is easier to see your work.

Step 7. Play with the different options. I added a three-color gradient based on the alpha channel for the layer.

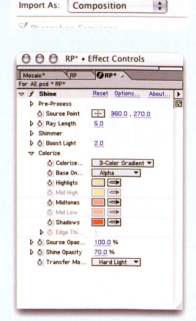

Step 8. This step is critical. Make sure all layers have their quality switches set to Final quality (/). Then ensure that your Comp Window is set to Full Quality and 100% viewing.

Step 9. Save the file out to the PSD format by choosing Composition>Save Frame As>Photoshop Layers. If you receive a warning about unsupported blending modes you can ignore it.

Step 10. When you open up the file into Photoshop, the new effect is visible. All opacity changes, blending modes, or additional layers are accessible.

This is an excellent way to harness powerful After Effects plug-ins that have no Photoshop equivalent.

Hands On | 05

Using Data Sets and Lower Thirds

Photoshop CS2 has introduced a new feature called Data Sets. This feature allows you to create a set of data that applies different text to the text layers, different visibility settings to all layers, or pixel replacement for art layers in your document. This is a great feature for use with templates. You can create a template file, then apply data sets to that template and save out individual variations of the template file as individual files.

By harnessing the power of data sets, you can dramatically speed up the production of repetitive graphics. In fact, by feeding in a text file, hundreds of lower third graphics can be generated in a few clicks. The advantage of this method is that a producer or production assistant can gather all of the needed names and titles into a single text file (easily created with any word processor). This file can then be loaded to generate as many graphics as needed. While the process is a little tricky at first, its pretty easy to get the hang of. Let's take a look (not you must have Photoshop CS2 or later installed) .

You'll find Exercise 05 on the DVD-ROM.

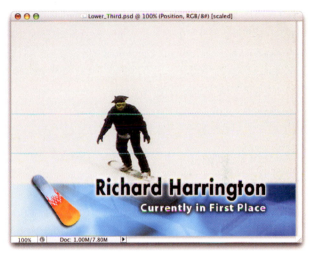

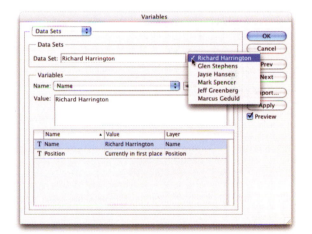

Spotlight on Type – Chank Diesel

Whenever my projects need a unique twist, I find myself turning to the Chank Company. This Minneapolis-based, full-service design firm specializes in fonts. Their sources of inspiration include historical signs from industrial districts, distinctive handwriting, and playful display fonts.

Mr. Chank Diesel, president and CEO, began making fonts in 1992, when he worked as creative director of the alternative music magazine, *Cake*. The first font he created, Mister Frisky, remains his most popular.

Compared to most foundries, you'll think the cold has gotten to the Chank Company when you see how affordable their fonts are. My favorite is the Font-of-the-Month club, which drops a new creative font (and idea or two) in my e-mail box each month. The Web site also contains several free fonts as well that are works-in-progress. Be sure to link to the Chank Army Web site, where you will find yourself plugged into the vibrant world of typographic design practiced by many affiliated artists.

Chank Diesel took the time to answer some of my questions on type. I think the interview has some great stuff that will make you think differently when designing type-based graphics such as lower thirds and full-screen titles.

Harrington: How is a font created? What software is used, what skills are needed?

Diesel: Fonts can be drawn on paper or in the computer. Use Adobe Photoshop to scan your artwork in and clean it up if you want. Adobe Streamline converts your grayscale scan into an EPS (Encapsulated PostScript) file, which you can open and edit in Illustrator. Use Adobe Illustrator as a clipboard for importing your outlines into Fontographer. You can also use Illustrator as the original drawing board for your characters. Macromedia Fontographer is the program that makes fonts. You can also draw characters directly in this program if that is best.

Harrington: What issues exist when working cross-platform?

Diesel: Most Mac users prefer PostScript fonts, and most PC users prefer TrueType. TrueType is becoming more popular for Mac, though. If you design something on a Mac and a PC user has that same font installed, ideally, they should have no problem seeing that font. A new system called Open Type is supposed to become the industry standard, used by both Mac and PC (www.microsoft.com/typography).

Harrington: What is the difference between free fonts on the Web and professional fonts that you must purchase?

Diesel: The Chank free fonts are experimental in nature and do not typically have complete character sets. The Chank fonts that I sell have full character sets, including foreign symbols and

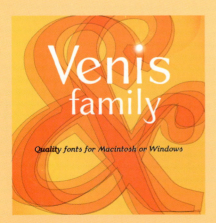

Chank's Venis family, featured on a limited-edition CD packaging.

Chank's Top Ten Fonts are conveniently packaged in one CD. Liquorstore is used for the packaging display.

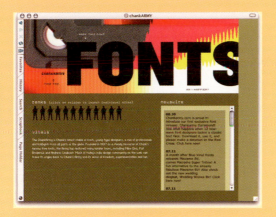

Chank Army's site is a great launching pad to find fonts from affiliated designers. Start here as a portal site into the world of contemporary typographic design.

In 1996, Taco Bell used Mister Frisky for their Halloween campaign.

some ligatures. A lot more design time goes into the professional fonts, and they are more useful overall.

There are other free fonts on the Web that are similarly experimental. However, there are also some pirates out there who illegally distribute free and professional fonts. Watch out for those because they are not legally licensed, and there can be problems with the files.

Harrington: How do you come up with the inspiration for a font?

Diesel: Sometimes I like the letters in an old hand-painted or neon sign. Using a few letters as the basis, I will interpret the entire character set in that style. Other times, a functional or aesthetic design need will inspire a font's creation. For example, Futura Condensed Extrabold is an extremely useful font for legible bold text displays, but I decided there needed to be an alternative design that functioned similarly, so I created the Mingler Fonts.

Harrington: What advice would you give when picking a font?

Diesel: A font is a great way to reinforce an image or message. Think of the image you want your words to portray. Try two or three different fonts for each project. Plug 'em in and see how they work. Choose fonts that complement your design work. Don't

force fonts into a design. If you need a font that dances, pick one with a little bounce instead of forcing a straight font to jump up and down. If you're working on a cowboy piece, for example, look for letterpress-style fonts to reflect the time period.

Harrington: Any general guidelines about using fonts in a composition? What's the total number of fonts I should to use? What about using font families?

Diesel: Make sure they are legible! Don't use display fonts for massive amounts of text. They're intended for headlines and such. Text fonts are made to be legible at small point sizes; display fonts are not.

You usually don't need more than three or four fonts for a project. Sticking with a family of fonts is a good way to have clean design. Use an extrabold version for headlines and lighter versions for text or captions.

The best tip I can offer is that you should not use the automatic Bold and Italic buttons to change your fonts for design work. If you compare letters created with those functions to a true bold or italic of the font, you'll notice that characters have spacing problems and may be awkwardly shaped. When font designers create true bold and italic versions of a font, they carefully create each character to avoid those problems.

Chank also distributes fonts by other designers. Joseph Churchward of New Zealand has more than a dozen fonts in Chank's library.

Chank's painting of Dizzy Gillespie and handwriting font Corndog grace the cover of a CD by Minneapolis jazz ensemble GST.

Harrington: If you are on a budget, where should you invest first?

Diesel: Fonts are an inexpensive way to make a difference in design. Fonts can easily be changed. Fonts visually reinforce the message of the words they display. Fonts can often carry an entire design, and also tie together a campaign. I offer fonts at an afford-able rate so that freelance designers can have easy access to them.

Be sure to look on the disc for some freebies and a special offer from the Chank Company, 1-877-GO-CHANK or www. chank.com.

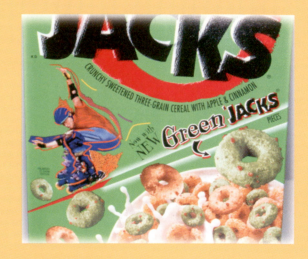

PRO*file*: Frank Rogers

Frank Rogers has a diverse background in film and video. He's designed props, make-up, prosthetics, table top and special effects for movies such as "True Lies," "Homicide," "Contact," and "Mars Attacks." Frank started working for Interface Media in all the same capacities, but beginning to add more digital tools to his palette.

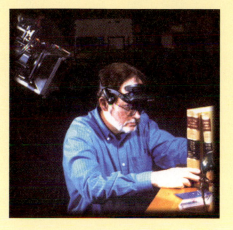

"Coming from a traditional effects background and moving more and more to computer/real effects has made sense to me," said Rogers. "I do motion control, miniatures, set building and all the traditional art department effects work. That's lead to working on a miniature world with cel animation characters for PBS or working out how to shoot an Eskimo in the Arctic (in a studio) believably or how to run down a Arab street and through a hole in a wall to see the Ark of the Covenant."

"Rather than a friction between traditional and CG effects worlds, I see the digital world driving clients to ask for more effects," said Rogers. "In the case of recent movies, more are still nondigital than digital. Of course, the real beauty of digital world is the ability to finesse those floor effects miniatures and CG into a believable whole. Most people aren't aware of how many of the "CG" backgrounds in the Rings films are actually miniatures beautifully finessed in the comping stage.

One area where several purists disagree is motion control photography. Rogers says that there's room for digital tools there as well.

"Even though you would think real world Motion Control would be antithetical to Photoshop, clients really enjoy showing up with double spread of the Sistine Chapel and hoping that I'll be able to take the staple out of God's navel," said Rogers. "Photoshop and a decent DeskJet sit next to the Moco. Motion control can whip through 15 to 20 setups in an hour and I've yet to have that kind of turnout in CG."

Rogers is among a growing group that is harnessing Photoshop's powerful text engine to produce effects. The flexibility of the Character and Paragraph palettes, along with Layer Effects, makes it a powerful "CG" machine.

"I like title creation because I have so many choices and inputs to nudge my approach to type," said Rogers. "I also do storyboards in Photoshop to widen my choices."

This open attitude has allowed Rogers to adapt and grow with changing technology. When you sit down with him, you quickly discover that he is as "tech-savvy" as a recent college grad, current with what the industry is doing. Combine that with his extensive background and you have a key individual, one who is indispensable to the production team.

"I see a lot of people get very comfortable in one set of skills and I've seen highly paid experts in fields like Airbrush Retouching suddenly be unemployable," said Rogers. "Even if you are God's gift to _____ , pray that _____ stays around."

This realization has lead to a lifelong approach to learning. Rogers is working to be solid in type, color correction, photo retouching, and effects; all of these are skills important to the video and film industry. The most important skill, however, is still speed.

"I really admire people with speed and shortcut ability. I find that each job I do in a specific area is a chance to repeat and learn a new set of shortcuts."

Two of Frank Rogers' favorites:

- The ability to change type styles on a line of type that's already been set
- The ability to scroll blending modes using the *Shift* and + or − keys.

Rogers encourages other pros to put the time into learning Photoshop.

"Learning to use Photoshop well is like knowing how to play piano in music or type in the real world," said Rogers. "It's a core program you wind up back in whether you are a compositor, motion graphic expert, or 3D code warrior."

BEFORE

AFTER

6

LAYER STYLES: BEVELS, SHADOWS, GLOWS, AND MORE!

While many graphics are easy to read at print resolutions, they quickly become lost in the frame when keyed over moving video. In the print world, type is generally placed over a solid color (such as white paper). In the video space, we frequently mix type with motion, and this results in an issue referred to as type on pattern.

There are several strategies for assisting with readability in these situations. Common techniques include adding bevels, glows, or contrasting drop shadows. While there are many excellent Photoshop techniques and software products developed over the years, nothing is better suited for the video world than proper use of Layer Styles.

What are Layer Styles?

Imagine effects that never need rendering. Did I mention that they are infinitely customizable? Oh, and if you make a change on the layer, they instantly update. Photoshop offers several customizable effects that can be applied to a layer. The effects that are applied to a layer become the layer's custom style.

Layer Styles are the perfect tools for a video pro with deadlines. Layer Styles are fast. They can be embedded into the document or easily transported, eliminating the need for identical plug-ins and cross-platform issues. Better yet, there are thousands of Layer Styles available online for free. And best of all, the effects are "live" (much like After Effects), which gives you the ability to apply, stack, undo, or remove as many times as you (or the producer) wants.

Styles aka Effects

Layer styles are often referred to as *layer effects*. Do not get confused if looking at articles or tutorials.

141

More Styles from the Mothership

 Looking for more Layer Styles? Be sure to check out the incredible adobexchange.com site and you will find a generous community offering free Layer Styles.

The best way to understand Layer Styles is to simply apply them. Of course, there are a few gotchas—it wouldn't be a computer application if there weren't. Layer Styles are designed to work inside of Photoshop, which means they aren't particularly friendly when you import layered files into a video application. They also don't work perfectly with alpha channels. However, both problems can be solved in 15 seconds, still leaving Layer Styles well ahead of the race against the clock. There are four major ways to apply styles:

- The Add a Layer Style pop-up menu at the bottom of the Layers palette
- The Style palette
- The Layer Style dialog box
- The Layer menu (Layer>Layer Style)

Each provides unique advantages, depending upon your situation. We will cover all four in this chapter, but let's start with the pop-up menu.

Step 1. Create a new document sized for video using the NTSC D1 preset.

Step 2. Place an element such as text on an empty layer. Choose a thick, sans serif font and type a short word.

Step 3. Go to the bottom of the Layers palette; click on the *fx* icon (older versions use a circular *f*). Choose the first effect, Drop Shadow.

Step 4. The Layer Style dialog box appears, and you have the chance to tweak your effect.

Blending Options...

Drop Shadow...
Inner Shadow...
Outer Glow...
Inner Glow...
Bevel and Emboss...
Satin...
Color Overlay...
Gradient Overlay...
Pattern Overlay...
Stroke...

Drop Shadow

The drop shadow is a straightforward effect that will serve well as an introduction to the other Layer Styles. Many of the options presented will reoccur in other Layer Styles.

Blend Mode: You can specify the blending mode for the shadow. Different colors and modes will produce very different results. Remember, shadows aren't always black; they often pick up the color of the light source or background on which they are cast. The Multiply blending mode is the most common for shadows.

Color: By default, the shadow is set to black. To change the color of the shadow, click on the colored rectangle to load the Adobe Color Picker. You can also pick a contrasting color to help offset your type or logo on a busy background. This allows the shadow to more realistically blend with lower layers.

Shadows...Go Forth and Multiply

The most practical blending mode for shadows is Multiply. This causes the shadows to mix with the background on which they are lying and create a darkening effect.

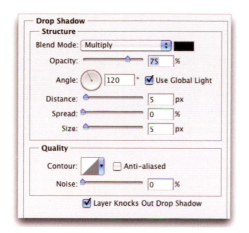

Opacity: You will want to adjust the opacity to taste. Opacity is the opposite of transparency; the higher the number, the less you can see through the layer.

Angle: This setting affects the direction of the shadow.

Use Global Light: The Global Light option allows for a consistent light source for all layer effects. It's a good idea to leave the Global Light box checked so that your designs have realistic lighting. You can adjust the angle to modify all your effects.

Distance: The Distance option affects how far the shadow is cast. If numbers aren't your thing, you can simply click in the window and manually drag the shadow into a new position.

Spread: This affects how much the shadow disperses. Higher numbers create greater dispersal.

Size: This modifies the softness of the shadow. Higher numbers create softer edges.

Contour: While most users skip the Contour settings, you will not. The Contour is a curve; it represents how Photoshop fades transparency. We'll explore this powerful option later in this chapter.

Anti-aliased: Don't forget to check the Anti-aliased box. Anti-aliasing will give you smoother on-screen results, especially at video resolutions.

Noise: Noise can add random dispersion to your style. This can help make the effect look more natural as well as reduce banding on a video monitor.

Layer Knocks Out Drop Shadow: This option is checked by default (and should probably stay that way). It ensures that the shadow does not bleed through partially transparent text.

Uncheck the Drop Shadow box to remove the shadow, and then click on the Inner Shadow box.

Global Light is Important

The Global Light of a Layer Style affects important aspects like the direction of shadows and reflections. It is important to keep your Layer Styles consistent, so be sure to use a consistent global light setting to drive the effects.

More is Better

You'll find the Layer Styles shown in this chapter on the book's disc, as well as 55 styles from Action FX.

Inner Shadow

Inner shadows cause a shadow to be cast in front of your layer. This effect can be used to create a "punch-out" or recessed look. Inner shadows look best when they are soft. Play with the distance and size sliders to get a desirable effect. Inner shadows work well with other Layer Styles, but look distracting when overused. The controls of this effect are nearly identical to those of drop shadow. There is one new setting called Choke.

Choke: You can use a slider to shrink the boundaries of the Inner Shadow prior to blurring.

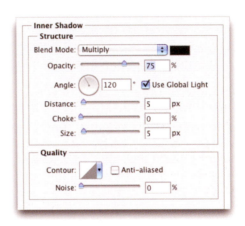

Go Softly

Soft-Edged Stroke? Sure—it's called Outer Glow. Adjust the size and spread for better appearance.

Outer Glow and Inner Glow

These two effects offer similar controls. Both enable you to set color, amount, and shape of the glow. The key difference is that the inner glow lets you set where the glow emanates, the edges of the layer or the center of the layer. Inner glows signify light coming from behind the layer. It is unlikely that you would need to apply a drop shadow and a glow simultaneously. Tweak the contour and quality for a variety of shapes to your glows.

Technique: You can choose to use the Softer option, which does not preserve as many details. Alternately, choose Precise if the source has hard edges (like s logo or text).

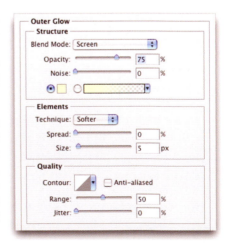

Source: An Inner Glow can originate either from the edges or the center of a layer.

Range: This helps target which portion of the glow is impacted by the contour.

Jitter: This will vary the application of the glow's color gradient. It affects color and opacity. Modify to make subtle changes to the effect.

Bevel and Emboss

This versatile effect enables you to access five different types of edge effects. These work very well for offsetting a layer. Bevels complement inner and outer glows to produce a realistic depth effect.

- An Outer Bevel adds a three-dimensional beveled edge around the outside of a layer; this is generated by adding a clear edge.
- Inner Bevel generates a similar effect inside the edge but uses the layer's own pixels.
- The Emboss effect combines inner and outer bevels.
- Pillow Emboss combines the inner and outer bevel, but reverses the outer bevel, causing the image to appear stamped into the composition.
- The last effect, Stroke Emboss, must be used in combination with the Stroke layer effect. These two combine to create a colored, beveled edge along the outside of a layer.

The beveled edges allow a great deal of control. It is possible to change the lighting source and direction of the bevel, as well as thickness, softness, and depth. It is also possible to use the power of blending modes to create extremely photorealistic effects, such as plastic or chrome.

Check Yourself

 Don't over-bevel. A subtle bevel helps a text or logo element lift off the screen and adds subtle depth. Overuse, however, looks amateurish.

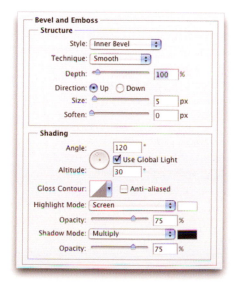

Depth: This is the thickness of the bevel.

Direction: You can set the bevel to go up or down. This can dramatically change the look of the bevel.

Altitude: You can set the altitude of the light source between 0° and 90°. The higher the number, the more the bevel appears to go straight back.

Gloss Contour: Use this command to create a glossy or metallic appearance. The Gloss Contour is applied after shading the bevel or emboss.

Highlight Mode and Opacity: This specifies the blending mode and opacity of the highlight.

Shadow Mode and Opacity: This specifies the blending mode and opacity of the shadow used in the bevel.

Contour: The flexibility of the Contour controls is the bevel effect's best feature. There are many presets to try, or create your own. There are two contour settings: the first pane affects the lighting of the bevel, and the Specialized Contour pane alters the shape of the edge.

Texture: The final option is Texture, which can be applied to the bevel or entire surface. Many presets can be used by clicking on the triangular menus. Additional patterns can be loaded or created. Many textures exist at online creative sites; you'll also find a variety of textures included on the bundled DVD. Creating unique textures is also easy, as we'll see in future chapters.

Uncheck the Bevel and Emboss boxes to remove the bevel, and then click on the Satin box.

A Soft Touch

Satin is an underused effect that can add soft highlights to a layer.

Satin

Satin is used to add regular ripples or waves in your Layer Style. With a little practice, you can create liquid effects and subtle highlights. This style requires some experimentation because its controls are very sensitive. Choosing different colors, contour settings, and blending modes will produce widely different results. Satin works very well in combination with other effects.

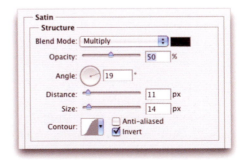

Uncheck the Satin box to remove the Satin effect, and then click on the Color Overlay box.

Color, Gradient, and Pattern Overlays

These three styles all serve a similar purpose: to replace the contents of your layer with new fill colors or textures. A great time-saver is the ability to quickly swap colors on a group of layers without having to repaint or edit each layer. It is possible to switch the color of text by applying a new color in the Layer Style. This same style can be applied to multiple layers simultaneously.

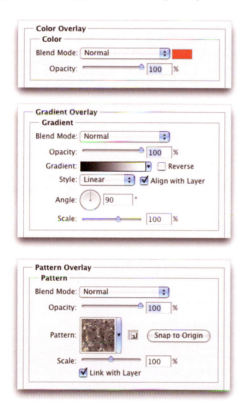

Step 1. Copy the Layer Style by *ctrl* +clicking (right-clicking) on the small *fx* (*f*) icon.

Step 2. Link all of the layers together.

Step 3. Then *ctrl* +click (right-click) and choose Paste Layer Style to Linked.

Gradient and pattern overlays are useful in creating new looks, especially when using photorealistic patterns or seamless tiles. To create more believable effects, be sure to combine pattern usage with blending modes. All three of these overlay effects are useful in creating your own Layer Styles.

Stroke

The Stroke effect places a colored border around the outside edge of a layer. This is a great replacement for using the Stroke command under the Edit menu. It is now possible to keep the stroke as an easy-to-update effect without needing to place it on its own layer. All of the needed controls are

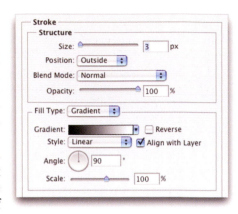

here: you can choose from inner, outer, or center strokes, as well as advanced controls such a blending modes, textures, and gradients. The Stroke effect can be further enhanced by combining it with the Stroke Emboss effect.

Designing with Layer Styles

Harnessing Layer Styles is an important part of a professional user's workflow. The efficiency and flexibility offered by styles are huge time-savers. They can also add consistency to a designer's techniques. Be sure to fully explore all the ways that styles can be useful to you.

Loading Prebuilt Styles

Sometimes the best way to start is with a preset. Photoshop includes some good styles to work with. The easiest way to work with styles is to call up the Styles palette, which by default is docked with the Color and Swatches tabs. If you've closed that window, look under the Window menu and call up the Styles palette.

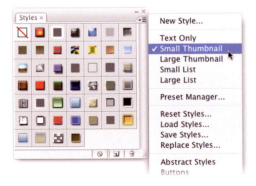

You'll notice a small swatch that represents each style. To apply a style, highlight any layer (other than the Background layer or a locked layer) and click on a swatch. You can view these preset icons in many ways. Click on the triangular submenu icon in the upper right corner of the Styles window and choose from different sized thumbnails or lists. For the visually minded, I recommend a thumbnail view. If you have many presets to choose from, the large list view is helpful because it combines a name and thumbnail.

Accessing Additional Built-In Styles

When you need more styles to choose from, simply pick from the drop-down list in the submenu (Photoshop comes with 10 styles to choose from). When you select a new set of styles from the Preset list, you are presented a choice. You can:

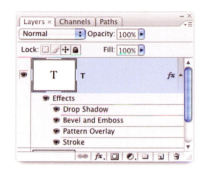

- **Append:** Adds the new styles to the bottom of the current list.
- **Cancel:** Does not load anything new.
- **OK:** Replaces the current list with new presets.

Step 1. Open up the `Ch06_Start.psd` file in the chapter's folder. If you do not have access to this file, create a new document with a floating text layer.

Step 2. Select the Text layer so that the layer is highlighted. Call up your Styles palette. From the submenu, choose Text Effects 2. Click OK to add the styles.

Step 3. Click on each preset, pausing to study the end results. See how quickly the simple text layer changes from organic effects, to shiny metal, to jelly-like letters? This is just the beginning.

To fully appreciate the power of Layer Styles, have your Layers palette open. As you change styles on a layer, the palette updates. Double-click on each component to call up the dialog window. You'll discover how the effect was made. Better yet, these presets are merely starting points! You can modify them and save them for later use or sharing with others.

Accessing Additional Styles

If you'd like to load new styles that don't appear in the preset list, choose Load Styles from the Styles window submenu. For inspiration, we've included a large collection of styles in the chapter's folder on the DVD. If you'd like these to appear in your preset list, find the *Presets* folder inside your Photoshop application folder and look for the *Styles* folder. Any Layer Styles copied into the *Styles* folder will appear as a preset the next time you launch the program.

Technology is only as good as it is customizable. Fortunately, Layer Styles are infinitely "tweakable." You can create your own entirely from scratch, or build off an existing style. The practice of building styles is booming in Photoshop user groups. One of the best places to look is Adobe Exchange (http://www.adobe.com/exchange). This popular site is free. (Don't be thrown off when it asks you to register.) Here you will find tons of content available for all Adobe products. On first visit, stick to Photoshop and look at the styles available. You will find that many users have been busy posting their own creations. Download a few styles to help on your next project and see what's possible with Layer Styles.

Sizing Styles

When changing Image Size (Image>Image Size), you can now specify that you'd like styles to scale proportionately.

Building Your Own Styles

Creating a style is a straightforward process. You can apply any combination of the previously mentioned 10 effects. Change the options, use a new texture, apply gradients and blending modes, and so on. If you are unsure how each Layer Style is applied, flip back to "Layer Styles" on page 141. Styles are quick to learn and easy to master; just continue to experiment with many options. Advanced customization through contours, gradients, and textures will be covered later on in this chapter.

Saving Styles

Once you've created an original style (or even modified an existing one), you will likely want to save it. Sharing styles can be accomplished two ways:

- First, you can give someone the project in which you used the style. The styles remain attached to the layered document. Choose a layered format such as PSD, Layered TIFF, or Photoshop PDF. This will allow the information to be called back up later. So six months from now, when your project comes back, you can open up your source files and start making changes.
- The second method is more efficient for the Web. You can save the styles as self-contained .asl files. These library files can then be shared between users and machines.

Sharing Styles

Whatever items currently appear in the Styles palette will be included in the style library. It is a good idea to remove unwanted or preset styles from the palette first. You can drag these into the palette's Trashcan, or ⌥+click (*alt*+click) on the ones you wish to delete. When ready, choose Save Styles from the Style palette submenu. The resulting file is small and can easily be e-mailed to others. To prevent the file from being garbled in e-mail, make sure that you include the .asl extension.

Save Yourself

If you add new styles to a library, you must *resave* the .asl file to update it. Otherwise, the new styles will be cleared when you load another library.

Updating Your Presets

A good place to store styles is in Application folder>Presets> Styles. By using the default location, Photoshop will recognize the libraries on start-up. This will allow you to click on the Styles palette submenu and load them from the presets list.

Step 1. When you create a style worth sharing, load the library where you want to save it. It's a good idea to create a custom set for yourself.

Step 2. Select the affected layer in the Layers palette, and then click on an empty space in the Styles palette.

Step 3. Now choose Save Styles; name the file with the same name it had before, and save it to the same location.

Action FX

Known best for its many action files, Action FX has an impressive collection of Layer Styles as well. What started as a site for Photoshop hobbyists has quickly become a popular stop for Actions, Layer Styles, Brush Sets, and Textures.

There are many tutorials and articles created by Photoshop author Al Ward. Al calls himself a certified Photoshop addict and is the webmaster of Action FX Photoshop Resources. He also contributes to the official NAPP Web site as the Actions area coordinator (www.photoshopuser.com).

Action FX has included 55 Layer Styles on the book's disc. You'll find these to be great time-savers in your upcoming projects. There are many more styles and resources available at the Web site as well. Action FX offers tons of free downloads that will generate fast results. If you like what you find, there are also many other great things to be had by joining.

Besides creating cool software, Al is an accomplished author and is worth looking up the next time you are in the market for a book on special effects. You can count on more great things from Al Ward, as he lists coffee as his favorite food group and sleep as the one pastime he'd like to take up some day.

The Power of Contour Settings

Perhaps the least understood option of the Layer Styles dialog boxes is the Contour setting. Most users leave it set to the default linear slope setting. The easiest way to understand the contour is to think of it as a cross-section of the bevel. The contour represents the shape of the bevel from a parallel point of view. A simple linear contour reflects light with predictable results. Irregularly shaped contours can generate metallic highlights or multiple rings to the bevel. When you think you've tried every option, the contour settings will unlock many more. Just make sure to pick the Anti-aliased option.

Contours to Try Out

You'll find a collection of contour settings to try out on the disc.

To modify a contour, you can click on the drop-down menu and select a preset. If you don't like the 12 included settings, feel free to load some or make your own. Loading contours is similar to loading styles: just click on the submenu triangle. Making your own involves defining the shape of the curve. Click on the curve and add points. If the Preview box is selected, your curve will update in near real time. This is the best way to learn how the contour controls work. Contour controls are available on glows, shadows, and bevels.

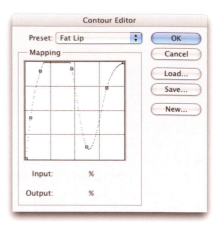

Think of the contour as a cross-section of the bevel. It represents the shape of the bevel from a parallel point of view.

Gradients and Textures

Another way to create a unique look is to use custom overlays for your layer. These can be a gradient or a texture. You have precise control of how the overlay is blended and scaled to the layer. These tools behave the same way throughout Photoshop, so if you are experienced with gradients or textures, this will be easy!

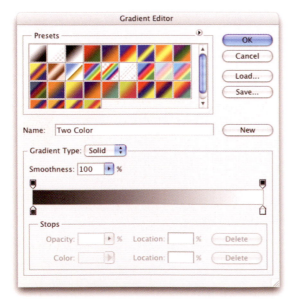

Using Gradients

A gradient is simply a gradual blend between two or more colors. Photoshop offers many gradient libraries in the Presets menu. To access these, follow the triangles to access the submenus. Try different styles of gradients (radial, linear, angle, reflected, or diamond) for a new look. The angle setting will also change the gradient's appearance. To go even further, change the blend mode.

Creating your own gradients is a simple process. Clicking on the image of the gradient will bring up the Gradient Editor, where the color stops and opacity stops define the color and opacity throughout the gradient. The midpoint can also be adjusted to favor one color over the other. To add new stops, click in an empty space above (for opacity) or below (for color). You can also create copies of existing stops by holding down the

 key and dragging left or right. Gradients are useful for adding depth and life to an image. Be careful to avoid extreme contrast between stops, or you will get visible banding or patterns on your video output. For more on gradients, be sure to see Chapter 11, "Creating Backgrounds for Video."

Using Patterns

The introduction of photorealistic patterns goes a long way towards adding life to your layers. Patterns can be created from any scan or digital photo. You may also choose to paint your own. There is an abundance of patterns available online and from third-party vendors. The trick is to use a seamless pattern that tiles smoothly. Creating a seamless pattern is now simple, thanks to the Pattern Maker filter. In total, the process of creating and saving a seamless pattern should take you less than two minutes. To get started, open the file `Ch06_Stone_Texture.tiff` from the chapter's folder on the DVD-ROM.

Step 1. Select the *Background* layer and then choose the Crop tool.

Step 2. In the Options bar, enter a target size of 800 px by 800 px. Crop the image to size and press Enter to apply the crop.

Step 3. Choose Edit>Select All and then Filter>Pattern Maker. The Smoothness and Sample Details should be adjusted to produce best results. Higher numbers warrant better patterns but will take longer to generate. Be sure to click on the Use Image Size button to generate a large texture.

Step 4. Click the Generate button to create the first pattern. Repeated clicks will generate multiple results, all of which are tracked in the lower right corner. You can go back to earlier versions by clicking the arrows in the bottom corner.

Step 5. When you are happy with the results, click OK.

Step 6. With the entire layer selected (Edit>Select All), choose Edit>Define Pattern.

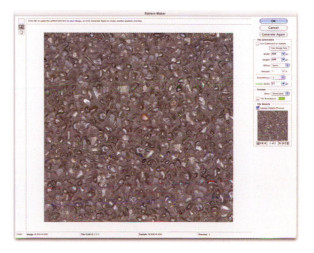

Once a pattern is created, it can be used from the Pattern Overlay Layer Style or Pattern Fill Layer. Choose the pattern from the pop-up list. If you'd like, you can access the submenu in the Layer Styles palette and choose to save your currently loaded patterns. (This process is identical to saving contours.)

Creating Duotones and Sepia Tones with Layer Styles

The Color, Gradient, and Pattern overlays are useful when working with photos. If working with groups of historical sources or grayscale photos, you can use Layer Styles for consistent tinting effects.

Step 1. If working with a historical photo, strip all of the color data out the photo before restoring it. You can do this by choosing Image> Adjustments>Desaturate.

Step 2. Add a layer effect such as Color Overlay or Gradient Overlay. Adjust the blending mode of the effects to tint the layer.

If you'd like to see effects in action, load the style library `PhotoStyles.asl` from the book's DVD-ROM.

Importing Layer Styles into an NLE

Importing Layer Styles into a nonlinear editing system generally warrants undesirable results. While most NLE software will recognize a layered PSD file, Layer Styles are ignored. To get around this, there are two approaches. The first approach is to attempt to recreate the effects within the NLE environment. This works well for basic effects like drop shadows, but not for the more advanced features.

The second approach is to use merging to permanently apply the Layer Styles. If you are going to choose this approach, be sure to save a copy of the original file before proceeding.

Step 1. Create a text layer and apply a Layer Style to it.

Step 2. Create a new layer by pressing `Shift`+`⌘`+`N` (`Shift`+`ctrl`+`N`). Drag the new layer below the stylized layer in the Layers palette.

Step 3. Select both layers, `Shift`+clicking their layers in the Layers palette (older versions of Photoshop require that you link the layers).

Step 4. Choose Layer>Merge Layers.

Step 5. Repeat for any other layers that have Layer Styles applied.

Alternately, you can take merging layers a step further; see "Targeted Flattening" at the end of this chapter.

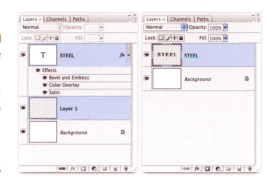

The left image shows the original layers, the right image is after merging.

Importing Layer Styles into After Effects

The process of importing Layer Styles into Adobe After Effects has continued to improve with each software release. As both Photoshop and After Effects are made by Adobe, the expectation

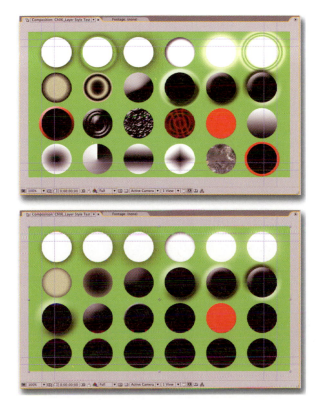

The top image shows the merged layers when imported into After Effects. The bottom image shows the errors generated when Layer Styles are brought into After Effects as a "live effect."

is that the two applications will exchange seamlessly. However, expectations are not always reality.

Layer Styles are very complex, especially when features like Contours and Patterns are used. After Effects does its best to recreate the Layer Style using its effects engine. Depending on the effects you have applied, After Effects may need to pre-compose layers or split the stylized layer into multiple tracks. If you have After Effects, we've included a test file on the book's DVD-ROM.

Step 1. Launch After Effects and select the Project window.

Step 2. Choose File>Import>File and select the file `Ch06_Layer Style Test.psd` from the chapter's folder on the DVD-ROM. Choose to Import As: Composition and click Open. The layered file is opened into After Effects.

Step 3. Double-click the composition icon in the Project window to load it.

Step 4. The topmost layer can be toggled off and on. It is a merged copy created in Photoshop that shows you how the Layer Styles *should* look. You'll notice that none of the advanced features like Contour or Noise translate. Additionally Texture, Gradient, Stroke, and Satin may be ignored (depending on which version of AE you are using). Even features like bevels don't translate exactly.

Depending on your desired results, you'll need to make a choice. You can take the approach we discussed for NLE import and merge stylized layers with empty layers to "flatten" the style. Otherwise, if you need the layer effect to be editable, you will need to modify the imported file until it matches your desired effect as closely as possible. It is important to keep in mind that After Effects and Photoshop are separate programs and you cannot expect all features to work seamlessly.

Final Advice when Working with Layer Styles

The following advice is offered to really make you an expert Layer Styles user. These techniques can really tip the balance of power and give you the speed and flexibility that video deadlines demand.

Shortcuts

How do you add shortcuts to a technology based on shortcuts? The designers at Adobe managed to squeeze a few in. Here are the most useful shortcuts related to Layer Styles:

- Double-click on a layer in the layer's palette (except on the name), and you will be in the Layer Style dialog box.
- To edit a specific effect, double-click that effect's name in the Layers palette.
- Turn effects off temporarily by clicking on the eyeball icon next to it.
- Copy and paste Layer Styles by right-clicking on the effect icon in the Layers palette and choose Copy Layer Style.
- You can also paste a copied effect to multiple layers that are selected or linked. Just right-click on the Effect icon and select Paste Layer Style.
- You can move a Layer Style from one layer to another by dragging it.
- You can ⌥+drag (*alt*+drag) a Layer Style from one layer to another to copy it.

Alpha Channels and Import Issues

You'd think alpha channels would be a snap with Layer Styles as such a perfect time-saver. Despite lobbying efforts, Layer Styles do not affect how a layer loads; this is a crucial step in creating the alpha channel. Simply put: loading a layer with a drop shadow or glow will ignore any pixels outside the initial shape. This makes generating an alpha channel nearly impossible.

To add to this problem, other applications have difficulty with Layer Styles. No NLE system correctly interprets all effects. Even After Effects imports Layer Styles as multiple layers and pre-compositions, with some features not fully supported. While the Create Layers command is often recommended as a solution, it is not a perfect fix. It generates messy results with grouped layers and some effects displaying incorrectly.

"Marching ants" don't lie…the light bulb on the left is loading incorrectly, as it does not recognize the outer glow layer effect. It is important to flatten layer effects before sending them out to other video applications.

Targeted Flattening

Many designers I know have given up on Layer Styles and reverted to using filters. But you can keep using Layer Styles without problems. The solution is simple: Flatten them! You can flatten the contents of an individual layer so that it loads perfectly and travels easily. Better yet, through a little Layers palette trickery, we can make a portable copy while still preserving an editable layer. This technique, which I call targeted flattening, is similar to a video mixdown or a nested composition.

Using Create Layers

You can right-click and choose Create Layers to turn a Layer Style into a multilayered effect. This command can assist in translating effects to another system, but you lose the ability to modify the effects.

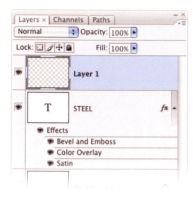

Step 1. Save your document under a different name by using Save As. This is an extra precaution against accidentally deleting your work. (I usually rename it Document Name for AE.psd or Document Name for FCP.psd, etc.)

Step 2. Double-click on the background and give it a new name, thus creating a floating layer. This procedure will not work correctly if the background layer is part of your linked set.

Step 3. Create a new (empty) layer and place it below the stylized layer.

Step 4. Select both layers by Shift-clicking. Older versions of Photoshop (pre-CS2) require you to link the two layers together.

Step 5. Leave the empty layer highlighted. While holding down the ⌥ (alt) key, click on the submenu and select Merge (or Merge Linked). This merges the layers to the target layer, but leaves the originals behind.

You should have a flattened copy on the target layer. Repeat for all layers and save your work. This method will produce a layered document, which can be cleanly imported into other editing applications that support layers. You will discard the layers that you don't need within the NLE or motion graphics application after import.

Updating Styles

You can easily jump into the Photoshop document to make updates. After Effects users can choose Edit Original (⌘+E / ctrl+E).

Step 1. Select the flattened layer, choose Select All, and press Delete.

Step 2. Pick the original (unflattened) layer and make your changes to the Layer Style or layer contents.

Step 3. Repeat the Targeted Flattening procedure.

This process works well with the Edit Original command in After Effects and Premiere Pro or Final Cut Pro's External Editor. It can also work with Avid's batch import command and support for Photoshop layers, as well on newer systems.

Create the Alpha Channel

If you need to create an alpha channel for an effected layer, you will need to create a merged copy.

Step 1. Create a new, empty layer.

Step 2. Disable the visibility on any background or reference layers that you don't want included in the alpha channel.

Step 3. With the empty layer selected, hold down the ⌥ (*alt*) key and choose Layer>Merge Visible.

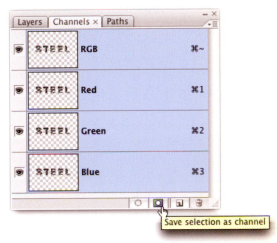

Step 4. You can now ⌘+click (*ctrl*+click) on the merged layer to load it as a selection. Throw away the merged layer as you are done with it. Creating an alpha channel is just one click away.

Step 5. With the "marching ants" circling, go to the Channels palette. Click on the Save Selection as Channel button (second from the left). You have now created the needed alpha channel.

Step 6. Choose File>Save As… and pick a format that your system recognizes and that will support an alpha channel (such as PICT, TIFF, or Targa). Be sure to only have one alpha channel in your Channels palette (visible or invisible). Additional channels will cause problems when you save your files out for video.

Hands On | 06

Creating Layer Styles with Photos

Layer Styles are one of the most exciting things to happen to Photoshop. Flat images can take on a rich depth and visual excitement. In this tutorial we'll explore using multiple layers and photographic sources to create a logo.

Unfortunately, most users resign themselves to only using the built-in styles. Many don't realize that there are more to load (just click on the palette's submenu). Better yet you can download more from great sites like www.adobe.com/exchange. But the true power lies in creating your own.

While the act of creation may seem intimidating, don't fret. Photoshop offers several easy ways to create your own styles. In this tutorial we'll explore using photographic sources as textures or patterns that will push Layer Styles into new possibilities.

You'll find Exercise 06 on the DVD-ROM.

PRO*file*: Michael H. Amundson

Michael Amundson studied film at The University of Iowa, and soon found himself a freelancer in film production. He worked as an operator and assistant on film and video productions as well as other duties ranging from dolly grip to sound recordist. He then went to work for a production company, where he became an Avid editor, making commercials, videos, and interactive media. Amundson then pulled up roots and moved across the country to Boston, Massachusetts to work for the PBS long-form public-affairs documentary series FRONTLINE.

"My duties at FRONTLINE were demanding and wide-ranging, including online and offline editing of the films and promos," said Amundson. "I also supervised restoration of archival documentary film. But I did a significant amount of design work for the open titles and credits, promo end-pages, and graphics, as well as the design and updating of packaging elements."

After five years Mike decided to get behind the camera again and is now with Vermont Studio, a boutique company not far from Boston. "I'm very lucky to have found a flexible environment where I can keep one foot in the edit suite and the other behind the lens." Mike has been shooting for FRONTLINE as well as providing post-production services for a variety of filmmakers and non-broadcast clients.

When graphics are involved, Amundson always turns to Adobe Photoshop. He uses Photoshop to prepare photographs and other scanned elements for use in the documentaries. Amundson says that Photoshop is "indispensable" to the broadcast TV business.

"Photoshop is great for retouching problem photos to eliminate scratches or distracting elements in the image," said Amundson. "I also create graphic elements such as main titles and credits in Photoshop, then animate or effect them in After Effects. Photoshop support is integrated perfectly in After Effects, making the work very easy and more creative. I then render a QuickTime movie with After Effects to be imported into the finishing system."

Amundson says Photoshop's accessible and affordable toolset is a perfect complement to an NLE suite.

"Our online system has excellent color correction and scratch removal tools, so I don't use Photoshop as much as I used to for that," said Amundson. "However, not everyone has access to expensive broadcast tools, and Photoshop can accomplish many of these tasks at a great price."

Amundson offers two pieces of advice for nonlinear editors.

- He says he relies heavily on the History palette. "I use the history palette to undo my screw-ups, which are many."
- He also points to the need for collaboration. "Being in tune with the people in your edit suite is half of the editing process."

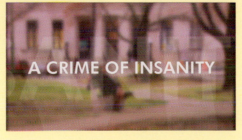

A SENSE OF HISTORY

A true test of how powerful a computer application is lies not in the ability to "do," but rather to "undo." Having the ability to create with a safety net is a liberating experience. By harnessing the power of the History palette, an editor or designer can manage to try new things without having the pressure of a missed deadline.

Configuring History States

By default, Photoshop has 20 history states. A history state is simply a level of undo. If 20 is not enough for you, then you can increase this number. To do so, activate Photoshop's Preferences by pressing ⌘+K (ctrl+K). In Photoshop CS3 you'll find History States under the Performance group (in earlier versions it can be found in the General group).

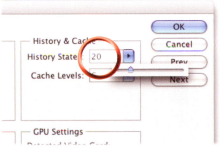

When adjusting history states, you should keep in mind that you are tying up your computer's RAM for each level of undo. Fortunately, Photoshop is very efficient in tracking changes. History states are stored in RAM, where you can access them quickly. If you run out of RAM, they are written to the available scratch disk.

Photoshop currently supports up to 1000 levels of undo. It would take some very fast mouse clicks to use those up. Since you are generally working with small file sizes, RAM requirements are low. I recommend 100 history states as a starting point. Go up or down as needed based on your workflow.

History States Use RAM

History states are stored only in RAM. If you close a document or your computer crashes, you lose your multiple undos. Be sure to save your work frequently.

Accessing History States

To make undos a little easier, you may want to change your Redo key settings. Most nonlinear editing systems will "walk backwards" when the Undo key is pressed. By default, Photoshop will dance

History States = Multiple Undos

Photoshop supports up to 1000 levels of undo. These history states eat up RAM, however. Set yours to taste, but I recommend a number less than 100 for better performance.

a two-step: undo/redo, undo/redo. To change this requires you to access your Keyboard Shortcuts.

Step 1. Choose Edit>Keyboard Shortcuts or press *Shift*+⌥+⌘+*K* (*Shift*+*alt*+*ctrl*+*K*).

Step 2. Access Shortcuts for Application Menus and twirl down the Edit Menu category.

Step 3. Delete the shortcut for Undo (which is set to ⌘+*Z*/*ctrl*+*Z*). Leave this field empty.

Step 4. Change Step Backwards to ⌘+*Z* (*ctrl*+*Z*) and accept the suggested changes for the History palette as well. Step Backwards will revert you to an earlier version of the document.

Step 5. Change the Step Forward command to ⌘+*Y* (*ctrl*+*Y*) if that is what your NLE system uses. Don't worry that you are replacing the proof colors shortcut, that's for print use only. Step Forward is used to move forward through states of a document after undos have been performed.

Step 6. You can save and back up your custom settings, or just click OK to apply them. This will speed up your access to multiple undos and make Photoshop act more like your NLE.

The History palette is not the most visible window. Most users have it shrunk down to just a few lines; some have it hidden completely. To make this wonderful palette more accessible, dock it in the palette well. Drag the tab to the upper right corner of your screen. The History palette will dock itself in the Options bar, always ready, never in the way.

Think of the History palette as an edit assistant that tracks your every move. As you move forward through your project, you can instantly jump back as many steps as you need. If you are decisive, set your history state number lower. If you are experimental, leave this number high. Every time you click and make a change that affects your canvas, that change is recorded. You can now access this list visually with the mouse, or through keyboard shortcuts. Take a deep breath, and jump in the pool of creative thinking.

Performing Multiple Undos

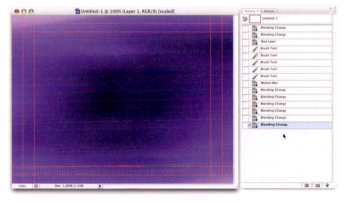

The best way to understand the History palette is to simply try it out. For this exercise you will regress a little and finger paint. This is a great opportunity to try out the flexibility of Photoshop's Brushes.

Step 1. Create a new document sized for video using the NTSC D1 720×486 pixels template.

Step 2. Start painting an abstract background that you could use in your next video or motion graphics project. Combine different brush strokes and colors. Don't hold back; just create.

Step 3. Continue to experiment until you are satisfied with the image. After you've finished painting, look at what you've created.

Step 4. Select the History palette tab (if not visible choose Window>History).

In the History palette you will see a comprehensive list of every step you took (up to your number of history states limit). Your final step is highlighted at the bottom of the list. To go backwards, click on the state you wish to return to. The change is instant.

The speed and flexibility of the History palette will let you explore different approaches without having to keep multiple copies of an image open. For those who prefer keyboard shortcuts, cycling through your undos will take you backwards through the History palette. Earlier you changed the Redo key to ⌘+Y (ctrl+Y) under the Keyboard Shortcuts window, ; this is a faster way to access previous history states.

By default, you should be working with history states using the linear mode. This is the standard mode for the History palette; it can be accessed by going to the palette's submenu. Click on the small triangle on the right corner of the palette's tab. Choose History Options and make certain the Allow Nonlinear History box is unchecked.

As you step backwards through each state, you should notice how states become grayed out and italicized. This lets you know that you are working in the linear mode. As you move backwards, Photoshop is alerting you that these steps are undone. Moving forward, by applying a change to the image, will result in these grayed items being dropped off the list. Once an item has been removed from the History palette, it is gone.

It is possible to create your own time-stamped backups. Photoshop can automatically create a snapshot each time you save. Snapshots are useful, but are only temporary, because they are stored in RAM.

Revert is slow and painful. Your computer has to reload the original file into memory. Instead, use the first snapshot for an instant "go back to start" jump.

It is very important to remember that the History palette is tied to RAM. Power failures, computer crashes, or kicked power strips will all interrupt your computer's power supply and, therefore, your RAM data. Do not think of the History palette as a replacement for saving your work. It's also important to note that the history information is not stored with the document when you save it.

The History palette for a specific document resets each time you open that document. However, you can toggle between open documents, and each will retain its own history states and levels of undo. Program-wide changes to palettes, user preferences, actions, or color settings are not recorded to the History palette.

Using Snapshots

A snapshot is exactly as its name implies, a captured moment in time. Making a snapshot creates a point that you can quickly jump to (think of them as digital breadcrumbs).

Proper use of snapshots will expand flexibility. Since the changes are stored in RAM, you can jump from one point to another very quickly.

Making a snapshot is easy. At the bottom of the History palette, click on the Create New Snapshot icon (the icon looks like a camera icon). If you want more advanced options hold down the (*alt*) key when clicking. This will give you advanced options, including the ability to name the state when you create it.

Snapshots appear at the top of the History palette. Photoshop will create the first snapshot by default when you open the document. This gives you a very quick return path to revert to the original document, and is significantly faster than reloading the file back from disk. You can add new snapshots whenever you want a milestone to return to. Photoshop supports more than 1000 snapshots, depending upon available RAM and scratch disk space.

One particularly helpful option for snapshots is to have Photoshop create a new snapshot every time you save. This is similar to the "attic" or "vault" features of many nonlinear editing systems. To access this feature, access the triangular submenu in the History palette. Choose History Options and enable the Automatically Create New Snapshot When Saving check box.

Now each time you save your document, a new snapshot will be generated. Jumping between different versions is as simple as clicking on the icon for each in the History palette. Photoshop names the new state with the exact time it was created. This feature is invaluable when the client or producer is sitting next to you and wants to make "just a few" changes. It now becomes possible to jump through numerous hoops, yet always return to any given point in a near instant.

On the subject of frequent changes, you can generate a new document from any history point by clicking the Create New Document icon at the bottom of the palette. This will open a new document (with its own History palette) based upon your current history state. Dragging a snapshot on the Create New Document icon will create a new document based on that state. This is identical to a common editing practice of making a duplicate sequence before undertaking significant revisions.

Create new document from current state

Saving Snapshots

 Be sure to check out Adobe Evangelists (http://www.adobeevangelists.com) for their great tips and actions on using the History palette. One killer action, **Saving out Snapshots**, allows you to create new documents from each snapshot (up to five) with just one click!

Linear versus Nonlinear Mode

While nonlinear video editing saves time and adds flexibility, the nonlinear mode of the History palette is not as useful. By default, the nonlinear option is disabled, for good reason. The nonlinear mode opens up an incredible amount of increased flexibility, but making sense of that flexibility often becomes a brainteaser not worth solving.

The Nonlinear History mode can be accessed from the History palette submenu. When enabled, a user can go back in time and make changes without losing the subsequent history states. In practice, this can be seen as branching. You can jump back to step 3 and design in a new direction. Your old steps (which are currently unused) still appear at the bottom of your list; they do not drop off.

While editing video in a nonlinear fashion may seem natural, most users (rightfully) avoid this option in the History palette.

The designer eventually needs to make a choice: return to the bottom of the list, thus abandoning the sidetracked design, or manually remove the unwanted items at the bottom of the list by dragging them onto the Delete (trash can) icon. Sound confusing? It is. A more logical approach that does not involve organizing "alternative realties" would be employing the previously mentioned Create New Document feature. Other users prefer using multiple snapshots to simplify this process.

Using the Edit History Log

Have you ever wished that you had someone to take notes while you worked? Well now you can. … Photoshop can help keep careful track of what's been modified or done to a file. This can be useful for several reasons:

- You are experimenting and would like to track the design process.
- You need to be able to explain to a peer or a client what changes were made.
- You need to show for legal purposes what sort of modifications have been made to an image (such as images used in forensic videos).

To use the History Log, you must enable it in your General Preferences group by pressing ⌘+K (ctrl+K).

Step 1. In the History Log Options pane, specify how you want to store the log information:

- Metadata to store log info in the metadata of each file.
- Text File to export the text to an external file.
- Both to store metadata in the image file as well as in a text file.

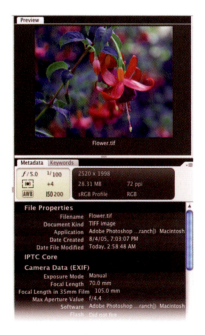

Step 2. From the Edit Log items menu, you must choose what to store:

- Sessions includes information for each time Photoshop is launched or exited. It also tracks each time files are opened and closed.
- Concise includes the text from the History palette as well as the Sessions information.
- Detailed to include Actions palette in addition to the Concise information. Detailed will give you the complete history of a file.

If storing the information as metadata, keep in mind that it adds to your file size. This can slow down the opening, saving, and closing of a document. However embedding the information is convenient, as it is stored with the file. To view the metadata, look in the Metadata window of Adobe Bridge.

What are Those Weird Brushes?

Your toolbox contains two tools with the word history in their titles: the History Brush tool and the Art History Brush tool. Both of these tools require you to use snapshots to define the source of the brush. The first tool lets you paint backward in time. The second tool is used to create impressionistic painting effects. The best way to understand these tools is to see them in action.

These two brushes have very little to do with multiple undos. But you can paint back in time or create a painterly look with them.

History Brush

Let's give the History Brush tool a try. You can open any source photo with a single subject. You may use the photo called `Ch07_Fish.tif,` which can be found in the Chapter 7 folder on the DVD. Ensure that Photoshop created a new snapshot when the document was opened.

Step 1. In order to see the brush in action, you'll want to filter the photo. Choose Filter>Brush Strokes>Crosshatch. You may use the default values or modify to create your own. Click OK to apply the filter.

Step 2. Examine the image closely. Notice how the photo is now filtered evenly, including facial details. By employing the History Brush tool, you can restore this missing information.

Step 3. Click next to the desired snapshot in the History palette so the Paintbrush icon becomes visible. By default, the icon will already appear next to the original snapshot (which will work for this exercise).

Step 4. Select the History Brush tool from the Toolbox. Using the History Brush, you can paint back the unfiltered photo. This is a good idea for restoring missing facial detail. Paint in detail to restore the image near the eyes and mouth.

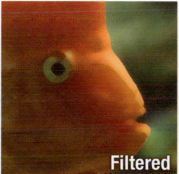
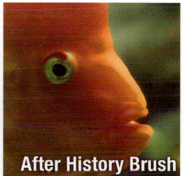

Using the History Brush tool, it is possible to "paint backwards in time." The first image is the original, the second is filtered, and the third has details painted back into the face and mouth area.

Before the History Brush tool, designers would often duplicate the photo, filter the top copy, and then erase back down to the unfiltered version below. The History Brush is essentially giving you the same results without the need for extraneous layers.

Art History Brush

So the History Brush can be truly useful. But what about that other one? The Art History Brush is an attempt to simulate natural media effects. You deploy it in an identical way to the History Brush. You will also notice advanced features in the Options bar that affect the shape of the strokes, as well as tolerance and style.

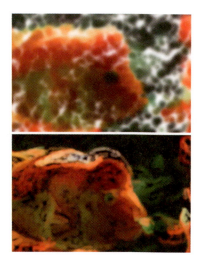

The end result will vary, but the official stance is that you can create paintings from photos. This is often useful for backgrounds, but the Art History Brush tool is not always a practical tool for a deadline-focused environment. Getting good results will often take a lot of time. Other alternatives would include filters or third-party applications like Synthetik Software's Studio Artist or Procreate's Painter. This is an interesting area to explore, but not an essential skill for use in digital video.

These two images were created using the Art History Brush tool.

Want to Try the Art History Brush?

If you're looking to give the Art History Brush a spin, you'll find two tutorials in the Chapter 07 folder. They were written by Daniel Brown and Julieanne Kost from www.AdobeEvangelists.com.

Don't Panic!

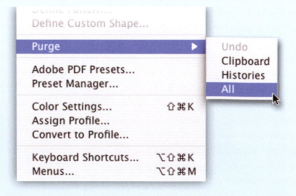

If you get a scratch disk warning, it's not the end of the world. Photoshop uses RAM to store open documents; when RAM fills up, it switches to scratch disk space. It is a cosmic law that hard drives will eventually fill to capacity. If this happens to you, there are four possible solutions:

1. Purge your history states, undo memory, and clipboard to finish the current task. (Choose Edit>Purge>and the appropriate category).
2. Buy more RAM.
3. Back up old files on your drive then trash and erase.
4. If you have multiple drives or partitions, specify them as additional scratch disks (Preferences>Performance or Plug-Ins and Scratch Disks).

Creating a DVD Overlay for Motion Menu Design

The art of DVD menu design is an evolving practice. One of its most enjoyable aspects is the creation of motion menus. These can give your DVD a truly polished look. Motion menus will often use a black & white (or subpicture) highlight layer. This layer is used to signify overlays that will be placed over the motion background when a button is highlighted.

Creating buttons for a motion menu can be a time consuming task, figuring out the highlights, complex selection techniques, and getting the perfect edge. Unless you do it the east way! This tutorial will show you two approaches that work very well for both Adobe After Effects and Apple's LiveType. You can adapt the techniques to work with other motion graphics software as well.

You'll find Exercise 07 on the DVD-ROM.

PRO*file*: Greg Mitchell

Greg Mitchell is a well-established creative director who has completed Avid's Master Editor Workshop. Not content to just cut and dissolve his way through a timeline, Mitchell is a big fan of graphic-rich videos. Before he co-founded his own company, Greg worked as a producer/editor for a full-service production facility.

"It's funny to think how I used to long for the green grass over at the big post houses in town. Hearing about those cool boxes with names like Flame, Smoke, Flint, etc., used to make me all warm and fuzzy inside," said Mitchell. "I love compositing – 'going vertical' as I like to call it – stacking track upon track, layer upon layer. Using all sorts of crazy plug-ins, transfer modes, and processors to rack focus back and forth through gooey glowing layers of all sorts of what-have-you… yum. I often felt compelled to outsource stuff just to get that high-end look that my clients expected, because that's what they saw on TV every night."

Fortunately the current crop of digital tools allows Mitchell to produce a high-end look right from his desktop.

"I have always been fairly comfortable mixing it up (Photoshop and Avid have always been a match made in heaven). But it has not been until the past few years that a technology has existed that really allows the two worlds to integrate so seamlessly (and affordably!)," said Mitchell. "With the advent of the 'Holy Trinity' (Photoshop, After Effects and Avid or similar NLE), all of a sudden I've got my *own* little incendiary device that's warming me up just fine. Photoshop is no longer just a high-end title generator for my NLE. It's now the springboard for some pretty wild creativity in the edit suite."

Although most of Mitchell's work is only for the small screen, he cautions against building graphics at low-resolution. He says that higher resolution graphics allow more flexibility in compositing and for dealing with client requests.

"I develop all graphics using Illustrator and Photoshop, making sure that the art is vector or at least very big (e.g., 300 dpi). Even if you're only creating some elements for video that don't need to be any bigger than 720×540 pixels, you would be surprised how often your client will ask you to 'send me those graphics you made for the video so I can make an 8×6 ft. banner out of it,'" said Mitchell. "Once you're happy with your design, just make some copies and dumb them down for video… 720×540 – 72dpi, flatten the image with an alpha channel, and you're ready to import and edit."

Mitchell says he relies heavily on Avid's ability to import layered Photoshop files with alpha channels intact. He will frequently animate right within the Avid to take advantage of its ability to sync audio. He says his emphasis on graphics to complement his stories is essential to meet clients' demands.

"If you are not interested in expanding your craft beyond classic video editing, you may soon be facing some fierce competition in the marketplace (if you're not already)," said Mitchell. "Though forever a staple of video editing, cuts and dissolves alone just don't cut and dissolve it anymore. At least not with the clients I've been working with. The most successful editors these days are the ones who are just as comfortable working in a graphics program as they are in their NLE."

Greg recently co-founded JuiceBox Design Communications, Inc. in 2001 (www.juiceboxdc.com). A company founded and operated by creatives, it's like an agency, only without all the suits.

8

FILTERS

Filters are one of Photoshop's most popular features: specialized add-ons that boost performance. Some people collect them, entire books are written on them, and the variety available is overwhelming. They are also completely overused and underutilized.

How can that be? A look becomes popular, and everyone wants to use it. Because people don't fully understand Photoshop, they rush out and buy add-on after add-on. Don't get me wrong—I'm always happy to try out new filters, and I'm amazed at what wonderfully creative software designers come up with. However, you can do a lot with a little, and a better understanding of how to use filters will help you maximize your investment of time and dollars.

This entire "3D" scene was created in Photoshop using a variety of filters from Flaming Pear (www.flamingpear.com)

Filters Defined

Proper application of filters significantly extends the abilities of Photoshop. It is possible to achieve results quickly that are time consuming (or even impossible) otherwise. By definition, a filter must reside in your Photoshop Plug-Ins folder. Other special effect options such as actions and styles should not be confused with filters.

When buying filters, be sure to check compatibility. Make sure that the filters you buy are compatible with your operating system and version of Photoshop. You will want to visit the developer's Web site and see when the filters were last updated. Some filters have yet to be updated for Intel-based Macs or Windows Vista. Many old favorites have been retired as developers move on to the next new thing. Some filters will never be revised because their publishers no longer exist. Why bring this up? Because many catalogs and stores will continue to sell old products that don't work with the new operating systems, always check a manufacturer's Web site for compatibility before purchase. *Caveat emptor.*

Before Running a Filter

Before you rush in and try out every filter in the application and on the disc, you need to make sure the image is ready to be processed. If the image needs to be cropped, sized, or rotated, do that first. Many filters are render-intensive; there's no reason to spend extra render time on pixels you were going to throw away.

Fix Major Errors

If the image needs to be touched up, do that first. Filtering mistakes only seems to draw further attention to them. It's very important to make sure the image is properly exposed. This can most easily be accomplished using a Levels Adjustment (Image>Adjustments>Levels). For now, you can click Auto or, if you've had previous experience, adjust the gamma (midpoint) for a proper exposure. For more on Levels, see Chapter 9, "Color Correction: How to Get It Right."

Check Color Mode

Make sure you are working in RGB mode (Image>Mode>RGB). Many stock images come in CMYK mode; you'll need to convert them to RGB. The majority of filters only work in RGB mode. Only those filters that are meant for print work have been optimized to work in CMYK mode. You do not have to worry about color shift when converting from CMYK to RGB. Because CMYK has fewer colors than RGB, no information will be lost.

Set Your View

Filtering an image is easiest when you can see all your pixels (otherwise resampling occurs). For best results, zoom into 100% or choose View>Actual Pixels. You can also double-click on the magnifying glass in the toolbox, or press ⌘+⌥+0 (*ctrl*+*alt*+0.) You can always use the Navigator palette to get a global overview and to move quickly around an image that is zoomed in.

Check Bit Depth

Photoshop continues to adds new support for layered 16-bit images and 32-bit (High Dynamic Range) images. This increase in bit depth can significantly improve the color and exposure range in digital images. While these images offer greater flexibility, they don't support filters as well as their 8-bit brethren. Often this is because filters are legacy software, and

GIGO

An image should be color-corrected properly before filtering. Remember: garbage in = garbage out (GIGO). For more on image adjustments, see Chapter 9.

were written before Photoshop worked with 16- and 32-bit images. While Adobe has gone back and re-engineered old filters, many have been ignored in favor of more important software features.

Despite the drawbacks of filters, working in 16-bit mode is becoming the new standard. This is because 16-bit mode images are a tremendous leap forward in quality (one that most NLEs can't fully utilize yet). A 16-bit image is far less likely to show banding or posterization, especially when running multiple filters. So you're thinking, maybe you should switch...go for it, but keep in mind the limitations:

- 16-bit images can only access 37 of Photoshop's built-in filters.
- 32-bit images can't access any of Photoshop's built-in filters.
- The majority of third-party filters do not work in 16-bit mode.
- Most NLEs cannot import 16-bit images.
- Adobe After Effects can read layered 16-bit images.

Many users will scan at 16 bits if their scanner supports it. You can also try working in 16 bits, especially if your piece has a lot of glows or gradients. A flattened 16 bit-image imports into most NLEs with no problem as long as it's in RGB mode. Most motion graphics applications now support 16-bit layered files. If you need an 8-bit layered version, simply duplicate the file and convert to 8-bit mode by choosing Image>Mode>8 bits/channel.

General Advice about Filters

Making time for "research and development" is tough in a production-driven world. The investment pays off, however, because you don't want to be sitting in the edit suite with the manual open trying to achieve the look your client is asking for. There are three key steps to maximizing your investment in filters.

Stage one: Run them through a full test.

Before you run out and buy more filters, discover what you already own. Filters are highly specialized mini-programs, and they can accomplish a lot! You need to try out every filter: pull every pull-down, slide every slider, try the presets that came with it, and don't forget to try blending modes with the Fade command (Edit>Fade Filter) immediately after running the filter. You can streamline this testing process by working on a small, low-resolution source image.

Stage two: Put them into new environments.

Sure, that Unsharp Mask filter is for sharpening, but what happens when I crank it all the way up on a flattened text layer? What would happen if I used the Wave filter on a gradient layer? What if I try the Minimum filter on an image? You

Free Your Mind...

Many filters will produce pleasantly unexpected results when used in situations they weren't designed for.

A little experimentation can go a long way. This night scene was heavily stylized with filters to change the mood of the scene. When working with filters, try unusual combos, especially with filters being used for reasons other than their "official" purpose.

might be surprised what happens when you try doing Western swing to heavy metal for a change.

Stage three: Combine them in unlikely ways.
The true power of filters is in the combinations. You will see several techniques used throughout this book. Be sure to check out the tutorials on the disc. (These tutorials are referenced in callout boxes throughout the book.) I also employ filters heavily in Chapters 5, 9, 10, and 11, so be sure to check those out.

While you are experimenting, don't forget other parameters such as which colors are loaded, because the foreground and background will change the way many filters perform. The resolution of your source file will also impact how dramatically the input values affect the image. For example, a 20-pixel blur on a 72-ppi image will behave very differently than on a 300-ppi source. Keep this in mind when working with Photoshop cookbooks. Many are written for print audiences.

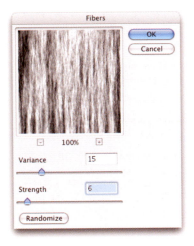

Understanding Filter Interfaces

Some filters have no user interface; for example, Blur More and Despeckle. These limited filters will quickly fall off your favorites list. Most filters will have some form of a user interface. When you launch, ensure that the Preview box option is checked; I know very few people who can make artistic decisions without previewing the edit.

Here are some general tips regarding standard filter interfaces that contain preview boxes:

- Hold down ⌥ (*alt*) while dragging a slider for a real-time preview of the effect.
- Click in the Preview window and pull your view around. The size and quality of the preview image has been significantly improved in recent versions of Photoshop.
- Use the + or − button under the preview window to zoom in or out. You can also zoom in to the Preview window using ⌘+= (*ctrl*+=) and zoom out with ⌘+− (*ctrl*+−).
- Click in the image window to adjust the center point of the preview window. (This may not work in all cases.)

Once in the dialog box, make the most of it. If there's a variable, change it. If there's a Load button, try loading presets that shipped with the product. Many manufacturers and Web sites offer additional presets that you can download. The support of textures or bump maps allows you to load grayscale images as textures. There are many of these included on the Photoshop Install CD, and I've included an assortment on this book's DVD as well.

Is There an Interface?

If a filter name is followed by ellipsis dots (…) then it has a dialog box that will open. If not, then the filter is as-is and cannot be tweaked before application (but you can still use the Fade command afterwards).

Using the Filter Gallery

Adobe renovated the filter interface for several filters even further with the arrival of Photoshop CS. You'll find that 47 of Adobe's built-in filters have moved to the Filter Gallery. This large window allows you to apply multiple filters in one pass and preview their results in a large window.

Why not all of the filters? According to Adobe, the gallery is designed to make it easier to try out filters that are experimental (such as the Sketch filters), rather than surgical (like Unsharp Mask). The key benefit of using the filter gallery is that you can see the results of combination effects without having to render each effect out.

When you first launch the gallery (Choose Filter> Filter Gallery), you are presented with an obnoxious thumbnail area. You can click on a category name to show a representative image. This abuse of screen real estate gets old fast and you'll want to click the Show/Hide button at the top of the dialog box. This will significantly expand the preview area. You can drag inside the preview area to pan around just like in standard filter interfaces. The same keyboard shortcuts and zoom controls can be used to move closer into (or out of) your image as well.

After adding the first filter, you can choose to add additional ones by clicking on New Effect Layer button. Effect layers can also be deleted or rearranged. Changing the stacking order often results in new looks. If you'd like to temporarily disable an effect layer, just click on the eyeball visibility icon. When satisfied with your results, click OK to apply the effect.

If you find yourself missing the "old" way, you are unfortunately out of luck. The 47 filters have all been moved into a single plug-in called Filter Gallery. Hopefully, Adobe will continue to add information about which filters are included in the gallery, as there are many omissions that would come in handy.

Defining the Area to be Affected by a Filter

The key to achieving results with filters is accurately specifying the area to be affected. Depending on the desired outcome, filters may be run on the entire image, a small portion, or even a single channel. It is a good idea to test a filter by running it on a small area first. With no selection made, a filter will process the entire image, even those parts that extend beyond the work area. Running a filter with no selection assures that you will filter all pixels on a layer, even those that are not currently visible.

In Need of Textures?

Look for a huge collection of seamless textures from Auto FX on this book's disc. These can be used as bump maps for many filters that support loading textures.

You can hide the filter thumbnails to make more room for image previews by clicking the triangle in the upper right corner.

Stacking Matters

Be sure to try changing "stacking order" in the Filter Gallery. The order in which you run an effect will impact its results.

Master Selections

Good filtering requires good selections. Be sure to see Chapter 4.

To affect only a portion of the image, you must make a selection with the Marquee, Lasso, or Wand tools. For more details on additional selections, see Chapter 4, "What About Transparency?"

Using the Color Range Command

The most useful selection technique for filters is the Select Color Range command from the Select menu.

Step 1. With an image open, choose Select>Color Range. The key to making a good selection is to use the eyedropper on the initial area you'd like to use to build your selection.

Step 2. Next, with Eyedropper Plus and Eyedropper Minus, you can add or subtract to the new selection.

Step 3. Adjust the Fuzziness to be more tolerant and form a smoother selection.

Step 4. Finally, click OK, and you can start to work with your selection.

Smoothing Out a Selection

One final piece of advice: soften your selections. There are two keys to achieving smoother edges:

Step 1. The first step is to smooth your selections (Select>Modify> Smooth). This rounds out hard corners in your selection.

Step 2. The second step is to feather the edges with Select> Feather or **⌘**+**⌥**+**D** (*ctrl*+*alt*+**D**). This modification will produce a gradual edge. This is similar to the difference between a line drawn by a ballpoint pen and one by a felt-tip pen. In Mac OS X, the keyboard shortcut is used to show/hide the Dock (damn that Dock). You can remap Photoshop's default shortcut to an unused key combo. Adjust your feathering to get a soft transition between filtered and unfiltered areas.

The Select Color Range command is invaluable for selecting large areas of an image. It is significantly faster (and easier) to use than other commands.

Fading and Blending Filters

You will read about and see several examples of fading filters in the coming pages. Fading is one of those little-known secrets about Photoshop. You can further modify filters by harnessing the power of blending modes (See Chapter 3, "Why Layers?").

You will not believe how much more life your filters will have with blend modes. Photoshop CS3 currently has 24 blend modes besides normal. That means your filter collection is 24 times bigger than you thought. Through Fading, you can mix the filtered image with its previous state. This leads to entirely new results with the filter.

The Fade command must be invoked immediately after the filter is run, even before you deselect the active selection. You can find it under the Edit menu (Edit>Fade [name of filter or image adjustment last run]). The quickest way to access this command is to use the shortcut Shift + ⌘ + F (Shift + ctrl + F). Think of it as you want to command (or ctrl) the shifting (fading) of the filter.

If you forget to invoke Fade, step backwards through your History palette until the filter is removed. Run the last filter with the same settings by pressing ⌘ + F (ctrl + F) and then fade it. Now that you've have an understanding of running filters, let's explore the built-in tools.

The Guide to Standard Filters

So you say you know filters? Let's take a look at all of the filters that come bundled with Adobe Photoshop. We'll explore both common and uncommon uses for the filters. You'll find a video-friendly intro to each filter with hidden features that most users don't touch, such as the Fade command—the key to unlocking a filter's power.

The guide presents filters in the order you'll find them. This is for ease of use for when you are trying to memorize where a filter can be found. Feel free to skip around; read the text when an image catches your eye. I guarantee you'll see a lot of new things.

Similar But Not the Same...

Many effects in Adobe After Effects have very similar names to Photoshop filters. You will find a lot in common with these two programs, but they have their own unique differences. Be sure to fully explore each filter interface and not make any assumptions as to how filters work.

Fade (Immediately) Away

The Fade command must be invoked immediately after the filter is run. Choose Edit>Fade (name of filter or image adjustment last run). You can also press Shift + ⌘ + F (Shift + ctrl + F).

Essential Filter Shortcuts

Repeat last filter:
⌘ + F (ctrl + F)
Reopen last filter with same settings:
⌘ + ⌥ + F (ctrl + alt + F)
Fade last filter: ⌘ + Shift + F
(ctrl + Shift + F)

Essential Filters

Artistic Filters

The Artistic Filters are direct descendants of the Gallery Effects filter package that was originally a stand-alone product. These filters are "old" and their looks have been frequently used. Be careful about overusing the artistic filters. You should try blending them or combining them to get a new look.

Colored Pencil

The Colored Pencil filter produces a very predictable result. The key to achieving variety is the color loaded as your Background color, as this becomes the "paper" that shows through. Shorter stroke width combined with a higher pressure setting generally produces the best results. Using white as the background produces a natural look. To further enhance the filter, choose fade immediately after running it and set the filter to Hard Light Mode.

Cutout

This effect produces a very pleasing look that is quite suitable for a video background. The image is simplified to the point that it looks like pieces of colored paper that have been roughly cut out and glued together to form an image. A higher setting of edge simplicity produces a better look. You will likely need to run the Gaussian Blur filter on the resulting image to anti-alias the edges to avoid on-screen flicker.

Dry Brush

The Dry Brush produces a very traditional paint effect, somewhere between oil and watercolor. The strokes are very defined, and it is possible to introduce a visible texture. This effect is typically employed to make a video freeze frame look like a painting. Be sure to De-Interlace the freeze frame first by choosing Filter>Video>De-Interlace.

Film Grain

At low values, Film Grain can be used to introduce a fairly realistic grain. This can be employed when mixing computer-generated graphics with material shot on film. I often run this filter at a low value (then fade it additionally) for lower thirds and logos that I cut into commercial spots shot on film. At high values, the effect produces a gritty, posterization look. This can be useful for stylizing items for an aggressive, youthful look.

Fresco

Fresco is a traditional art technique by which earth colors are dissolved in water, then pressed into fresh plaster. Knowing this, it's safe to say the filter could be accused of false advertising. What you get is a darker image with small swirls. The look can be useful for simple photos, but gets too "mushy" on photos of people or small objects.

Neon Glow

The Neon Glow filter uses three colors to produce its results: the foreground, background, and one additional color specified within the filter's dialog box. This can be used to add a variety of glows to an image, as well as colorizing and softening. This stylized effect can work well on video backgrounds.

Paint Daubs

This filter is the most versatile of Photoshop's artistic filters. It comes with 6 paint styles and 50 brush sizes, which give you a lot of variety. Brush types include simple, light rough, dark rough, wide sharp, wide blurry, and sparkle. If your client wants a painterly look, choose Paint Daubs. You can get a lot of mileage out of this one.

Palette Knife

A palette knife is a thin flexible blade used by artist to mix paints. The only thing in common here is that the filter reduces detail in an image, giving the effect of a thinly painted canvas. This gives the appearance of the canvas's texture showing through.

Plastic Wrap

This filter is better suited for producing text effects, although most of its results can be generated by layer styles. When using it on an image, it simulates the effect of coating the object in shiny plastic. To gain finer control, choose to fade this filter, and adjust blending and opacity controls.

Poster Edges

This filter posterizes an image (removes the number of color steps or gradients). It also finds the edges of the image and draws black lines throughout the image. This filter is not very useful for video as it provides too much detail in the resulting image.

Rough Pastels

This pleasant effect simulates the image being drawn with strokes of colored pastel chalk on a textured background. The chalk appears thick in light areas, and the textures shows through more in darker areas. This filter is very flexible as it lets you load your own textures. Be careful though not to have too much detail in your texture, or your image will "shake" on-screen.

Smudge Stick

This video-friendly filter softens an image using short diagonal strokes. These strokes smudge or smear the dark areas of an image. The light areas lose some detail and become brighter. Be sure to check that your whites aren't too "hot" for video.

Sponge

This filter simulates the traditional art technique of painting with a sponge. Images are highly textured, with areas of contrasting color. The resulting images will be clearer if you fade the filter. Be sure to use a high smoothness setting, or the results will be unusable for video.

Underpainting

This filter is very similar to Rough Pastels. Its texture controls are where its true power lies. The filter gives the appearance of a softly painted image over a textured background. Because the resulting textures are generally thick and soft, this one is considered video-friendly.

Watercolor

This final artistic filter paints the image in a watercolor style. Details are simplified, because of the larger brush size. Saturated areas will become darker as well. This is a nice look for print, but contains too many fine details for video purposes.

Blur Filters

These filters are useful to the video pro, as they will help you soften or retouch an image so it is screen-ready. Beyond their obvious uses, Motion Blur and Radial Blur can be used as design effects, especially when faded or blended. These filters are surprisingly diverse and worth exploring. If you are applying a filter to a layer with transparency, make sure the Preserve Transparency option in the Layers palette is turned off; otherwise the image will defocus, but have crisp edges.

Average

This new filter is a welcome addition to Photoshop CS. The Average filter analyzes the selected pixels, then fills with that color. This filter is often run on areas of "flat" color that contain too much noise. While this may sound pretty tame, it's a great way to kill off noise in a sky or grain in your shadows.

Blur and Blur More

If ever two filters could be replaced (or simply forgotten), these are they. Blur will slightly (practically unnoticeably) soften an image. Blur More will do the same about three times more. Both require repeated applications, and are inferior to the Gaussian Blur filter. In two words, don't bother.

Box Blur

A Box Blur softens an image based on the average color value of the neighboring pixels. This filter can be used to create special effects. For best results, try adjusting the size of the area used to calculate the average value for a given pixel. A larger radius will achieve greater blurring.

Gaussian Blur

This is the blur filter and you will use it often for video work. The term Gaussian is frequently used to signify normal distribution. This filter is appropriately named as generates a bell-shaped curve when Photoshop applies a weighted average to the pixels. This filter is very fast and has great controls. It is typically used to defocus an area or an entire image. It can be run on drop shadows or glows to add natural softness. Blurring an image, then fading it, opens up a whole new world of stylized color correction.

Lens Blur

The Lens Blur filter adds a very needed depth of field blur to Photoshop. Before running this filter, create an alpha channel to serve as the depth map. This filter is great when creating chroma key backgrounds as it allows you to manipulate the apparent depth of the background and produce a more realistic composite. Be sure to check out Chapter 10 for more information.

Motion Blur

The Motion Blur produces a very photo-realistic simulation of a delayed exposure. This can be used to simulate motion, or to add streaks of light from an image. This filter blurs and equal amount in two directions, which can be set from an angle dial. The intensity settings range from 1 to 999 (though higher values are meant for print resolution images). This filter also produces very nice results when it is faded. This is an effective way to liven up stills or text effects for use on-screen. Applying a 1- or 2-pixel Motion Blur (set to a 90° angle) can help reduce interlace flicker on text or logos.

Radial Blur

This filter is plagued by a poor interface, but can be used to produce nice effects. It is designed to simulate the blur of a zooming or rotating camera. Spin blurs along concentric circles, zoom blurs along radial lines. Both allow a variable between 1 and 100. Move the center point in the filter dialog box to aim the blur's center. Avoid the Draft quality mode and stick with Good. If you have patience and time (which you probably don't), Best produces nice results.

Shape Blur

This filter allows you to use a specified kernel (or shape) to create the blur. You can choose the kernel from a list of custom shape presets, then adjust the radius slider to change its size. For greater flexibility, you can load different shape libraries by clicking the triangular submenu.

Smart Blur

This filter can be thought of as a "selective" blur. The filter allows you to set a tolerance setting (threshold) for finding dissimilar pixels and specify a radius so it knows how far to search. These pixels can then be blurred a specified amount and quality setting. The filter can blur the entire image (normal mode) or focus on the edges (Edge Only and Overlay). These last two modes often produce unexpected results.

Surface Blur

This filter blurs an image while preserving edge detail. It can be used to remove noise or graininess. Adjust the Radius option to specify the size of the area sampled for the blur. Threshold controls how much the tonal values of neighboring pixels must differ from the center-value pixels with sufficiently different tonal value (less than the Threshold value) are not blurred.

The Plug-in Site – http://thepluginsite.com

I stumbled across this site and was amazed at the diverse content. There are several different filter packs available (including plug-ins for After Effects and Premiere). The several freebies here give you a great taste for what's possible. Make sure to download the gradients, edges, and actions (they're free). The site favors the Windows platform, and offers an excellent program for managing Windows plug-ins called Plug-In Commander. Mac users shouldn't be too disappointed however, because there are several great things here for them, too. Be sure to sign up for the free newsletter about plug-ins; I am amazed at some of the cool Photoshop things I discover in that e-mail (it often beats the major publications to the story.)

Zoom Blur

This effect produces a nice light blast from the focal point of an object. Crop and size your image for video and make sure you are in RGB mode.

Step 1. Duplicate the background layer by pressing ⌘+J (ctrl+J).

Step 2. Desaturate the duplicate layer by pressing ⌘+Shift+U (ctrl+Shift+U).

Step 3. Apply a Zoom Blur by selecting Filter>Radial Blur>Zoom. Use an amount of 100 at Good quality (High quality takes *forever*. Move the center-point by dragging within the dialog box).

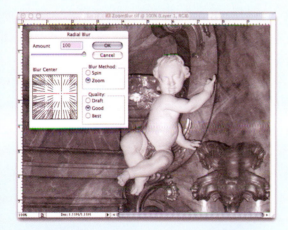

Step 4. Specify the maximum blur and position the focal point for the blur at the focal point of your object. Click OK.

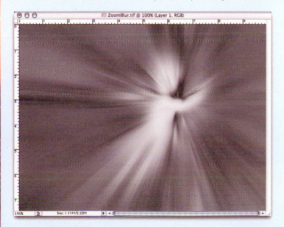

Step 5. Repeat the blur filter by pressing ⌘+F (ctrl+F).

Step 6. On the background, make a Levels Adjustment (Image>Adjustments>Levels). Bring the black and white sliders towards center. Move the gray slider (the midpoint) away from black.

Step 7. Change the blend mode of the layer to taste. In this case I used Screen mode.

Step 8. Run a levels adjustment on the background to add some contrast. Using a soft-edge brush and the eraser tool set to 30% opacity, erase away parts of the blast layer, leaving just the image below. I did this over detailed areas such as the face.

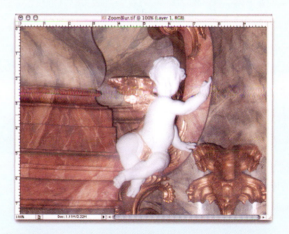

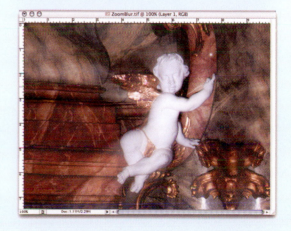

Brush Stroke Filters

The Brush Stroke filters could have simply been named Artistic Filters Part II. They are more leftovers from the Gallery Effects package, and are meant to give a painterly or fine arts look. These filters use different brush-and-ink-stroke effects to produce a variety of looks. They also will add grain and texture to an image, for a pointillist effect. Be sure to chooser larger brush sizes to keep these effects broadcast-safe. You will likely need to soften the images as well with a Gaussian Blur or Median filter to avoid flickering lines.

Accented Edges

As expected, this filter accentuates the edges of an image. This filter generates a traced edges look. When the edge brightness is set to a low value, the accents resemble black ink. When set to a high value, the accents look like white chalk. This look is very pleasing and has a nice softening effect for video.

Angled Strokes

This filter "repaints" an image using diagonal strokes. You can choose the balance between right and left strokes. The lighter areas of the image are painted in strokes going down to the right, while the darker areas are painted going down to the left. Avoid high sharpness values, as the excessive detail will cause buzzing on screen.

Crosshatch

The Crosshatch technique shades an image with two or more sets of parallel lines. This filter preserves the original details of an image, but adds texture and roughens the edges. The technique resembles the use of a pencil hatching. To avoid moiré patterns, keep the strength option controls, which specify the number of hatching passes, set to 1.

Dark Strokes

This filter is a bit unusual in that it appears to "burn" the image. The dark areas of an image are moved closer to black with short, tight strokes. The lighter areas of the image are brushed with long, white strokes. This filter can be used as a "grunge" filter, especially when combined with blend modes and fading. This one is very video-friendly.

Ink Outlines

This filter redraws an image with fine narrow lines. These lines go over the original details, simulating a pen-and-ink style. The amount of detail produced makes this filter essentially unusable for video purposes.

Spatter

Thus filter produces rough edges, while simulating the effect of a spatter airbrush. If you are going to use this effect, be sure to simplify it. The fine details of this filter produces results unfit for video.

Sprayed Strokes

This filter is similar to Spatter, and has the same problems on-screen. It produces rough strokes of the dominant colors in the image.

Sumi-e

This filter tries to simulate a popular Japanese painting style. The image "looks" like it was painted with a wet brush full of black ink on rice paper. The result is a soft, blurry image with rich blacks. This filter closely resembles Dark Strokes. To find out more on this style of artwork, visit http://www.sumiesociety.org.

Distort Filters

The Distort filters allow you to bend, push, squish, and completely reshape your photo. These tools can help simulate 3-D space, and can be quite useful when building storyboards or backgrounds.

Diffuse Glow

This filter acts very much like diffusion applied to a camera. It is possible to get a very subtle or dramatic effect. The glow color is driven by your loaded background color; a white, or off-white looks best. If you get strange results, choose a different color. The image will be rendered with Film Grain and white noise, with the glow fading from the center of the selection.

Displace

In our two examples, I've used a grayscale file (inset) to displace (distort) the source photo. As soon as I say this, I will get 150 e-mails telling me otherwise…but I find the Displace filter to be overly complex and unrewarding. Can this filter do a lot? Yes. But it requires you to build your own displacement maps (grayscale files) for it to work. I generally use filters to save steps, not add more.

But don't take my word for it, try it and form your own opinion. Here are the essential steps needed to make the filter work:

Step 1. Create or locate a grayscale file to act as a displacement map. Black areas will move pixels to the right, down, or both. White pixels will move the image left, up, or both. 50% Gray will have no effect. You must save the map as a flattened Photoshop format file.

Step 2. Choose Filter>Distort>Displace.

Step 3. Enter the scale for the magnitude of the displacement. You can specify the horizontal and vertical displacement separately.

Step 4. If the map is a different size than your image, specify whether the edges should wrap or repeat to fill in empty pixels. Click OK.

Step 5. Navigate to and select the displacement map. The distortion is applied to the image rather quickly.

Step 6. Ask yourself, "Was it was worth it?" If you have to perform a displacement to map an image to a surface, then this is your filter. After Effects users will find themselves missing AE's much better Displacement Map effect.

Glass

This versatile filter allows you to distort an image so it appears as if it is being viewed through different types of glass. There are some presets to choose from, or you can create your own glass surface as a Photoshop file and apply it. With controls for scaling, distortion, and smoothness settings, quite a bit is possible. This filter can also be used as for creating pleasant ripple or haze effects. To create your own map, follow the instructions for the Displace filter.

Lens Correction

The Lens Correction filter can be used to fix common lens flaws such as barrel and pincushion distortion from camera lenses. It can also remove vignetting and chromatic aberration.

- Barrel distortion is a defect that causes straight lines to bow out toward the edges.
- Pincushion distortion is the opposite, where straight lines bend inward.
- Vignetting is considered a defect where edges of an image are darker than the center.
- Chromatic aberration appears as color fringe along the edges of your subject as the camera is attempting to focus on different colors of light in different planes.

You can store settings that match your lens. Additionally, the filter can be used to fix perspective problems caused by vertical or horizontal camera tilt.

Ocean Ripple

This filter should have been called Glass LE. It does a very similar effect, adding randomly spaced ripples to the image's surface. The intent of the effect is to make the image appear as if it were under water. The effect is not very convincing, but can be useful as another Glass filter.

Pinch

Think of this more as a "pucker & bloat" filter. It is possible to take a selection and squeeze it in with a positive value (up to 100%). The opposite effect of pushing the image out can be achieved with a negative value (up to −100%). Applying this to only a portion of the image adds a nice "pop-up" effect (useful on maps or other "blow-ups.")

Polar Coordinates

Rule number one: Give up on understanding the Polar Coordinates filter. Rule number two: Don't forget about it when creating backgrounds. This filter is designed to change an image or selection from its rectangular to polar coordinates, and vice versa, according to a selected option. Technically, it is designed to counteract shooting with curved lenses or mirrors; however, some cool effects can be generated.

When combined with other filters, the Polar Coordinates filter provides a nice way to "scramble" an image. This can be quite useful in creating backgrounds or patterns for use in video. This way the source image is unrecognizable, but the colors come through nicely.

Ripple

This filter adds a pattern similar to ripples on the surface of water. You have three sizes of ripples to choose from, as well as control of quantity of ripples. For greater control, use the Wave filter instead.

Shear

This filter uses a curve to distort the image. To form a curve, simply drag the line in the filter control box. You can add additional points by clicking on the line and pulling. Click Default to reset the curve to a straight line. You can also specify if edge pixels wrap or repeat.

Spherize

This filter is very similar to the Pinch filter. It simulates a 3-D effect by wrapping a selection around a spherical shape. It can distort an image by making it appear to wrap around the outside or inside of a sphere. Here, I have spherized a portion of the image, then applied a stroked border. This provides an easy way to achieve a "magnifying glass" effect.

Twirl

This effect rotates a selection more sharply in the center than at the edges. I like to think of this as a "spin-art" effect, although it is often called the "toilet-bowl" filter. If you fade this filter immediately after running it, you can get a nice effect. The only control of this filter is specifying an angle that produces the twirl pattern. To produce a more realistic effect, run this filter several times with a lower twirl amount.

Wave

The Wave filter is very powerful. You have tremendous control over the shape of waves, quantity, amplitude, and wavelength. The randomize option is also helpful. This filter produces very realistic wave distortions.

Even better though, this filter is very useful in generating background patterns. Just push the number of generators way up, and play with the other settings. You can quickly create random backgrounds that make great starting points for video background and lower thirds.

ZigZag

This filter produces a different kind of ripple, one that radiates from a center point, much like a drop hitting a flat surface of water. You have three types of ridges to choose from, as well as a quantity slider. This filter also produces a nice effect on text.

Back in the Day...

Gallery Effects used to be a stand-alone product. Originally released by Silicon Beach, they were then sold to Aldus (the originally makers of PageMaker and FreeHand). Adobe acquired them in a package deal, and wasn't sure what to do with them. They first shipped with PageMaker, then as a stand-alone product.

Originally there were 48 filters available in three collections. Don't look for them in stores; all but one (an alternate emboss filter) have migrated into Photoshop. They're now living in the Artistic, Brush Strokes, Sketch, and Textures submenus. If you can find it for nostalgia's sake in a bargain bin or on eBay, buy it; the manual is actually well written.

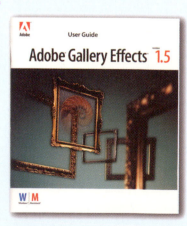

Show Me, Show Me, Show Me...

Want to simulate a magnifying glass passing over your image? By combining three effects, we can pull this off. Open an image that has a focal point you want to magnify. Crop and size the image for your video system.

Step 1. With the Elliptical marquee, draw a circular selection around the subject. Hold the *Shift* key to constrain the selection to be circular.

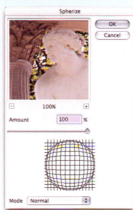

Step 2. Choose Filter> Distort>Spherize and enter the maximum value.

Step 3. Press ⌘+*T* (*ctrl*+*T*) to enter Free Transform mode. Scale the magnifying glass amount up approximately 20%. You can enter the scale into the Options bar or drag with the mouse (while holding down *⌥*/ *alt* to scale from center). Click Apply Transformation or press *Return*/*Enter* twice.

Step 4. With the selection still active, create a new (empty) layer.

Step 5. Stroke your selection with a 12-pixel centered stroke in an off-white color (Edit > Stroke).

Step 6. Apply the Bevel & Emboss Layer Style and modify to taste. I used an Inner Bevel with a Smooth Technique. I set the depth to 510%, Direction Up, and a 5-pixel size.

Step 7. Apply the Outer Glow Layer Style and adjust to your preference. I used a 27-pixel softer blur.

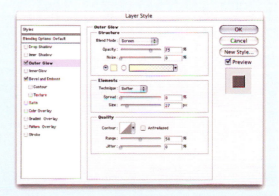

Noise Filters

Noise filters can create textures or grain. They can also remove problems that cause a moiré effect. You will find yourself using these a lot to counteract video's limitations for small detail.

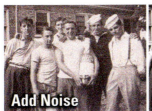

Add Noise

The Add Noise filter introduces random noise to the image. It can be grayscale (monochromatic) or multicolored. The filter is also useful for reducing banding in gradients. If you have done a lot of retouching, add noise in to match the previous grain. You have two distribution methods for adding noise. Uniform distributes noise using random numbers for a subtle effect; Gaussian distributes noise for a speckled effect.

Despeckle

This filter combines edge detection with blurring. It is useful for finding speckles in an image, and softening them. This produces the effect of removing or limiting noise. There are no sliders to adjust, just keep repeating the filter (⌘+F / ctrl+F) until the desired result is achieved.

Dust & Scratches

This filter provides a more powerful way to remove noise from an image. Dissimilar pixels are modified to achieve a balance between sharpening and hiding defects. It is a good idea to try different settings on your image, as a wide variety of results are possible. It may be helpful to run the filter on only part of your image at a time.

Step 1. Make a selection or use the entire image.

Step 2. Choose Filter>Noise>Dust & Scratches.

Step 3. It is a good idea to keep the preview zoomed into 100% and pan to see the scratches.

Step 4. Set the Threshold slider to 0. This turns off the value so that all pixels can be examined. Threshold is used to determine how different pixels must be before they are removed.

Step 5. Move the Radius slider left or right, or choose a value from 1 to 16 pixels. The radius determines how far to search for differences among pixels. Overuse of Radius blurs the image, so stop or balance where noise is removed versus where softening occurs.

Step 6. Gradually increase the threshold to the highest value possible, which still has an effect.

Median

This filter is most useful as a way to eliminate moiré patterns. If your scanner does not have a descreen option, run this filter on your scans. This filter is very sensitive; so only use a low value for image correction. High values can be used to get an interesting softening effect. The filter examines the radius of a pixel for pixels of similar brightness. Any nonmatching pixels are discarded and replaced with the median brightness value of the searched pixels.

Reduce Noise

The Reduce Noise filter can be used for noise reduction as well as for smoothing out JPEG artifacts. To use the filter:

Step 1. Choose Filter>Noise>Reduce Noise.

Step 2. Zoom the preview image to get a better view of noise. Be sure to view the image at 100%.

Step 3. Adjust the following options:
- **Strength:** The amount of luminance noise reduction applied to the image's channels.
- **Preserve Details:** This preserves edges and image details such as hair. A value of 100 preserves the most image detail, but reduces luminance noise the least. You'll need to play with the balance of Strength and Preserve Details to fine-tune noise reduction.
- **Reduce Color Noise:** This removes random color. Use a higher value to reduce more color noise.
- **Sharpen Details:** This sharpens the image. Removing noise will reduce image sharpness.
- **Remove JPEG Artifacts:** This removes blocky image artifacts step and halos caused by JPEG compression.

Step 4. If noise is more prevalent in one or two color channels, click the Advanced button. Now you can choose individual color channels from the Channel menu. Next, use the Strength and Preserve Details controls to reduce noise in the problem channels.

Pixelate Filters

These filters produce a variety of pixel types. Similar color values in cells are clumped together into new pixels. They allow you to process an image into a different look, often slightly stylized. These filters also work well at high pixel sizes for creating background layers. I've included two examples for each filter. The first is a more "standard" setting, and the second combines fading and high pixel values in the slider settings.

Color Halftone

This filter simulates the effect of getting too close to your Sunday Comics. An enlarged halftone screen is very visible on each channel. The image is divided into rectangles, and each rectangle then becomes a circle (sized proportionally the brightness of the rectangle). This one is not very useful, but at a large diameter setting, it can create nice texture layers.

Crystallize

Pixels are clumped into polygons with a solid color. This filter can generate a stained glass look at small cell size, or simplify a complex image into a bed of color for use in composite building.

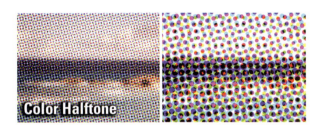

Facet

This filter produces a very subtle change to pixels. Don't be confused when you run it; no dialog box appears. It may take several repetitions to notice the effect, so keep pressing ⌘+F (ctrl+F). Similar colored pixels are clumped together into blocks of like-colored pixels. This provides for a nice painterly effect. This filter is really a Brush Strokes filter that got lost when Adobe sorted filters.

Fragment

This filter produces the same effect of an editor without coffee. Four copies of the image are created, averaged, and then offset from each other. This filter produces a blur effect that may make you feel "groggy."

Mezzotint

Mezzotints are a traditional Italian process of engraving copper or steel plates by scraping and burnishing. This produces areas of extreme light and dark. These plates were often used to make prints that would contain random pattern of black-and-white areas or of fully saturated colors. Stick with the longer dot patterns from the type menu in the dialog box; you may also need to soften the resulting image. This is a nice effect for stylizing images.

Mosaic

This filter replicates the effect of sitting too close to a television. Pixels are clumped into larger pixels (square blocks) to form images. These new pixels are the averaging of the original colors in the selection. Think of this as your Atari 2600 filter. If you ever need to "cop-blur" something, use the Mosaic filter over that portion of an image.

Pointillize

This filter simulates a pointillist painting. The image is broken up into randomly placed dots. The background color loaded acts as the "paper's" color. This filter is not very useful for video work. If you set the cell size extremely large, you can generate acceptable texture plates.

Cop-Blur: The Names of the Innocent Have Been Changed

Need to hide someone's identity but can't remove them from the picture? This technique is particularly useful for news organizations.

Step 1. Draw a selection around the subject you are trying to obscure with the elliptical marquee You can use the ⌥ (*alt*) key modifier to draw from center.

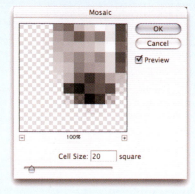

Step 2. Duplicate this selection to a new layer by pressing ⌘+J (*ctrl*+J).

Step 3. Run the Mosaic Filter at a 20-pixel amount (Filter>Pixelate>Mosaic).

Step 4. We are now going to feather the edges to blend the effect in more.

Step 5. Load the layer by ⌘+Clicking (*ctrl*+Clicking).

Step 6. Feather the selection 8 pixels by pressing ⌘+⌥+D (*ctrl*+*alt*+D).

Step 7. Select the Inverse by pressing *Shift*+⌘+I (*Shift*+*ctrl*+I).

Step 8. Hide the selection by pressing ⌘+H (*ctrl*+H).

Step 9. Press *Delete* until the desired feathering is achieved.

Render Filters

The Render filters are a mixed bag. Some, like Clouds and Lighting Effects produce beautiful photorealistic results. Others, like 3D Transform are clunky and slow. Spend a little extra time on these as they can be quite handy when you have to perform Photoshop magic. I find myself using these a lot on freelance or off-site jobs when the client has no stock materials and access to a scanner is limited. You can truly create something from nothing with these.

Clouds

This filter is incredibly useful, really! It generates a soft cloud pattern from random values that between the foreground and the background colors. Every time you run this filter, you get new results, so if you don't like the clouds generated, simply press ⌘+F (ctrl+F) to get more. To create a more stark cloud pattern, hold down the ⌥ key (alt key) when you run the filter.

Clouds

For retouching work it can create nice clouds that you add into blown-out skies. Simply load your foreground and background as off-white for the clouds and blue for the sky. This filter is also the starting point for many background textures. For After Effects users, simply render your clouds out as a black-and-white file, import them into AE, place into screen mode, and use them as cloud layers. You'll shave tons of time off your renders.

Difference Clouds

This filter is very similar to the Clouds filter, but it blends the new cloud data with the existing data using a difference-blending mode. Running the filter for the first time will invert portions of the image. Applying the filter several times creates a marble-like effect. This filter is driven by your foreground and background colors.

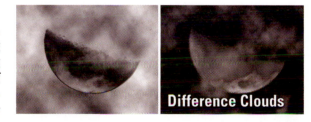

Difference Clouds

Fibers

Photoshop CS adds a new texture generator called Fibers to simulate natural fibers. Your foreground and background swatch affect the fibers, but you can always recolor them with an image adjustment or gradient map. Be sure to experiment by clicking the Randomize button.

Fibers

Lens Flare

This filter generates what many see as mistakes. A lens flare is the refraction caused by shining a bright light into the camera lens. You can specify where the flare occurs by clicking on the image thumbnail or by moving the cross hair. Many designers use this as an element, or for down-and-dirty lighting effects. Photoshop CS adds a new flare type, Move Prime. The very popular AE plug-in Knoll Light Factory also comes with an equally powerful Photoshop Plug-In.

Lighting Effects

This diverse filter lets you simulate 3-D lights being added to your "scene." You have a lot of choices with this filter, so start with the presets. You can pick from 17 light styles, 3 light types, and 4 sets of light properties. All of these can be tweaked and repositioned. You can also use a bump map (grayscale texture) to produce 3-D-like effects. This filter is very useful for creating focus, generating backgrounds, and adding a high-end look to bumper graphics. Digital Film Tools Light! is a big step up from this filter.

I Need to "Render" a Background

The render filters are a big help in creating backgrounds for video use. Here we employ two of them to create a nice "3-D" look.

Step 1. Select a foreground and background color that are complementary.

Step 2. Open or create a safe-title document.

Step 3. Run the Clouds filter; if you don't like the first pass, repeat.

Step 4. Go back to the Distort menu and access Ripple.

Step 5. You will likely need to soften your image with a Gaussian Blur.

Step 6. Now the cool part, access Lighting Effects and add a spotlight to the scene. Play with different settings. I chose to cast a light across the bottom corner.

Sharpen Filters

The sharpen filters can be used to focus soft images by increasing the contrast of adjacent pixels. You can have moderate success with sharpening, but be careful not to oversharpen, or you will get distortion. This can lead to grain and pixelization.

Sharpen and Sharpen More

These two filters offer an all-or-nothing approach; thus, they are not very useful. While they add focus to a selection, they have no controls. The Sharpen More filter applies a stronger effect than the Sharpen filter. Skip these and just use the Unsharp Mask or Smart Sharpen.

Sharpen and Sharpen More

Sharpen Edges and Unsharp Mask

These two filters attempt to find areas where significant color changes occur and sharpen them. While the Sharpen Edges filter has no controls, it still does a good job. It only affects edges, thus preserving overall image smoothness.

The Unsharp Mask filter is the better way to go. This filter lets you adjust the contrast of edges by producing a lighter and darker line on each side of the edge. This helps add emphasis to edges, and produces a very satisfactory result.

Sharpen Edges and Unsharp Mask

Smart Sharpen

The Smart Sharpen filter is was added to Photoshop CS2. It offers superior sharpening controls not available with the Unsharp Mask filter. Most importantly, it gives you a choice of sharpening algorithms and control over the amount of sharpening that occurs in the shadow and highlight areas.

Smart Sharpen

Change Your "Mode" of Sharpening

For color images, run the Unsharp Mask in the Lab mode. Select the Lightness channel and adjust the sharpness. Be sure to switch the image back to the RGB mode when finished.

Sketch Filters

OK, it's time for the Artistic Filters Return, Part 3. The filters in the Sketch category add texture to the images. They are useful for creating a hand-drawn look (I know, big surprise). These filters almost all rely upon the foreground and background colors you have chosen. Experiment with different colors for very different looks. These all produce results that are generally acceptable for video usage.

 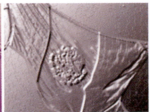

Bas Relief

This filter does an excellent job of transforming the image to appear carved into stone. You also can control the direction of light and how soft it gets. Dark areas of the image use the foreground color; light colors use the background color.

Chalk & Charcoal

This filter simulates an artist using chalk and charcoal to form an image. The midtones are turned to gray, the highlights are turned to chalk (in the foreground color), and the dark areas are turned to charcoal (in the background color).

Charcoal

This redraws an image, creating a smudged, posterized effect. Charcoal is the foreground color; the paper is the background color. This can create a nice, simplified look that works well in video.

Chrome

This filter attempts to make the image act like it is polished chrome. Adobe recommend using the levels adjustment after running this filter to get a better look. I recommend you just skip this one.

Conté Crayon

This effect reproduces a pleasant look for use on-screen. Conté crayons are usually very dark or pure white. The Conté Crayon filter uses the foreground for dark areas and the background for light ones. To replicate the traditional look, use a dark red, brown, or black for the foreground color. You can also use a texture for the canvas, but I find the look more pleasing without. This filter can also be used as an optional way to achieve a historic-looking sepia tone.

Graphic Pen

This filter uses fine (perhaps too fine) strokes to replicate the original image. It is a nice look however, and after a little softening with the median filter, it is ready for the screen. The foreground color acts as ink; the background color acts as the paper.

Halftone Pattern

This filter can be very useful in stylizing an image. You can choose between dots, circles, and lines. This can be used to create a scan-line look or a unique twist on pixelization. The foreground and background colors are important here. Using the Fade command on this filter will also generate a lot of possibilities.

Note Paper

This is another one of those filters that just sort of sits there. No one is deeply impressed by its abilities. The official stance is that it creates a look constructed of handmade paper. I'm not convinced.

Photocopy

Photocopy does what its name implies: it makes it look like you made a photocopy of a color image on one of those 1970 copy machines at the back of the public library. Large areas of darkness will copy only around their edges. Midtones tend to drop off to pure black or white. This filter is useful for simplifying a photo down for use as a design element.

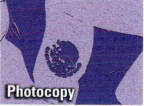

Plaster

This filter simulates a molded image made of plaster. The foreground and background colors are both used to colorize the image. Dark areas are raised, light areas are recessed. This is another filter that doesn't generate too much excitement.

Reticulation

Reticulation is a developing technique where the controlled shrinking and distorting of film emulsion generates an image that appears clustered in the shadows and grained in the highlights. This is a nice alternative duotone effect.

Stamp

This filter creates a woodcut or rubber stamp look. This is a good way to simplify images for use in multilayered designs. The foreground and background colors play a major role here.

Torn Edges

This filter works well on high-contrast images and text. It makes the image appear to be constructed of torn paper. The foreground and background colors then tint the image. The softening effect of this filter makes it well suited for video.

Water Paper

This painterly effect uses blotchy daubs of paint on fibrous, damp paper. The colors of the source appear to flow and blend. This filter also softens the original image, which makes it a good candidate for your videos.

Like to Paint?

If you find yourself needing that fine art or hand-drawn look a lot, it may be time to add an excellent companion program. Studio Artist from Synthetik Software is a graphic synthesizer. There are more than 2000 paint style presets, as well as 300 adjustable parameters. You can run the program in automatic mode like a filter or take control, even using a tablet and pen.

Everything is vector-based so you can go back and make changes. Vectors make it possible to greatly enlarge a low-resolution file. You can

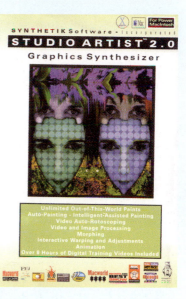

also process QuickTime MooVs as well, producing much better results than an After Effects plug-in. The software is only available for Macs, and you'll find a demo on this book's disc. For more information, visit: http://www.synthetik.com.

Stylize Filters

These filters are useful for creating stylized images. They work by displacing pixels and adding contrast to edges. Use of the Fade command and Blending Modes will significantly extend the usefulness of these filters. I find these helpful for creating texture layers for use in lower thirds and backgrounds.

Diffuse

This filter is very subtle and may take a few passes to be noticed. It attempts to diffuse an image to make the selection look less focused. Normal moves pixels randomly. Darken Only replaces light pixels with darker pixels. Lighten Only replaces dark pixels with lighter pixels. Anisotropic shuffles pixels towards the direction of least change in color.

Emboss

Emboss gives the appearance of a raised or stamped image. You can specify the angle, height, and amount of color. To better preserve color, fade the filter immediately after running it. I generally prefer using the Bevel & Emboss layer style for greater flexibility.

Extrude

This filter is fun. It's great for making backgrounds as it creates a 3-D texture. You can choose from Blocks or Pyramids, as well as specify the size and depth. This is a nice look for background images; it looks particularly good on simple backgrounds or even solid colors.

Find Edges

This filter creates a very nice stroked edge effect. Blending this filter is particularly useful for generating a cel-shaded, cartoon look. Experiment with this one as it is very useful for bumper graphics.

Glowing Edges

This filter is basically an inverse of the Find Edges filter. It also identifies edges, but produces an inverted color scheme. This filter looks best when blended via the Fade command.

Solarize

This filter blends a negative and a positive image together. Once again, choose Fade after running the filter to open it up to more possibilities.

Tiles

This filter breaks the image up into tiles. You can specify the size, amount of movement, and what lies beneath. This filter is overused and not very impressive.

Trace Contour

This filter locates the transitions of major brightness areas and thinly outlines them. Each color channel is identified. Adobe says the effect is similar to contour lines on a map; I say lose it.

Trace Contour

Wind

This filter creates small horizontal lines to simulate a wind effect. You can choose left or right, as well as three methods: Wind; Blast, and Stagger. You may have to soften the image after this effect to avoid "buzz."

Wind

Is There a Cartoonist in the House?

Have you ever been asked for a Cartoon filter? If so, the following technique works well. It's been said several times, but remember the true power in a filter lies in the Fade command (Edit>Fade).

Step 1. Open and size the image.

Step 2. Run the Find Edges Filter (Filter>Stylize>Find Edges). There is no dialog box for this effect.

Step 3. Immediately after running the filter, fade it by choosing Edit>Fade Find Edges or pressing `⌘` + `Shift` + `F` (`ctrl` + `Shift` + `F`). I remember this shortcut by saying I want to command (or control) how the filter shifts (i.e., Fades).

Step 4. Try Overlay mode and adjust the opacity slider to taste. Depending on your source image, different Blending Modes may be used.

Texture Filters

The Texture filters can give the appearance of depth in an image. They also can make an image appear to be on an organic surface. I often use these effects on text layers to add some depth. When run on images, they give the appearance of the image being mapped or repainted on additional surfaces.

Craquelure

This filter simulates paint on a plaster surface. It creates cracks that follow the image's contours. The fine details required for this filter make it unusable for video output.

Grain

This filter offers several styles of grain to add texture to an image. Choose between regular, soft, sprinkles, clumped, contrasty, enlarged, stippled, horizontal, vertical, and speckle grain. This filter is very useful for stylizing images and backgrounds.

Mosaic Tiles

Don't confuse this with the much more useful Mosaic filter. This filter is just another version of Craquelure and just as useless for video work.

 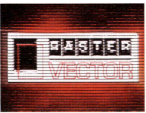

Patchwork

This filter can be thought of as an alternate Mosaic filter. It cuts the image into smaller squares filled with the predominant color in that area. The squares have a random depth assigned to them.

Stained Glass

This filter does a nice job simulating stained glass windows. The image is repainted as single colored cells, outlined in the foreground color. I find this is a nice effect partially superimposed over video.

Texturizer

This filter is very diverse if you have textures. Any flattened grayscale Photoshop format file can be used as a texture. Look in your Photoshop folder or on your install disc for extra textures.

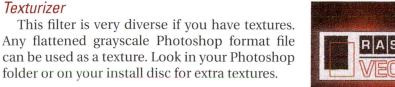

Video Filters

The Video filters aren't very deep: one is useful, the other is not very. Hopefully Adobe (hint) will develop more (hint) video filters.

De-Interlace

This filter can smooth fast-moving images captured on video. It will remove the odd or even field in your frame grab. If you are working in After Effects, this is not necessary, but if processing in Photoshop, it is generally important. You can replace the discarded line via interpolation or duplication. Generally speaking, replacing odd or even fields does not matter, but interpolation generates better results than duplication.

The De-Interlace filter has removed the field rendering from this still graphic. Fields are useful in motion sources, but not in Photoshop.

NTSC Colors

Unfortunately, this filter hard clips color information that falls outside the safe color range for the NTSC model. Instead of gently fading these colors, a hard clip is quite visible. Use this filter to check for problem areas, and then adjust by hand with the sponge tool set to desaturate. This filter does not take the place of a dedicated NTSC monitor, or better yet, a scope.

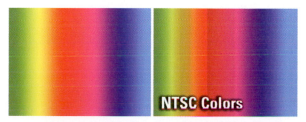

The NTSC Colors filter in Photoshop is used to remove colors that are too saturated for broadcast. Unfortunately, the filter creates clipping and banding. Instead, use the Broadcast Safe Saturation action in the Video Actions set that can be found in the submenu of the Actions palette.

Other Filters

These filters apparently did not fit into any of the other categories. So the descriptive term "other" was put through months of development and testing. You can use these filters to make your own filters, modify masks, or adjust colors.

Custom

I am going to be a wimp here. This filter is for people who like to program their appliances to operate as independent robots. I have read (and reread) the manual's description. Try it yourself; launch Photoshop Help ⌘+? (ctrl+?). Essentially you are multiplying, adding, and subtracting color information. I am sure this will excite a few of you, but my math skills allow me to do three things: understand the Z-axis; add hours, minutes, seconds, and frames accurately; and balance my checkbook (although I have been known to try and carry the one when I hit :60). This filter is not worth struggling with when you are on a deadline. Play with it when you are bored (after you've counted all the holes in your edit suite's ceiling).

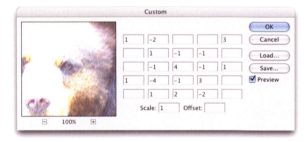

High Pass

This helps keep edge details within the specified radius while suppressing the rest of the image. The filter is sort of an anti-Gaussian Blur filter. This filter is sometimes used before running a threshold adjustment to help simplify edges, but it's not terribly useful.

Minimum and Maximum

These two filters are for modifying masks or alpha channels. The Minimum filter acts as a matte or channel choker. Black is expanded, while white is shrunk. The Maximum filter has the opposite effect as a matte spreader; white is expanded, while dark is contracted. These filters can also be run as a different pixelization effect, thus producing a nice mosaic look for an image.

Offset

You can use this filter to move an image a specified distance, either horizontally or vertically. The pixels can leave an empty place; wrap around to the other side, or continue the color at the edges. This filter can be used to create a seamless tile, for use in motion graphics. Simply offset the image, then heal the seam with the Healing Brush or Clone Stamp tools. Then in your compositing program, use its offset filter to animate the cycle. I've included a tutorial specifically on this technique for the book's disc.

"Loose" Filters

You'll find a few filters randomly inserted in the Filter menu. These filters are "late" additions and seem placed into the Filter> Menu simply because they had nowhere else to locate them.

Extract

The Extract filter is generally referred to as the Extract command. It was addressed in Chapter 4, "What About Transparency?" It is a somewhat useful command for extracting images, but many pros prefer layer masks that offer nondestructive touchup.

Filter Gallery

The Filter Gallery can be invoked two ways: by choosing it from the top level of the filter menu or by launching one of the 47 filters that it contains. The Filter Gallery was discussed in depth at the start of this chapter.

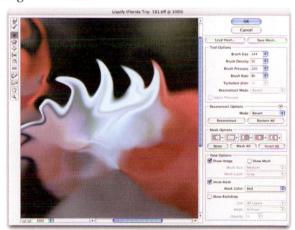

Liquify

The Liquify filter essentially turns the pixels in your image into "wet paint." This allows you to move them around as if you were finger-painting.

Pattern Maker

The Pattern Maker filter can create a seamless texture based upon the details of your image. This command is explored in depth in Chapter 11, "Creating Backgrounds for Video."

Vanishing Point

The Vanishing Point filter allows for Perspective Cloning within an image. By drawing a series of grids within the image, you can reposition or remap elements within the photo and Photoshop will compensate for perspective when it scales. You'll find a video demo about this command on the DVD-ROM.

Third-Party Filters

Smart Filters in Action

 See the DVD-ROM for more on Smart Filters.

When looking for filters, two great starting places come to mind. *Photoshop User* magazine frequently reviews plug-ins. Members of NAPP often get discounts as well. Go to their site (http://www.photoshopuser.com) and click on the about the magazine link to find out more.

The second resource is this book's disc, where you'll find free filters, trial versions, and time-limited demos. I've saved you the trouble of big downloads and have included the documentation packages as well.

How to "Age" Your Photos—*with Robert Lawson*

Oftentimes during a video production, you will need to mix photos from different decades. You may need to take a modern photo and mix with historical images. By aging a photo, you can use it as part of your narrative without jarring the viewer.

If you want to make a photo look much older, then explore this tutorial. This quick technique can significantly age any modern photo. No third-party plug-ins are needed, as everything is done with Photoshop's built-in tools. Additionally, these steps can easily be recorded as an Action so you can batch process several images.

You'll find Exercise 08 on the DVD-ROM.

PRO*file*: Liane G. Rozzell

After freelancing as an editor for four years, Rozzell accepted a staff job editing for a company that specializes in producing programs for museum exhibits. While she's worked in many genres, she's most well known for her documentary work. Because documentaries rely heavily on photos, Rozzell frequently turns to Photoshop. She finds it gives her the necessary creative leverage to solve her production problems.

"How do I use Photoshop? Let me count the ways. My most basic use is in preparing a still image for import: cropping it, sizing it, adjusting the levels, and adjusting the color. Scans almost always need this sort of work. With archival photos, I'll often have to do some retouching," said Rozzell. "Sometimes I use it to prepare images that will then be animated in After Effects or using the Moving Picture plug-in inside the NLE. Every now and then, I've used Photoshop to fix a frame of an image that comes from video."

Why does she rely so much on Photoshop?

"Most of the things I do in Photoshop can't be done in the NLE itself, at least not as powerfully. For example, I can't create backgrounds as well in an NLE. I can make titles, but if I want to rotate them or create a better gradient effect, I have to do it in Photoshop," said Rozzell. "Right now, I have more control over color and levels in Photoshop, but that is changing as NLEs gain more color correction tools."

Rozzell equates mastering Photoshop to learning another language. She says a power user is one who is fluent in Photoshop: "Just as you'll never learn every word of another language (who even knows every word in their native language?), you don't have to know everything about Photoshop."

"You start learning another language by building practical knowledge, learning how to say "please" and "thank you," and learning a few idioms or expressions. You can consider yourself pretty fluent when you can do the equivalent of ordering off the menu or reading a book or newspaper without having to think hard about it," said Rozzell. "Translating this to Photoshop, it means learning the basics about how the application works. How to use layers, selections, alpha channels and paths, learning what the filters do, learning how and when to use the various tools. Add 'idioms' — keyboard shortcuts and plug-ins — for efficiency. And, as with a language, there is no substitute for practice, repetition and interaction with graphic artists and other Photoshop speakers!"

To get you on your way, Rozzell offers two speed tips for Photoshop users:

- "My favorite shortcut is the simple ability to set the crop tool to the dimensions I need to create a static image. Boring, but so often necessary."
- "The tool I've gotten most excited about when it came out was the one I call "The Magic Transform Tool:" (⌘ + *T* / *ctrl* + *T*). I just love the fact that with one tool I can resize, re-position and rotate all at the same time."

Her final advice is also important: she warns about losing track of why we use all of these great tools.

"For editors, as much as we use computers, I always get back to the fact that our work is about telling stories. Learn to use your tools to tell stories well. When you do that, your work will be good, and you'll be able to get more work!"

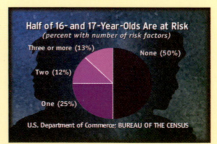

9

COLOR CORRECTION: HOW TO GET IT RIGHT

How often do you need to color-correct your video? Chances are, every edit session. The same issues that plague video also affect still photography (especially digital photography). The bad news is that you won't find a waveform monitor inside Photoshop. The good news is that all of your knowledge about fixing video signals will translate to Photoshop (with a little practice). If you think you're SOL because you don't have much experience "onlining" an edit, don't worry, you'll be up to speed quickly.

The Five Most Useful Image Adjustments for Video:

1. Levels
2. Curves
3. Hue/Saturation
4. Color Balance
5. Shadow/Highlights

The Approach

When working in Photoshop, the most common type of color correction you will need to perform is scene-to-scene correction. That is to say, you will need to bring a variety of shots, from a variety of sources, closer together. They will need to look as if the same photographer shot them under similar lighting conditions. This is an extremely challenging task if you consider the likelihood that you will pull images from several different stock libraries, client-provided sources, and video frame grabs.

The key when starting out is to work on a copy of the image. This way you always have a copy to return to if something goes wrong. Open the image in question, then choose File>Save As..., and give the corrected version a new name. In fact, this is always a good idea. Image correction is often destructive editing, meaning that you cannot revert to the original state at a later date. Once the modified file is closed and saved, you lose the ability for multiple undos. By preserving an original version, or employing adjustment layers, nondestructive editing is possible.

Color Correction allows you to make important improvements to color and exposure within an image. The top image is the original image; the bottom image has been enhanced.

Choosing a Bit Depth for Color Correction

When fixing images, bit depth is an important consideration. While most Photoshop users are most comfortable working with

8-bit images, there is a strong case to switch to a 16-bit workflow. The extra bit depth gives you more image details (especially in areas such as shadows and highlights). The extra bit depth can also reduce banding and posterization in gradient areas (such as skies). Since most digital cameras and scanners now offer 16-bit modes, be sure to explore this option.

Mode	Pros	Cons
8-bit	More filters. Faster image processing. Greater compatibility with older video and motion graphic tools.	Banding in gradients. Image can show "wear" more quickly after application of filters or adjustments.
16-bit	Greater range for color and exposure. Allows for more processing of image without visible pixelization.	Larger file sizes. Not as many filters or adjustments available. Overkill for users working with 8-bit video formats.

Using the Histogram Palette

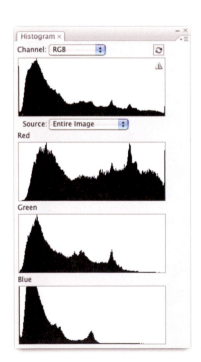

While Photoshop doesn't offer the same scopes that you are used to, there is a useful palette that you can leave open. The Histogram palette shows you the data within your image (including the ability to view per-channel data).

Step 1. Choose Window>Histogram.

Step 2. Click the triangular submenu in the upper right corner of the palette and choose All Channels View to see each channel in your image.

Step 3. Leave this palette open as you work on images. We will explore reading a histogram as we work on repairing images in this chapter.

How to Spot a Problem

Color correction, like editing, is a never-ending process. It's done when the budget runs out, all the time is used up, or the client is satisfied. The end product could always be better if you only had more time/money/processing power. So understand that it is important to be able to spot problems quickly. What sort of problems? There are several. We will analyze the most important tools in Photoshop and evaluate which situations they might help you in. This evaluation will give you a better understanding of color correction.

Levels

There's a very good reason this image adjustment comes first in the menu. You will need to make a Levels adjustment on every image. The Levels command allows you to correct tonal ranges and color-balance issues. That is to say, that you can fix poor exposure and adjust your white and black point. If you understand the need to white-balance a video camera, the Levels command will soon make sense.

Video #13   Using the Levels Adjustment

The Levels adjustment is a powerful command that will serve you well. To learn more, see the DVD-ROM for a video tutorial.

Working with a Histogram

The key to understanding the Levels adjustment is the histogram. If you can learn to read this graph, it can serve as a visual guide for adjusting the image. To illustrate this powerful command, let's try it on an image.

Step 1. Open the file `Ch09_Levels1.tif` from the chapter's folder on the DVD-ROM.

Step 2. Launch the Levels dialog by choosing Image>Adjust>Levels or by pressing ⌘+L (ctrl+L). Make sure that the Preview box is checked so that you can see your changes update.

By adjusting the black and white input sliders, you can set the black and white points in the image. This can be useful for fixing both the brightness and contrast in the image.

The midtones are way too dark in this image. (Photo by James Ball.)

Step 3. Move the black Input slider to the right until it reaches the rise in the histogram data. This will increase the intensity of the blacks in the image.

Step 4. Move the white Input slider to the left until it reaches the rise in the histogram data. This will increase the intensity of the whites in the image.

By adjusting these to sliders, you have told Photoshop to map the pixels to the values set for black and white in the Output levels area. The pixels that fall in between are adjusted proportionally in order to maintain a proper color balance. For this photo, adjust the Input and Output levels to restore some of the missing contrast in the image. While a separate command exists for brightness and contrast, the Levels adjustment lets you perform several improvements with one adjustment, thus cutting down on quantization (loss of quality) introduced from multiple image processing steps.

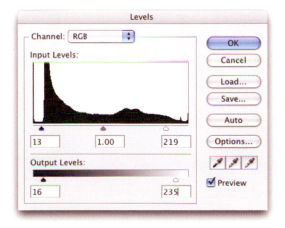

Output levels are often clamped for analog video and some nonlinear editing software.

The true power lies in the middle slider. Here you can modify the gamma setting. Effectively, you can use the middle Input slider to change the intensity of the midtones without making dramatic changes to the highlights and shadows. In a sense, you can better expose the picture, adding or subtracting "light" from the midtones. This adjustment is critical to creating a continuous flow between images. Levels adjustments do not offer as many precise adjustment points as Curves adjustments, but they are significantly easier to perform, and they generally create very good results.

Step 5. Adjust the middle Input slider to affect exposure. Pull the slider both left and right to see the changes to the document. Adjust the slider until you are happy with the exposure of the image.

So far you have been making Levels adjustments across all channels evenly. You can choose to isolate your corrections to a specific channel by clicking on the drop-down list of channels. This can be used to remove colorcast issues, such as spill from a background or a photo shot under colored lighting.

Step 6. Switch to the Red channel by choosing it from the drop-down list or by pressing ⌘+1 (ctrl+1).

Step 7. Adjust the middle slider for the Red channel to help balance the color in the skin tones.

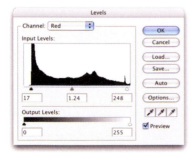

Adjust the levels for the red channel separately to improve color balance.

This color balancing process can also be automated a bit by using the eyedroppers. Use the black or white eyedroppers to click on an area to define its target color. For example, if you have a blue cast, clicking on a white area with the Set White Point eyedropper will remove the blue cast from the image.

What about all those other buttons?

- The Save and Load buttons can be used to save a color-correction setting. If you have several images from the same camera or photographer that need a common adjustment, you can save that adjustment, then load it back and run it again.

- The Auto button tells Photoshop to attempt to fix the image by making a "best-guess." I generally recommend avoiding this option unless you are *very* pressed for time. You will need to make a conscious decision about every image; don't trust the computer to make accurate, artistic decisions about color.

Curves

Curves aren't easy, but they are powerful. The Levels adjustment just gives you three control points (highlights, midtones, and shadows). The Curves dialog gives you up to 16 control points, opening significantly more possibilities. One option is to add a single control point and pull it up to lighten the image or down to darken. The adjustment is applied evenly throughout the entire image. Multiple points can be employed for contrast adjustments based on tonal range.

Let's take a look at Curves in action. I've chosen a grayscale file for the exercise because it is easier to work only on contrast issues when first using Curves. When you feel comfortable with grayscale images, switch to color ones, being sure to keep an eye on color shift.

Control Points Made Easy

When the Curves Editor is open, you can automat-ically add control points by ⌘+clicking (*ctrl*+clicking) within the image. The control points will appear in the editor. These can be moved up to lighten or down to darken.

Step 1. Open the file `Ch09_Curves1.tif`.

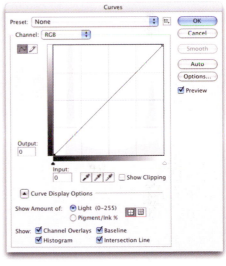

Step 2. Launch the Curves dialog box by choosing Image> Adjust>Curves or by pressing ⌘+M (*ctrl*+M).

Step 3. Under Photoshop CS3 (or newer) click the Curve Display Options triangle and make sure that the Curves is set to Show Amount of Light (0–255). If you are using an older version of Photoshop, click on the small right-hand triangle on the bottom of the x-axis. This will place white at the top and right in the Curves dialog box, thus using the more familiar 0–255 scale.

Currently your curve has two points on it: one representing the black point, the other, the white point. When you add additional curves and move them, you are reassigning values.

Step 4. Click in the middle of the Curve line to a control point at the midpoint, then move that point up (towards the lighter area on the y-axis); the image will lighten. Notice that the input and output values update as you drag.

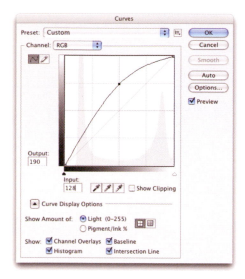

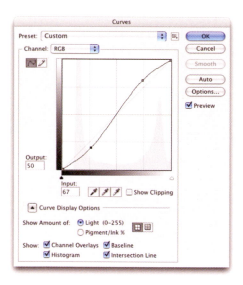

What differentiates Curves is that you have precise control over what points get mapped, whereas in Levels, you do not. Additionally, a Curves adjustment uses a curved line (rather than Levels' linear) to make adjustments that are eased through the image. It is possible to create adjustments that are easier to blend in with existing data, as opposed to Levels' frequent problem of hard clipping.

So how do you know what points to pick? You click on the image itself (actually, ⌘+click on the Mac and *ctrl*+click for PCs). In the Curves dialog box, you can then move these new points up to lighten or down to darken.

You will notice as you drag on a point that the others react as well. Be careful, because as you add contrast in one area, it is removed from another. Radical adjustments will leave you with an undesirable posterization effect.

Because Curves are so complex, most people use a Curves adjustment layer instead of applying the adjustment directly to the source layer. An adjustment layer affects everything beneath it and has the added ability to support masks and blending modes. The results are just as effective as a traditional adjustment, but significantly more flexible. We'll look at adjustment layers in greater detail later in this chapter.

Special FX

To create Special FX, try using:
- Curves (with arbitrary settings)
- Channel Mixer (load presets from Photoshop's *Goodies* folder)
- Gradient Map

Color Balance

This is a simple yet useful tool. By using the Color Balance command, you can change the overall mixture of colors in a particular tonal range. This is quite useful for generalized color correction. When you think an image is too blue or red, a quick adjustment allows you to tone down specific colors. The adjustment is constrained to the shadows, midtones, or highlights as specified in the dialog box.

Step 1. Open up the file `Ch09_Color_Balance1.tif.` Notice how the light from the candles is a bit green?

Step 2. Make sure the composite channel is selected in the Channels palette, or the command won't work.

Step 3. Launch the Color Balance dialog box, or press ⌘+B (ctrl+B).

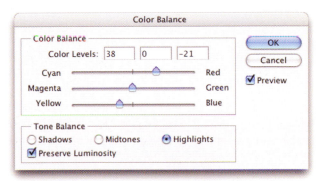

Step 4. Select the Highlights radio button so the command only affects the brighter areas of the image.

Step 5. Leave the Preserve Luminosity box checked to prevent changing exposure. This option will allow you to maintain tonal balance throughout editing the image.

The original image is too green. A Color Balance adjustment can help.

The new image feels warmer. (Photo by James Ball.)

Step 6. Drag the sliders towards Red and Yellow; those colors will increase while the opposite colors decrease.

Hue/Saturation and Desaturate

These two commands are incredibly important for video graphics. If colors are too saturated, you will need to tone them down. Otherwise, you will get "bleeding" onscreen with color data spreading from its original areas into other parts of your graphic. This can severely impact readability and is distracting to the viewer.

Video #14   Fixing Saturation

Fixing saturation problems can be very tricky. See the video tutorial on the DVD-ROM.

These rich, saturated colors may cause us problems on a video monitor (Photo by James Ball.)

Notice color shift in the red and yellow?

Equalize will force the matte.

Blur the matte for softer edges in the color correction.

Oversaturation Test

How do you know an image is oversaturated? The best way is to import the graphics into your NLE and use features such as Final Cut Pro's Range Check option. Better yet, put the image onto a vectorscope and see if the image exceeds the target values. If hardware scopes aren't available, you can purchase software alternatives such as Scopo Gigio from http://www.metadma.com/.

But if you are looking for a built-in option for Photoshop, you'll need to settle for the NTSC Colors filter. While this filter is designed to fix saturation problems, it generally produces posterization and banding that make it an unacceptable fix. However, it can be used to check whether the image has issues.

Step 1. Open up the file `Ch09_Saturation1.tif`.

Step 2. If the bottom-most layer is called *Background,* double-click and name it so that it's a floating layer.

Step 3. Create a copy of the photo layer by pressing ⌘+J (ctrl+J). Make sure that you do not have a selection made.

Step 4. Run the NTSC Colors filter on the layer. Look for any color shift. In our example, there are two areas that should show up: the juice bottles and the red tower of chalk.

Step 5. Set the filtered layer to Difference blending mode. The problem areas should be quite clear now.

Isolate for Saturation Adjustment

You now need to create a selection matte to isolate the saturation adjustment. You can create this matte by using existing layer data.

Step 1. Select (or Link) the two layers.

Step 2. Select the top layer, which is set to Difference mode.

Step 3. Hold down the ⌥ or alt key and choose Merge Layers (or Merge Linked) from the Layer menu. A flattened copy set to Normal mode is now available.

Step 4. Desaturate this new layer by selecting Image>Adjust> Desaturate, or press Shift+⌘+U (Shift+ctrl+U).

Step 5. You need to expand this matte to make it more useful. To get a larger white area, choose Image>Adjust>Equalize.

This will assign the lightest area to white (255) and the darkest area to black (0). The remaining pixels are dispersed evenly, thus creating a more useful high-contrast layer.

Step 6. Soften the matte by running the Gaussian Blur filter. Choose a value that generates soft edges. Depending on your image's resolution, this number will vary.

Step 7. Now the high-contrast layer will be used as a selection guide. Switch to the Channels palette (by default, it is docked with Layers. If it isn't visible, choose Windows>Show Channels).

Step 8. Hold down the ⌘ key (*ctrl*) and click on the layer's thumbnail. You should now see the appropriate "marching ants."

Step 9. Further soften the selection by choosing Select>Feather if desired.

Step 10. Switch back to the layer's palette; turn off the visibility indicator for the high-contrast matte. Select the photo layer that needs desaturating.

Step 11. Add a Hue/Saturation adjustment layer by choosing Layer>New Adjustment Layer>Hue/Saturation. Click OK to create the layer then make sure the Preview box is checked.

Step 12. Pull down the saturation and lightness sliders in small amounts. If you overdo it, you will get undesirable posterization. Click OK to apply the adjustment. You can double-click the adjustment layer to modify the Hue/Saturation adjustment if needed.

Automate Broadcast-Safe Color

The above correction is now available as a prerecorded action. If you have Photoshop CS2 or newer, then load the Video Actions set by clicking on the Actions palette submenu.

Mask Touchup

When touching up mattes, masks, or alpha channels, you will use:

- Levels
- Invert
- Equalize
- Threshold

The final image has the oversaturated areas corrected.

With experience, you will learn to spot saturation problems visually. You can, however, always use the NTSC Colors filter as a way to spot potential issues.

Exposure

If you are working with 32-bit images, you will turn to the Exposure command for fixing your images. Generally referred to as High Dynamic Range (HDR), 32-bit images offer great flexibility in exposure. These images are well suited to re-creating the wide range of exposures found in outdoor scenes or intense lighting conditions. This image function usually exists in 32-bit space, and is said to be 32-bit floating point (often shortened to "float").

HDR images are generally created in one of two ways. First, they can be generated with 3D software tools. The second method requires that the camera be secured firmly to a tripod and that you are careful when triggering or adjusting the camera to not move it. Several photos at various exposures are taken of the same scene (a minimum of three, but usually five to seven is adequate). The camera should have its auto-bracket and ISO features disabled. Each shot should be about two f-stops apart. The user then harnesses the Merge to HDR command (File>Automate>Merge to HDR…) to create the 32-bit image.

We created a HDR image in Chapter 2, so you can use that one. If you skipped that exercise, then open the sample `Ch09_HDR1.psd` from the chapter's folder on the DVD-ROM.

Step 1. Open the file `Ch09_HDR1.psd.` You'll notice that several features are grayed out. Most image adjustments do not work. Additionally, only Photoshop CS3 Extended allows for the use of layers (including Adjustment Layers).

Step 2. Choose Image>Adjustments>Exposure. This command makes tonal adjustments by performing calculations in a linear color space (gamma 1.0) rather than the current color space. This offers extreme flexibility for future changes, as every adjustment goes back to the original image data in a nondestructive manner.

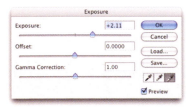

Step 3. There are three properties than can be modified with the Exposure command:
- **Exposure**. This modifies the highlight end of the tonal range. It has little effect on the extreme shadows.
- **Offset**. This darkens the shadows and midtones of the image. It has little effect on highlights.
- **Gamma**. This adjusts the gamma of the image.

Step 4. The Exposure command offers three eyedroppers that adjust the image's luminance values:
- **Set Black Point Eyedropper**. This sets the Offset, which shifts the selected pixel to zero black.
- **Set White Point Eyedropper**. This sets the Exposure, which shifts the selected pixel to white (1.0 for HDR images).
- **Midtone Eyedropper**. This sets the Exposure, which shifts the selected pixel to the middle gray.

Step 5. Apply a dramatic adjustment and Click OK. Let the image blow out, so you can see the flexibility of HDR images.

Step 6. Apply a second Exposure adjustment. Use it to bring the image back into a more accurate exposure. Notice the blown-out areas are restored (this is impossible with 8- or 16-bit images as overexposed data is discarded).

Useful Commands in Brief

Channel Mixer

By using the Channel Mixer, current channels can be combined to form a new channel. This has two distinct purposes:

- **Scenario 1.** A digital photo had a write error and one of the channels is damaged. You can use the two good channels to create a replacement for the third.
- **Scenario 2.** You want better grayscales. You can choose the monochromatic option and produce much better grayscales than by simply switching modes or desaturating.

Let's try the second scenario out and manually create a new grayscale image.

Step 1. Open the file `Ch09_Channel_Mixer.tif` from the chapter's folder on the DVD-ROM.

Step 2. Choose Layer>New Adjustment Layer>Channel Mixer… and click OK to create the adjustment layer.

Step 3. Check the Monochrome box and adjust the Red, Green, and Blue sliders to taste. Depending on your source image, you'll want to emphasize different channels. In general, emphasize Red when skin tones are involved.

Step 4. When satisfied with the new grayscale conversion, click OK.

Step 5. To permanently apply the image adjustment, choose Image>Mode>Grayscale.

Gradient Map

The Gradient Map is an extremely useful effect for stylizing images. With that said, you should always choose to use the Gradient Map adjustment layer instead of the Image Adjustment command.

What does the Gradient Map do? The name says it all; it takes a gradient and then maps it based on luminance values. The effect is particularly useful for colorizing backgrounds and textures. When used on photos, however, it can create some dynamic looks, especially when used with blending modes.

After Effects users have an extremely similar effect too; in AE, it's called Colorama. To see Gradient Maps in action, open the file `Ch09_Gradient_Map.psd` and turn on the individual gradient maps.

When Gradient Maps are used as adjustment layers, they can be masked and blended. All of the effects shown used a single Gradient Map. There is no rendering time involved, and the original color data is preserved. (Photo by James Ball.)

Invert

This image adjustment creates an image that is a direct inverse or negative. This is very useful for reversing grayscale images—for example, reversing the masked areas of a layer mask. It can also be used to make a positive from a scanned 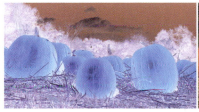 black-and-white or color negative. When an image is inverted, the brightness of each pixel is assigned the inverse value from the 256 color-values scale. This means that a 0 value would map to 255, while a 15 value would map to 240.

Equalize

If an image appears too dark or washed out, Equalize is the sledgehammer way to pound it into a usable state. The command attempts to redistribute pixels so that they are equally balanced across the entire range of brightness values. You can tell Photoshop to look at the  entire image when equalizing, or sample a smaller area that will drive the overall adjustment. The command will take the lightest area and map it to pure white (255) and the darkest area to pure black (0). Since the equalize command uses the full 0–255 range, you will need to adjust levels to keep the image broadcast safe.

Threshold

This command is used to set the "continental divide." All pixels on one side of the new midpoint are black; the others are white. This adjustment can be used to clean up a mask made from individual channels.

Don't Bother

Skip these (unless you have no time at all):
• Auto Levels
• Auto Contrast
• Auto Color
• Variations

Not-So-Useful Tools

Brightness/Contrast

These controls are an inferior substitute for Levels and Curves, because the overall brightness or darkness is affected. Most of the time, the problem is in the midtones or gamma. A brightness and contrast adjustment will often leave your image washed out. Skip it. While this command has been improved in Photoshop CS3, it is still inferior to a proper Levels or Curves adjustment.

Replace Color and Selective Color

These are not the most useful commands. Replace Color combines the select color range interface with a fill command. I personally prefer to split this step out and have fine control. The Selective Color command is similar to Color Balance (but not as easy to use) and does not produce the high-quality results that are possible with Levels or Curves. You are better off using the individual Color Range command (Select>Color Range) and then creating a Levels or Curves adjustment layer.

Even More Problems

These may introduce *new* problems to your image:
• Brightness/Contrast
• Replace Color
• Selective Color
• Posterize

Posterize

Posterization cuts down on the number of colors used, thus producing banding. Reduced color palettes and banding are both extremely poor for video use. Skip the Posterize adjustment.

Variations

Inexperienced users try Variations. This wizard feels a lot like a visit to the eye doctor with its "more-and-less" approach to image adjustments. While it is initially attractive, it will ultimately leave you wanting more. Don't bother with this command.

Standard Definition Broadcast-Safe Concerns

Have you ever watched a low-budget commercial on late-night TV? Listen closely, as you may actually *hear* the graphics. If whites are too hot, the video track bleeds over into the audio track of a broadcast signal. This can also cause problems when tapes are duplicated. It is an accepted industry practice to keep video signals broadcast-safe.

Recently, creating broadcast-safe graphics has gotten trickier. Many video editing tools have begun to automatically adjust graphics to make them broadcast-safe during import. The system will automatically remap the white and black points to a broadcast-safe value. For example, both Premiere Pro and Final Cut Pro

will properly interpret a zero black as 7.5 IRE on a Waveform monitor. Avid systems continue to offer you a choice and will ask if the graphics have RGB levels (0–255) or 601 Levels (16–235).

While this can take care of graphics where luminance is the only concern, it generally does not solve the problem of too much saturation. Whenever you adjust an image, you have to be concerned about modifying its colors to the point where they are no longer "broadcast-safe."

It is important to read the documentation that comes with your video software (or see the guides that come in the Appendixes of this book). If you do need to remap your graphics, then it is better to make this adjustment in Photoshop.

If you need to clamp your graphic to 601 levels, then you'll want to pull things into the 16–235 broadcast-safe range. In doing so, however, you don't want to overdo it, so you must monitor the adjustment. By placing targets using the Color Sampler tool (stored in the same well as the Eyedropper and Measure tools), you can monitor the values of white and black.

In the example (`Ch09_BSC.tif`), I have placed targets on the clouds (for white) and the deepest shadows (for black). In the Info palette, it is clear that these colors are out of the safe range. Add a Levels adjustment layer and set the output levels to 16 and 235. The colors are now in the safe range. You can leave the adjustment layer floating and modify it at any time within Photoshop.

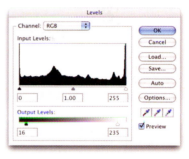

High-Definition Color Space

When creating graphics for high-definition video, you must keep in mind that SD and HD define colors differently. For standard definition, the International Telecommunication Union (ITU) 601 color space is used, while HD normally uses ITU 709. The most common problems occur when conversion occurs between SD and HD video sources. If the codec or video software doesn't automatically convert the color space, then a slight shift in color will occur.

These color shifts are only visible on a properly calibrated HD monitor that supports the 709 color space. However, most users are not designing with these hooked up so they won't see the issue.

Fortunately, it is rarely a problem as the color conversion process is fairly transparent and is generally handled internally by the video software application. For example, when Adobe After Effects converts from RGB to Y'CbCr in a video codec, the codec handles the conversion internally. When you export the same After Effects project to both an SD and an HD output, the process should work without issue.

Adjustment Layers

I've already mentioned adjustment layers as a helpful tool for pulling down Levels and for use in the Gradient Map feature. Adjustment Layers are the only true way to perform nondestructive editing on an image. The adjustment layer can be blended, masked, or deleted at any time. Additionally, if you double-click on the Adjustment Layer's thumbnail, the Image Adjustment dialog box comes back. Nearly every image adjustment available in the Image>Adjustments menu and is offered as an Adjustment Layer (the notable exceptions are the Shadow/Highlights, Equalize, Match Color, and Replace Color commands).

Masking Adjustment Layers

If you want to apply an adjustment only to part of a layer, make an active selection as you would for any other change (see Chapter 4, "What About Transparency?"). Then, when you create the Adjustment Layer, it will automatically mask the adjustment to apply only to your selection. It is a good idea to feather the edges of your selection (Select>Modify>Feather) for a more believable adjustment. Otherwise, you will see a hard edge that makes the adjustment very easy to spot.

The sign can use a little "punching up." (Photo by James Ball.)

The new image has a different "feel." If I change my mind, editing is a double-click away.

Video #15 The Power of Adjustment Layers

Adjustment Layers offer the flexibility you need to edit images non-destructively. Check out the video tutorial on the DVD-ROM.

Adjustment Layers can also have gradient masks applied. The Adjustment Layer automatically comes with a mask applied. Just click on its thumbnail (the big, empty white one), and you will see a border around the mask's icon. You can now add a gradient or hand-painted mask in which to blend the adjustment. To see these two techniques applied, open up the file `Ch09_AL_.psd.`

Photo Filter Adjustment Layers

Adobe added to the "real-time" color-correction tools with the introduction of Photo Filter Adjustment Layers. These 20 different adjustments simulate using colored glass filters when the photo was taken. These "filters" can be used to adjust the color balance and color temperature of the light in the scene. Besides the built-in presets, you can also choose custom colors from the Photo Filter interface using the standard color picker.

The filter offers several choices, but they can be simplified into three groupings:

- **Warming Filter (85 and LBA) and Cooling Filter (80 and LBB).** These are meant to even out photos that were not properly white-balanced. The Cooling Filter (80 or LBB) makes images bluer to simulate cooler ambient light. The Warming Filter (85 or LBA) makes images warmer to simulate hotter ambient light.
- **Warming Filter (81) and Cooling Filter (82).** These are similar to the previous filters but cast a more distinct color. The Warming Filter (81) makes the image more yellow and the Cooling Filter (82) makes the image bluer.
- **Individual colors.** The Photo Filter also has several preset colors to choose from. These can be used for two primary purposes: (1) to add a complementary color to a scene to remove color cast, or (2) to introduce a color cast for stylistic reasons.

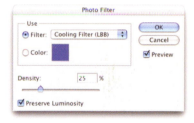

Let's try adding a Photo Filter to an image. Open the file `Ch09_Photo_Filter1.tif` from the chapter's folder on the DVD-ROM. To apply a Photo Filter, do the following:

Step 1. Ensure that you are on the top-most layer (or above the photo layers) that you want to affect. The image must also be in RGB mode.

Step 2. Click on the adjustment layer icon at the bottom of the Layers palette and choose Photo Filter or choose Layer> New Adjustment Layer>Photo Filter.

Step 3. Be sure the Preview box is checked.

Step 4. Select the Color Option by choosing a preset or defining a custom color.

Step 5. If you don't want the image to get darker from the adjustment, check the Preserve Luminosity box.

Step 6. Adjust the Density slider to control the intensity of the effect.

Step 7. Click OK. At any point in time, you can double-click on the adjustment layer's icon to refine the effect.

Color is Easy

Photos that look useless can often be restored quickly. Color problems are one of the easiest things to fix in Photoshop.

Fixing Common Problems

Our next chapter, Chapter 10, "Repairing Damaged Photos," will tackle more difficult photo damage. Here we will look at six common color problems that will affect you frequently.

Red Eye

I'm not talking about what you have after a late-night editing session. The fill flash bouncing off the back of the eyeball causes red eye. This is a common problem for photos taken with consumer-quality cameras, because the flash and lens are very close together. Dark rooms only aggravate the problem, because the pupils are open wider. If it's your camera, look for a red eye reduction mode; it will strobe the flash, thus cutting down on the red eye. You can also use a secondary flash with a sync cable if you are using a professional camera.

However, chances are you didn't take the pictures. Unless the photos are from a visit to the Inferno, you will need to clean up this problem. The discoloration won't necessarily be red, just look for glowing eyeballs that shouldn't be there.

Step 1. Open the file `Ch09_Red_Eye.tif` from the chapter folder on the DVD-ROM.

Step 2. Zoom into the red eye area in the eyes. You only need to select one eye at first. An easy way is to take the Zoom tool and drag around the problem area.

Step 3. Select the Red Eye tool from the toolbox (it is nested with the Healing Brush and Patch tools).

Step 4. Click in the red eye area to remove it. If too little of an area is affected, you will need to undo and modify the tools setting in the option bar. Similarly if too large an area is processed (you'll notice if the skin around the eyeball turns gray), you'll want to tweak settings.

Step 5. Adjust the Pupil Size to a higher number if you need to convert a larger area (smaller if too great a range is modified). Adjust the Darken Pupil setting to adjust how dark the pupil will be after the conversion.

Step 6. You may want to touch up the pupil using the Burn tool as well.

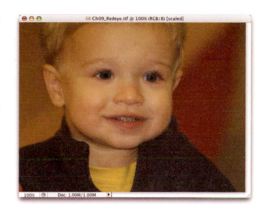

Color Cast

Sometimes the light cast conditions are universally off. This could be seen as a blue cast throughout the entire shot. Maybe the wrong filter was used, or the image was not white-balanced. Sometimes the problem is simply at the developing end. (When you go to a one-hour photo center at your local superstore, chances are the machine is on autopilot and is being run by someone with little or no experience.)

Step 1. Open up the file `Ch09_Color_Cast.tif`, and you will see how easy this is to fix.

Step 2. Examine the photo. Identify a suitable white, gray, and black point. The gray point will be tricky, but you can make multiple attempts.

Step 3. Add a Levels Adjustment Layer.

Step 4. Select the black eyedropper and click on the darkest point in the picture.

Step 5. Select the white eyedropper and click on the lightest point in the picture.

Step 6. Look for a gray point. With the gray eyedropper, click on a gray area that is representative of midtones. It may take a few attempts to find the right point in the picture.

Reset an Adjustment Layer

 If you need to reset the adjustment layer hold down the ⌥ (*alt*) key and the Cancel button becomes Reset.

Video #16 Using Shadow/Highlights

The Shadow/Highlight command allows you to fix several problems at once. Be sure to see the video tutorial on the DVD-ROM.

Fixing Shadows and Highlights

One of the most flexible image adjustment commands is called Shadow/Highlight. The purpose of the adjustment is to help salvage images where the subject is silhouetted due to strong backlight. It can also be used to improve subjects who have been washed out by the camera's flashbulb. The command does not just lighten or darken an image; rather it makes adjustments based on neighboring pixels.

When first opened the tool is too basic, offering just two sliders. However, clicking on the Show More Options box opens this tool up significantly. Let's give it a try:

Step 1. Open the file `Ch09_Shadow_Highlights1.tif`.

Step 2. Choose Image>Adjustments>Shadow/Highlight.

Step 3. Be sure that both the Preview box and Show More Options box are checked.

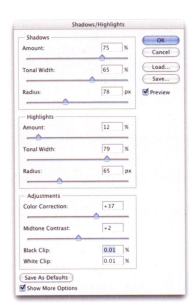

Step 4. Adjust the Shadows and Highlights.
- **Amount:** How strong of an adjustment is made.
- **Tonal Width:** Small values affect a smaller region; larger values will begin to include the midtones. If you push these values too high, you will get halos around the images.
- **Radius:** A tolerance setting that looks at neighboring pixels to determine the affected area.

Step 5. Apply Image Adjustments to improve image quality.
- **Color Correction:** Essentially adjusts the saturation of the adjusted areas. This allows you to counterbalance washed-out images. This is only available for color images.
- **Brightness:** If you are working with a grayscale image, Color Correction is replaced by a control for Brightness.
- **Midtone Contrast:** This command affects missing contrast in the midtones of an image. Negative values reduce contrast, positive values increase contrast.

- **Black Clip and White Clip:** Raises the black point of shadows and lowers the white point of highlights. This is good to lower the intensity of the effect. You will still want to adjust broadcast-safe levels using the Levels command for finer control.

Step 6. Click Save if you want to reuse the adjustment later, otherwise Click OK.

While this command simplifies the process of fixing shadow/highlight problems, it is not available as an Adjustment Layer. Therefore, it is a destructive editing command, which means you should work with a duplicate file or layer so you can return to the original photo if needed.

Skin Tones

It seems like old photos tend to have problems with skin tones. I look back at childhood photos from the 1970s and 1980s, and I know that my skin was never that red. Improvements in film quality and processing have cut down on these color shifts, but the proliferation of digital cameras has made this problem all too prevalent. Picture fading can cause a photo to lighten or darken over time. Generally, this is an even distortion, however, so a slight adjustment is all that is needed.

Step 1. Open up the file `Ch09_Skin_Tones.psd`.

Step 2. Add a Levels Adjustment Layer and click Auto. The individual channels have been automatically adjusted. Closer, but not quite right yet.

Step 3. Now you can tweak. Switch to each channel by selecting it from the pull-down list at the top of the Levels window.

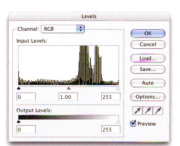

For each channel, adjust the spread of the histogram. Bring the black and white point sliders closer to the pixel spread. Adjust the gamma or midpoint slightly until you are happy with the overall color. You will likely need to take two passes through each channel to get it "just" right.

Nondestructive Shadow/Highlight Adjustment in CS3

If working in Photoshop CS3, you can use the Shadow/Highlight command nondestructively. You must first turn the photo into a Smart Object (this can be done by right-clicking and choosing Convert to Smart Object). You can then apply the Shadow/Highlight command and make an adjustment. For future changes just double-click the Shadow/Highlight command in the Layers palette.

Over time, the reds in this photo have become too dominant.

A proper Levels adjustment makes everything right.

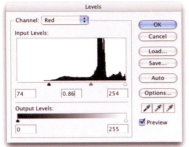
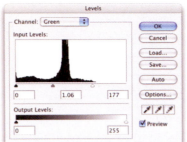
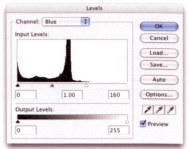

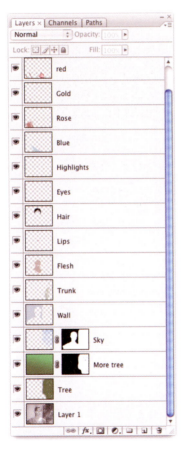

While it can be time consuming, you can hand-paint a grayscale photo to look realistic. Place each color on its own layer and set the layer to Color blending mode.

Tinting a Photo

Imagine that you are working on a project showing different people, and all of your sources are full color, except one. What do you do? Dump it? Look for a tornado to carry you over the rainbow? No, you regress a bit and color it.

This technique is simple, but often overlooked.

Step 1. Create a new layer for each color you need and place the layer in Color mode.

Step 2. Paint on the layer, and it will tint the photo below. Soften the colors with the occasional use of Dodge, Burn, Blur, and Smudge. Be sure to isolate each color on a separate layer so you have better control over the image.

To see this technique open the image `Ch09_Recolor.psd` from the chapter's folder.

Can you spot the fake? The top picture is actually a hand-colored grayscale version. The original photo is on the lower right. (Photo by James Ball.)

Hands On | 09

Enhancing Still Images for Video—*with Jayse Hansen*

As an editor or motion graphic artist, you will often be sent still images to include in your video. These images will often be rather uninspiring and may not fit the overall mood of your video. By harnessing some basic techniques, images can quickly be made to look more professional and meaningful using Photoshop.

For example, you might be tasked with creating a somber biographical video about an individual. The client hands you a box of mismatched photos. Some are color, some are black and white, and some are an awful orange color from the seventies. Simply adding these photos "as-is" to your video would make the end result look messy, inconsistent and amateur.

Therefore, in order to make the video piece have a uniform quality—we want to adjust the photos so they all have a similar look to them. Because this hypothetical piece is somber, we will make the photos a classic sepia-toned. Keep in mind, however, that this same process can be used to create wildly different looks and variations.

You'll find Exercise 09 on the DVD-ROM.

PRO*file*: Glen Stephens

Glen Stephens is an experienced broadcast designer who makes time to actively contribute to the Photoshop community. Stephens is the developer of Tools for Television, a Photoshop add-on that brings many features that are needed for broadcast design. He also contributes a monthly column on video graphics to Photoshop User Magazine (www.photoshopuser.com).

"I've spent many years studying and researching to find resources and techniques that help me as a designer for video," said Stephens. "Because Photoshop users in the video industry are hard to come by, those sharing resources and tips are equally elusive. This is why I do everything I can to make the learning process easier for those eager to expand their skills."

Stephens would not be in a position to offer all of this advice if he were not actively involved in the production community. To get his designs done, Stephens relies heavily on Photoshop.

"Photoshop is my scratch pad and design platform. In most situations, the images for projects, lower thirds, opens, bumpers and closes are all created or conceptualized in Photoshop. If the client doesn't want or require any animation then Photoshop is my final output. If motion is needed then to After Effects and Motion I go," said Stephens. "All photographs, scans, digital images, frame grabs, or any clipart that are used in my composites always get color corrected, and stylized in Photoshop before it is used anywhere."

Stephens also uses Photoshop's superior text handling to complement his Final Cut Pro editing system. "Photoshop is my character generator. All of my lower thirds, full screen images, Over-The-Shoulder graphics are all created in Photoshop."

Stephens sees a definite need for any video pro to focus on Photoshop. In fact he sees it as the single most important complement to any video application.

"In my opinion, it is critical to anyone's career. Doesn't matter what industry you are in, Photoshop will be there. Even if it is only a supplemental application for you, learn it," said Stephens. "Many times Photoshop is all you have, and the more you know the less you will turn to other applications for other tasks. It is the single most powerful image creation/manipulation tool and failing to learn it is career suicide."

Stephens also encourages you to try the Tools for Television PRO package. "I may have written and created it, but I use the tools on it everyday!"

While the process of learning may be challenging due to time constraints and workload, Stephens encourages editors and graphic artists to push themselves further.

"Take seminars, classes, read, interface with others, and just get in and use Photoshop. Then learn After Effects, Illustrator, Motion, Final Cut Pro, and any other desktop video/graphic tool you can," said Stephens. "The more you know, the more marketable you will be, and the quicker you can get your work done and surprise your client with fresh ideas and the correct execution of them."

Stephens' web sites are http://www.pixelpoststudios.com and http://www.toolsfortelevision.com. He is always open to ideas, input and suggestions for products and tools that make graphic design easier and more intuitive. He is also available for training, consulting and graphic design contracting for a wide variety of broadcast and video projects. For questions, suggestions, or good old work you can contact him at glen@pixelpoststudios.com.

10

REPAIRING DAMAGED PHOTOS

Damage, like beauty, is in the eye of the beholder. Show the same series of photos to five people and ask them to point out the mistakes; you'll get five totally different answers. Always ask your clients if there is anything they wish were different; you'll be surprised at the answers. I have had several instances where the request was as simple as cloning someone out of a group shot because they no longer worked for the company. Sometimes it will be a simple crop or color change. Always ask; don't assume that what they gave you was perfect.

Then look for the obvious things. Color-correct the image first. (If you skipped it, take a look at Chapter 9, "Color Correction: How to Get It Right.") Then look for physical damage such as rips, wrinkles, pushpin holes, scratches, and ballpoint pen marks. On the second pass, look for printing or scanning errors. Is there a texture present, streaks, a misregistered scan? Finally, check for alignment and title-safe issues; you may have to rotate and clone the image to make it work. In five minutes? Yes, with practice you can fix 90% of the problems in five minutes; the other 10% you learn to live with (or ask for more time).

Working with Historical Sources

Historical or archival photos present additional problems. There is an increased likelihood for physical damage such as tearing, water damage, or adhesive stains. The photos have also faded with time and will need touch-up. It will often be easier to remove color altogether from a historical source and reintroduce an overlay or sepia tone as the final step.

Look and Learn

You'll find several of this chapter's examples on the disc. Feel free to use these for trying out the techniques.

Time is not kind to prints. Read on and learn how to fix the damage.

A USB slide scanner is an affordable option these days.

Working with Modern Sources

All of the problems with historical sources can be present in modern photographs. However, the most likely problem with modern photos, especially digital ones, is color issues, followed by physical abuse. If a photo is wrinkled, creased, punched, or scratched, look for the negative and either reprint or use a negative scanner. If the photo is dusty, smudged, or fingerprinted, gently wipe it clean with a soft cloth, and then rescan. If rescanning or reprinting is not an option, you can fix several issues without going back to the negative.

Stamp It Out

Photoshop has several powerful options available to fix problem areas. Often the solution is to replace bad pixels with good ones. Do not think of these tools as being exclusive; it is common to employ two or more when tackling a tough problem. For all of these tools, be sure your painting tools are set to Brush size and your other tools to Precise (in your Preferences pane). This will allow you to better see your tools in action.

Clone Stamp

The Clone Stamp works very well, especially if a lower-opacity brush is combined with multiple sample points.

The Clone Stamp (**S**) is an old favorite of Photoshop users. It's been there forever, and with a little practice, produces predictable and accurate results. It works by sampling pixels from one area and applying them in another. This technique goes beyond copy and paste, however, because it uses the flexibility of Photoshop's Brush palette.

Step 1. Open the file `Ch10_Clone_Stamp.psd` from the DVD-ROM and select the Clone Stamp tool by pressing **S**.

Step 2. Select a brush from the Options bar or Brush palette.

Step 3. Experiment with blending modes. This can be useful when retouching to avoid visible cloning.

Step 4. Specify the alignment. If Aligned is selected, the sample point and painting point move parallel as you move. If the user clicks and starts over, the sample point picks up where it was last. If Aligned is deselected, the initial sample point is used (even after you stop and resume cloning.) The second method ensures that you are always sampling from the same area. You can clone from all visible layers by specifying Use All Layers. If this is deselected, only the active layer is used.

Step 5. ⌥+click (*alt*+click) within the current document, or another open document set to the same color mode. This defines the source point for sampled pixel data.

Step 6. Click and start to paint as if you were using the Brush tool (you are essentially sampling pixels from one area and painting them into another). The sampled pixels are drawn from before you click. Therefore, it may be necessary to release and start over occasionally to avoid cloning the problem area.

Step 7. Try cloning at a lower opacity from several different places to fill in a problem area. This way you can avoid too much repetition.

Step 8. Try to "follow the line" by looking for edges to follow. Straight lines such as creases in clothing are easier to follow than random spots. Look to follow the natural folds and linear paths that are present.

Healing Brush

The Healing Brush (**J**) is a tool that is designed to correct imperfections in a photo. Similar in handling to the Clone Stamp, it successfully hides blemishes by taking cloned pixels and matching the texture, lighting, and shading of the sampled to the original pixels. This can often generate results in which the repaired pixels blend seamlessly together. To get better results on an area with strong contrast, make a selection before using the Healing Brush tool. The selection should be bigger than the area to be healed and should follow the boundary of high-contrast pixels. For example, if healing a person's face, make a selection over the problem area that excludes the adjacent sky or clothing. This way, when painting with the Healing Brush, the selection will prevent color bleed-in from outside areas.

Step 1. Open the file `Ch10_Healing_Brush.psd` from the DVD-ROM. Select the Healing Brush tool by pressing **J**. (Be careful not to select the Spot Healing Brush.)

Step 2. Select a brush from the Options bar or Brush palette.

Step 3. Choose a blending mode. (This can be useful to avoid visible cloning when retouching.) The Replace option preserves noise and texture at the stroke's edges.

The Healing Brush was designed for challenges like this.

Step 4. Choose a source for repairing pixels in the Options bar. The standard source is sampled. Here pixels are taken from the area surrounding your sample point. As the brush moves, the sample point also moves accordingly to ensure

Spot Healing Brush

The Spot Healing Brush is similar in function to the Healing Brush. However, it does not require you to set a source point and will automatically blend neighboring pixels.

Video #17   Using the Healing Brush

The DVD-ROM includes a video tutorial on the Healing Brush.

variety in the sampled source. The Pattern option uses a pattern from the current pattern library (accessible from a pop-up list).

Step 5. Specify the alignment. If Aligned is selected, the sample point and painting point move parallel as you move. If the user clicks and starts over, the sample point picks up where it was last. If Aligned is deselected, the initial sample point is used (even after you stop and resume cloning). The second method ensures that you are always sampling from the same area.

Step 6. You can clone from all visible layers by specifying Use All Layers. If this is deselected, only the active layer is used. You can sample on one layer then apply the healing to a new empty layer above. This will provide greater flexibility in your workflow.

Try to "follow the line" for better results.

Step 7. If you are using the Sampling mode, [⌥]+click (*alt*+click) within the current document or another open document set to the same color mode.

Step 8. Click and start to paint as if you were using a brush. Because the sampled pixels are drawn from before you click, it may be necessary to release and start over occasionally to avoid cloning the problem area.

Step 9. Release the mouse to merge the sampled pixels. The stroke will look strange until then.

Step 10. Try to "follow the line" by looking for edges to follow. Straight lines such as creases in clothing are easier to follow than random spots. Look to follow the natural creases and linear paths that are present.

Patch Tool

The Patch tool uses similar technology as the Healing Brush, but Patch is better suited to fix larger problems or empty areas. You can repair an area using pixels from another region or a pattern. To get the best results, select a smaller area.

Using a Selection

Step 1. Open the file `Ch10_Patch_Tool.psd` from the DVD-ROM. Select the Patch tool by pressing J. (It's in the same well as the Healing Brush.)

Step 2. The Patch tool can be used two different ways. You can make a selection in the area you want to repair, and then select Source in the Options bar. Or you can make a selection in the area from which you want to sample, and then select Destination in the Options bar. You can also make a selection first, and then activate the Patch tool.

Step 3. Modify a selection with the standard modifier keys.

- Hold down the Shift key, and you can add to the selection.
- Hold down the ⌥ key (alt key), and you can subtract from the selection.
- To create an intersected selection, ⌥+Shift+drag (alt+Shift+drag) to make a new selection.

Step 4. Place the cursor inside the selection, and then do one of the following:

- If Source is selected in the Options bar, drag the selection border to the area you want to sample. When you release the mouse button, the original area will be patched with the sampled pixels.
- You can use any selection tool to create your active selection and then switch to the Patch tool.
- If Destination is selected in the Options bar, drag the selection border to the area you want to patch. When you release the mouse button, the sampled area will be patched over the new area.
- With both options, you will get a useful real-time preview of the results. This makes it significantly easier to drag and get the expected results.

Hide It: Blur and Smudge, Dodge, and Burn

The Tools palette offers several hands-on tools that help touch up photo damage. All of these tools are driven by brush settings: diameter, angle, roundness, and hardness will all affect the way these tools behave. If you are not familiar with the new Brushes palette, be sure to "brush up" first. Remember, if the Caps Lock key is down, brush previews are disabled.

Blur and Sharpen

There are two focus tools in Photoshop: the Blur tool and the Sharpen tool. The Blur tool (**R**) gives you the ability to manually soften problem areas. The Sharpen tool (**R**) helps focus soft edges.

Step 1. Select the Blur tool or Sharpen tool by pressing **R**.

Step 2. Specify the brush and brush options.

Step 3. Choose a blending mode. The Darken and Lighten modes are particularly useful for isolating the blurring effect.

Step 4. Adjust the strength for the tool. It is generally better to use a lower strength with several applications.

Step 5. Specify Use All Layers to use data from all visible layers.

Step 6. Paint over the areas that need touching up.

Be careful not to over-sharpen; it will quickly introduce visible noise and distortion.

Smudge

Think of the Smudge tool as the original Liquify command. This tool simulates dragging a finger through wet paint. The pixels are liquid and can be easily pushed around the screen. The tool uses color from where you first click and pushes it in the direction you move the mouse. This tool is useful for cleaning up mattes and is also a quick way to clean up specks or flakes in a photo. Set the tool's blending mode to Lighten or Darken (depending on the area to be affected), and you have virtual concealer to touch up any problem.

Step 1. Select the Smudge tool by pressing **R**.

Step 2. Specify the brush and brush options.

Step 3. Choose a blending mode. The Darken and Lighten modes are particularly useful for isolating the smudge.

Step 4. Adjust the strength for the tool. It is generally better to use a lower strength with several applications. If you are in a hurry, bump the strength up.

Step 5. Specify Use All Layers to use data from all visible layers.

Step 6. Paint over the areas that need touching up.

Step 7. The Finger Painting option can be accessed from the Options bar or activated temporarily by holding down the ⌥ (*alt*) key while painting. This technique, also known as *dipping*, smudges and introduces the foreground color.

Dodge and Burn

Known as the toning tools, Dodge and Burn allow you finer control over lightening or darkening your image. They are similar to traditional techniques used in a darkroom, where a photographer would regulate the amount of light on a particular area on a print. These tools are helpful when touching up faded photos, especially when repairing water damage.

Step 1. Select the Dodge or Burn tool by pressing ⓞ.

Step 2. Specify the brush and brush options.

Step 3. Choose a range of shadows, midtones, or highlights to isolate the effect.

Step 4. Adjust the exposure for the tool. It is generally better to use a lower exposure with several applications.

Step 5. Paint over the areas that need touching up.

Sponge

The Sponge is a toning tool that can be used for subtle changes in color saturation or grayscale contrast. This tool is useful for touching up spots that are too bright for television's color range. It can also be used to reduce digital grain that appears in an image.

Step 1. Select the Sponge tool by pressing ⓞ.

Step 2. Specify the brush and brush options.

Step 3. Choose Saturate or Desaturate, depending upon your needs.

Step 4. Adjust the flow for the tool. It is generally better to use a slower flow with several applications.

Step 5. Paint over the areas that need touching up.

Soak or Dry?

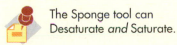

The Sponge tool can Desaturate *and* Saturate.

Use a small brush and short strokes with the Healing Brush for best results. The Smudge tool set to Lighten or Darken mode is also useful for correcting minor blemishes.

Video #18   Restoration in Action

 You can see a video demonstration of the restoration process on the DVD-ROM.

Restoration in Action

Fixing photo damage is not a step-by-step solution or recipe. Practice is the best way to become skillful, but you can expect good results if you know which tools to use. I have seen students become proficient in just a few weeks using Photoshop's rich suite of tools. The challenge is knowing which tools to use, and when to use them. With that in mind, I present some common scenarios and the most likely solutions.

Wrinkles, Holes, and Tears

To simplify the problem, you have areas that are missing and need to be replaced. For small areas like pushpin holes, you can easily use the Clone Stamp to sample an adjacent area and fill in the space. It is possible to just "finger-paint" the problem away using the Smudge tool as well. If the hole is in a dark area, set the Smudge tool to Darken, and push the pixels in. This virtual spackle works extremely well. Tears of a significant size benefit from the Clone Stamp tool. To avoid repeating patterns, try cloning at a low opacity and sample from different areas. A little bit of randomness goes a long way.

If things are really bad, consider a vignette effect and blur the outside edges. Make an elliptical selection, then reverse it by pressing *Shift* + ⌘ + *I* (*Shift* + *ctrl* + *I*). Then feather the edges extensively and run the Gaussian Blur filter.

Goop, Sludge, Schmutz

There are several names for the problem. What I'm talking about are physical blemishes attached to the photo that could have/should have been wiped off before scanning. This problem is often caused by food or environmental debris. If the photo is still in your possession, gently clean it and rescan.

If all you have is the scan, then use the Patch tool. Set the Patch tool to Source Mode and lasso around the problem spot (feather edges for a softer transition). Drag the selection to a clear area of similar texture (using the *Shift* key to constrain movement to a straight line, if desired). If you want perfection, touch up with the Blur and Smudge tools. Problem solved.

For little blemishes, use the Smudge tool. If you have dark spots on a lighter background, smudge in the Lighten mode. For light spots on a dark background, smudge in the Darken mode. Because you are outputting to such a lo-res medium, these touchups are virtually unnoticeable, and they are fast. The key again is to "follow the line."

Moiré Patterns and "Buzz"

Fine patterns are often desirable in print…in video, they will give you a headache. Lines thinner than three pixels will appear to vibrate, especially if they are in motion or fall diagonally. In Photoshop, we create these items to be anti-aliased. In stock photos, you may need to go through and soften these up with the blur or smudge tools. The smudge tool set to darken or lighten mode will isolate your smudging to the dark and light areas, respectively. As this is a timely process to get right (but not overdo) it is a good idea to import the graphic into the NLE and test, or view it on an NTSC or PAL monitor throughout the process.

If your NLE or compositing application has a flicker filter (such as After Effect's Reduce Interlace Flicker effect or Final Cut Pro's Flicker filter) you may choose to skip this step. But remember, a 10-second clip means you are running a filter between 250 and 300 times (depending on video format) versus only one processing pass in Photoshop.

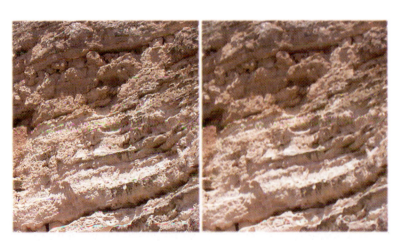

The fine details in the image on the left will "buzz" or vibrate on-screen. Be sure to soften the image to cut down on this problem.

Fixing Flicker During Scan

If you are scanning in previously printed items, such as newspapers, magazines, books, or inkjet prints, you will likely get a moiré pattern. This is caused by Photoshop scanning the small spaces between the previously printed dots. Most scanners have a de-screen filter in their software. If available use it when scanning previously printed items.

Fixing Flicker in Photoshop

If going back to the scan is not an option (or the problem persists), you can try the following options.

- Run the Median filter at a low value (Filter>Noise> Median).
- Run the Motion Blur filter (Filter>Blur>Motion Blur). Run at a value of 1 to 4 pixels at an angle of 90°.

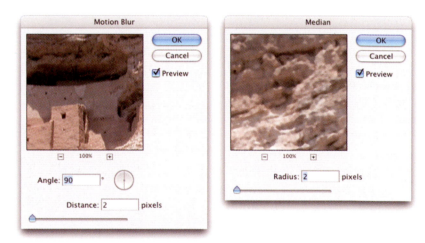

The Median and Motion Blur filters are useful for de-emphasizing details in the image.

Automatic Flicker Fix in Photoshop

If you are using Photoshop CS2 or newer, be sure to load the Video Actions set from the Actions palette submenu. Within, you'll find the Interlace Flicker Removal action. This applies a gentle but effective flicker removal (and only to the areas that really need it). If you are using an older version of Photoshop, be sure to visit the fine folks at Adobe Evangelists, where you can download the action (http://www.adobeevangelists.com/deflickerator.zip).

Alignment

The world is not flat, and sometimes it shows. Thin, crooked lines look very bad in video. If a photo is not straight (because it was shot or scanned at a slight angle), it is easy to fix.

Step 1. Open the file `Ch10_Alignment.tif` from the DVD-ROM. Access the Measure tool (**I**) and find a surface you think should be horizontal (or vertical).

Step 2. Click and drag a line to measure the angle.

Step 3. Select Image>Rotate Canvas>Arbitrary. The correct value is inserted automatically from the Measure tool.

Step 4. Crop the image or patch the gaps and make any additional repairs.

Shot Composition

Don't forget about cropping. At print resolution, a wide shot works. On video (especially if it ends up on the Internet), tighter is better. Always scan your photos at a higher resolution setting so that you can zoom in for fine corrections, and still have pixel data if you need to crop.

Step 1. Open the file `Ch10_Composition.tif` from the DVD-ROM, then select the Crop tool (**C**).

Step 2. Specify a target size (such as 720×540 for NTSC standard or 720×534 for NTSC DV in square pixels) in the Options bar. Be sure to type *px* for pixels if your rulers are set to inches.

Step 3. Crop the photo tighter, being sure to allow a 10% gutter on each side for action-safe purposes.

Zoom out and resize so you have room to expand the crop.

Aspect Ratio

Half the time your photos will be in the portrait aspect ratio. Chances are you can't send out instructions for people to rotate their TVs 90°. The Crop tool makes this an easy fix.

Step 1. Make sure the photo layer is floating. If it's called Background, double-click and rename the layer.

Step 2. Zoom out and resize the window so that you can see some of the gray area around the photo.

Step 3. Select the Crop tool (**C**).

Step 4. Specify a target size (such as 720×540 for standard or 720×534 for DV in square pixels) in the Options bar. Be sure to type *px* for pixels if your rulers are set to inches.

Step 5. Draw the crop; initially you will be constrained to the image's area. After releasing, you can grab the individual anchor points and crop beyond the image's border.

Step 6. You can clone the missing areas in with the Clone Stamp or Patch tool.

A little Clone Stamping and stretching of the background, and the aspect ratio is changed.

Step 7. Alternately, you may be able to "stretch" the edges by using the Free Transform feature. This works particularly well if the image is a portrait against a standard backdrop, or the background is nondescript, such as a sky. This down-and-dirty technique works very well if the sections to be filled fall outside the title-safe area.

Crop and Straighten Photos with Automation

When scanning, it's tempting to get lazy. Instead of putting every photo one at a time on the scanner bed, it's often easier to load up the flatbed. Photoshop CS adds the Crop and Straighten Photos command that creates separate files from multiple images in a single scan.

Performing the Crop and Straighten Photos Command

Step 1. Scan multiple images directly into Photoshop, or open a composite scan. For specific scanning instructions, see your owner's manual for the scanner; for general scanning tips see Chapter 2, "Pixels: Time for Tech."

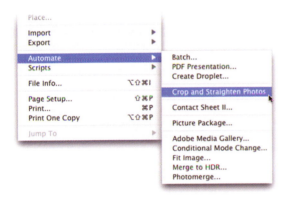

Step 2. Highlight the layer that contains the images. You can also draw rough selections with the lasso tools (hold shift to add more selections) to specify to capture only specific images to be processed.

Step 3. Choose File>Automate>Crop and Straighten Photos. Each image will be processed and open into a separate window.

If the Crop and Straighten Photos Command Fails

Step 1. Make a selection border around the image and some background.

Step 2. Hold down the key (*alt*) and pick File>Automate> Crop and Straighten Photos. This tells Photoshop that you only want to crop a single image with the command.

Step 3. If unsuccessful, just grab the Crop Tool and make the crop manually.

Better Edges for Crop & Straighten

You should keep an eighth of an inch between the images on your scanner bed. This should be an even color, such as the white or black from the scanner lid. Clear edges are the key to this command succeeding.

Keystoning

If a photo is taken from a low angle, distortion is likely to appear. Open the file `Ch10_Keystone.psd`. The strong horizontal and vertical lines make the distortion easy to see.

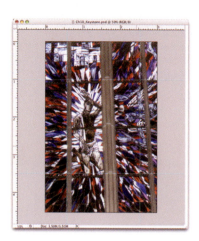

Original image has noticeable distortion.

Step 1. First get the picture properly aligned horizontally using the previous technique with the Measure tool. Don't worry about cropping yet.

Step 2. Zoom out and resize the window so that you can see some of the gray area around the photo.

Step 3. Make sure your rulers are visible. If not, press ⌘+R (ctrl+R).

Step 4. Drag two guides out to match the vertical lines. Line them up along the bottom edge if the photo was taken from a low angle (use the top edge for a high-angle shot).

Step 5. Make sure the photo layer is floating. If it's called Background, double-click and rename the layer.

Step 6. Access the Free Transform command by pressing ⌘+T (ctrl+T).

Step 7. Enable the Perspective transform by ctrl+clicking or right-clicking on a two-button mouse. Drag the top handles apart to correct the keystoning of the image.

Step 8. Enable the Distort transform by ctrl+clicking or right-clicking on a two-button mouse. Drag the corners individually to finalize the correction. Make sure snapping is off (View>Snap) or the fine-tuning will be difficult.

Step 9. Apply the transformation by pressing the Enter key or clicking the Apply button.

Step 10. Crop the image or clone in the missing areas.

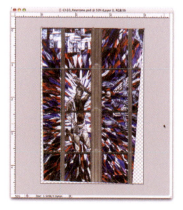

Once the distortion is corrected, proper perspective is regained.

Soft Focus

Under low light, cameras are more likely to generate a soft focus. The Unsharp Mask filter can fix blurring that is introduced during scanning, resizing, developing, or even when the image was first photographed. It works by finding pixels that differ from their surrounding neighbors (specified by the threshold) and then increases their contrast by a specified amount. The effect can be limited by specifying the radius of comparison. The filter works best in the Lab color mode when run on the Lightness channel.

Step 1. Choose Filter>Sharpen>Unsharp Mask. Select the Preview option so that you can see your changes. It is better to run the filter on the entire image rather than on a specific area.

Step 2. When you click on the thumbnail in the Filter dialog, it reverts to the prefiltered state. You can also uncheck the Preview box to A/B the effect. It is a good idea to set your Preview window to a 100% or 50% magnification to get the most accurate preview of the filter.

Step 3. Specify a value for how much to increase the contrast of the pixels.

Step 4. Adjust the radius slider slightly.

Step 5. Modify the Threshold slider, which determines how different the sharpened pixels must be from the surrounding area before they are treated as edge pixels. A value of 2 to 20 is often useful for preserving flesh tones and eliminating additional noise. The default value of 0 sharpens all pixels in the image.

If you get oversaturated colors, switch to the Lab image mode. Apply the filter only to the Lightness channel.

Step 6. You may choose to defocus grainy backgrounds manually with the Blur tool, or make selections, feather the edges, and run a blur filter.

You can open the file `Ch10_Soft_Focus.psd` to see this technique in action.

Fading Historical Sources

A common problem with old black-and-whites or sepia tones is that they fade. Attempting to adjust the Levels or Curves often introduces color artifacts.

Step 1. Leave the image in RGB mode, but strip away the color by choosing Image>Adjust>Desaturate or by pressing `Shift`+`⌘`+`U` (`Shift`+`ctrl`+`U`).

Step 2. Make a Levels adjustment and restore the white and black points.

Step 3. Make any additional adjustments as needed.

Step 4. Create a Hue/Saturation adjustment layer. Click the Colorize box and adjust the sliders until your photo is tinted to match your desired look. This adjustment layer can be used on other photos as well.

You can open the file `Ch10_Historical_Stamp.psd` to see this technique in action.

Digital Blues

Many digital cameras tend to roll towards the blue tones. A simple adjustment using the Color Balance command can help you restore the missing reds in the shadows, midtones, and highlights. Be careful not to overdo it, because a consumer television will tend to make an image redder on its own.

Color Balance is a quick way to replace the often-missing reds from a digital picture.

Missing Sky

Professional photographers spend a lot of time searching (and waiting) for the perfect sky. Unfortunately, professionals do not take many of your pictures. Skies will often be washed out and missing. By combining a few techniques, we can restore the sky in no time.

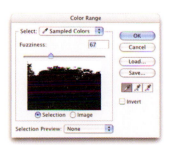

Step 1. Open the files `Ch10_Fix_the_Sky.psd`. Double-click on the Background layer and name it building.

Step 2. Select the sky using the Color Range method (Select>Color Range).

Step 3. Subtract any stray selections in the lower half of the photo by using the Marquee tool and holding down the ⌥ (*alt*) key.

Adjust the fuzziness slider for a smoother selection.

Need the Perfect Sky?

Be sure to check the demo of Aurora (The Natural Plug-In) from Digital Element. This Photoshop plug-in harnesses true 3D power and lets you restore missing details from photos. You can add:

- Sun and star effects
- Volumetric, ambient, and point lighting
- Water and reflections
- Haze and atmosphere

Try out the demo, and then visit www.digi-element.com to find out more.

Step 4. Reverse the selection by choosing Select>Inverse then click the Add Layer Mask button at the bottom of the Layers palette.

Step 5. Open the file `Ch10_Fix_the_Sky2.tif` from the DVD-ROM.

Step 6. Copy the cloud layer to your clipboard, then paste it into the `Ch10_Fix_the_Sky.psd` window.

Step 7. Place the layer on the bottom of the stack in your Layers window.

More Clouds?

Check out the free cloud plug-in called Cumulus from Flaming Pear on the DVD-ROM.

Step 8. Press ⌘+T (ctrl+T) to access Free Transform. Scale and position the clouds to taste. You may find it helpful to press ⌘+0 (ctrl+0) to zoom your view out when moving the layer.

Step 9. Apply the Transformation.

Damage Control

Every time I show people how to fix a problem or take something out, someone in the audience wants to know how to add damage back in. At some point, "mistakes" like flash frames, video snow, and light leaks became "cool." So in turn, clients will ask for a distressed photo look. Here are some of my secrets.

Grain

Sometimes you may want to add some noise back into a picture. The key is to put the noise on its own layer so it's easier to control and adjust.

Step 1. Open the file `Ch10_Grain.tif` from the DVD-ROM.

Step 2. Add a new layer above the photo and fill it with 50% gray (Edit>Fill and choose 50% gray from the pop-up list).

Step 3. Create grain by choosing Filter>Artistic>Film Grain.

Step 4. Set the layer to Overlay mode.

Step 5. Duplicate the grainy layer to increase the noise.

Scan Lines

The digital distortion look continues to remain popular due to several Web sites employing this technique. There are really several ways of doing this look. Here is one that can easily be accomplished within Photoshop.

Step 1. Open the photo `Ch10_Scanlines.tif` from the DVD-ROM.

Step 2. Duplicate the background layer.

Step 3. Run the Gaussian Blur filter on the duplicate layer to soften it. I used a value of 10 pixels.

Step 4. Load the default colors by pressing D.

Step 5. Run the Halftone Pattern filter (Filter>Sketch>Halftone Pattern…) Choose Line as the pattern and specify a width of at least 3 pixels. Apply the filter.

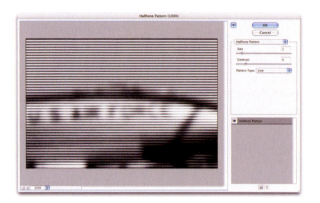

Step 6. Select the Move tool by pressing V. We need a tool without blend modes for the next shortcut to work.

Step 7. Cycle through the blend modes by pressing Shift + = or Shift + −. Adjust the opacity of the layer to taste. I used the Luminosity mode set to 50% Opacity.

As an option, you can add a Levels adjustment layer to boost contrast.

The lower image has had its focus area better defined by using the Lens Blur filter.

Lens Blur

Blurring an image can help your viewer find a focus point. Photoshop CS adds the long-requested ability for depth of field blurring. This allows some objects to remain in focus while others fall gently out of focus. Photoshop allows you to be very specific about how the ramping occurs, by using a depth map. This can be best be expressed by using an alpha channel.

- Black areas in the alpha channel are seen as being the foreground on the photo.
- White areas are seen as being in the distance.

Step 1. Create a new alpha channel.

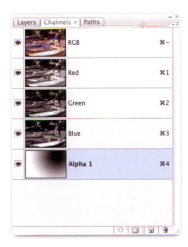

Step 2. Apply a gradient to the alpha channel; the linear or radial gradients work well for this. Be sure to use a black-to-white gradient, if needed reset the Gradient tool to load the default set back in.

Step 3. Run the Lens Blur filter (Filter>Blur>Lens Blur)

Step 4. Select the alpha channel from the Source menu. If needed click the Invert box to reverse the blur's direction.

Step 5. To get quicker previews, choose Faster. When ready to check the final appearance, select More Accurate.

Step 6. Adjust the Iris shape to curve or rotate them. This mimics a traditional lens operation. If you are familiar with how a true lens works, the experience is familiar. If you are more of an editor than a Director of Photography, then adjust to taste.

Step 7. Adjust the Blur Focal Distance slider until the desired pixels are in focus. Easier yet, you can click inside the preview image to set the point.

Step 8. If you want Specular Highlights, adjust the Threshold slider to set the cutoff point for highlights. Then increase the highlights with the Brightness slider.

Step 9. You can also choose too add or remove noise from the image. It's a good idea to add a little noise back into the image after blurring to keep the image evenly grainy.

Step 10. Click OK. If you no longer need it, you can trash the alpha channel.

Ripped Edges

The key to pulling off this effect is to use real paper for the ripped edge. Find a piece of poster board or cardstock and rip the edge. Make sure the paper is a different color than your scanner's lid.

Step 1. Scan the ripped paper.

Step 2. Make the layer float, then delete away the white.

Step 3. Open the photo that needs a "ripped" edge. Make sure the photo layer is floating. If it's called Background, double-click and rename the layer.

Step 4. Copy and paste the ripped layer into the photo's composition. Position the rip so the edge lines up in the desired area in the photo. Use Free Transform to modify the ripped layer. If there is an empty space, make a selection with the rectangular marquee; then Free Transform it to fill in the gap.

Step 5. Place the photo layer on top in the Layers palette; then create a Clipping Mask by pressing ⌘+⌥+G (ctrl+alt+G).

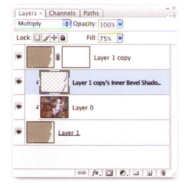

Step 6. To add a little more depth, place a copy of the ripped paper on top. Change its blending mode and add a beveled edge. Then ctrl+click on the layer effect and tell it to create layers. Isolate the carved edge, and throw away the other highlights effect layer.

To see this effect, open `Ch10_Ripped_Photo.psd`.

Old Photo

Want to make your own old photo? Just add noise and some tinting and you're there! The technique can even be turned into a layer style or action for quicker processing.

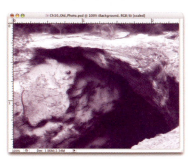

Step 1. Open the target photo.

Step 2. Desaturate it by pressing *Shift*+⌘+**U** (*Shift*+*ctrl*+**U**).

Step 3. Duplicate the photo by pressing ⌘+**J** (*ctrl*+**J**).

Step 4. Blur this copy using Gaussian Blur (Filter>Blur>Gaussian Blur). I used a 6-pixel blur.

Step 5. Add some Film Grain (Filter>Artistic>Film Grain).

Step 6. Select the Move tool by pressing **V**. We need a tool without blend modes for the next shortcut to work.

Step 7. Cycle through the blend modes by pressing *Shift*+▬ or *Shift*+▬. Adjust the opacity of the layer to taste. I used the Multiply mode.

Step 8. Add a Solid Color adjustment layer set to the tint color you want to use. Place this layer in Color or Soft Light mode for different results. Alternately, you could use a Gradient Map in a similar way.

To see this effect, open `Ch10_Old_Photo.psd`.

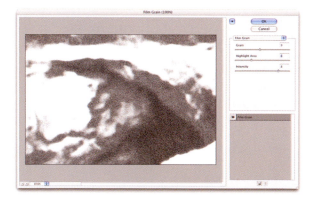

Distressed Photo

In typical fashion, I stumbled across this technique while trying to get more out of my filters. I frequently will push filters into situations they weren't designed for. As a case in point, we're going to use Flaming Pear's cool cosmos/starscape generator, Glitterato, to distress a photo. You'll find a fully functional demo of the plug-in on the book's disc.

Step 1. Open the target photo.

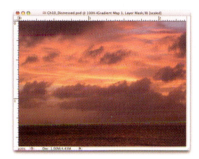

Step 2. Duplicate the photo by pressing ⌘+J (ctrl+J).

Step 3. Blur this copy using Gaussian Blur (Filter>Blur>Gaussian Blur). I used a 10-pixel blur.

Step 4. Duplicate the blurred layer by pressing ⌘+J (ctrl+J). Set the blurred layer to Multiply mode.

Step 5. Run the Glitterato filter and choose the Yellow Weave preset (Filter>Flaming Pear>Glitterato). Scale to taste with the Free Transform Command.

Glitterato from Flaming Pear does some really cool things!

Step 6. Soften the Glitterato layer by running the Median filter (Filter>Noise>Median). I used a 2-pixel average.

Step 7. Select the Move tool by pressing V. We need a tool without blend modes for the next shortcut to work.

Step 8. Cycle through the blend modes by pressing *Shift*+= or *Shift*+−. Adjust the opacity of the layer to taste. I used the Screen mode set to 50% opacity.

Step 9. Add a Gradient Map adjustment layer set to the Black-to-White gradient. Experiment with blending modes and opacity to achieve the desired look.

Step 10. Add a Saturation Adjustment Layer. Strip 70% to 90% of the chroma out of the layer.

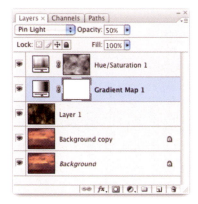

Step 11. Click on the Adjustment Layer's layer mask. Press *D* for default colors. Run the Clouds filter (Filter>Render>Clouds). Repeat by pressing *⌘*+*F* (*ctrl*+*F*) until you are happy with the random splotches.

To see this effect, open `Ch10_Distressed.psd`.

Hands On | 10

Motion Control 3D

Imagine if you could introduce the illusion of motion in the third dimension into a static image. By harnessing the power of Photoshop and After Effects it is possible. Add subtle motion and bring your photos to life. Make your audience do a double take to determine if the images are really moving.

By splitting up the image in virtual space, each individual element comes to exist on its own layer. Shift the layers in conjunction with one another or rack focus from foreground to background. The delicate movement created within the frame brings forth an unusual and attention grabbing effect.

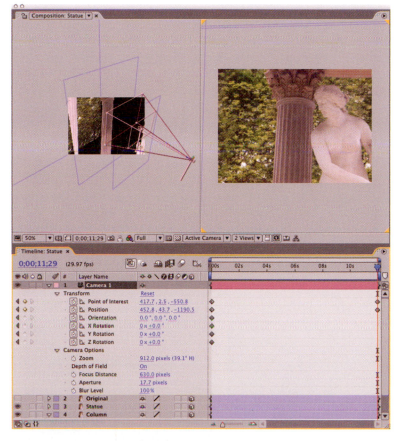

These techniques are not for the meek. You will need to have a strong comfort level with layer masking in Photoshop as well as a basic understanding of 3D cameras in After Effects. To complete this tutorial, we've prepped files, which will allow you to complete the exercise even if you haven't mastered these two skills. But if you'd like to take this technique to its full potential, then be sure to practice layer masking and working in 3D space.

You'll find Exercise 10 on the DVD-ROM.

PRO*file*: Larry Hawk

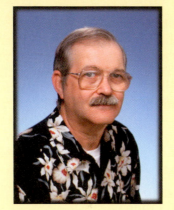

Larry Hawk is one of those Pros that is not well known, but should be. He has been making broadcast graphics since 1978. He is a pioneer and was among one of the first video pros to switch to designing on-air graphics exclusively on a Macintosh using desktop software such as Adobe Photoshop and Illustrator. Hawk works for KCCI in Des Moines, Iowa as their Senior Broadcast Designer.

"I use Photoshop and Macs as the ONLY graphic 2D paint program here at KCCI. That includes on-air news graphics for every newscast, promotion support graphics for the Avids, and sales graphics for use in the Avids and production studio," said Hawk. "I use Photoshop to design virtual sets for chroma-key walls and to visualize studio sets before they are built. I use Photoshop in almost all the stations print graphics like newspaper ads, billboards, banners, sales materials and KCCI stationary and business cards."

Hawk's reliance on Photoshop over the years has led to him developing specific skills. Long before editable type or even layers, Hawk refined his Photoshop skills so he could meet a tough broadcast schedule. Hawks use of keyboard shortcuts and power tools has enabled him to turn out more than 50 graphics in a single day.

"The use of Photoshop for television graphic requires some special tricks and skills to get the final result and remember to watch your levels of black and white and NTSC colors," said Hawk. "Using the correct fonts and colors in video graphics is always a challenge and I see a lot of bad fonts on television today—local and network broadcasts."

Hawk has mentored several interns and newbies (this author included). He truly is a power user, often leaving others wondering: "How did he do that?"

"I have had many college interns here at KCCI and new production employees that want to help or learn television graphics. First I ask how much Mac/PC experience they have and second 'Do you know the basics of Photoshop?'" said Hawk. "It's the MOST important program to learn if you are going to do any multimedia graphics. That includes television, film, Web and presentations."

To speed your Photoshop work up, Hawk offers this expert level tip:

"When removing light or dark spots from scanned photos, use the "Blur Tool" at 100% set to the Lighten mode for light spots and set to Darken mode to darken the spot without using the Clone Stamp Tool. This works best with a soft edge medium brush."

Hawk also extends some helpful advice to those working in broadcasting:

"Never stop learning or expanding your Photoshop skills, and if you are lucky enough to work at a broadcast television station, NEVER stand still in the hallway or someone from the newsroom will run you down on their way to the ENG room."

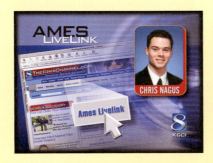

11

CREATING BACKGROUNDS FOR VIDEO

Backgrounds should match the "mood" of the piece. Don't just tile the client's logo.

While the video world often constrains itself to a 4×3 or 16×9 aspect ratio, the real world does not. When incorporating photos, type, and logos, there is often empty space. Some choose to leave this area empty (or filled with black). I like the color black more than most people—in fact, half my wardrobe is gray, charcoal, or black. But even I'll admit that it can get pretty boring for video.

To combat this, you can wallpaper the screen. You may choose to fill the screen with blended colors, repeating patterns, or soft textures. In all cases, Photoshop proves to be an excellent tool for creating backgrounds for video. If you choose to animate these backgrounds, they can easily be imported as layered images into After Effects, Combustion, and most nonlinear editing packages these days. In fact, 75% of my After Effects work starts in Photoshop. With this wide-open box of possibilities, let's begin.

Be sure to go with less saturated red tones. The use of gradual blends helps hold this background together. (Image courtesy American Diabetes Association.)

Gradients

Video has difficulty dealing with high-contrast ratios. Proper use of gradients exploits video's greatest weakness. A gradient is a gradual blend between two or more colors. These gradual transitions work very well on video, even after duplication to lower-quality consumer tape stock or being broadcast.

There are three major ways to access gradients:

- Gradient tool
- Gradient Fill layer
- Gradient Map

However, all three use a similar interface: the Gradient Editor.

Proper use of gradients can lift your work off the screen. Gradients are essential to natural color.

Gradient Editor

All gradients are edited using the common Gradient Editor. To access it, click on the thumbnail of the gradient that is loaded in the pop-up window or the Options bar.

Presets (A). You have several presets to choose from. If you want to load additional preset gradients, access them from the submenu (triangle icon). You can choose to replace the existing gradients, or append (add-on) to the loaded gradients. You can also load gradients that live outside the presets folder by clicking the Load button. There are several gradients available online, as well as with this book's DVD. You can also choose to save your own creations. The best place to store them is inside your Presets Folder (Application Folder> Presets>Gradients). This way they will appear in the submenu for faster loading.

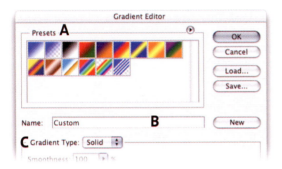

Name (B). For ease of recall, gradients can be named. If you are having a particularly boring day, express yourself here.

Type (C). There are two gradients to choose from: Solid and Noise. Solid gradients involve color and opacity stops, with gradual blends in between. Noise gradients contain randomly distributed colors within a specified range. Each has a different interface and will be discussed separately.

Solid Editor

Smoothness (D). Controls the rate at which colors blend into each other. It can be gradual or steep.

Opacity stops (E). Gradients can contain blends between opacity values as well. To add another stop, click in an empty area on the top of the gradient spectrum. To adjust a stop, click on it, and then modify the opacity field.

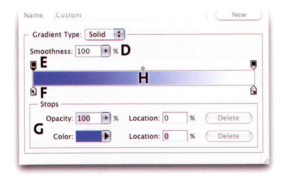

Color stops (F). The simplest gradients contain only two colors, but who said clients were simple? Often you may choose to use several colors (or even repeat colors) to achieve a desired effect. Double-click on the color stop to access the Adobe Color Picker.

Stop Editor (G). Selected gradient stops can be adjusted numerically. You can edit the opacity, color, and location (0%–100%, read left to right.)

Midpoint (H). Between stops are midpoints. By default, the midpoint is halfway between two stops. However, it wouldn't be Photoshop if you couldn't tweak it.

Noise Editor

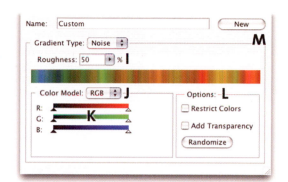

Roughness (I). Noise gradients use a roughness setting to determine how many different colors are used to create noise. Use the ▸ (comma) and ▪ (period) keys to cycle through your gradient presets.

Color Model (J). You can choose between three models: Red-Green-Blue, Hue-Saturation-Brightness, or L*a*b.

Color Range Sliders (K). Adjust the range of colors available to the gradient.

Options (L). You can choose to restrict colors (which has no apparent effect for broadcast-safe colors). You can also introduce random transparency. To create a new gradient, click on the Randomize button. Every time you click, a new gradient will be generated.

New Button (M). To add a gradient to the Presets window, type a name into the name field. Click the New button, and an icon will be added in the Presets window. This new gradient is not yet permanently saved, but stored temporarily in the Preferences file. If this file is deleted or damaged, or if you change presets, the new gradient set will be lost. You must click the Save button and navigate to the desired folder. Be sure to append the file name with .grd to inform Photoshop that it is a gradient set.

Gradient Tool

The Gradient tool can be used to manually draw gradients on a layer. To access the Gradient tool, select it from the toolbar, or press **G**. The Paint Bucket shares the same well as the Gradient tool, so if you can't find the Gradient tool, press **Shift** + **G** to cycle through your tools.

The Gradient tool can use any gradient created from the gradient editor or from the Presets menu. To select a gradient, choose from the available ones in the Options bar. You can also load preset libraries or manually load gradients by accessing the palette's submenu. To access the gradient editor, double-click a Gradient icon.

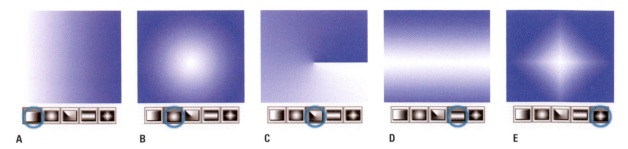

A   B   C   D   E

You now must choose between five options to build your gradient:

Linear gradient (A). Shades from the starting point to the ending point in a straight line.

Radial gradient (B). Shades from the starting point to the ending point in a circular pattern.

Angle gradient (C). Draws the gradient in a counterclockwise sweep from the starting point.

Reflected gradient (D). Draws a linear gradient symmetrically on both sides of the starting point.

Diamond gradient (E). Draws the gradient in a diamond-shaped pattern outward from the starting point.

You have a few available options to further modify the gradient. You can specify a blend mode to affect how the gradient is applied to the layer. (For more on the versatile blend modes, see Chapter 3, "Why Layers?")

- To swap the direction of colors in the gradient, select Reverse.
- To create a smoother blend by adding noise, choose Dither.
- To use a gradient's built-in transparency, check the Transparency box. If a preset gradient does not contain transparency, edit it and add opacity stops.
- To draw the gradient, click to set the starting point. Continue to hold the mouse button down and draw to the endpoint.
- To constrain the angle to multiples of 45°, hold down the *Shift* key as you drag.

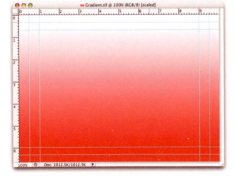

Gradient Fill Layer

A Gradient Fill layer creates a new gradient layer in your document (Layer>New Fill Layer>Gradient or from the Create New Adjustment or Fill Layer menu at the bottom of the layer's palette). Instead of drawing the gradient, you access its controls from the editor and a pop-up window. The gradient can be positioned by dragging in the open document. You can

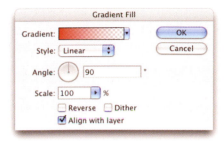

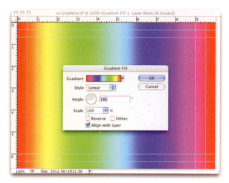

also change the direction and shape of the gradient. When you are satisfied, click OK. While this gradient is not very flexible, it can be included when creating an action. To confine the new gradient to a specific area, make a selection first. This will add a layer mask to the gradient layer. You can edit this mask at any time by highlighting the layer and using any painting tool or filter.

You can click the gradient to display the Gradient Editor. You can also click on the drop-down arrow to access the pop-up gradient palette. You can choose to set additional options, or edit the gradient if desired. All of the previous options and styles are available to modify the gradient. Additionally, you can move the center of the gradient by clicking and dragging inside the Image window.

Double-clicking on the adjustment layer's icon launches the gradient controls. You can then click and drag within the window to reposition the gradient.

Gradient Map

A frequently underused feature is the Gradient Map (Layer> New Adjustment Layer>Gradient Map). The Gradient Map applies a new gradient to the grayscale range of an image. A two-color gradient produces a nice duotone effect. Shadows map to one of the color stops of the gradient fill; highlights map to the other. The midtones map to the gradations in between.

A multicolored gradient or noise gradient can add interesting colors to an image. This is an effective technique for colorizing textures or photos for a background. I recommend using the Gradient Map from the Adjustment Layers menu, because it will provide the necessary flexibility to tweak your look. To modify the Gradient Map, access the Gradient Editor and adjust the previously

Gradient Map in AE?

Looking for the gradient map in After Effects? It's called Colorama. It's great for special looks and color treatments.

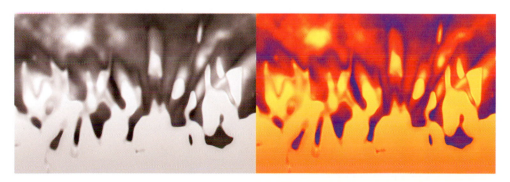

The Gradient Map adjustment layer is fast and flexible. You can also change the adjustment layer's blending mode to extend the effect's possibilities.

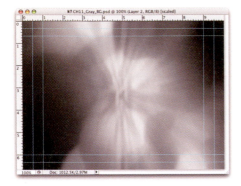

mentioned options. Remember, Dither adds random noise, which can smooth the appearance of the gradient fill, thus reducing banding. Let's try it out.

Step 1. Open the file `Ch11_Gray_BG.psd` from the DVD-ROM.

Step 2. Add a new Gradient Map adjustment layer by choosing Layer>New Adjustment Layer>Gradient Map. Then click OK.

Step 3. In the Gradient Map window, click the drop-down list near the gradient preview to see a list of thumbnails. These would work fine, but let's load some more.

Step 4. In the thumbnail area, click the triangular submenu to the right to show the list of gradient presets. Choose Color Harmonies 2 and click OK to load it.

Step 5. Choose the Orange, Yellow preset and click OK.

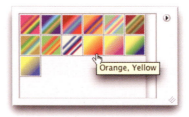

Step 6. It is now time to experiment with Blending modes. Press *V* to select the Move tool then press *Shift*+*=* to cycle modes. Color Burn, Linear Light, and Color look good in my opinion. Choose one you like (to move backwards through the blending list press *Shift*+*−*).

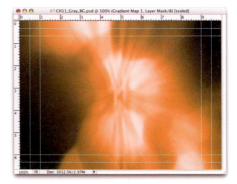

Working with Photo Sources

Using a photo as a background can be a very effective technique if handled properly. Remember this guiding advice: it's a background. Sounds simple, right? But be careful that the image you put behind your text or logos does not compete for attention or you will distract your viewers and reduce their comprehension. Here are a few techniques to try.

Defocusing

Gently softening an image works well. This can create a sense of image without dominating the screen. One of the most effective filters for this is the Lens Blur filter first introduced in Photoshop CS (if this is not available to you, then go for Gaussian Blur). Let's try it out:

Step 1. Open the file `Ch11_BG_Market.psd` from the DVD-ROM.

Step 2. Duplicate the Background layer by pressing ⌘+J (ctrl+J). By filtering a copy of the background, you can reduce the opacity of the blurred copy to modify the strength of blurring.

Step 3. Apply the Lens Blur filter by choosing Filter>Blur>Lens Blur. Adjust the filter to taste, but favor an out of focus image. Click OK when satisfied.

Creating a Screened Area

Another technique to make a "cleared" area for text involves using a screen. This is a very traditional print process, but it works well for video as well. Let's use the same image we had open for our last example.

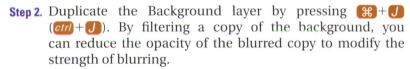
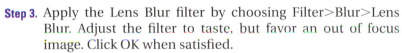

Step 1. Use (or open) the file `Ch11_BG_Market.psd` from the DVD-ROM.

Step 2. With the Rectangular Marquee, draw an area for your text (often referred to as the text block).

Step 3. Add a Levels adjustment layer by choosing Layer>New Adjustment Layer>Levels and click OK to create the layer.

Step 4. Drag the Gray Midpoint slider for Input to the left (a value of approximately 1.75 should work).

Step 5. Lighten the box by dragging the Black Output slider to the right (a value of 100 should work).

The advantage to using an adjustment layer is that you can continue to modify the background layers.

Gradient Maps

Gradient Maps aren't just for amorphous backgrounds; in fact they also work quite well on photographic backgrounds.

Step 1. Open the file `Ch11_Flower_Market.psd` from the DVD-ROM.

Step 2. Strip the color from the source using one of two techniques. The first Image>Adjustments>Desaturate is good if you are in a hurry. The second, a Black&White adjustment layer (available in CS3), does a much nicer job of making the grayscale file.

Step 3. We'll now soften the image with a gentle blur. Press ⌘+A (ctrl+A) to select All then choose Edit> Copy Merged to copy al layers to your clipboard. Paste this layer into the Layers Palette by pressing ⌘+V (ctrl+V). Blur the layer with a 15-pixel Gaussian Blur and set its Blending Mode to Screen.

Step 4. Add the Gradient Map by choosing it from the Adjustment Layer pop-up menu at the bottom of the Layers palette.

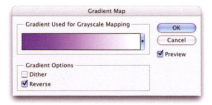

Step 5. Experiment with different Gradient Maps and Blending Modes to see the full range of design options.

Filtering

To further modify photos into backdrops, experiment with filters. While frequently overused, judicious application of the Artistic or Brush Stroke filters can simplify a photo to a pleasant image. Combine filters with fading and blending to achieve a modern look.

Sometimes the photo may serve just as a painter's palette. By applying several distortions and filters, it is possible to render a photo unrecognizable. All that is left behind are the dominant colors originally contained in the source. This is an excellent way to generate random color fields to use as backgrounds.

Using Patterned Tiles

Tiling a pattern or texture is a nice way to fill up space. The key is to make sure the texture size is large enough that the seams are not visible. You can find several collections of patterns available, but the key is to look for seamless ones. Thanks to the folks at Auto FX, I was able to include a sampler of seamless textures on the book's DVD. You can find 3000 textures as well as hundreds of free fonts at their Web site, http://www.autofx.com.

The easiest way to make a tiled background is to use a pattern adjustment layer. The adjustment layer will create a pattern that can be easily resized and positioned. Let's begin.

These utterly useless patterns are built in Photoshop. Don't let them scare you away. The Artist Surfaces, Rock Patterns, and Texture Fills collection are very useful.

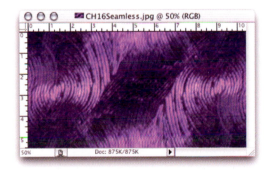

Step 1. Open the file `Ch11_Seamless.jpg` in this chapter's folder or any other seamless texture.

Step 2. Select the entire object by pressing ⌘+**A** (*ctrl*+**A**).

Step 3. Define the pattern and name it (Edit>Define Pattern). The pattern is now temporarily stored in your Preferences file.

Step 4. Create or open a safe-title document sized for your edit system.

Step 5. From the Fill Layer menu on the Layers palette, choose Pattern. The last-added pattern will automatically be selected. Adjust the scaling of the pattern, but do not exceed 100%, or the pattern will soften.

Step 6. You can click in the palette and reposition the pattern by dragging.

The end result, perfectly tiled and scalable. And at any time, the Pattern Fill layer is editable.

Step 7. To save the pattern, click on the drop-down arrow, then the triangular submenu icon. Select Save Patterns and give it a unique name, adding .pat at the end to inform Photoshop that this is a pattern library. All of the visible presets in the window will be stored into this library (you can ⌥/*alt* click to remove a thumbnail from the library). The best place to store them is inside your *Presets* folder (Application Folder>Presets>Patterns). This way, they will appear in the submenu for faster loading.

Step 8. Click OK to apply the pattern to the layer.

If you change the size of your document, the pattern will automatically expand or contract to fill the work area.

More Free Patterns

You'll also find a huge collection of seamless textures on this book's disc provided by the generous folks at Auto FX Software (http://www.autofx. com).

Creating Patterns from Photos

If you have a photo that you'd like to turn into a seamless background, there are two key techniques: Offset (with cloning), and the Pattern Maker filter introduced in Photoshop 7. If you are scanning the photo, scan it at a higher resolution so you have plenty of pixels to work with. Tiled patterns look best when the tiles have fewer repetitions.

Offset and Clone

The "original" method of creating seamless patterns involves the Offset filter. By shifting an image, the seams become clearly visible. You can then employ the Clone Stamp or Healing Brush to smooth out the edges.

Step 1. Open the file `Ch11_Brick.tif` to try out this technique.

Step 2. The brick photo contains several repeating patterns. However, the photo is slightly misaligned, which will cause problems. If you have horizontal or vertical lines, check alignment using guides.

The original image.

- You need to determine the specific misalignment. Select the Measure tool; it is in the same well as the Eyedropper tools. (To cycle, press _Shift_ + _I_.)
- Measure along a straight line to determine the misalignment.
- Select Image>Rotate Canvas>Arbitrary. The appropriate measurement is automatically plugged in and will correct misalignment.

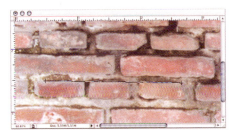

Use the Measure tool to determine if the image needs to be rotated into alignment.

Step 3. Crop a small portion of the tile. Try to get some of the mortar along the edges as shown. This will make a more natural tile.

The cropped image.

Step 4. Choose Filter>Other>Offset to push the image over; be sure to offset horizontally and vertically. Be certain to select the Wrap Around option. This step will show the seams that must be removed to create a tile.

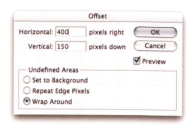

Step 5. Erase the seams using a combination of the Clone Stamp, Healing Brush, Smudge, and Blur tools. Remember to clone from several parts of the image to avoid "twins" syndrome. You can compare your pattern source with the file `Ch11_Brick_Processed.tif.`

Step 6. Select>All and choose Edit>Define Pattern. You can now use the pattern as a seamless tile.

Step 7. To use a seamless tile, add a pattern adjustment layer. Be sure to save your custom patterns to your *Presets* folder. The Save menu can be accessed from the Pattern palette's submenu. You can move the pattern at any time to tweak the fill. Highlight the adjustment layer, and then click in the composition's window and drag.

Open the file `Ch11_Wall.psd` to see the results.

After cloning the seams, the tile is ready.

Pattern Maker

The Pattern Maker can be found under the Filter menu in Photoshop 7 or newer. It can be used to generate tiling patterns. These patterns do not often match their initial source; the pixels are "scrambled" to generate a seamless tile. Because the pattern is based on the pixels in a sample, it shares visual characteristics with the original image. This filter works well for small patterns, but not on large objects. The Pattern Maker command is available only for 8-bit images, so you'll need to down-convert 16-bit or 32-bit sources. Let's explore this useful filter.

Step 1. Open the file `Ch11_Pattern_Maker.tif.`

Step 2. Size the image for your video editing system by cropping or using the Canvas Size command.

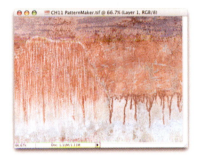

Step 3. The layer from which you make the selection will be replaced by the generated pattern. It is a good idea to copy the layer by pressing ⌘+J (ctrl+J).

Step 4. Make a selection with the rectangular Marquee tool around the area you want to use as the basis for the tile.

Step 5. Choose Filter>Pattern Maker.

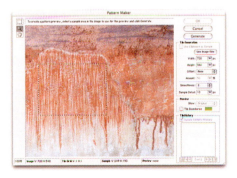

Sample and Remix for Better Patterns

 Increasing the Sample Detail and Smoothness improves the appearance, but significantly increases render time.

Depending on your source, you may need to increase the Smoothness and Sample Detail to a higher value. If the pixels in the sample lack contrast, increase the Smoothness value to decrease edges. If the sample contains details that are being chopped up, increase the Sample Detail value. Increasing the Smoothness and Sample Detail increases render time.

Step 6. Tell the Pattern Maker filter that you want to generate a full-size tile by clicking on the Use Image Size button. This produces the best results as the pattern is sized to fill the whole layer.

Step 7. Click Generate Again to create additional patterns. You can use the same options, or make adjustments and click Generate Again. You can flip back through all generated tiles using the Tile History panel.

Step 8. When you're happy with the preview, click OK.

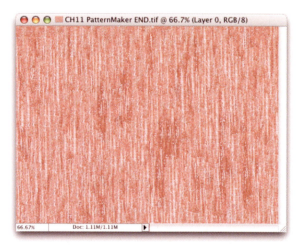

Step 9. You can now define the image as a seamless pattern using the previously described techniques of Edit>Define Pattern.

Softening the Background

Getting the right balance between focus and detail will require some experimentation. To produce a natural defocused effect, you can harness the powerful Gaussian Blur or Lens Blur filters. Unfortunately, there are no Blur of Focus adjustment layers (although you can harness Smart Filters in Photoshop CS3).

One way is to flatten the layered background, or make a copy and flatten it. This is inefficient, because it requires backing up and managing multiple files. A better option is targeted flattening, first introduced in Chapter 3 (page 60) as an alpha channel solution. The technique is relatively simple, but it opens up several new design options.

Step 1. For this technique to work, all layers must be floating. The bottom layer is likely named Background and is technically not a layer yet. ⌥ (*alt*)+double-click to float the layer.

Step 2. Select the topmost layer by clicking or pressing ⌥+ *Shift*+*]* (*alt*+*Shift*+*]*).

Step 3. Create a new layer by pressing *Shift*+⌘+*N* (*Shift*+ *ctrl*+*N*).

Step 4. Hold down the ⌥ key (*alt*) and select Merge Visible from the Layer palette's submenu. All layers will be flattened to the target layer.

Step 5. You can now defocus this layer by using one of the natural blurs such as Gaussian Blur or Motion Blur.

Be sure to hold down the ⌥ (*alt*) key when choosing Merged Visible. This will preserve your layers.

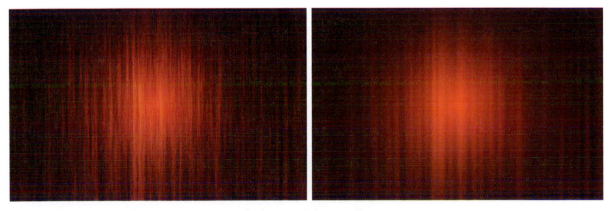

The softened background will make a better backdrop for foreground elements. Use blurred copies and blending modes for new looks.

This technique has many other implications, especially when blending multiple copies of layers together. Try targeted flattening periodically while building a composition. Apply assorted filters, such as Radial Blur (Zoom) to these intermediary copies, and then adjust blending modes. Several new techniques can be developed.

Some Recipes

To get you started, 12 backgrounds created entirely within Photoshop are included on the DVD. Instead of eating up page space printing long lists, I've captured these backgrounds as Photoshop actions.

Step 1. To load a set of actions, call up the Actions palette.

Step 2. Go to the palette's submenu and choose Load Actions.

Step 3. Open the `PSV Backgrounds Ch11.atn` file in the chapter's folder on the DVD-ROM. You can view each step by flipping down all of the triangles in the palette. You can also use these actions to quickly create the featured backgrounds.

Step 4. To watch the individual steps in an action, change the action's playback speed. From the Actions palette submenu, choose Playback Options>Pause for (X) seconds. You can now see the action playback one step at a time.

Remember, there is no exact science to these backgrounds, just some controlled experimentation and a little bit of luck. By employing the Actions palette, you can capture these experiments for later use. For more on Actions, see Chapter 12, "Automation."

You can see the recipe by flipping down the action. Feel free to modify these to create more automatic backgrounds.

Backgrounds in Action

You'll find an Actions file on the DVD for all of these backgrounds. Feel free to modify these backgrounds and use them in your projects.

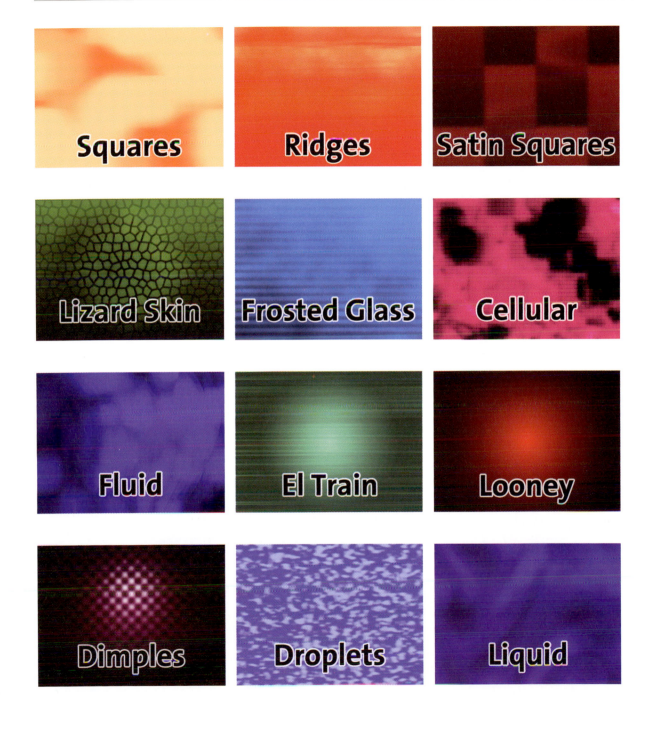

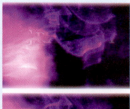

The Most Versatile Effect: Gradient Wipe

I couldn't discuss gradients without talking about the incredible Gradient Wipe. After Effects can use any gradient layer as a "transition map." Create or modify a gradient in Photoshop first. You can combine gradient layers, blend modes, and filters to create an interesting map.

Step 1. Import the gradient into After Effects.

Step 2. Add the gradient to your timeline but leave its visibility off. Make sure the gradient layer is the length of your composition.

Step 3. Apply the Gradient Wipe (Effect> Transition>Gradient Wipe) to the intended layer.

Step 4. Define the Gradient Layer source.

Step 5. Turn up the Transition's softness for a smoother transition.

Step 6. Start the transition 100% complete, and then set a second keyframe to 0% where you want the transition to end.

A linear gradient blends with the Clouds and Flaming Pear's Glitterato filters.

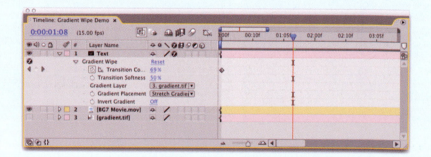

Not an AE user (yet)? Final Cut Pro has the same effect, conveniently called Gradient Wipe. Other NLE users should look for the Spice Master AVX from Pixélan software (http://www.pixelan.com).

See It Move

A sample project is provided on the DVD.

Hands On | 11

A Loop is a Loop is a Loop

Would you like to learn a technique that can save you thousands of dollars? If you produce videos, television, motion graphics, or DVDs you are probably quite familiar with looping backgrounds. These essential elements get used all the time under title graphics, inserted into lower-thirds, or as DVD menus. There are plenty of outlets available for purchasing looping backgrounds (chances are you already own some).

But this gets expensive, and does not give your video a unique look. There are several approaches to looping backgrounds, several companies (including the major players) take a lazy way out and don't make a full loop, but instead just dissolve to a graphic or different source.

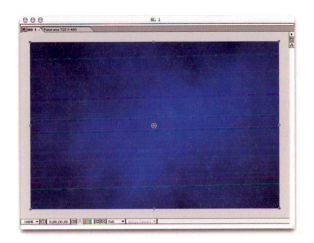

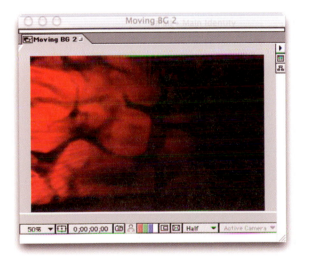

By combining the power of Photoshop and After Effects, you can create custom looping backgrounds. In this tutorial, we'll create two different looping backgrounds. You can harness these techniques to create very different backgrounds with just a little bit of effort and variation. Let's explore your options.

You'll find Exercise 11 on the DVD-ROM.

PRO*file*: Kevin Oleksy

Kevin Oleksy is an experienced video pro working for the U.S. Government. He produces re-enactments, documentaries, training pieces, and live satellite talk shows.

"I've been in video production for about 20 years and spent time in news as a cameraman, reporter, anchor, producer, technical director, and director. However, I've spent the majority of my career in post-production, doing military, corporate, and commercial editing and finishing," said Oleksy. "I was first introduced to the Avid back in the 5.0 days and haven't looked back."

Oleksy soon discovered the power of Photoshop to enhance his video projects. He started with Photoshop version 4 and has been a huge fan since. Photoshop also helped him expand into After Effects as well.

"When I worked for the military I mainly used Photoshop for Over-The-Shoulder graphics within the nightly newscast and the week in review. I would take still shots that highlighted the story and create a layered and keyable graphics that I could either fly in layer-by-layer live or import into the Avid for post work," said Oleksy. "I continue to use Photoshop to make mattes and backgrounds as well as titling. I do all of my titling in Photoshop... the flexibility and power for titles is awesome."

Oleksy thinks that Photoshop is the perfect companion application for any NLE package. He says it is a required skill for editors.

"Learning Photoshop is crucial in the video world. The flexibility and versatility it provides, allows you to create more visually appealing and hard-hitting productions. NLE's are great for editing, but their titling, masking and background abilities are often limited and weak."

To lean and keep his skills sharp, Oleksy takes every opportunity to attend training sessions and conferences. He's a firm believer in pushing himself to learn more.

"No matter how far you get, there's always somewhere further to get to. You can never say 'I have enough knowledge to be the best that I can.' Take every opportunity to attend training and tradeshows," said Oleksy. "Also, watch what other's are doing and try to build on that; some of the best ideas are generated by something you saw by someone else. No one is the be-all, know-all editing or graphics god, but the more you learn, the more you can learn!"

12

AUTOMATION

If you work in the video industry, chances are you're used to deadlines. Whether it's a rush to get the show on-air, a client sitting over your shoulder in the edit suite, or a replication due date, you've got hard deadlines to make. While we can't extend your FedEx drop-off times, we can get you some of your life back. You can save precious minutes (even hours) by learning to harness the power of Photoshop's awesome automation tools to meet your next production deadline.

Actions at Your Fingertips

Customize your keyboard! Photoshop actions can be mapped to the keyboard, giving you up to 60 customizable keys by using the f-keys and modifiers.

The Tools of the Trade

There's a lot of different ways to speed up your workflow in Photoshop. You have several built-in choices (and even a few third-party choices). Finding the right one requires an understanding of each. Photoshop's automation tools can be a huge time-saver, and most video pros find they are pretty easy to use. There are four major categories of automation techniques:

> **Actions.** Actions offer the ability to generate extremely complex results. Batch processing allows you to run an action on an entire folder of images.
>
> **Droplets.** By turning an action into a droplet, you can place the convenience of Photoshop Actions into a drag-and-drop utility on your desktop.
>
> **Automate commands.** These perform complex production-oriented tasks with minimal effort.
>
> **Scripts.** You can harness scripts to perform tasks that are more complex than actions. Creating scripts requires programming skill, but Photoshop ships with several useful scripts built in.

289

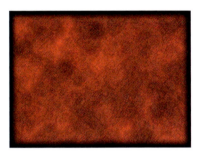

The built-in Rusted Metal action can be useful for text effects or backgrounds.

Actions

Virtually every command (and better yet, series of commands) can be captured and played back later. Basic actions will play back one command, such as a resize command or image mode change. In fact, these simple actions often can take advantage of your empty function keys on the keyboard. By combining the *Shift* and 🔧 (*alt*) key modifiers, a standard keyboard has 48 to 60 customizable keys.

An Overview of the Actions Palette

Call up the Actions palette (Window>Actions). Go to the palette's submenu and make sure that the Button mode is not checked. One of the first things you'll notice is a familiar interface. This is one tool that is clearly video-influenced: the Stop, Record, and Play buttons function like their video counterparts. The other three buttons appear similar to those found in other palettes. The Folder icon creates sets; a set holds individual actions just as bins hold clips. The Page icon creates a new (empty) action. The Trash icon performs the obvious role of deleting items.

To get started, let's work with one of Photoshop's built-in collections. Go to the Actions palette submenu and choose Textures.atn. (This file should have been loaded when you installed Photoshop.) Any actions stored inside of the Presets folder will appear in the submenu's list (Application Folder>Presets>Photoshop Actions). These texture actions are not specifically designed for video, although you may find them useful for creating texture layers.

Step 1. Create a new document using one of the video presets (File>New. . .).

Step 2. In the Actions palette, open the Textures set by clicking the triangle next to its name to twirl it down.

Step 3. Click on the Obsidian action and press Play. Photoshop quickly creates a realistic texture by combining several built-in filters and image adjustment techniques. Let's try another.

Step 4. Next, try the Rusted Metal option. Highlight the name and press Play.

Depending on your processor speed, Photoshop should have finished rendering about. . .now. I hope you are impressed. Flip down the triangles in the Actions palette and look at how elaborate some actions are. You may be thinking that these are somewhat interesting, but surely they will get old quickly.

This is not the case. Modifying actions is simple. The easiest way is to turn Dialog Boxes on. Normally, an action will play all the way through, using the original values assigned to the filters or image adjustments. By clicking in the column next to the action's name (the empty space next to the checkmark), you can enable dialog boxes for a filter or adjustment. These dialog boxes let you enter variables and influence an action's outcome.

Step 5. Try this out: turn on Dialog Boxes for the Rippled Oil action. Then press the play button.

Step 6. Click through the first few options about naming layers. Try different values for the Clouds, Chrome, Gaussian Blur, and Unsharp Mask filters.

Enable Dialog Boxes for future variations.

Same action, different outcomes. Turn on the dialog boxes for new results.

By modifying an action, several different outcomes are possible. Flip down the triangle next to an action's name, and you will see the list of steps. It is possible to turn on only some of the dialog boxes by clicking next to the specific step.

If you are excited by the little you've seen so far, keep reading. We have only scratched the surface. Actions open up all sorts of options, both for creative and technical outcomes.

The Best Things Are Free—A sample of Photoshop's built-in Image Effects Actions.

Commands
Frames
Image Effects
Production
Sample Actions
Text Effects
Textures
Video Actions

Using Built-In Actions

Photoshop ships with several built-in actions for various tasks. These actions are meant to solve basic problems as well as serve as a source of inspiration. You'll find eight different action sets built in; each set contains multiple actions.

Commands. This set adds function key shortcuts for several useful commands. This set is really unnecessary, since Photoshop now allows you to customize menus.

Frames. This set can be used to add border effects to your images. There are several attractive borders included.

Image Effects. These actions can process an image for specialty looks. There are some good actions in here worth trying.

Production. If production means print or Web to you, these are great. . . but then why would you be reading this book?

Sample Actions. A literal grab bag meant to generate ideas. Have a quick look just to see what is possible.

Text Effects. These are useful for creating some stylized text treatments. Unlike Layer Styles, these are not editable, so you may want to duplicate the text layer before applying the action.

Textures. These actions can be used to creating background layers or textures to overlay on top of a logo or text.

Video Actions. I made these actions just for you. . . really! I cowrote these actions with Daniel Brown from Adobe Evangelists. They automate several of the techniques we've covered in this book. So if things are automated, why learn the "slow" way? My goal is to teach you they why and the how. . . so use these actions to save time, but still know how they work. Each action contains a Stop command at the top, which explains how the action works. When you have a hold on how the action works, delete the stop so the action runs uninterrupted.

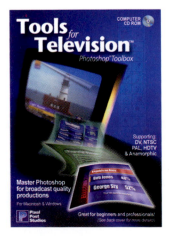

Finding Actions That Help the Video Editor

Entire Web sites and commercial products have been developed that significantly extend Photoshop's ability as a video tool. The accompanying DVD includes samples of some of these products.

Tools for Television. The Tools for Television Photoshop Toolbox package (http://www.toolsfortelevision.com) builds safe-title documents for every format, resizes square pixel documents, and helps build alpha channels.

ActionFX. One source that has both free and for-sale actions is the diverse Web site ActionFX (http://www.actionfx.com).

Members have access to thousands of Photoshop actions, as well as other add-ons. You'll find free items to try out before joining. You'll also find some great samples on the DVD-ROM.

PanosFX. A newer site that is really becoming one to watch is PanosFX (http://www.panosfx.com). This site has some incredible free actions as well as some very affordable and powerful tools for sale. You'll also find some great samples on the DVD-ROM.

Adobe Exchange. If you're not in a position to purchase add-ons to your system, there's one incredible free resource worth mentioning. With the release of Photoshop 5.5, Adobe launched a website originally called Action Xchange where users could share their actions; see http://www.adobe.com/exchange.

If you download actions from a Web site, they are probably compressed. After you extract or decompress the files, they should have the extension .atn after them, so Photoshop knows that they are actions.

When you successfully download actions (or create your own), you will want to store them in two places. If you install them into your Presets folder (Photoshop Application>Presets>Photoshop Actions), they will be available from the Actions palette submenu. Storing them in your Presets folder is convenient, but if you have to reinstall Photoshop, it will erase the Photoshop Actions and replace them with the defaults. Therefore, back up a copy of your actions to another location so that you can quickly load them in after future upgrades.

Creating and Saving Actions

Throughout this book, I've offered several keyboard shortcuts. Many of them will be useful, but I have no doubt that you've wished for more. Starting with Photoshop CS, keyboard shortcuts can now be remapped by choosing Edit>Keyboard Shortcuts... or pressing *Shift* + ⌥ + ⌘ + *K* (*Shift* + *alt* + *ctrl* + *K*). Despite this ability, you'll discover that not all commands are available in the Customize menu.

Wouldn't it be nice to have a single click for a new DVD menu sized document or create safe-title area button? You can by mapping an action to an f-key. Most keyboard have 12 to 15 function keys and 2 modifier keys, for a total of up to 60 keys that you can customize.

Mapping complex commands to your keyboard involves a few steps. First, you must create a set to hold your actions. Sets hold actions, and there's no limit to how many actions in a set, or how many sets you can load. For example, you could create a set with 60 actions mapped to the f-keys. You could have another set mapped to the same keys and simply swap it out. The possibilities are endless. Let's try it out.

Step 1. Open an image.

Step 2. Call up the Actions palette and click on the Create New Set Icon (looks like a Folder icon).

Step 3. Name the set, making sure to add the extension .atn at the end.

Step 4. Click on the new Action icon.

Step 5. Name the action and assign it to F2. If you want, you can also assign a color to the action. Colors help identify actions when you are in the simplified Button mode.

Step 6. Under the Filter menu, choose the De-Interlace filter (Filter>Video>De-Interlace).

Step 7. Click Stop. Congratulations! You've just made Photoshop faster and more video-friendly.

Step 8. Now save your work. Click on the action set (not the individual action, the entire set). Go to the Actions palette submenu and choose Save Actions. By default, the Photoshop Actions folder will be chosen. If it isn't, search for it in your presets folder. Name the set and make sure that the extension .atn is added after the name.

Repeat these steps as needed. Virtually every menu command or button can be recorded (although manual items from the toolbox do not record properly). Actions can be duplicated, modified, and deleted. Explore all of the options in the Actions palette submenu, look at other people's actions, and experiment by creating your own actions. With a little practice and imagination, you'll be amazed at what you can accomplish.

Another Action to Record

While layer styles are a great design option in Photoshop, they don't often travel well. After Effects can only import a limited amount of layer style options, and other video application essentially ignore them altogether. The approach we take in our studio is to save a layered PSD file, then a second layered file with layer styles flattened for import.

Step 1. Make a new empty layer and call it "Flat."

Step 2. Press ⌘+[(ctrl+[) to move the current layer below your styled layer.

Step 3. Press ⌥+] (alt+]) to select the forward layer.

Step 4. Link the selected layer to the layer called flat by clicking the link icon at the bottom of the layers palette.

Step 5. Choose Layer>Merge Layers.

Video #20   Using Batch Processing Commands

To learn more about batch processing, watch the video tutorial on the DVD-ROM.

General Tips for Better Actions

The Actions palette provides a video-friendly graphic user interface (GUI) for computer programming. Here's some general advice to get results quickly.

- Brush strokes, cloning, and most manual tools from the toolbox do not work. There are several alternatives, such as using a Gradient Fill layer instead of the Gradient tool.
- To play a single step of an action, double-click on it.
- Button mode lets you launch actions quickly; it's in the Actions palette's submenu. You'll need to disable it to get recording and editing features.
- Set the Playback Options from the Actions palette submenu to play back an action accelerated. Photoshop can process faster than it can redraw the screen.
- You can choose File>Automate>Batch to run an action on an entire folder of images.
- You can batch multiple folders at once. Create aliases or shortcuts within one folder that point to the desired folders. Be sure to click the Include All Subfolders option.
- Back up your custom actions to two folders, the default location and a secondary backup. This way, a reinstall or upgrade won't blow your custom actions away.
- To create an action that will work on all files, you must record some commands with the rulers set to percentage.
- Use File>Automate>Fit Image to resize images for a specific height or width.
- Photoshop will record the names of layers as you select them. This may cause playback issues, because the action will look for specific names.
- Use keyboard shortcuts to select layers and such so that the action won't look for a specific name for that step.
  - Choose layer above ⌥+] (Shift+alt+])
  - Choose layer below ⌥+[(alt+[)

- Choose top layer *Shift* + ⌥ + **]** (*Shift* + *alt* + **]**)
- Choose bottom layer *Shift* + ⌥ + **[** (*Shift* + *alt* + **[**)
- You can also arrange layers with shortcuts:
  — Move the current layer up the layer stack ⌘ + **]** (*ctrl* + **]**)
  — Move the current layer down the layer stack ⌘ + **[** (*ctrl* + **[**)
  — Move the current layer to the top *Shift* + ⌘ + **]** (*Shift* + ⌘ + **]**)
  — Move the current layer to the bottom *Shift* + ⌘ + **[** (*Shift* + ⌘ + **[**)

More Options with Actions

Turning on Dialog Boxes allows you to interact more with an action. In fact, it can open up hundreds of new possibilities.

Automate Commands

The Automate menu contains several useful commands that automate complex and repetitive tasks inside of Photoshop. These are worth fully exploiting, as they can shave hours (or even days) off a large project. When first starting, you may want to process a copy of your files to ensure that you do not accidentally overwrite a needed image. After a little bit of practice, this safety precaution can be bypassed.

Batch Processing

Photoshop allows you to run actions on an entire folder of images. This can significantly cut down your production time. You can resize a folder of images, de-interlace a bunch of screen captures, or remove the blue tint from a group of improperly exposed photos. Anything you may need to do to one image, you can do to several.

Batch...
PDF Presentation...
Create Droplet...

Crop and Straighten Photos

Contact Sheet II...

Picture Package...

Adobe Media Gallery...
Conditional Mode Change...
Fit Image...
Merge to HDR...
Photomerge...

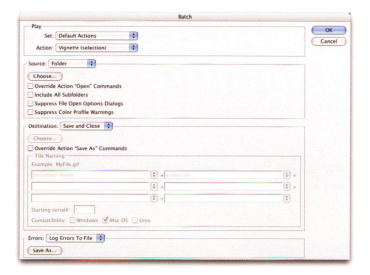

More Time. . . Less Work

Batch processing is a great thing for lunch breaks or overnight.

Batch Choices

You have flexible options when specifying the sources for your batch. You can choose to use Opened Files from the Source area to process all open documents. Additionally, you can opt to use the selected images in Adobe Bridge.

File Format Conversion

The Batch command cannot convert between file formats. Fortunately, this can easily be done using the Image Processor script that ships with Photoshop CS2 (or later).

PDF to Go (and Fast)

Be sure to check out the PDF Presentation command. It allows you to create self-contained slide shows that run in Adobe Reader (formerly Acrobat Reader). You can specify a folder of images and even set a transition and slide duration.

Step 1. To apply an action to a group of images, place those images into one folder.

Step 2. Make sure the action you want to run is loaded in the Actions palette.

Step 3. Choose File>Automate>Batch.

Step 4. Select the desired set and the action.

Step 5. Select the folder to process in the Source area. When you first start out, it's a good idea to work with a duplicate copy so that you don't accidentally erase your images.
- Select Override Action "Open" Commands in order to ignore open commands recorded in the original action.
- Select Include All Subfolders to process even nested files in the original folder.
- Select Suppress Color Profile Warnings to ignore any profile warnings.

Step 6. Choose a destination folder for the new images from the Destination menu. Choose None to leave the files open or Save and Close to overwrite the original images.

Step 7. Be sure to choose an error-processing method: Stop for Errors or Log Errors to File. By logging errors to file a large batch won't stop because of a single error.

Step 8. Click OK.

PDF Presentation

Adobe provides a useful Automation command called PDF Presentation that allows you to merge multiple images into a single PDF document. This is a useful way to send a lot of images to a client or as a way to present your work.

Step 1. Choose File>Automate>PDF Presentation.

Step 2. In the PDF Presentation dialog box, click the Browse button to select the images you want to include. Navigate to the folder that contains the images you want to use. In this case, navigate to the folder PDF Presentation in the Chapter 12 folder on the DVD and open it. You can now *Shift*+click to select multiple files or ⌘+click (*ctrl*+click) to select discontiguous files in a list. Additionally, you could also choose Add Open Files option to add files already open in Photoshop.

Step 3. Drag the files into the order you want the pages (or slides) to present. The topmost file is presented first. Simply drag them to reorder the images.

Step 4. In the Output Options area of the PDF Presentation dialog box, you need to choose from the following options:

- **Multi-Page Document.** This creates a PDF file with each image on an individual page.
- **Presentation.** This creates a PDF slide show presentation. This can be run as a stand-alone slide show.

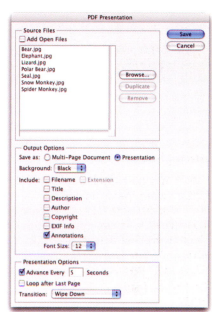

Step 5. If the Presentation option is chosen, you can specify the following options:

- **Advance Every [5] Seconds.** This allows you to specify how long each image is held. The default duration is 5 seconds. Unchecking this option causes the slides to be manually advanced. For this exercise, choose every 5 seconds.
- **Loop After Last Page.** This tells the presentation to automatically start over after reaching the end. This can be useful if the presentation is to be self-running at a kiosk.
- **Transition.** You can specify a transition to use between slides. For this presentation, choose Wipe Down.

Step 6. Click Save to create a PDF file. Navigate to the Desktop and name the file Slideshow.pdf.

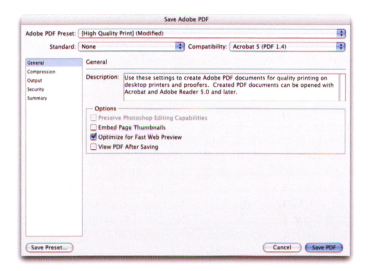

Slideshow.pdf

Step 7. The Save Adobe PDF dialog box opens. This allows you to pick a default compression setup or specify detailed options for the PDF document. Choose Smallest File Size to make the file easier to e-mail. If desired, you can also choose to add Security restrictions to the PDF.

Step 8. Click Save PDF to create the PDF file. A dialog box appears telling you when the PDF presentation is created successfully.

DVD Slideshow

Save your droplets in a convenient location for drag-and-drop.

Droplets

If you live in a drag-and-drop world, then droplets are for you. A droplet is a Photoshop action conveniently stored as an icon on your desktop. Files or folders can be dragged on top and batch processed. For example, I have created an action and then a droplet that converts an image to RGB mode while preserving layers. I could use this to ensure that all my graphics were in the proper mode for my edit. The important thing to remember is that you can't have a droplet without first having the action you want to put in it.

Step 1. Choose File>Automate>Create Droplet.

Video #21   Creating a Droplet

Droplets can make an action easier to use. To see how, watch the video-tutorial on the DVD-ROM.

Step 2. Click Choose in the Save Droplet In section of the dialog box. Specify a location to save the droplet where you can get to it easily. Many users set the target as the Desktop.

Step 3. Choose the specific set and action from the Set and Action menus. The action you want to use must be currently loaded.

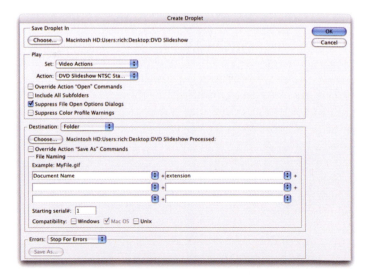

Step 4. Specify Play options for the droplet:
- Override Action "Open" Commands ignores any file names specified in the action.
- Deselect Override Action "Open" Commands if the action is designed to work only on open files or if the action contains Open commands for specific files needed by the action.

Step 5. Decide if you want to include all subfolders to process files in subdirectories of drag-and-drop.

Step 6. Select Suppress Color Profile Warnings to ignore color policy messages. These can cause a batch to hang waiting for your input.

Step 7. Specify a destination for the batch-processed files in the Destination menu:
- None leaves the files open without saving changes (unless the action contains a Save command).
- Save and Close rewrites the files to their current location.
- Folder lets you specify a new location.

Step 8. If Folder is the chosen destination, specify a file-naming convention for the batch-processed files.

Step 9. Specify an error-processing option from the Errors pop-up menu. Log Errors to File is generally best for batching. I use a similar approach in my batch digitizing, because this is when I stand up to stretch my legs a bit.

Web Photo Gallery

Here's a real-world scenario: Imagine that you're working on a video that needs some stock photos of the healthcare industry. Your clients provided you with a shot list, but they are across town and can't approve things until they come in tomorrow. After searching for the right stock photos, you've narrowed it down to 25 choices, about three per each shot needed. You could: (a) sit on your hands, (b) e-mail the client a bunch of attachments that are likely too big and will get stuck in their corporate firewall, or (c) just go ahead with your gut (and then redo things later).

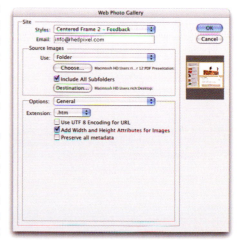

Photoshop provides you with a fourth option: one of the hugest time-savers of all, the Web Photo Gallery feature. After a couple of clicks, Photoshop can take an entire folder of images, instantly resize them for the Web, author a preview page complete with thumbnails, and set up the whole site while you take a break. Don't worry; it's perfectly safe and leaves your original files and layers intact. Just think

Storyboards Plus

Use the Web Gallery for dynamic storyboards.

Customize It

Photoshop gives you several templates to choose from for use in the Web Photo Gallery command. If you know HTML, or if you have a Web developer on staff, you can use a customized style for pages that feature your company logo and colors.

of the timesavings. You can e-mail the whole folder to your client or post it to your company's site with a blind link. (The folder is there, but there is no visual link on your Web site's home page; customers access it through a text link you send them.)

Best of all, Photoshop offers templates for gathering client comments. Be sure to check out the feedback templates, which create elaborate (but easy to use) Web pages. You can use these styles to collect precise client comments on a project's images. These comments are then e-mailed directly back to you so you can integrate the feedback into your show. Let's give it a try.

Step 1. Choose File>Automate>Web Photo Gallery.

Step 2. Specify the site's appearance:

- Choose a style from the pop-up menu. For this sample, choose one of the Feedback templates.
- Enter an e-mail or other contact info to be displayed on the page.
- Choose an extension (.htm or .html) for your pages. To determine which one, look at your corporate page. The .htm is more likely these days.

Step 3. Under Folders, specify the image source:
- Choose or Browse to identify the folder that contains the images you need. Don't worry about making copies first, the originals will not be permanently modified. You can reuse the PDF presentation images to try the Web Gallery out.

- Include All Subdirectories if there are folders inside your targeted folder.
- Specify the destination. You cannot save the images into the same folder they came from, because this would cause an endless loop. Specify a final destination.

Step 4. Modify the banner options with the rest of the site information that you want displayed.
- For Site Name, enter the project's name.
- For Photographer, enter your client's name.
- For Contact Info, tell the client whom to call with questions.
- For Date, enter the date that the page was built or modified.
- Specify fonts and font size. Remember, the default Web sizes on Macs and PCs differ. Text that looks just right on a Mac will be significantly bigger on a PC.

Step 5. Choose Large Images from the Options pop-up menu and specify how big the display images should be. A higher-quality JPEG will take up more space and take longer to load. A setting of 6 to 8 is usually sufficient for preview purposes. Be sure to tell Photoshop to display the file name as a caption so that you and your clients are speaking the same language when they call.

Step 6. Next, modify the thumbnails from the Options pop-up menu. Choose a size for the thumbnails, and then specify how many columns and rows that you want on each index page (if the style you choose uses index pages).

Step 7. If you want, modify the colors for the page.

Step 8. You can add a watermark over each image (such as Confidential or For Approval Purposes) by choosing Security from the Options pop-up menu.

When you run the automation, Photoshop will go into autopilot and begin building the site. In the destination folder, you will find an image's subfolder, a thumbnail subfolder, an htm subfolder, and an index page. The index page should be opened in a standard browser to view the preview site (or lightbox).

Posting Animations

Looking for a way to post animations on a Web page for clients with very low-bandwidth connections? I have found that the Web Photo Gallery works well for those clients who are stuck on dialup or mobile phones.

Step 1. In After Effects you can change a composition's setting to be 2 frames per second. This technique can also be used as a way to get an animation's storyboard approval. You can render out a PICT or TARGA sequence, then post two or three frames from each second to a thumbnail page.

Step 2. Add the Composition to the Render Queue.

Step 3. Specify a target folder and output an image sequence.

Step 4. Return to Photoshop and use the Web Photo Gallery feature.

If you don't have access to After Effects, many applications can output an image sequence. In fact, QuickTime Pro can convert a .mov file into an image sequence. Just be sure to throw away the frames that you don't want before creating a gallery.

The Web browser is an easy way to show your clients animations or storyboards, especially if your client has a slower-speed Internet connection or is traveling.

Contact Sheet II

A common practice is to send several photos to a client for review. Earlier we explored a dynamic photo gallery; let's take a look at a more static option called a contact sheet. Traditionally, it has been a common practice to create a contact sheet from rolls of film. This is done so the photographer or client could select images for printing at full size. This step was done for both convenience and costsavings.

A video pro can harness the practice of contact sheets to save time and money. By pulling multiple images into a PDF document, you can quickly send several photos to a client via e-mail. Let's give it a try.

Step 1. Choose File>Automate>Contact Sheet II

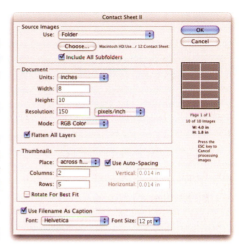

Step 2. The Contact Sheet II dialog box opens and prompts you to specify which images to use. This can be done by choosing from the Use menu in the Source Images area:

- **Current Open Documents**. This uses all images that are currently open in Photoshop.
- **Folder**. Click the Choose button, then navigate to a folder containing images. You can choose to Include All Subfolders to use images within any subfolders. For this example, click Choose and select the folder called Contact Sheet in the Chapter 12 folder on the DVD-ROM.
- **Selected Images From Bridge**. If you've selected images in Bridge *before* invoking this command, Photoshop will use those for the contact sheet.

Step 3. In the Document area, specify the dimensions of the paper, a resolution, and a color mode for the contact sheet. For e-mail uses, enter a page size of 8 × 10 inches and a resolution of 150 ppi, and use the RGB color mode.

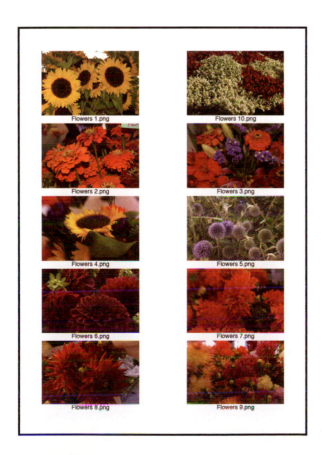

Step 4. Choose Flatten All Layers to put all images and text onto a single layer. This will reduce the overall size of the files. If you need the ability to edit photo captions, then leave this box unchecked.

Step 5. In the Thumbnails area, specify options for the thumbnail previews and document layout.
- Place—You can choose to arrange thumbnails across (from left to right, then top to bottom) or down (from top to bottom, then left to right).
- Enter the number of columns and rows you want for each contact sheet. When a page is full, Photoshop will automatically create new contact sheets. As you modify settings, a visual preview of the specified layout updates. For this, the folder contains 10 images, so choose 2 columns and 5 rows to maximize thumbnail size.
- Choose to Use Auto-Spacing so Photoshop will optimize the amount of space between each thumbnail.
- Deselect Rotate For Best Fit so the images appear properly oriented.

Step 6. Choose Use Filename As Caption to label each image with the source file name. This will allow the client to give better feedback.

Step 7. Click OK to run the action.

Step 8. Choose Layer>Flatten Image to merge all layers.

Step 9. When the file is done. . . Choose Save As and choose to save the file as a Photoshop PDF file for maximum compatibility and easy e-mail use.

A Little Space Is Needed

For best results, keep a minimum of 1/8 inch between the images in your scan. If the Crop And Straighten Photos command fails (which is very rare) then manually crop the images with the Crop tool.

Crop and Straighten Photos

Looking to save some time when scanning images? You can often fit more that one image onto a scanner bed at a time. When placing the images, be sure to allow a small space between each photo. You can then use the Crop and Straighten Photos command to separate each image into its own document window. Let's give it a try.

Step 1. Open the file Crop and Straighten.tiff from the Chapter 12 folder on the DVD-ROM. If you prefer to use your own scanner, just scan in a few images simultaneously on your own scanner.

Step 2. Choose File>Automate>Crop and Straighten Photos.

Step 3. Each image should be cropped, straightened, and moved into its own document window.

Scripting

Scripting in Photoshop offers a more powerful automation technology than actions. With scripts, you can choose to perform more elaborate tasks than an action can perform. Scripting was first introduced with Photoshop CS, and each version has added greater support. Photoshop ships with built-in scripts that are very useful.

Export Layers to Files

As you work with different video applications, you will find that support for Photoshop layers is not universal. To get past this limitation, Photoshop offers a useful script called Export Layers to Files. Photoshop allows you to convert a layered file into a series of individual files. You can choose to create a PSD, BMP, JPEG, PDF, Targa, or TIFF file for each layer. Layers are named automatically as they are

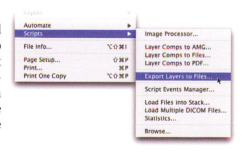

Sending Layers to Files

Need to import a layered file into a program that doesn't recognize layers (such as Apple's LiveType)? Be sure to check out the great script called Export Layers to Files.

created; however, you have options that you can use for naming. Let's give it a try.

Step 1. Open the file `Scripts_Demo.psd` from the Chapter 12 folder on the DVD-ROM.

Step 2. Choose File>Scripts>Export Layers to Files. . . to run the script.

Step 3. In the Export Layers to Files dialog box, choose a destination by clicking the Browse button. For this sample, create a new folder on the desktop called Export.

Step 4. Enter a descriptive name into the File Name Prefix text box.

Step 5. Choose a File Type and set any options for the exported file. For our sample, choose PSD and check the Maximize Compatibility box.

Select the Visible Layers Only option if you want to export only layers that are visible.

For video workflow, you can leave the ICC Profile option unchecked

Step 6. Click Run.

Image Processor

The Image Processor command is an extremely useful production tool that will allow you to quickly reformat and size images to meet your workflow. The Image Processor script made its official debut in Photoshop CS2, but you can find also find it online under the name Dr. Brown's Image Processor.

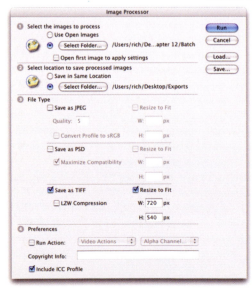

The Image Processor script can be used to convert and process multiple images. It differs from the Batch command in that you don't need to first create an action. The image processor can be used for any of the following tasks:

- To convert images to JPEG, PSD, or TIFF format. You can also convert files simultaneously to all three formats.
- To process a set of Camera Raw files using the same Camera Raw options.
- To resize images to fit within a specified pixel dimension.
- To embed a color profile into images or convert files to sRGB and save them as JPEG images for the web.
- To include copyright metadata into the processed images.

The Image Processor can be used with PSD, TIFF, JPEG, or camera raw files. Let's give it a try.

Step 1. Choose>File>Scripts>Image Processor.

Step 2. Select the images that you want to process. You can use the open images or navigate to a folder to select images. Click the Select Folder button and navigate to the folder called Batch in the Chapter 12 folder on the DVD-ROM.

Step 3. Select a location to save the processed images. You can choose the Exports folder you created previously on your Desktop.

Step 4. Select the file types and options you wish to convert to.
- **Save As JPEG.** This sets the JPEG quality between 0 and 12. You can also choose to resize the image and convert it to sRGB color profile.
- **Save As PSD.** This sets the PSD options. You can also resize the image and choose to Maximize Compatibility.
- **Save As TIFF.** This saves images in the TIFF format with LZW compression. You can also resize the image.
- For our example, choose TIFF and choose to resize to 720×540 pixels.

Step 5. You can choose from other processing options.
- **Run Action.** If an action is loaded into your Actions palette, you can run it on the image during the process.
- **Copyright Info.** You can add copyright metadata to the image.
- For our example, add the your name to the copyright information.

Step 6. Click Run to process the multiple images.

Video #23   Using the Image Processor

If you need to convert or resize several images, then be sure to check out the Image Processor command. See how it works by watching the video tutorial on the DVD-ROM.

Creating and Using Additional Scripts

Writing scripts is far more challenging than actions. Actions use a GUI with obvious controls (Play, Record, Stop). Scripting, on the other hand, requires you to use a scripting language. Depending on the version of Photoshop that you are using, as well as the operating system, you can use AppleScript, Visual Basic, or JavaScript.

If you've successfully tried your hand at writing an After Effects expression, then you may feel at home scripting. To find out (a lot) more about scripting, look inside your Photoshop Application

Photoshop CS3 AppleScript Ref.pdf

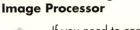

Photoshop CS3 JavaScript Ref.pdf

Photoshop CS3 Scripting Guide.pdf

Photoshop CS3 VBScript Ref.pdf

Sample Scripts

Utilities

folder. Inside the Scripting Guide folder you'll find four PDFs to help you learn scripting.

If the thought of computer programming makes you want to shutdown your computer and hide, you can rely on others for scripts. Inside the same Scripting Guide folder, you'll find sample scripts to try out (although most are gimmicky). There are some truly wonderful examples of scripting available at the Adobe Exchange Web site, http://www.adobe.com/exchange.

You can load scripts by choosing File>Script>Browse. If you'd like a script to permanently appear in the scripts menu, place it into the Scripts folder inside your Presets folder.

Using Adobe Bridge

All Adobe applications support the use of Adobe Bridge, which functions as a robust file browser. Besides sifting through images, it can also be harnessed as an automation tool. Bridge allows you to do simple tasks such as rename items as well as move, copy, and delete files. One of the most useful features is the ability to modify a group of images.

Accessing Bridge

By default, Adobe Bridge is not visible. To enable it you can choose File>Browse to launch Adobe Bridge. You may also want to modify your Photoshop preferences to tell Bridge to launch whenever you open Photoshop. Open your Preferences window by pressing ⌘+K (ctrl+K), then check the box next to Automatically Launch Bridge from the General area.

To select a file in Bridge, click on it. To choose multiple files, hold down the Shift key; for noncontiguous files hold down the ⌘ key (ctrl key). When you have the desired images selected, press Return/Enter on the keyboard, or double-click.

Bridge for Organization

You can rotate, delete, and move images from within Bridge.

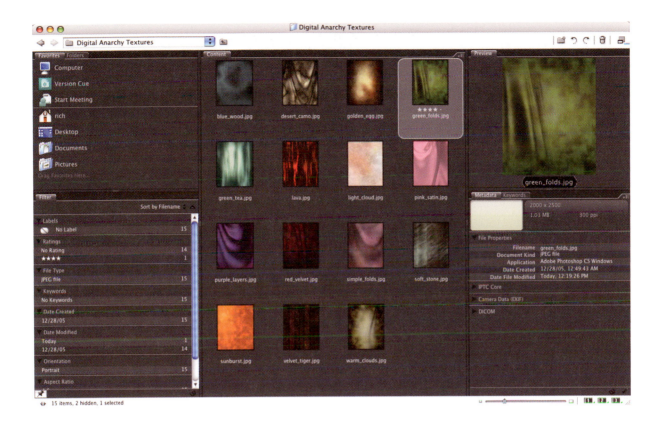

Batching Items

There are several items you can batch-process in Bridge. You can choose Tools>Batch Rename and rename a group of images. You can *Shift*+click to select a group of images, and then press the *Delete* key to erase the images. You can also move a group of images from one folder to another. Experienced Photoshop users may tend to overlook Bridge, but it's worth the effort to learn it because Bridge can save a lot of time.

There's a lot more to Adobe Bridge. Be sure to check out the Help menu within Bridge to see more about the program. If you like what you find, you can dig much deeper and explore Bridge. There are dedicated books all about Bridge; be sure to check out the one by author Terry White, who is recognized as the leading expert.

Hands On | 12

Creating a DVD Slideshow

One of the best things about DVDs is the bonus material, whether it's a behind the scenes feature, extra interviews, or a look at the storyboards. DVD slideshows are also a mainstay of DVDs because they take up very little space on the disc.

But making slideshows isn't as easy as you might think. Sure, the authoring side is pretty straightforward; most DVD authoring applications support drag-and-dropping folders of images. But, if those images aren't sized right, you'll have problems: strange cropping, bad aliasing, and softening. Just because DVD software can process still photos doesn't mean it should (after all, the word Photo appears nowhere in the name DVD Studio Pro or Encore DVD).

When it comes to photo slideshows, its Photoshop you'll want to turn to. But with all that cropping, and resizing, it sounds like you've got a lot of work ahead of you… or not. By harnessing the power of actions and automation, Photoshop can get the job done in a jiffy.

You'll find Exercise 12 on the DVD-ROM.

DVD Slideshow

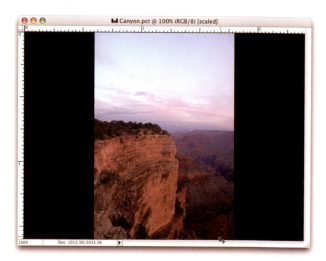

PRO*file*: John Mark Seck

John Mark Seck is the President of BlackCherry Digital Media Inc., a company providing high-end 3D animation, visual fx and motion graphics to film, broadcast and corporate clients. At BlackCherry Photoshop is the Swiss army knife in their arsenal of digital content creation programs.

"Every project we work on uses Photoshop as an integral part of the process," says Seck. "From texture creation, graphics creation and layout, digital matte painting, keying, roto it just gets used everywhere."

Seck emphasizes that Photoshop skills are essential for anyone involved in digital content creation today and especially for animation and motion graphics.

"At BlackCherry we've made extensive use of Photoshop for our museum exhibit work", say Seck. "It gives us the ability to retouch, color correct, and make levels adjustments to increase production value.

"The dust and scratches filter is a handy quick fix for retouching a photo. I think many people starting out think this filter will add rather then correct dust and scratches," said Seck. "Everyone should become good friends with the clone stamp tool and the healing brush when it comes to retouching photos."

Seck offers additional advice on getting the most out of Photoshop:

- "The layer blending modes are probably my favorite options in Photoshop," said Seck. "I think when people are starting out they tend to avoid these effects. It doesn't really matter if you understand exactly what each mode is doing. The best thing is to dive in and try out the different looks each mode will achieve."

- "Actions combined with batch processing is a tremendously powerful combination and a huge timesaver," said Seck. "If you ever do anything more than once you should have an action for that function."

- "We tend to use Photoshop layers in conjunction with After Effects and Maya a lot. We layout multi-layered animation and texture elements for import into our animation apps."

"While technology changes quickly some aspects of production are now very standardized and hence skill sets are more clearly defined. For content creation employers it really means there is a base level of knowledge and skill expected from any potential employee and strong Photoshop skills are at or near top of the list", say Seck.

Seck further emphasizes the need for diversification in the digital artist. "Develop a variety of skills. These may include editing, graphic design, motion graphics, 3D animation and visual effects. This is a big chunk to chew on, but if you give yourself time, you find they all start to tie together and you develop a very marketable skill set. You have to be flexible, have a broad base of skills but also make sure you have a focus, something you do really well."

Diversification goes way beyond what software packages you can run however. To get back to content creation as an art form, it's necessary to reach beyond software "party" lines.

"I would say often these days there is too much emphasis on what software package(s) you know," said Seck. "While very important software is just a starting point and is the easy part. Design skills and artistic aesthetics are much more elusive. Visit your local art galleries, stay in touch with current trends and be open to new ideas."

13

THE ROAD TO VIDEO

If you bought this book, then you must intend for your graphics to end up on video. If you're on a deadline (okay, you're always on a deadline), you may have jumped to this chapter right away. Please go back and start at the beginning of the book. In one chapter, it would be impossible to discuss the several issues that make designing video graphics a challenge.

If you've made it through most of the book, then you are likely anxious to see your work on screen, on air, or on tape. I realize that Photoshop can be painful at times. Unlike your NLE, Photoshop is not designed to exclusively be a video application. There are very few safety nets to keep you from choosing an adjustment or filter that will send your graphic reeling into the land of nonbroadcast-safe.

Copyright Breany/iStockphoto.

Purpose of this Chapter

What you will find in this chapter are several methods to check your work to ensure it is ready for video. We'll also explore techniques for getting your client to buy in and sign off, as well as some general tips on resizing and deciding upon the right file format. Finally, we'll discuss the importance of file extensions and reinforce methods to prepare for future changes (because "approved" only means "for now").

The tips in this chapter come from years of experience. What you'll find here are strategies for success. Techniques for tiny budgets, as well as those for deeper pockets, are offered. Please go with the best solution you can afford.

Copyright Hemera PhotoObjects

Copyright SoundSnaps/iStockphoto

Final Testing on an NTSC/PAL Monitor

There's no way around it: you have to test your graphics. If you're building them in the edit suite, this should be easy. But what happens if you're building them for someone else, or you're on the road, or you don't own a vectorscope? There are lots of challenges in creating video graphics; it is essential that you test the graphics on your final intended output device.

Testing During the Design Stage on Your Computer

The best situation when designing video graphics is to have a broadcast monitor hooked up to your system while you are designing the graphics. This will allow you to check for interlace flicker, safe-color concerns, and contrast issues while you design. There are several possible solutions for this setup; the right solution will depend upon your budget and available technology.

Video Preview Command

In Photoshop CS2, Adobe introduced the Video Preview command. This allows Photoshop to send a preview of the graphic over a FireWire cable to a DV device. Photoshop gives you several options for specifying aspect ratio.

Video Preview Tech In-Depth

- The Video Preview plug-in only works if you are using RGB, Grayscale, or Indexed Color mode (but you should *NEVER* work in Indexed Color mode for video anyway).
- The plug-in will convert 16-bit images to 8-bit images on the fly (but will not function on a 32-bit image).
- Transparency data such as alpha channels are ignored.

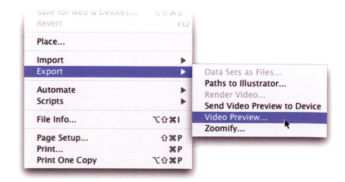

Step 1. Attach a FireWire based device that uses the DV protocol to your computer. Then attach a broadcast quality display. Let the devices warm up for a minute before launching Photoshop.

Step 2. Launch Photoshop and open or create a video-sized document.

Step 3. To set up the Video Preview properties, choose File>Export> Video Preview . . . . This will give you full control over output options. For future outputs where nothing has changed in hardware, you can just choose File>Export>Send Video Preview to Device.

Step 4. In the Device Settings area, you can adjust the following options for a more accurate preview.
- **Output Mode.** You can choose NTSC or PAL to match your hardware. If you are seeing black patches, then you have likely picked the wrong standard.
- **Aspect Ratio.** Here you specify the aspect ration for the device you have hooked up (not of the Photoshop file). This setting is important, as it impacts the Image Options.

Frame Size Issues

 While the Video Preview plug-in works with all sizes of documents, only those that match the DV standard (such as NTSC DV, NTSC DV Widescreen, and PAL D1/DV) will appear at their full size. Others such as HD (or even NTSC D1) may need to be scaled to match your output format. Scaling can diminish the accuracy of the preview.

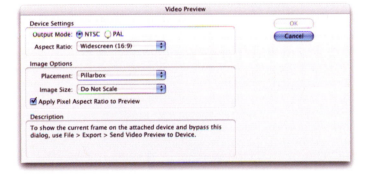

Step 5. In the Image Options area, you can adjust additional options that impact how the image is displayed when aspect ratios of graphics and monitors aren't identical. Remember, the Placement options available will vary based upon the Aspect Ratio you set in Step 4.
- **Center.** This places the center of the image at the center of the screen. Any edges that fall outside the display edges of the video monitor will be cropped.
- **Pillarbox.** When a 4:3 image is shown on a 16:9 display, the image is centered. On the outside, gray bands appear to the left and right of the image. This option is only available if the device aspect ratio is set to Widescreen (16:9).
- **Crop to 4:3.** When a 16:9 image is shown on a 4:3 display, the image is centered. The left and right edges must then

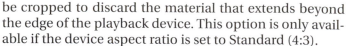

Need a FireWire Bridge?

Looking for a digital to analog converter (also called a DA)? I highly recommend those from Canopus (www.canopus.com). They offer several different models with many features at a variety of price points.

be cropped to discard the material that extends beyond the edge of the playback device. This option is only available if the device aspect ratio is set to Standard (4:3).

- **Letterbox.** When a 16:9 image is shown on a 4:3 display, the image is centered. This maintains the aspect ratio without distortion. On the outside, gray bands appear to the top and bottom of the image. This option is only available if the device aspect ratio is set to Standard (4:3).
- **Crop To 14:9/Letterbox.** This option is an alternative to displaying widescreen content on a 4:3 monitor. The widescreen image cropped to a 14:9 aspect ratio with black bands on the top and bottom of the image.

Step 6. You must next specify in the Image Size pull-down menu how you want document pixels to be scaled to match the output device.

- **Do Not Scale.** This is the most common choice. It will apply no vertical scaling to the image. The image must then be cropped using the methods addressed in Step 5.
- **Scale To Fit Within Frame.** The image frame will either increase or decrease. For example, a 16:9 image appears on a 4:3 display as letterboxed, and a 4:3 image appears on a 16:9 display as pillarboxed.
- **Apply Pixel Aspect Ratio to Preview.** Leave this checked to utilize the document's own pixel aspect ratio settings.

Step 7. Click OK to invoke the Video Preview.

High-End Video Cards

There is no better way to preview your graphics than using a high-end video card and a broadcast monitor. You can purchase a video card for your system such as one made by DigitalVoodoo, BlueFish444, BlackMagic, or AJA. These cards not only give you video I/O for your editing system, but they also allow you to extend your desktop to the card and work correctly on a video display.

These solutions can be pricey, but they open up several possibilities. A video card with Serial Digital Interface or component output will allow you to check your graphics. Hands down, this is the best solution, but prepare to dig deep into your pockets. Cards will range between $800 and $14,000, depending on the types of inputs and outputs you want. If you already have a nonlinear edit system hooked up at your facility, you may just choose to harness its ability to output to a video monitor or a scope for testing purposes.

The extended desktop or mirroring option will vary based on your video card manufacturer. Many will ship with their own specialty software to extend Photoshop's capabilities. Others depend upon additional software, such as Synthetic Aperture's Echo Fire.

Digital Voodoo manufactures several popular video cards designed for video editors and broadcast designers.

Low-End Video Cards and Laptops

The proliferation of computers with video ports is on the rise, due in part to features like Media Center from Microsoft and Front Row from Apple. Additionally, several laptops come with AV or S-Video ports. These are primarily designed so that business-people can send presentations out to a TV.

These types of connections allow you to plug in an S-Video cable. You can then check your Displays or Monitors control panel to enable the port. You may have to restart your machine. If you have enough VRAM, you may be able to drive the main screen and video monitor simultaneously.

Step 1. Hook the video card up to a consumer television.

Step 2. Set Photoshop to Full Screen Mode (press **F** two or three times).

Step 3. To remove palettes, press the Tab key.

Step 4. You can now output and test your graphics on consumer equipment, which is where your audience will probably see them.

These cards do not necessarily scale the video properly and may have interlace issues. There is also a chance that the luminance/chrominance will be slightly off. But even with those negatives, this method is still a better option than *not* previewing on a television.

Software Solutions for Checking Graphics

If you have the budget, there is extra software you may want to add to extend Photoshop's capabilities. These three tools overlap, so you will likely need only one of the three. They are arranged with the most full-featured (and expensive) first.

Echo Fire

This tool has long been regarded as an absolute essential. While Photoshop's newer ability to send video out over FireWire slightly diminishes EchoFire's value, it does not eliminate it by any

means. Photoshop and After Effects users have the ability to send their work to a video monitor for immediate previews. With After Effects, this includes full-motion previews with audio. The plug-in works with Mac and PC FireWire devices or several cards from Digital Voodoo, AJA, Pinnacle Systems, Aurora, and Media 100.

Features that come in handy for Photoshop include:

Echo Fire offers a very flexible solution for video previews, for both Photoshop and After Effects.

- Video previews in Photoshop by pressing a key or from the Export menu.

- Ability to handle 4×3 and 16×9 aspect ratios.
- Direct overlays of a waveform monitor, vector scope, and test-pattern displays within Photoshop.
- A video-safe color picker.
- Proper handling of video interlace and color for accurate previews. You'll find a full-featured demo on this book's disc that will let you try it out for three days. If you like it, be sure to visit Synthetic Aperture's site.

ScopoGigio

This flexible plug-in is cross-platform and works with both RGB and 601 video levels. It allows you to check a Waveform Monitor or Vectorscope right within Photoshop. The plug-in loads as a filter, and you invoke it by choosing Filter>Video>ScopoGigio. The dialog box opens and gives you the ability to set several different options. The filter cannot actually be applied; clicking OK merely dismisses the dialog box. For more information, visit http://www.metadma.com.

VideoScope

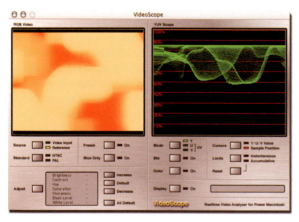

This Mac-only product is an affordable option, at only $30 US. It is designed to monitor video input; however, it works quite well to check graphics. You can drag and drop a graphic into the viewer monitor and then have access to a software-based waveform and vectorscope. It appears to be as accurate as several NLEs' built-in scopes, but cannot fully replace a hardware-based scope. This application gives you the ability to use a software scope on systems that are not running a full NLE package. For more information, visit http://www.evological.com.

External Testing Options

If you are unable to attach a television or broadcast monitor to your computer system, external testing may be the way to go. You can always output your graphics to traditional media for testing on an external device.

VHS

There is absolutely no replacement for the least common denominator. If your graphics look good on VHS, they will certainly look good on beta or broadcast. Just batch import your graphics into an NLE and go straight to VHS. With the right video card, you may be able to go right out of your Mac or PC. Most video makers hate VHS for its low quality, but it is the "ultimate" test for all graphics.

DVD-RW/DVD-R

Have a DVD recorder? Chances are it shipped with all the software you need. Most DVD authoring applications will allow you to import full-screen graphics. Look for a slideshow feature to bring in a folder full of graphics.

The DVD-RW format is not as widely promoted. Discs cost about three times more than a burn-once disc. These have the benefit of being able to be reused hundreds of times. The DVD-RW discs generally take longer to burn, but you are likely only testing a small amount of data.

While the DVD+R format is relatively common, it is not as desirable. The discs are not as compatible as the DVD-R format. In fact, the DVD+R format is not recognized as a true DVD and does not feature the DVD logo.

Getting Client Approval

The Internet is proving to be a popular means to seek client approval. By harnessing Photoshop's Save for Web command (File>Save for Web & Devices. . .), you can reduce the file size to a comfortably portable 60 KB. Be sure to stick with JPEG compression. The Save for Web feature will not alter your original file; all size and layer data is preserved. It also saves the file in the smallest format possible, automatically leaving off features such as image previews and custom icons, which just beef up file size and serve no purpose on the Internet.

Another great Web approval method is the Web Photo Gallery (File>Automate>Web Photo Gallery). This automation command allows you to instantly build an entire Web site with thumbnail

Save for Web Gets Better!

You can resize your Web approval graphics in the Save for Web dialog box.
1. Click on the Image Size tab.
2. Uncheck Constrain Proportions.
3. Size your non-square documents to square pixel for viewing on the Web. For example, 720×480 DV graphics become 640×480.
4. Click the Apply Button.
5. Specify the Compression and Save. Your Web-ready graphic is created, and your original layered document with non-square pixels is preserved.

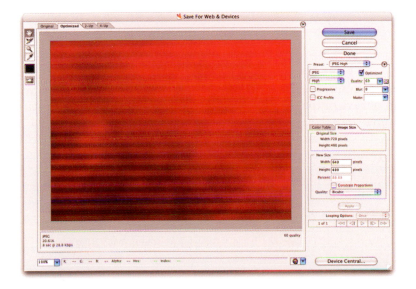

How to Get NLE-specific Information:

- **Adobe:** http://www.adobe.com/support/main.html
- **Apple:** http://www.apple.com/support
- **Autodesk:** http://www.autodesk.com/support/
- **Avid:** http://www.avid.com/support/index.html
- **Canopus:** http://www.canopus.com/support/
- **Media 100:** http://www.media100.com/support_training/
- **Pinnacle Systems:** http://www.pinnaclesys.com/support
- **Sony Vegas:** http://www.sonymediasoftware.com/

preview pages and larger images to view online. Additional features like contact information and watermarking allow you to quickly get client feedback while protecting your content online. The Feedback templates offer an outstanding way to collect client comments and avoid confusion. For more on this great feature, see Chapter 11, "Automation."

For both Web options, be sure to explain the concept of safe-title area to your clients. They may be bothered by "all that extra space around the edges." The PowerPoint user in them will rise up and command you to fill every pixel with small, unreadable text. Fight the power!

Non-Square Pixels: When to Resize

At some point, you will need to make a conscious decision about non-square pixels and document size. How do you find out what size and Pixel Aspect Ratio (PAR) your NLE needs? The best piece of advice I ever received was RTFM (Read the Frickin' Manual).

Every edit system expects that you will want to import graphics. Photoshop is the #1 choice for that need. Inside of every NLE's manual or the online help section, you will find a section on Photoshop and still graphics. A quick visit to a manufacturer's Web site will often have a PDF available for download as well.

But to show that I didn't try to dodge this bullet, check out Appendix C, "Working with Other Applications." You'll find guides for several popular NLEs and motion graphics applications.

Photoshop CS or Later

If you are working Photoshop CS or later, this question has gotten a lot easier to answer. Resize at the very beginning. You can choose to work with non-square pixels from the start when setting up a new document. You can also convert a logo, digital photo, or scanned image when you open it by pasting, dragging, or placing it into a document that has been set up for non-square pixels.

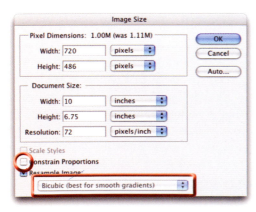

It's a good idea to build your original NTSC graphics using the NTSC D1 720×486 template. This way the graphic can work for both Standard Definition and Digital Video purposes. If you have interlaced material, choose to crop two lines from the top and four from the bottom using the Canvas Size command (Image> Canvas Size). First anchor the bottom edge, and then crop two lines. Repeat the step, but anchor the top edge, and crop four lines. If the material is entirely created in Photoshop CS (with no interlace issues), just change the canvas size to 480.

What about PAL? PAL DV and D1 are both the same frame size—720×576.

Photoshop 7 or Earlier (Square Pixels)

If you are working with an earlier version of Photoshop (or choose to stick with square pixels out of habit), you have a little more work cut out for you. Every edit system is different, as is every version. You simply must keep up on what your manufacturer recommends for graphics. It would be impossible to keep this chapter 100% current because every NLE has a different upgrade cycle.

If you are working in an NTSC environment, design at 720×540 pixels. This way you have the option to go to DV or D1 at any time during the design process. The final step is to resize to a non-square pixel size. A 720×540 file resizes for D1 at 720×486. If you designed at 720×540 but need to go to DV, first resize to 720×486, and then crop to 720×480.

If you are working with interlaced material, be sure to crop two lines from the top and four from the bottom using the Canvas Size command (Image>Canvas Size). First anchor the bottom edge, and then crop two lines. Repeat the step, but anchor the top edge, and crop four lines. If the graphic was entirely created inside Photoshop (with no interlace issues), just change the canvas size to 480.

Again, for PAL users, the PAL square pixel preset of 768×576 works for both D1 and DV.

Choosing the Right File Format

You used to have two choices for file formats that NLEs recognized. Macs took PICT files; PCs took TARGA files. That list has gotten significantly longer over the years to include virtually every file format that Photoshop can export. Here are six general tips:

1. There's a reason that PICT and TARGA were the first video-friendly formats. Stick with them. Be sure to not add any compression, and use with the maximum bit size.

2. A layered TIFF file can also be useful. It will import into an NLE or motion graphics application as a flattened file. However, when you edit the file, all layers are intact. The layered TIFF supports all options that a PSD file does.

3. Just because you can import a .psd file doesn't mean you want to. Most NLEs cannot handle blending modes and Layer Styles. Even After Effects chokes on some items. Be sure to selectively flatten items that don't travel well.

4. Always save your design files. These are essential for future changes. Save a separate version using the Save A Copy option (now joined with Save As), which can be accessed by pressing ⌘+⌥+S (ctrl+alt+S).

5. Be sure to include an alpha channel if you have transparency. For more on alpha channels see Chapter 4, "What about Transparency?"

✓ Photoshop
BMP
CompuServe GIF
Dicom
Photoshop EPS
JPEG
Large Document Format
PCX
Photoshop PDF
Photoshop 2.0
Photoshop Raw
PICT File
PICT Resource
Pixar
PNG
Portable Bit Map
Scitex CT
Targa
TIFF
Photoshop DCS 1.0
Photoshop DCS 2.0

6. Avoid Web formats at all costs; these are delivery formats, not authoring formats. The compression artifacts will taint your project.

File Extensions

Repeat after me: "I will always use file extensions." That two- or three-letter code is critical to preserving your file. The extension tells the computer (which is the least intelligent creation ever made) which application created the graphic and what can open it. Mac users have been historically lazy with extensions, because the Mac OS had written the file type into the header information. This does you no good if, for example, the file is copied to a PC-formatted disc, moves across a PC or UNIX network, or travels the Internet. Always use file extensions.

Not seeing your file extensions at all?

- Windows machines may have these turned off by default. Go to the Folder Options control panel and access the View pane. Disable the setting called Hide Extensions For Known File Types.
- Under OSX, you must access the Finder preferences. Choose Finder>Preferences. Click the Advanced button and check the box for Show all file extensions.

But what are all the file extensions? Don't worry about it; simply tell Photoshop to always use them. Open the Preferences menu by pressing ⌘+K (ctrl+K) and access the File Handling options. Tell Photoshop to Append File Extension Always, and check the Use Lower Case checkbox. Problem solved; you can now work cross-platform.

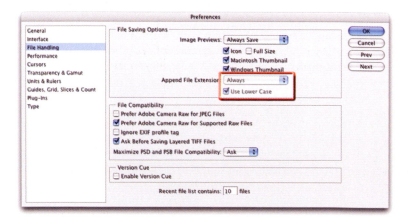

In our cross-platform world, file extension types are critical (especially for Mac users). Be sure to change your preferences to always append file extensions so that you don't have to memorize a bunch of two- and three-letter codes.

Common File Formats Used by the Video Industry

Photoshop supports many diverse file formats. As a tool that is used by video, print, Web, medical, and engineering professionals, it must offer several choices. Here are some common file formats used by video and motion graphics software.

Photoshop (.psd)

Layers	X	8-bit	X	16-bit	X	32-bit	X
Bitmap	X	Grayscale	X	Duotone	X	Indexed Color	X
RGB	X	CMYK	X	Lab	X	Multichannel	X

*Not all color spaces work in 16- and 32-bit modes

The Photoshop format is the default file format; it supports all of Photoshop's features. It's a good idea to save your design files in this format for maximum editability. Additionally, many other software packages recognize Photoshop layers.

Cineon (.cin or .dpx)

Layers		8-bit		16-bit	X	32-bit	
Bitmap		Grayscale		Duotone		Indexed Color	
RGB	X	CMYK		Lab		Multichannel	

The Cineon format is a common file format for digital film work. It is most often used in the motion picture industry. It is a subset of the ANSI/SMPTE DPX file format, which represents each color channel of a scanned film negative in a "10-bit log" format. Photoshop does not have a 10-bit space, so instead handles the images in 16-bit mode. The DPX file format is derived from the output file format of the Kodak Cineon film scanner. The Cineon format has been replaced by a related format called DPX.

OpenEXR (.exr)

Layers		8-bit		16-bit		32-bit	X
Bitmap		Grayscale		Duotone		Indexed Color	
RGB	X	CMYK		Lab		Multichannel	

The OpenEXR format is used by the visual effects industry for high dynamic range images. It was developed by Industrial Light and Magic and was released under an open source license.

The format supports multiple lossless or lossy compression methods. It is designed to supports both 16-bit and 32-bit images. Its primary benefit is that it allows for over 30 stops of exposure (which gives it incredible range of lights to dark). For much more information, see http://www.openexr.com/about.html.

PICT (.pct)

Layers		8-bit	X	16-bit		32-bit	
Bitmap	X	Grayscale	X	Duotone		Indexed Color	X
RGB	X	CMYK		Lab		Multichannel	

The Macintosh Picture format is mostly widely used by video editors, especially those on Macintosh-based computers. Its popularity can be traced back to many software packages that historically required graphics to be in the PICT format. The PICT format is very effective at compressing large areas of solid color. This compression results in huge file savings for alpha channels, which are mostly black or white.

PNG (.png)

Layers		8-bit	X	16-bit		32-bit	
Bitmap	X	Grayscale	X	Duotone		Indexed Color	X
RGB	X	CMYK		Lab		Multichannel	

The Portable Network Graphics is growing in popularity with many computer manufacturers. It is becoming increasingly more common on the Internet, but not all browsers support it. The PNG format was created to be a patent-free alternative to GIF. Its major advantage is the PNG-24 file, which allows for 24-bit images (8 bits per channel) and embedded transparency. It is technically superior to GIF.

Targa (.tga)

Layers		8-bit	X	16-bit		32-bit	
Bitmap		Grayscale	X	Duotone		Indexed Color	X
RGB	X	CMYK		Lab		Multichannel	

The Targa format was originally designed to be used with the Truevision® video board. The full name is in fact an acronym meaning Truevision Advanced Raster Graphics Adapter. The Targa format predates Photoshop.

TIFF (.tif)

Layers	X	8-bit	X	16-bit	X	32-bit	X
Bitmap	X	Grayscale	X	Duotone	X	Indexed Color	X
RGB	X	CMYK	X	Lab	X	Multichannel	

The Tagged-Image File Format is widely used to exchange files between applications and computer platforms. Additionally, TIFF is the one of the few formats to work in a bit depth of 8, 16, or 32 bits per channel. High dynamic range images can be saved as 32-bits-per-channel TIFF files.

Preserving Flexibility

While "done" is a four-letter word you like, it frequently leads to several others you may not want your mother to hear. Thanks to nonlinear editing and the Internet, nothing is ever done. It is always subject to tweaks, revisions, and repurposing. If you cut corners in the design and archiving stages, you will regret it later.

Never flatten your Photoshop Design files. Create a second copy for production purposes, or use the Save A Copy feature mentioned earlier. Chances are you archive your source tapes, project files, and EDLs for your video programs, not just the finished master. For the same reasons, you must save your Photoshop layered files.

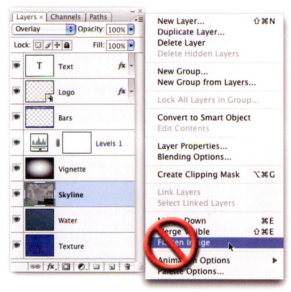

Do not flatten the layers on your PSD design files.

- Thanks to Adjustment Layers, several of the image adjustments and filters previously used can now be applied to the layered file.
- Additionally, you can apply effects to a layer filled with 50% gray; this can then be blended with layers below it, providing an AE-style adjustment layer.
- Lastly, use the Copy Merged command to Flatten Visible Layers to an intermediate copy. This will allow several filter and blend mode combinations.
- Change the way you work, and it won't be as much work to make changes.

Annotation Tools

Annotating a file is a helpful way to insert "sticky notes" for later use. Photoshop offers two annotation options, one for notes and one for audio. The Audio option is generally a waste of file space, so stick with the Notes Tool ().

What should you put into notes? Information such as fonts or colors used. It may also be helpful to specify which filters were used. Better yet, save an action for the look and include a note identifying it. Video treatments often drive the appearance of Web and print collateral materials. Follow the Golden Rule; make it easy for someone else to do their job, and the karma will return to you eventually.

What about clients? If they have Photoshop, they can easily add notes, but most clients don't have (or understand) Photoshop. Save your file in the Portable Document Format (PDF). You can then open up the PDF in Adobe Acrobat Professional and enable comments for Adobe Reader. Then send the file to the client and ask them to add annotations. To bring these into Photoshop, choose File>Import>Annotations and identify the PDF file.

Archiving Your Work

Storage-media prices have fallen to incredible levels. A DVD-R disc can hold 4.4 GB and is priced less than $2 per disc. Don't need that much room? CD-R discs have fallen in price to the point where you can find spindles on sale that end up being free after rebate. You have no economic reason not to save your work.

I keep binders with project files burned to CD-R and DVD-R. This proves invaluable for future projects for clients and for revisions. (Don't ever believe "it's done" actually means something.) To make the whole archive even more useful, enter the details of each disc into a database in a program like Filemaker Pro.

Several designers and companies I have worked with are nervous about giving clients all of the assets for a project. If you have a good relationship with the customer, you should at least be comfortable handing over your production files. If you are concerned about getting paid, hold onto things until the checks come in. Clients come back because of your creativity and level of service, not the fact that you hold their project's assets hostage.

What to Archive

 You should backup more than just your Photoshop files. Be sure to include the following:

- Fonts
- Original artwork
- Illustrator files
- After Effects files
- Source photos

Where To?

You made it through the final chapter. I'd like to say "Congratulations! You're finished." But you aren't. "Congratulations, you've come a long way" would be better. As soon as you think you are a Photoshop expert, new tools will come out and technology will change. Just as a video edit is never perfect, you can tweak and twiddle in Photoshop for the rest of your life and there would still be magical possibilities left to discover.

What Should You Focus on Next?

The most important skill you can have in Photoshop is speed. Mastering keyboard shortcuts, utilizing Layer Styles and actions, and building up your own resource library are essential.

Don't Stop Learning

Did you realize there are 12 full tutorials on the DVD-ROM and several video lessons? No rest for you!

Be sure to visit www.PhotoshopforVideo.com for book updates as well as the podcast and free resources.

My goal is to make you fast, so I've included hundreds of keyboard shortcuts throughout the book. Make your way through each chapter once again and try to incorporate these time-savers into your normal workflow.

While you're making your way back through, pay particular attention to Layer Effects and Actions, which are your two greatest time-savers. Collect these, build your own, and share them on http://www.adobe.com/exchange. Creating actions and styles should be a daily activity.

A large toolbox will serve you well as you go forward. Regularly archive your work to optical media. You should build your own stock image library, being sure to save valuable project sources. Start acquiring your own photos as well, harnessing the flexible power of a digital camera. When you have time to breathe, enroll in a photography class. In the meantime, shoot away. There's a very thin line between creative and unusable.

And above all, keep in touch. Be sure to keep an eye on my blog and resource site at www.PhotoshopforVideo.com. You'll find news, book updates, bonus videos, and articles. I update the site every week with new resources.

PRO*file*: Rachel Max

Max is originally Irish, born and raised in Dublin, but has considered herself fully assimilated to American culture since watching 'Pee-Wee's Big Adventure' on video in 1997. Perhaps drawing inspiration from that unlikely source, Max is a professional animator and has been screening her work in festivals since 1999. Her films have won several awards and recognition.

Awards don't pay bills, so Max also combines her love for animation and video into her day job as an animator and broadcast designer in NYC. Max is well-known in the After Effects community. She co-authored After Effects On The Spot and After Effects @ Work and has been featured in several other publications including Angie Taylor's Creative After Effects 7. As much as she uses After Effects, Photoshop has an important role in her production pipeline.

"I use Photoshop for 90% of my design work. I use it to create storyboards and style frames for clients, to design menus in DVD Studio Pro, and to do illustration for my personal work."

Max harnesses Photoshop's speed to cut down on her rendering times for her motion work as well.

"I do a lot of preliminary compositing in Photoshop. If there are effects that I'm not actually animating, I'll apply them in Photoshop and flatten the layer. This speeds up rendering in After Effects. The two programs work so well together now."

Max has a few of her own favorite tricks to make Photoshop easier:

- She scrolls through blending modes with the `Shift` `+` or `−` key combo

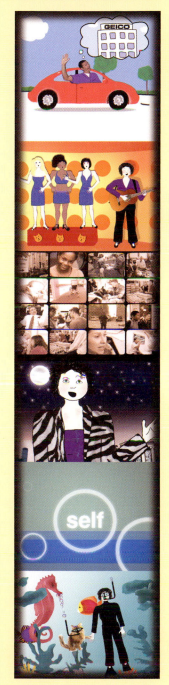

- When using the Crop Tool, she rotates it to straighten images or to select a new angle
- She uses the clone tool at 30% opacity for blending seams and blemishes
- She says actions are a huge timesaver (go to http://www.Adobe. com/exchange)
- Complete as many tutorials as you can (even if you are a power user).

The key to success for Max is continuous learning.

"Sometimes you can feel very overwhelmed by graphics and digital media programs," said Max. "I've worked with top professionals who admit that although they use Photoshop 8 hours a day, 5–6 days a week, that they still don't know how all the ins and outs. Never stop wanting to learn."

To find out more about Rachel and see her work, visit http://www.rachelmax. com.

ADVANCED LEARNING OPPORTUNITIES

I love books. I own hundreds of them. I hope you keep this book next to your nonlinear editing or motion graphics system so that it can be truly useful. Books aren't people, however, and no matter how conversationally I try to write, this book will never replace the personal connection you may experience with a trainer, instructor, or professor.

You need to look for a personal training opportunity that matches your needs. I am not a fan of those big, rolling caravans that advertise three-day "master workshops" where you will sit in an auditorium and learn everything. Education needs to be a personal and balanced experience.

I tell folks to consider enrolling in a college class. This will most likely place you with 20 or so other people for a few months. Chances are the class will focus on print and Web and not video. There are exceptions, however, with several schools offering Digital Media Production or Broadcast Journalism programs. A college class has the benefit of homework and the subsequent feedback loop. I spent about a third of my professional life teaching college students the ins and outs of video and motion graphics. I am sure that these students frequently fail to realize just how new and exciting this field is.

Adobe's training page offers several alternatives to advance your skills. Be sure to visit http://www.adobe.com/misc/training.html and look for authorized learning opportunities near you.

Adobe Certified Training Providers

There's a high likelihood that you don't have the time to take a college course. For working pros, there's a better solution: Adobe Certified Training Providers. There are several classes and resources to choose from. The best place to start is Adobe's website at http://www.adobe.com/misc/training.html.

Adobe carefully selects and screens its training centers and trainers. By ensuring that all of the trainers have passed a standardized exam, an objective level of quality control is maintained. Carrie B. Cooper, Training Partner Relations Manager within the Adobe Solutions Network, said that Adobe tries to offer variety.

"Adobe Certified Training Providers (ACTP) offer beginning, intermediate, advanced to more specific courses like Photoshop for Photographers," said Cooper. "The best thing to do is to check out the training centers' Web sites and catalogs."

One of those centers is Future Media Concepts. With offices in six East Coast cities and Chicago, FMC offers a full range of Photoshop and video-oriented courses (http://www.FMCtraining.com). Ben Kozuch, President and cofounder of FMC, explained his company's approach to training:

"We offer hands-on training in an intimate environment of no more than six people. Instructors are certified by Adobe, so participants are assured the highest-level quality training. Instructors are not professors, but industry professionals. We offer training on all Adobe software, varying in level from beginner through advanced."

When searching for a center, be sure to check their references. Ask for customer testimonials, and be sure to check Adobe's site to make sure they are listed as an ACTP (http://partners.adobe.com/asn/partnerfinder/search_training.jsp). You should also expect flexible and accessible scheduling (including weekend classes). Ask if instructors are working professionals. Some centers also offer a satisfaction-guaranteed policy and financing plans.

"Training is a major investment of time and money. You want to make sure that it is done right first time so you don't have to spend time again after a bad experience," said Kozuch. "Bad habits are tough to unlearn. At an authorized training center, you learn the software the way the manufacturer intended it to work."

Industry Certifications

So you want proof that you are as good as you think? Certifications offer Photoshop pros a chance test their mettle. The most recognized certification is the Adobe Certified Expert or ACE. To become certified, one must pass the Adobe Product Proficiency Exams for Photoshop. (While you're at it, you can pick one up for After Effects, Premiere, and most other Adobe products.)

Adobe Certified Expert

Exams are computer-delivered, closed-book tests. The exam consists of 60 to 90 multiple-choice questions. The tests are administered locally at Prometric computing exam centers located around the world. You'll know whether you passed immediately after the exam. Diagnostic information is also included in your exam's report to help identify strengths and weaknesses. The ACE program was created by Adobe to fill a specific need for users and instructors.

"It started as a vehicle to objectively measure instructors' ability on the products," said Carrie B. Cooper, Training Partner Relations Manager within the Adobe Solutions Network. "We expanded that audience to include all types of experts on the products, be they consultants, students, designers, etc."

To become certified, Adobe recommends the following five steps:

Step 1. Study for the Exam. You need to be familiar with the topic areas and objectives in the Exam Bulletin for the Photoshop exam (http://partners.adobe.com/public/en/ace/ACE_Exam_Guide_Photoshop.pdf).

Step 2. Review the Adobe Certified Expert Program Agreement. The ACE agreement is available as a PDF for your review (http://www.adobe.com/support/certification/pdfs/ace_agmt.pdf).

Step 3. Register for the Adobe Product Proficiency Exam. In the United States and Canada, you can call 1-800-356-3926. Outside the United States and Canada (or if you don't like being on hold), visit the Prometric Web site (http://www.2test.com).

Step 4. Pass the Adobe Product Proficiency Exam. There is no limit on how many times you can retest, but you must pay for each exam. If you don't pass on the first attempt, when you register to retake, use the discount code RETEST, which will give you a 25 percent discount.

Step 5. Receive your welcome kit in four to six weeks and begin using your benefits. You'll get a certificate stating your achievement. You'll also have access to the ACE logo for your business cards and résumé.

Recommended Reading

Becoming a good designer is a continuous journey. Below you will find the favorite items from my bookshelf. I have personally read and used all of these books and training discs, and I recommend them strongly.

Books on Photoshop

Copyright gilas/stockphoto.

- *Broadcast Graphics on the Spot* by Richard Harrington, Glen Stephens, Chris Vadnais
- *Photoshop Restoration and Retouching* by Katrin Eismann, Steve Simmons
- *Creating Graphics for Avid Xpress DV 3.5 with Adobe Photoshop* by Avid Technology Inc.
- *Photoshop Channel Chops* by David Biendy, Bert Monroy, Nathan Moody
- *Photoshop Down & Dirty Tricks* by Scott Kelby
- *Photoshop Killer Tips* by Scott Kelby and Felix Nelson
- *The Photoshop Channels Book* by Scott Kelby
- *Photoshop Classic Effects* by Scott Kelby
- *Photoshop Bible* by Deke McClelland
- *The Photoshop Speed Clinic* by Matt Kloskowski
- *Commercial Photoshop with Bert Monroy* by Bert Monroy
- *Photoshop Masking & Compositing* by Katrin Eismann
- *Welcome to Oz: A Cinematic Approach to Digital Still Photography with Photoshop* by Vincent Versace
- *Adobe Photoshop Studio Techniques* by Ben Willmore

Books and CD-ROMs on Type

Need to know more about type? I dug deeper into typographic theory in Chapter 5, "Some Words on Words, Logos, and Symbols." There are many more aesthetic decisions to be made, as well as some guidelines on legibility, alignment, and white space that need to be reviewed.

- *Stop Stealing Sheep and Find Out How Type Works* by Erik Spiekermann, E. M. Ginger
- *The Mac is Not a Typewriter* by Robin Williams
- *Typographic Principles with Don Barnett* by Lynda.com

Books and Discs on Motion Graphics

- ***Creating Motion Graphics*** by Trish and Chris Meyer
- ***After Effects in Production*** by Trish and Chris Meyer
- ***Creative After Effects*** by Angie Taylor
- ***After Effects on the Spot*** by Richard Harrington, Marcus Geduld, Rachel Max
- ***After Effects @ Work*** edited by Richard Harrington
- ***Adobe After Effects Essentials*** by Jayse Hansen
- ***Motion Graphics*** by Steve Curran
- ***Moving Type*** by Matt Woolman, Jeff Bellatoni
- ***Motion Control*** by www.VASST.com
- ***The Anvel*** by www.theanvel.com

Books on Color

- ***Global Graphics: Color*** by L.K. Peterson, Cheryl Dangel Cullen
- ***Global Color Combinations*** by Leslie Cabarga
- ***Color Correction for Digital Video*** by Steve Hullfish, Jaime Fowler
- ***Color Index*** by Jim Krause
- ***Color Harmony Workbook*** by Lisa Sawahata

Books on Design

- ***Brain Darts*** by Turkel Schwartz and Partners
- ***Robin Williams Design Workshop*** by Robin Williams, John Tollett
- ***Idea Index*** by Jim Krause

Photoshop Web Sites

A quick online search will leave you overwhelmed. If you judge by quantity, Photoshop is a well-loved product. Since your time is limited, I offer a scaled-down list of some of the best sites out there. Be sure to look for valuable resources and alternative points of view. Also, keep in mind that the majority of these sites are written from Web and print perspectives. In general, Web-oriented sites are the next best thing because they discuss designing for the screen as well.

Tutorials and Support

- **Photoshop for Video:** www.PhotoshopforVideo.com
- **Adobe Evangelists:** www.adobeevangelists.com
- **National Association of Photoshop Professionals:** www.PhotoshopUser.com
- **Photoshop Café:** www.photoshopcafe.com
- **Raster|Vector:** www.rastervector.com
- **Lynda.com:** www.lynda.com
- **Photoshop Roadmap:** www.photoshoproadmap.com
- **Planet Photoshop:** www.planetphotoshop.com
- **Team Photoshop:** www.teamphotoshop.com

Filters

- **Alien Skin Software:** www.alienskin.com
- **Auto FX Software:** www.autofx.com
- **Camera Bits:** www.camerabits.com
- **Digital Film Tools:** www.digitalfilmtools.com
- **Flaming Pear Software:** www.flamingpear.com
- **Mister Retro:** www.mrretro.com
- **Nik Multimedia:** www.nikmultimedia.com
- **The Plugin Site:** www.thepluginsite.com

Actions, Styles, and Add-Ons

- **Action FX:** www.actionfx.com
- **Adobe Exchange:** www.adobe.com/exchange
- **Elated.com:** www.elated.com/actionkits
- **Panos FX:** www.panosfx.com
- **Tools for Television:** www.toolsfortelevision.com
- **Web Teknique:** www.webteknique.com

Publications with Frequent Stories about Photoshop

There are several great computer magazines that routinely discuss Photoshop and related topics such as third-party plug-ins, motion graphics, and video. A magazine has a certain timeliness to it, and can provide excellent tips on Photoshop updates and add-ons.

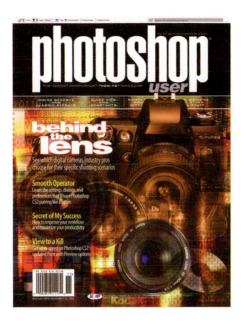

- **Photoshop User:** www.photoshopuser.com
- **Layers Magazine:** www.layersmagazine.com
- **Computer Arts:** www.computerarts.co.uk
- **DV Magazine:** www.dv.com
- **Cinefex:** www.cinefex.com

Conferences with Extensive Coverage of Photoshop for Video

Looking for some face-to-face training on Photoshop? The following is a list of conferences at which I have spoken. All offer coverage on Photoshop for Video.

- **Photoshop World:** www.photoshopworld.com
- **NAB Post|Production World:** www.nabshow.com
- **DV Expo:** www.DVExpo.com

TECH SUPPORT

Like anything related to computers, Photoshop will occasionally fail. I can safely say that it is rock solid, but not perfect. When pushing Photoshop's limits (yes there are a few) it is possible to "break it." There are several technical support options available from Adobe directly. Often a solution is available already; the documentation, however, just might not be available. Adobe also needs to hear about problems so they can release bug fixes and create new features that meet user's needs.

1. Limited complimentary phone support is available from 6 a.m. to 5 p.m. Pacific Time. You get 90 days of support with a new purchase of Photoshop and 30 days with a purchased upgrade. The counter starts when you first activate the phone support.

   Macintosh   206-675-6203
   Windows   206-675-6303

2. Pay-as-you-go service is also available for $39 per incident. Plans can be purchased by calling 1-866-MY-ADOBE.

3. Annual support agreements are available in a variety of packages. You can visit http://www.adobe.com/support/programs/photoshop/ to see your options.

4. Online information is plentiful. Start at www.adobe.com for many technical documents. You can also send an e-mail to techdocs@adobe.com to get a listing of more than 1,000 reference documents, FAQs, and technical articles. The Adobe Web site has a very good search feature. Software is dynamic, and with changes, there will be incompatibility issues. Frequent visits to the Adobe site will keep Photoshop (and you) up to date.

Support with Purchase

If you are a registered owner, you get 90 days of tech support for new copies and 30 days for upgrades.

More Tech Support

While straight from the horse's mouth is probably the best method, the horse isn't always available (and it ain't cheap to talk to). Since you will be working crazy hours, I am providing my Ten Tips for Tech Support. These steps will solve 95 percent of your problems. I've been using (and fighting with) personal computers for 25 years … so these are born from tough experience.

1. **Save (if you can).** Quit. Shutdown, count to 20, and restart. Believe it or not, this fixes 60 percent of computer errors. Sometimes a clean boot will do it.

2. **Try another file.** If you keep getting errors on your current document, open another file and see if the same problems occur. Sometimes individual Photoshop files get corrupted. If you isolate the problem to a single file, you can try running a disk repair utility to see if the individual file can be saved. Chances are pretty slim for corrupted files, however.

3. **Try another machine.** Open up the "questionable" document on another computer. If it works correctly, then your machine may be the culprit.

4. **Trash your preferences file.** Sometimes your preferences file goes bad and causes Photoshop to misbehave. Quit the application, then relaunch while holding down ⌘ + ⌥ + Shift keys (ctrl + alt + Shift).

5. **Check for updates.** Launch the Adobe Online utility and check for updates. Run your operating system updater. Visit third-party plug-in sites or go to VersionTracker.com. If you really think about it, it's amazing that our computers run at all, considering how much random code we stuff into them.

6. **Evaluate hardware.** Has anything changed? Any cables loose or unplugged? If you've added a new scanner, mouse, tablet, etc. it may be interfering with your OS or Photoshop. Remove the device and see what happens. Check the manufacturer's Web site and see if there are updates. Just because products are sold in stores doesn't mean the manufacturer supports them. Before adding hardware, visit the company's Web site and see when they last updated their tech support page. "Mac Compatible" doesn't mean it will work on OS X natively. Windows users frequently experience problems as well, especially with native support for Vista.

7. **Reinstall Photoshop.** Sometimes a fresh copy will solve your problems.

8. **Reinstall plug-ins and drivers.** Uninstall all third-party items and reload them one at a time. Check to see when the error occurs. Remove all the offending software.

9. **Repair or reinstall your operating system.** Some errors are tied directly to the operating system. For example, if Photoshop misbehaves when opening files, the Directory Services portion of the OS may be damaged. Remember, the OS and Photoshop work together. Some problems have nothing to do with Photoshop (even if that's where you first notice them.) Try disk utilities first, then if needed, you may have to freshen up the OS. Under OS X, you should launch the Disk Utility and repair the permissions file about once a month of after any software installs. A full system reinstall is the last resort.

10. **Take it to the Web.** There exists a wonderful assortment of online resources to help Photoshop users. There are several useful forums online. Members of the National Association of Photoshop Professionals have a dedicated members help desk. There are also useful forums at www.DV-forums.com and www.CreativeCow.net.

Technical Support on the Web

The Internet provides a wealth of knowledge—however, not all of it is good. Several users turn to community-based forums as an alternative. These moderated forums offer you a chance to post your questions and get answers (often in a very timely fashion). To improve your results, follow this advice:

1. Always specify what version software you are using.
2. Give details about the hardware and operating system you are using.
3. Avoid excessive abbreviations, as many are not standard. Laying the jargon on thick is also unnecessary.
4. Be sure to consult the built-in help features for the application. If an answer is obvious, you might not get a response at all (or can even be publicly ridiculed).
5. Run a search through recent posts. Your problem might have already been answered recently. Moderators will assume you've skimmed the post index first.
6. Post your question in the appropriate forums. If your question is about Photoshop and Final Cut Pro, post it to both forums.
7. If your problem is solved, confirm it so others don't keep posting answers. This is also helpful so future readers know that a suggestion worked.
8. Say thanks . . . I moderate a forum for free because I believe in giving back. I have drawn upon the advice and wisdom of many kind people in the past, and now I can return the favor. A thank you goes a long way . . . forums operate on karma.

Photoshop for Video Forum: www.DV-forums.com
Looking to create great-looking graphics for video? The folks at
DV Magazine host this forum, which is the only online forum
exclusively about Photoshop and Video. It's not as active as other
forums on the Net, but it is incredibly focused and on topic.
Post your questions and share ideas on making graphics for the
screen. This is the forum that I am most active in and it is a good
place to ask questions about Photoshop or this book.

2-Pop.com: www.2-pop.com
This site specializes in Final Cut Pro but has recently expanded
its vision. Avid, Apple, Media 100, and Adobe editing products all
have active forums. There is no specific graphics forum, but users
can post questions in their respective NLE's section.

Creative Cow: www.creativecow.net
This site offers an Adobe Photoshop and Illustrator forum. You
will also find a lot of After Effects resources and forums devoted
to most video editing, motion-graphics, and DVD-authoring
applications.

Worldwide Users Groups (WWUG): www.wwug.com
These forums are now part of Digital Media Net. Users can
come here for discussions on Adobe Photoshop as well. Several
threaded topics are available.

WORKING WITH OTHER APPLICATIONS

Integrating Adobe Photoshop with Adobe Production Studio

Why Photoshop Integration is Important for Adobe Production Studio

Adobe's Photoshop is an application that changed the way we all think about image editing. Adobe Premiere was one of the first software-based video editing applications on the scene. It's only natural that they would be designed to work hand-in-hand. Converting and processing still images and graphics and creating graphic elements and masks for compositing will always be a critical part of creating video programs.

- Whether you're creating a video for deployment on tape, CD-ROM, or DVD, Photoshop is a critical accessory for high quality video production with Adobe Premiere.
- Adobe After Effects relies heavily upon integration with Adobe Photoshop. This integration is explored through several of this book's tutorials.
- Encore DVD uses Photoshop as the basis of its menu systems.

What is the Proper Frame Size to Create Graphics for Premiere Pro?

Frames sizes will vary as project settings can have different sizes and pixel aspect ratios in Premiere Pro. Premiere Pro 1.5 added a menu selection to create a "New Photoshop Document."

This will open a Photoshop document that is configured properly for the Premiere Pro project you have open. Photoshop CS (or later) will create a document of both the proper dimension and pixel aspect ratio. If you are running an earlier version of Photoshop, the document will open with the proper pixel dimensions but will create the raster as square pixels only.

If you are capturing using FireWire, you are likely using the DV format. Regardless if you are using DV, DVCPRO, or DVCAM, your end result is a frame size of 720×480 for NTSC or 720×576 for PAL. If you are using Photoshop CS or later, you should design using the built-in non-square pixel document presets, which will match the native size of the video frame.

Format	4×3 Aspect Ratio Square Pixel	16×9 Aspect Ratio Square Pixel	Native Size* Non-Square Pixel
NTSC	720×534	864×534	720×480
PAL	768×576	1024×576	720×576

* Native size is the actual frame size stored by the Premiere Pro system and supported by Photoshop CS or later.

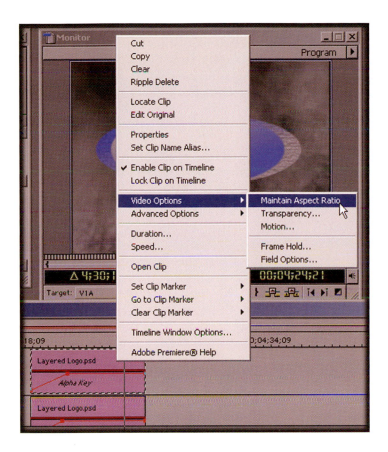

If you are working on a standard definition hardware-accelerated system, you are likely working at a standard frame size. The following offer general guidelines, but always consult the documentation that shipped with your hardware capture board or check the manufacturer's Web site. If you are using Photoshop CS or later, design using the built-in non-square pixel document presets, which will match the native size of the video frame.

Format	4×3 Aspect Ratio Square Pixel	16×9 Aspect Ratio Square Pixel	Native Size* Non-Square Pixel
NTSC	720×540	864×486	720×486
PAL	768×576	1024×576	720×576

* Native size is the actual frame size stored by the Premiere Pro system and supported by Photoshop CS or later.

If you build in square pixels, the final step is to resize the square pixel graphic to the desired non-square pixel size. To do this choose Image>Image Size. Uncheck the Constrain Proportions box and type in the native size from the chart above. The graphic will now display correctly when played back from the timeline.

What about HD Graphics?

Premiere Pro supports several different versions of HD. Sizing your graphics will depend greatly on the tape format you are using. The good news is that the presets in Photoshop work well for HD.

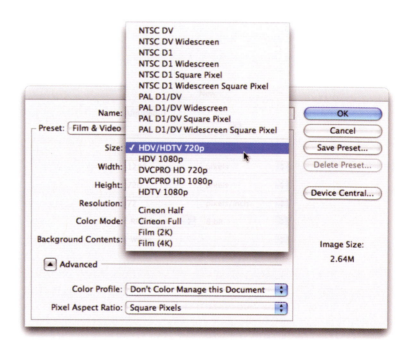

Format	Dimensions	Pixel Aspect Ratio
HDV/HDTV 720p	1280×720	Square (1.0)
HDV 1080	1440×1080	Non-square (1.33)
DVCPRO HD 720p	960×720	Non-square (1.33)
DVCPRO HD 1080	1280×1080	Non-square (1.5)
HDTV 1080	1920×1080	Square (1.0)

What is the Proper Frame Size to Create Graphics for After Effects?

Adobe After Effects is resolution-independent and meant for a variety of content creation tasks. As such, you can import Photoshop documents of any size. A general guideline is to bring the documents in at the size that you need. For example, if you were designing a motion menu for an NTSC DVD, you would use the 720×480 non-square pixels. However, if you plan to use a lot of elements in After Effects 3D space, you should strongly consider using square pixels.

What about Designing for Encore DVD?

The DVD specs and the DV specs line up precisely. As such, you can design using the following specs for DVD menus.

Format	4×3 Aspect Ratio Square Pixel	16×9 Aspect Ratio Square Pixel	Native Size* Non-Square Pixel
NTSC	720×534	864×534	720×480
PAL	768×576	1024×576	720×576

* Native size is the actual frame size stored by Encore DVD and supported by Photoshop CS or later.

What about Oversized Graphics?

It is possible to bring in a graphic that is larger than the screen. With Premiere Pro, you'll likely want to bring the graphic in as a flattened file. In After Effects, you will need to determine if you want to import as a composition to preserve a layered file for animation. Otherwise, you can import the item as footage.

What File Types are Supported

The Adobe video applications are capable of supporting several graphic formats. Because all of the applications are made by Adobe, they can work with almost any format. Some of the most popular formats include:

Format	Extension	Alpha?	Comments
BMP	.bmp	No	BMP: Windows bitmap format. This format supports color depths from dithered black and white to millions of colors.
JPEG	.jpg	No	CMYK images are not supported. A popular file format because it can create highly compressed yet good-looking graphics files. This format is not well suited for additional compression by editing into a video sequence.
Photoshop	.psd	Yes	CMYK images and files with more than four channels aren't supported. Supports color and grayscale 8-bit graphics, millions of colors, and alpha channels.
PICT	.pct	Yes	A common image format used on Mac computers.
PNG	.png	Yes	Allows color depths from black and white to millions of colors+.
Targa	.tga	Yes	An uncompressed file format that is supported by nearly every media application.
TIFF	.tiff	Yes	RGB and Grayscale images import correctly. Advanced TIFF files created with Adobe Photoshop 6 or newer mport correctly. CMYK and files with more than four channels do not import correctly.

Which Bit Depths are Supported?

Bit depth support will vary upon which versions of the application you have installed. While 8-bit support is universal (and the most common workflow), many will move to 16-bit imaging for greater color fidelity. If film output is in your site, then users may look to draw upon support for the newer 32-bit image formats.

Design With RGB or 601 Levels?

In their current versions, Adobe video applications correctly interpret RGB values (using the full 0-255 range). This will make it easier during the design process. Adobe Premiere Pro will properly map a 0 value to 7.5 IRE and a 255 value to 100 IRE. In Adobe After Effects, you design using the full color range, and color remapping will generally occur when the codec is applied in the Output Module.

For most users, the best practice is to design in full gamut RGB and apply the NTSC-safe filter on the file in Premiere Pro. This method ensures that all graphics are processed, but will cause the now-filtered graphic to be rendered when a properly prepared Photoshop document would not.

What Major Photoshop Features Import?

While subtle differences exist, Premiere Pro, After Effects, and Encore DVD all interpret Photoshop files the same way. You can choose to import Photoshop files as merged layers or load each or any independent layer of a document to use each layer as a separate element.

Additionally, importing a multi-layered Photoshop file as a "sequence" or "composition" will be a significant workflow improvement. When you load a file as a sequence or composition, a new sequence is created with each layer of your Photoshop document placed on its own track. You can easily manipulate the layers and nest the sequence into another sequence or use a "pre-comp" in After Effects.

The following properties transfer from Photoshop (accuracy and full support has improved with each new release):

1. **Opacity**
2. **Blending Modes**
3. **Grouped Layers**.
4. **Layer Set**—All layers within a layer set are imported to individual layers. After Effects treats them as "pre-comps" while Encore DVD uses the organization for rollover states for buttons.

5. **Type Layers**—Type is rasterized for Premiere Pro and After Effects. It can be converted back to vector text in newer versions of After Effects. Encore DVD preserves the editability of the text as vectors.

6. **Shape Layers**—Shape layers are rasterized by Premiere Pro. After Effects converts them to a solid with a Mask applied.

7. **Solid Color Fill Layers**—Solid Color Fill Layers are brought in as a graphic with a full-screen opaque alpha channel.

8. **Gradient Fill Layers**—Gradient Fill Layers are preserved upon import.

9. **Pattern Fill Layers**—Pattern Fill Layers import.

10. **Layer Styles**—The support of Layer Styles has improved with each release of the Adobe video applications. Older versions offered fair support. Newer versions have improved greatly.

11. **Layer Mask**—Layer Masks are applied upon import.

12. **Adjustment Layers**—These generally import into newer versions of After Effects and Encore DVD. Premiere Pro ignores them however.

How Do You Import Graphics into Adobe Production Studio?

Photoshop outputs image files in a variety of file types. Still graphics are represented in source clip bins just like video clips. Premiere Pro sees alpha channels when the clip is placed on video track 2 or above. Adobe applications offer three ways to interpret alpha channel transparency (pre-multiplied with white alpha, pre-multiplied with black alpha, or straight alpha channel). Default duration for still images can be set in the preferences, but length can be easily adjusted on the timeline after the clip is placed as well. To import, choose File>Import, or double-click in an empty area of the project window.

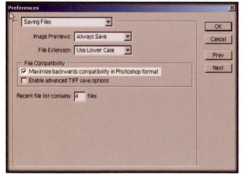

How Do You Export Video Frames from Your System?

Stills can be exported from Premiere Pro as Tagged Image Files or TIFF, Compuserve GIFs, Truevision Targa or TGA, Windows Bitmap or BMP. In After Effects you can choose Composition>Save frame as. . . . and choose from a wide variety of output options.

General Tips On Usage

Tip: Be sure the Maximize backwards compatibility in Photoshop format is checked in the Photoshop preferences for the broadest import capabilities. This will assure that Photoshop saves a rasterized version of vector layers within the Photoshop file for proper interpretation upon import into Premiere Pro.

Tip: Photoshop CS (or later) can use non-square pixel aspect ratios, so creating documents for video formats using non-square pixels is a fairly straightforward process. Previous versions of Photoshop work with square pixels only.

Author's Credit

Tim Kolb is an Emmy Award-winning director and author, and a veteran of video and television production. He serves as a program producer and first unit director for video programs, television commercials, CD-ROMs and DVDs. His work has been seen on the CBS Evening News, ESPN, ESPN 2, and CNN and he has been known to freelance for the likes of Court TV and ABC Sports. Besides Emmys, his shelf holds a Chicago Film Festival "Hugo", American Advertising Awards, Tellys, International Television Association Honors, and Communicator Awards. He judges Emmys and Tellys and is an advisor to Adobe Systems and Canopus Corporation. He tends to hang out at several industry-related forums at creativecow.net, where he is a host. Tim can be reached at tim@kolbproductions.com.

Special thanks to Daniel Brown and Richard Townhill of Adobe Systems for their critical assistance in assembling this appendix.

Integrating Adobe Photoshop with Apple Final Cut Studio

Why Photoshop Integration is Important for Final Cut Studio

Photoshop is tightly integrated with Apple's Final Cut Studio. Apple supports most Photoshop features and encourages Photoshop integration throughout the entire suite.

- Final Cut Pro can import layered PSD files with most blend modes intact.
- DVD Studio Pro can use a layered PSD file as the basis for a DVD menu. This support is well documented in the application's printed and online documentation.
- Motion can import a layered PSD file and can then be easily animated.

What is the Proper Frame Size to Create Graphics for this System?

If you are capturing using FireWire, you are likely using the DV format. Regardless if you are using DV, DVCPRO, or DVCAM, your end result is a frame size of 720×480 for NTSC or 720×576 for PAL. If you are using Photoshop CS or later, you should design using the built-in non-square pixel document presets which will match the native size of the video frame.

Format	4×3 Aspect Ratio Square Pixel	16×9 Aspect Ratio Square Pixel	Native Size* Non-Square Pixel
NTSC	720×534	864×534	720×480
PAL	768×576	1024×576	720×576

* Native size is the actual frame size stored by the FCP system and supported by Photoshop CS or later.

If you are working on a standard definition hardware-accelerated system, you are likely working at a standard frame size. The following offer general guidelines, but always consult the documentation that shipped with your hardware capture board or check the manufacturer's Web site. If you are using Photoshop CS or later, design using the built-in non-square pixel document presets, which will match the native size of the video frame.

Format	4×3 Aspect Ratio Square Pixel	16×9 Aspect Ratio Square Pixel	Native Size* Non-Square Pixel
NTSC	720×540	864×486	720×486
PAL	768×576	1024×576	720×576

* Native size is the actual frame size stored by the FCP system and supported by Photoshop CS or later.

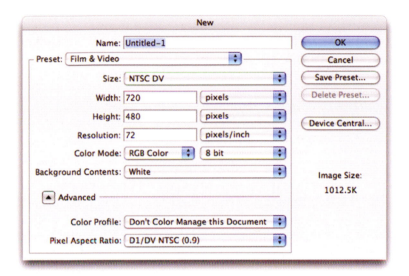

If you build in square pixels, the final step is to resize the square pixel graphic to the desired non-square pixel size. To do this choose Image>Image Size. Uncheck the Constrain Proportions box and type in the native size from the chart above. The graphic will now display correctly when played back from the timeline.

What about HD Graphics?

Final Cut Pro supports several different versions of HD. Sizing your graphics will depend greatly on the tape format you are using. The good news is that the presets in Photoshop work well for HD.

Format	Dimensions	Pixel Aspect Ratio
HDV/HDTV 720p	1280×720	Square (1.0)
HDV 1080	1440×1080	Non-square (1.33)
DVCPRO HD 720p	960×720	Non-square (1.33)
DVCPRO HD 1080	1280×1080	Non-square (1.5)
HDTV 1080	1920×1080	Square (1.0)

What about Designing for DVD Studio Pro?

The DVD specs and the DV specs line up precisely. As such you can design using the following specs for DVD menus.

Format	4×3 Aspect Ratio Square Pixel	16×9 Aspect Ratio Square Pixel	Native Size* Non-Square Pixel
NTSC	720×534	864×534	720×480
PAL	768×576	1024×576	720×576

* Native size is the actual frame size stored by DVD Studio Pro and supported by Photoshop CS or later.

What about Oversized Graphics?

It is possible to bring in a graphic that is larger than the screen. Make sure that the graphic is a single-layer document. This way FCP or Motion will recognize the square-pixel nature of the graphic and automatically compensate for you. Using a high-resolution image is useful for creating backgrounds or simulating motion control photography. Note: for DVD Studio Pro, it is best to bring graphics in at their final playback size.

In Final Cut Pro, keyframed motion parameters such as Center, Anchor Point, and Scale parameters in a clip's Motion tab allow panning and zooming (in Motion, you can apply behaviors to the object.) Be certain not to scale over 100%, or image softening will occur. You will also want to be sure to that the Timeline is set to maximum quality for processing the stills. Press ⌘+0 to open the Sequence Settings for the active sequence. Click the Video Processing tab then choose Best from the Motion Filtering Quality menu and click OK.

What File Types are Supported

Final Cut Studio is capable of supporting several graphic formats. Because Final Cut Studio is QuickTime-based, it can draw upon a wide variety of formats. Some of the most popular formats include:

Format	Extension	Alpha?	Comments
BMP	.bmp	No	BMP: Windows bitmap format. This format supports color depths from dithered black and white to millions of colors.
JPEG	.jpg	No	CMYK images are not supported. A popular file format because it can create highly compressed yet good-looking graphics files. This format is not well suited for additional compression by editing into a video sequence.
Photoshop	.psd	Yes	CMYK images and files with more than four channels aren't supported. Supports color and grayscale 8-bit graphics, millions of colors, and alpha channels.
PICT	.pct	Yes	A common image format used on Mac computers.
PNG	.png	Yes	Allows color depths from black and white to millions of colors+.
Targa	.tga	Yes	An uncompressed file format that is supported by nearly every media application.
TIFF	.tiff	Yes	RGB and Grayscale images import correctly. Advanced TIFF files created with Adobe Photoshop 6 or newer import correctly. CMYK and files with more than four channels do not import correctly.

Which Bit Depths are Supported?

Both 8-bit and 16-bit RGB are supported reliably. Note that at this time, Final Cut Pro cannot properly recognize Photoshop images that contain layers when working in the 16-bit mode. It will import them as a flattened file. Motion, on the other hand, is designed to work in up to 32-bit mode (or float). You can save Photoshop files in 32 Bits/Channel mode and import them. Other 32-bit formats, including Open EXR, are also supported.

Design With RGB or 601 Levels?

When a graphics clip is edited into a sequence, its levels are affected by the "Process maximum white as" pop-up menu in the Video Processing tab of the Sequence Settings. If it is set to White, then the brightest white in the graphic will appear at 100 percent when viewed on FCP's Waveform Monitor. If the sequence is set to Super-White, then the brightest white of the graphic will register 109 percent on FCP's Waveform Monitor.

Use the Super-White setting if matching the brightness of imported graphics to video that was shot and captured with the super-white luminance levels. This is generally the case with many consumer camcorders. If the video was shot under controlled conditions, a maximum white level of 100 IRE in the recorded video signal, you should have "Process maximum white as" set to White. This will help ensure that the white levels of the graphics match properly. You can design with the full 0–255 range when working with Final Cut Pro or Motion.

If an imported graphic triggers Final Cut Pro's range check feature, you should adjust the graphic's saturation back in Photoshop. While using a three-way color corrector may seem desirable, you are adding unnecessary render time. The quickest fix is to reopen the graphic in the appropriate external editor.

You can define which applications will open for editing specific kinds of clips. Set the still image tab to open Adobe Photoshop. To open the clip in Photoshop, do one of the following:

1. Control-click on a clip in the Canvas or Browser. Then select Open in Editor from the pop-up menu.

2. Select a clip in the Timeline or Browser. Then select Clip in Editor from the View menu.

Make any changes you need to the graphic. Then close and save changes. As long as you do not change the order or number of layers, the changes will automatically update in Final Cut Pro.

What Major Photoshop Features Import?

Final Cut Pro lets you import multilayered Photoshop files. It is possible to import any version of Photoshop files, but only those features that work in Photoshop 3.0 features are supported. Supported features include opacity, composite modes, layer order, and layer name.

The following properties transfer correctly from Photoshop:

1. **Opacity**—The imported layer's opacity becomes the Opacity control in the Motion Tab.
2. **Blending Modes**—For Final Cut Pro, the following blend modes transfer correctly: Add, Subtract, Difference, Multiply, Screen, Overlay, Hard Light, Soft Light, Darken and Lighten. In Motion, support for blending modes is much greater.
3. **Grouped Layers**—Layer grouping is ignored. However, all layers, including grouped layers, are imported as individual layers.
4. **Layer Set**—All layers within a Layer Set are imported to individual layers.
5. **Type Layers**—Type is rasterized.
6. **Shape Layers**—Shape Layers are rasterized.
7. **Solid Color Fill Layers**—Solid Color Fill Layers are brought in as a graphic with a full screen opaque alpha channel.
8. **Gradient Fill Layers**—Gradient Fill Layers are preserved upon import.
9. **Pattern Fill Layers**—Pattern Fill Layers import.

When importing a multilayered Photoshop document, Final Cut Pro creates a new sequence. All of the layers of the Photoshop file are composited together. The sequence uses a frame size identical to the imported file's frame size.

What Photoshop Features Do Not Import?

1. **Layer/Set Mask**—Layer and set masks are ignored. To keep the mask's transparency, you must merge the set or layer with an empty layer. Highlight the empty layer as a target.
2. **Layer Effects**—Layer effects must also be merged in order to travel.
3. **Adjustment Layers**—Merge the adjusted layers together.
4. **Photo Filter Layers**—Merge the adjusted layers together.
5. **Paths**—Paths cannot be imported.

How Do You Import Graphics into Final Cut Pro?

Importing graphics into your system is pretty straightforward. However, there are a few options that you need to understand. The steps are as follows.

To import a file or folder:

Step 1. At the Finder level, copy or move the files and folders that need to be imported to the project folder and hard disk. It is a good idea to keep all non-timecoded elements, such as graphics, sound files, and imported movies, in one folder. This facilitates the archival and backup procedures needed to preserve a project.

Step 2. In the Browser, select a destination.
  a. Click on a project's tab to import files or folders into the main (root) level of a project.
  b. To import files directly into a bin within a project, you most first open that bin. Double-click the bin; it will open in a separate window. Import your items directly into this bin.

Step 3. To import, do one of the following:
  a. Drag the files or folders from the finder to a project tab or bin in the Browser.
  b. Choose Import from the File menu (⌘+*I*). Select File or Folder from the submenu. Select a file or folder in the dialog box, and click Open.
  c. Control-click in the Browser or a bin's window. Next, choose Import File or Import Folder from the pop-up menu. Select a file or folder then click Open.

Step 4. Save the project.

How Do You Import Graphics into Motion?

Importing graphics into your Motion is an easy process. Motion gives you precise control on how to import a layered PSD file.

Step 1. Choose File>Import.

Step 2. Navigate to the file you want to import, then click Import. This will open the Pick Layer to Import dialog box.

Step 3. Choose a command from the Layer Name pop-up menu.
  a. **Merged Layers:** All layers of the Photoshop file are imported into a single object.
  b. **All Layers:** A new layer is created and nested within the currently selected layer in Motion. Each layer of the Photoshop document appears as an individual nested object.
  c. **Individual Layers:** Each layer in the the Photoshop file appears as a separate item a drop down menu.

How Do You Export Video Frames From Your System?

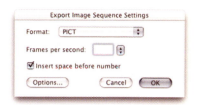

Step 1. In the Canvas, Viewer, or Timeline, place the playhead at the desired frame.

Step 2. From the File menu, choose Export. Then pick Using QuickTime Conversion from the submenu.

Step 3. Select a location and enter a name for the file.

Step 4. Select Still Image from the Format pop-up menu.

Step 5. Click the Options buttons and pick a setting from the pop-up menu. Ignore the frame rate (fps), as it doesn't apply to a single frame.

Step 6. You can customize the export setting by clicking on the second Options button. Adjust the options and export format, then click OK.

Step 7. When ready to export, click Save.

General Tips on Usage for Final Cut Pro

It is important to note that:

- An imported Photoshop file becomes a sequence in the Final Cut project.
- To import a layered Photoshop file as a single clip, it must be flattened in Photoshop first.
- A transparent background in the PSD file creates a transparent background in the new sequence.
- Layer opacity settings, some layer modes, fill layers, and visibility are preserved upon import.
- When making modifications to a PSD file that's already used in a Final Cut Pro project, do not add or delete layers.
- A great file format is the layered TIFF format. Final Cut Pro will read the file in as a flattened file, however Photoshop will open it as a layered image. This gives you all the flexibility you need to make changes with none of the overhead of a layered file.
- Photoshop's Save for Web command is a great way to save PNG-24 files. This is an easy way to save a flattened file with the transparency data intact.

Author's Credit

Richard Harrington is an Apple Certified Trainer and Adobe Certified Expert. He has worked with Final Cut Pro since the first version. Rich frequently instructs for Future Media Concepts and has spoken and industry events such as the NAB Post|Production World Conference, DV Expo, and Photoshop World.

Integrating Adobe Photoshop with Avid Editing Systems

Why Photoshop Integration is Important for Avid Editing Systems

Avid editing systems are the most widely used option for video postproduction. They are indeed edit systems and not paint packages, however. The proper use of Adobe Photoshop is important to give Avid users access to advanced titling opportunities as well as to enable them to prepare logos and photos for import into projects. Avid recognizes this important connection and even offers an advanced course through Avid Education Centers called *Creating Graphics and Mattes with Avid Media Composer and Adobe Photoshop.*

What is the Proper Frame Size to Create Graphics for this System?

Depending upon which Avid system you are using and which video standard (NTSC or PAL) used in your particular country, your graphic size may vary. All graphics should be properly sized before you import them. Improperly sized graphics are prone to distortion and loss of quality.

For those working with standard definition video, such as Avid Media Composer, Avid Symphony, and Avid Xpress, use the following sizes. If you are using Photoshop CS or later, you should design using the built-in non-square pixel document presets which will match the native size of the video frame.

Format	4×3 Aspect Ratio Square Pixel	16×9 Aspect Ratio Square Pixel	Native Size* Non-Square Pixel
NTSC	648×486 or 720×540	864×486	720×486
PAL	768×576 or 720×540	1024×576	720×576

* Native size is the actual frame size stored by the Avid system and supported by Photoshop CS or later.

There are two square pixel sizes listed for the 4×3 aspect ratio for flexibility. Designing at the 720×540 standard allows you to carry graphics to both NTSC and PAL. A small crop to 720×534 will also allow them to be used with DV footage or DVD titles.

For those working with the Digital Video formats on Avid Xpress DV, use the following sizes. If you are using Photoshop CS or later, design using the built-in non-square pixel document presets

Format	4×3 Aspect Ratio Square Pixel	16×9 Aspect Ratio Square Pixel	Native Size* Non-Square Pixel
NTSC	648×480 or 720×534	864×480	720×480
PAL	768×576 or 720×540	1024×576	720×576

* Native size is the actual frame size stored by the FCP system and supported by Photoshop CS or later.

If you build in square pixels, the final step is to resize the square pixel graphic to the desired non-square pixel size. To do this choose Image>Image Size. Uncheck the Constrain Proportions box and type in the native size from the chart above. The graphic will now display correctly when played back from the timeline.

What about HD Graphics?

Avid supports several different versions of HD. Sizing your graphics will depend greatly on the tape format you are using. The good news is that the presets in Photoshop work well for HD.

Format	Dimensions	Pixel Aspect Ratio
HDV/HDTV 720p	1280×720	Square (1.0)
HDV 1080	1440×1080	Non-square (1.33)
DVCPRO HD 720p	960×720	Non-square (1.33)
DVCPRO HD 1080	1280×1080	Non-square (1.5)
HDTV 1080	1920×1080	Square (1.0)

What about Oversized Graphics?

Avid editing systems require you to import your graphics at the proper size for editing. Larger graphics will be rescaled by Avid to fit. This is generally undesirable, as Avid systems do not scale at the same quality as Photoshop. There is one exception: many Avid systems include a Pan & Zoom plug-in. This can be used to load a larger image and create animated moves on the image.

Alias
BMP
Chyron
Cineon
ERIMovie
Framestore
IFF
JPEG
OMF
PCX
Photoshop
PICS
√ PICT
Pixar
PNG
QRT
Rendition
SGI
Softimage
SunRaster
TARGA
TIFF
Wavefront
XWindows
YUV

What File Types are Supported?

Avid systems support 24 still graphic file formats. The two most common formats that Avid recommends are TIFF and PICT. The following table lists the most common formats you will likely encounter. For a complete list, see your online help file or Avid user's manual.

Format	Extension	Alpha?	Comments
Alias	.als	No	Alpha must be a separate file.
BMP	.bmp	No	
Chyron	.chr	Yes	Images must be saved as a frame store file.
JPEG	.jpg	No	CMYK images are not supported.
Photoshop	.psd	Yes	CMYK images and files with more than four channels are not supported.
PICT	.pct	Yes	
PNG	.png	Yes	
Softimage	.pic	Yes	
Targa	.tga	Yes	
TIFF	.tif	Yes	RGB and Grayscale images import correctly, as do layered TIFF files created with Adobe Photoshop 6 or newer. CMYK and files with more than four channels do not import correctly.
Wavefront	.rla	Yes	

Which Bit Depths are Supported?

Both 8-bit and 16-bit RGB are supported reliably. Note that at this time, Avid systems cannot properly recognize Photoshop images that contain layers when working in the 16-bit mode. It will import them as a flattened file.

Design With RGB or 601 Levels?

You have three choices when for color levels when importing with an Avid system: RGB, RGB Dithered and 601. The method you choose to use will affect how you work in Photoshop.

- **RGB**—This is the most common color model used. Most computer-generated graphics use RGB graphics levels (0–255). If you choose RGB upon import to the Avid system, they will be remapped to appropriate ITU-R 601 (formerly CCIR 601) video color. The blackest black in the document will be assigned video black levels, and the whitest white will be mapped to video white.
- **RGB, dithered**—If your file contains complex color effects, such as a gradient or complex glow, and you are importing at a high resolution (2:1), choose this option. The 8-bit limit of 4:2:2 video encoding is prone to banding with fine gradients.
- **601**—This option is for use if the imported graphics file uses video levels based on the ITU-R 601 (formerly CCIR 601) standard. This would include frames of digitized video that were exported and processed in Photoshop. This also includes Avid color bars or images that include superblack for luma-keying.

If you are exporting a frame from your Avid system for touch-up in Photoshop, export it with 601 levels. Once you take it into Photoshop, be sure to avoid any adjustments to levels or saturation, or a visible color-shift will likely occur.

All other graphics that originate in Photoshop can be designed using the full color range of the RGB format. However, be certain to specify RGB or RGB, dithered levels when you import.

What Major Photoshop Features Import?

The following properties transfer correctly from Photoshop:

1. **Opacity**—The imported layer's opacity becomes the Foreground Level control in the Effect Editor.
2. **Layer Group**—Layer Grouping is ignored. However all layers, including grouped layers, are imported as individual layers.
3. **Layer Set**—All layers within a Layer Set are imported to individual layers.
4. **Type Layers**—Type is rasterized.
5. **Solid Layer**—Solid Layers are brought in as a graphic with a full-screen opaque alpha channel.
6. **Gradient Layer**—Gradient transparency is preserved upon import.
7. **Pattern Layer**—Pattern Adjustment Layers make the trip.

What Photoshop Features Do Not Import?

1. **Blending Modes**—Merge the blended layers together. Only normal mode is supported
2. **Layer/Set Mask**—Layer and Set Masks are ignored. To keep the mask's transparency, you must merge the set or layer with an empty layer. Highlight the empty layer as a target.
3. **Layer Effects**—Layer effects must also be merged in order to travel.
4. **Adjustment Layers**—Merge the adjusted layers together.
5. **Photo Filter Layers**—Merge the adjusted layers together.

How Do You Import Graphics into the System? Any Special Options?

Importing graphics into your system is pretty straightforward. However, there are a few options that you need to understand. The steps are as follows.

Step 1. Select the bin where you want the imported file(s) to be stored.

Step 2. Choose File>Import

Step 3. Navigate to where the files are located

Step 4. Select the files to import. Hold down the ⌘ or *Shift* key (*ctrl* or *Shift* key) to select multiple files. The *Shift* key selects contiguous files, the ⌘ (*ctrl*) key selects noncontiguous files.

Step 5. Choose a Media Drive and specify the resolution settings that best match your project. Remember that compressed and uncompressed footage cannot be mixed.

Step 6. Click the Options button and specify the options that best match your project and source materials.

   a. **Aspect Ratio, Pixel Aspect**

     i. **601, non-square**—This is the default setting. It assumes that your video has been properly sized for import to your Avid system. Use this option to import images with the native dimensions used by the Avid system: 720×480 (NTSC DV), 720×486 (NTSC), or 720×576 (PAL). Also use this option for 720×540 images or other images that match the 4:3 aspect ratio.

     ii. **Maintain, non-square**—This option never scales or resizes. In a D1 environment, use this with images sized for DVD or DV (720×480). The image is centered and padded with black at top and bottom to fill out the 486 scan lines for those systems that need it.

In Xpress DV, up to 480 (NTSC) or 576 (PAL) lines are preserved. The extras are removed, or missing lines are padded with video black. Use this option for DV sized material being used in a D1 project, or vice versa.

   iii. **Maintain, square**—This is for images that use square pixels, and are smaller than the video frame. This will prevent enlarging the image and thus softening it. Square pixels are resized for non-square usage and the empty areas are filled with video black.

   iv. **Maintain and Resize, square**—This option assumes that the image aspect ratio is incorrect. It will letterbox the image and scale to fit the 720-pixel width or the 480 (NTSC DV), 486 (NTSC), or 576 (PAL) size. It will also compensate for square pixels. For best full-screen resolution of files created with square pixels, use 648×480 (NTSC) or 768×576 (PAL). To create a single resolution for both NTSC and PAL, use 720×540. Do not use this option to bring in a full-screen square-pixel image that has already been stretched to non-square-pixel dimensions.

b. **File Field Order**—Leave set to non-interlaced for still graphics.

c. **Color Levels**—Choose from RGB, RGB, dithered or 601 based on the aforementioned criteria.

d. **Alpha**

   i. **Use Existing**—Applies only to images that have an attached alpha channel. If you create your alpha channels with the save selection as channel button, this method will not work properly

   ii. **Invert Existing**—This method inverts the Alpha Channel. This one is generally more useful to Photoshop users.

   iii. **Ignore**—Alpha channel is disregarded.

e. **Single Frame Import**—Specify a length for the clip.

Step 7. When satisfied with your options, click OK to close the dialog box.

Step 8. Click OK to begin import.

Step 9. Specify how you want the files imported. Your Avid system can import your Photoshop graphic three different ways: as a flattened image, or from some to all of the layers in a multilayered graphic. If you simply intend to key the graphic without any complex reveal or animation, such as a lower third, choose flattened.

If you are going to use the layers to build an animation or complex reveal, choose to import as a sequence of layers or select layers. Each layer imports as a separate object (a matte key or master clip). These can then be manipulated individually like any other matte key or master clip.

Upon import, the Avid system presents you with a sequence with each layer on a separate track. This will allow you to edit all of the layers into a final sequence. The names and order of the layers are preserved from the original Photoshop file.

How Do You Export Video Frames from Your System?

Step 1. Load the clip or sequence that contains the desired clip into your source or record monitor.

Step 2. Park on the desired position with the position indicator (blue bar).

Step 3. Choose File>Export.

Step 4. The pop-up list at the bottom of the dialog box contains saved Export settings. You can use these or create specialized exports.

Step 5. Click the options button to access the Export Settings dialog box.

Step 6. Choose Graphic from the Export As menu.

Step 7. Specify the following options:
  a. Use Marks—If selected, the in point is used. If deselected the position indicator is used.
  b. Use Enabled Tracks—If selected, the highest active track is used. If deselected, the highest monitored track is used.
  c. Graphic Format—Specify the output type. Avoid JPEG and GIF as they introduce undesirable compression.
  d. Format Options—Access specific options for each format.
  e. Width, Height—Use the presets to specify an output size. Use square pixels for print and web. Use Native size when touching up and re-importing or going to After Effects.
  f. Scale to Fit or Crop/Pad—How the image is forced to fit the export size.
  g. Color Levels—RGB is used most of the time. 601 levels if you plan to re-import after touchup.
  h. File Field Order—The Single Field option is best when exporting.

Step 8. Deselect Sequential Files option.

Step 9. Click Save As to save the setting for future use.

Step 10. Navigate to storage destination.

Step 11. Enter name for graphic with version number. Avoid alpha numeric characters and spaces.

Step 12. Click OK to save.

General Tips On Usage

It is important to note that:

- Opacity levels from Photoshop are converted to Foreground level in the Matte Key effect.
- Layer order and layer names are preserved during import to the system.
- A hidden layer will be imported as a matte key.
- Vector text and shape layers are rasterized during import to the Avid.
- Graphics must be RGB 8 or 16 bits, or grayscale.

Author's Credit

Richard Harrington is an Avid Certified Instructor and has participated in the Avid Master Editor Workshop. He has worked with Avid systems since 1994 and enjoys working with the entire lineup of Avid products (although he doesn't understand why the Transjammer AVX plug-ins went away). Rich frequently instructs for Future Media Concepts and has spoken at industry events such as the NAB Post|Production World Conference, DV Expo, Photoshop World, and the Avid Government Technology Symposium.

Integrating Adobe Photoshop with Autodesk Combustion

Why Photoshop Integration is Important for this System

It is to be expected that a client or designer will hand you resources created in Photoshop. The Photoshop file can be directly imported into Combustion retaining layers, transfer modes and opacity. While the discreet Combustion Paint Module itself uses image editing procedures similar to Adobe Photoshop, tools such as Custom Brushes, the Healing Brush, Liquify and Layer Styles are available only in Photoshop.

What is the Proper Frame Size to Create Graphics For this System With Square Pixels

Because Combustion is resolution-independent, it will not automatically resize images from square-pixel applications such as Photoshop. It is generally a good idea to design with the newer non-square pixel presets.

By default, the Combustion viewport(s) display a pixel ratio of 1:1 (square pixels), so an imported full frame Photoshop file may still appear to be squashed. In the Combustion menu, enable Window>Use Aspect Ratio to scale the viewport and display the output accordingly.

What File Types are Supported

File formats supported by Combustion are PSD (with layers, opacity and blend modes), BMP (24-bit only, no alpha support), GIF (32-bit, transparency support), JPG (24-bit, no alpha support), PNG (32-bit, full alpha support), TGA (32-bit, full alpha support), TIF (32-bit, full alpha support).

Which Image Modes are Supported

Combustion supports files created in Grayscale, Index and RGB modes. Combustion does not support files created in CMYK, Lab, or Mulltichannel modes. Newer versions of Combustion are also fully compatible with Photoshop's 16-bit and 32-bit formats.

Design With RGB or 601 Levels

Design in Photoshop RGB. If the composition is being used for broadcast, it may be necessary to bring the graphic within color safe. After importing the graphic into Combustion, apply a Broadcast Safe Color Operator (menu Operators>Video> Broadcast Safe Colors) to reduce the luminance or saturation or to identify NTSC illegal colors for manual correction, such as with the Color Corrector. If the composite contains numerous layers imported from Photoshop, the Broadcast Safe Color Operator can be applied on the final output and optionally nested; this makes all layers "safe." Of course, if you are doing genuine broadcast work, always make use of a vectorscope.

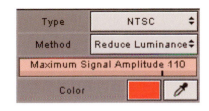

What Major Photoshop Features Import

Photoshop Layers are independently recognized by Combustion. Layers can be manipulated and modified individually or as a group. Photoshop Layers with visibility turned off will import into Combustion "off" and can be turned "on" by clicking the Layer icon in the Workspace. Photoshop Layer names are preserved on import.

Photoshop Layer Blend Modes are compatible with Combustion Layer Transfer Modes and can be changed easily in Combustion. However, new (Photoshop 7) Layer Blend modes will import as "Normal", these include Linear Burn, Linear Dodge, Vivid Light, Pin Light and Linear Light.

Photoshop Layer Opacity imports perfectly and the full range of Opacity can be modified and animated in Combustion. The Advanced Blending "Fill Opacity" is not acknowledged.

Photoshop Clipping Groups are imported seamlessly using Combustion's Stencil Layer option found in the Surface Controls. The Stencil Layer option is automatically set to Alpha.

What Photoshop Features Do Not Import

- Combustion does not recognize Layer Sets. All Layers are imported in order from top to bottom, disregarding Layer Sets and Layer Set names.
- Combustion does not recognize Layer Styles when the file is saved as a Photoshop file. Merge a Layer containing a Layer Style down into an empty Layer to rasterize it. However, if a Photoshop file is saved as a still image (BMP, GIF, JPG, PNG, TGA or TIF) Layer Styles are saved in the image and there is no need to rasterize.
- Adjustment Layers are not recognized by Combustion.
- Vector Type is rasterized on import into Combustion. If text needs to be scaled or edited, modify the original Photoshop file or use the Combustion Text Tools.
- Vector Shape Layers must be rasterized before being saved in Photoshop. Combustion ignores Vector Shape Layers on import.

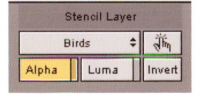

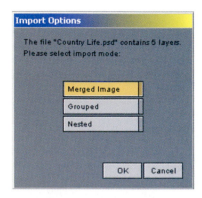

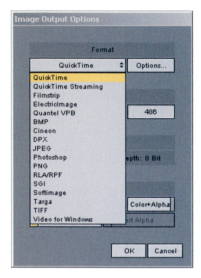

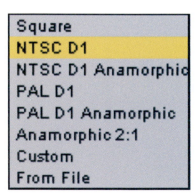

How Do You Import Graphics into the System?

Before importing a Photoshop file into Combustion 3, set your preference for Photoshop Import Behavior. File>Preferences> Footage>General: Photoshop Import Behavior>Import Mode: Choose either Color or Color + Alpha. By choosing "Color", no transparency information will be imported with the Photoshop file.

When importing Photoshop files into Combustion, a dialog gives details on how many layers are in the file and offers one of three Import Options:

Merged Image

The entire Photoshop file becomes a "flattened" single Layer in Combustion. Even after merging the file into a single Layer, individual Layers can be displayed one at a time through the Footage Controls>Source>Source Layer, uncheck Merge Layers and choose a layer from the drop-down.

Grouped

The Photoshop file is imported as individual layers parented to a Null Object. Each layer can be controlled and modified separately or manipulated together using the Transform Controls for the Null Object.

Nested

The Photoshop file is imported as individual layers parented to a Null Object within a Nested Composite. Each layer can be controlled and modified separately or manipulated together using the Transform Controls for the Null Object. The additional benefit of a Nested Import is that filters and Operators can be applied to the Nested Composite, affecting the entire group of layers uniformly.

How Do You Export Video Frames from Your System?

A single image can be exported from Combustion in over a dozen formats via File>Save Image with options for compression, frame size, bit depth and alpha channel. Be aware that the image is saved at Viewport Quality, so change the Viewport Display Quality to Best before saving an image.

An Image Sequence in any of the standard formats can be exported through Combustion in the menu File>Render.

General Tips On Usage

- If the Photoshop file is less than full frame (titles, icons), or larger than full frame (an image you want to "pan & zoom" around in) the square-to-non-square-pixel-ratio may not be as obvious. In this event, in the Combustion Footage Controls choose From File in the Pixel Aspect Ratio drop-down.

- If a file looks squashed or too wide in an NTSC Combustion composite and it's origin can't be determined, try scaling the Layer down 90% on the Y axis, if that fixes it, it was created with square pixels, most likely in Photoshop. Remember to enable Window>Use Aspect Ratio to display the proper aspect ratio in the viewport.

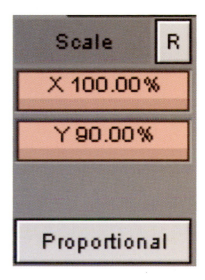

Author's Credit

Lee "Rod" Roderick was handed a life sentence in video production in 1984 with no possibility of parole. He teaches and works out of North Gate Studios, his facility in Walnut Creek, California and is a Certified discreet Training Specialist for Combustion as well as a co-author of Discreet's Combustion Courseware. Lee also produces the Combustion DVD training series "Combustion Underground" with Runaway Training – www.RunawayTraining.com. Lee's work is not limited to graphics, he is an editor, director, producer, CD-ROM/DVD author and photographer for a wide array of clients throughout California and beyond.

Lee can be contacted at rod@northgatestudios.com

Thank you to Josee Belhumeur, Gary M. Davis and Ken LaRue for contributing to this supplement.

Integrating Adobe Photoshop with Sony Vegas

Why Photoshop Integration is Important for Sony Vegas

At some point, the Vegas user may need the services of an image editing application, and Adobe Photoshop is the natural choice. With Photoshop, you can create a title graphic, tweak an alpha mask, re-touch a still image, or convert a vector graphic to a raster graphic for a Vegas project.

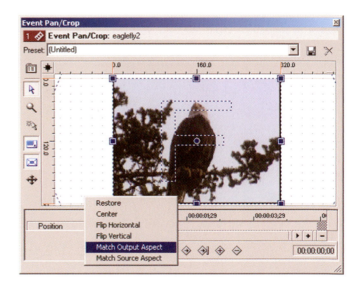

What is the Proper Frame Size to Create Graphics for this System?

If you are working in Photoshop CS or later, you can use the built-in templates for non-square pixels. These documents will import cleanly and at the native size.

If you choose to work with square pixels, Vegas can stretch images internally, so it is not mandatory to compensate for pixel aspect ratio at the still image creation stage. If you load the image into Vegas, choose event pan/crop> match output aspect (see following graphic). Vegas will stretch the image using high quality internal scaling algorithms—you will usually notice little if any distortion due to stretching. Additionally, using this method, you will not have to resize your still images if you are rendering to multiple formats with different pixel aspect ratios.

Of course there may be times when using a pixel aspect correct source file is desirable—for instance when creating masks that will be used along with video footage, or when ultra-high quality is desired.

For DV Based Projects

Format	4×3 Aspect Ratio Square Pixel	16×9 Aspect Ratio Square Pixel	Native Size* Non-Square Pixel
NTSC	720×534	864×534	720×480
PAL	768×576	1024×576	720×576

* Native size is the actual frame size stored by the Vegas system and supported by Photoshop CS or later.

For Standard Definition Based Projects

Format	4×3 Aspect Ratio Square Pixel	16×9 Aspect Ratio Square Pixel	Native Size* Non-Square Pixel
NTSC	720×540	864×486	720×486
PAL	768×576	1024×576	720×576

* Native size is the actual frame size stored by the Vegas system and supported by Photoshop CS or later.

What about HD Graphics?

Sony Vegas supports different versions of HD. Sizing your graphics will depend greatly on the tape format you are using. The good news is that the presets in Photoshop work well for HD.

Format	Dimensions	Pixel Aspect Ratio
HDV/HDTV 720p	1280×720	Square (1.0)
HDV 1080	1440×1080	Non-square (1.33)
DVCPRO HD 720p	960×720	Non-square (1.33)
DVCPRO HD 1080	1280×1080	Non-square (1.5)
HDTV 1080	1920×1080	Square (1.0)

What about Oversized Graphics?

It is possible to bring in a graphic that is larger than the screen. Make sure that the graphic is a single-layer document. If you are planning to zoom in on the graphic using motion effects within Vegas, it is a good idea to make the graphic larger than the video frame. If you double the frame size, you'll be able to zoom in on the image with no distortion and get the "Ken Burns" look.

What File Types are Supported?

The .png format, while a little less commonly used than .psd or .tga, is an excellent choice for graphics destined for Vegas. In addition to high quality, Vegas can auto-interpret the presence of alpha channel in .png files.

Format	Extension	Alpha?
BMP	.bmp	No
JPEG	.jpg	No
Photoshop	.psd	Yes
GIF	.gif	No
PNG	.png	Yes
Targa	.tga	Yes
TIFF	.tiff	Yes

Which Bit Depths are Supported?

Vegas offers great flexibility when working with graphics.
- Vegas provides support for both 8- and 16-bits per channel
- The following color modes are supported: RGB, Indexed, Grayscale, CMYK.
- The following color modes are not supported: LAB, Multichannel.

Design With RGB or 601 Levels?

You can choose RGB or 601, depending on the destination format you are working with. If needed, color correction filters can be applied in Vegas to deal with illegal color values in RGB files. These will take longer to render, but may offer a more flexible workflow.

What Photoshop Features Import?

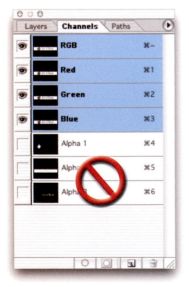

The first Alpha channel is properly understood on import. Do not save more than one alpha channel with your native .PSD file or it will be ignored. Feel free to use all of Photoshop's features. If your file contains, Layers, Layer Sets, Layer Styles, Blending Modes, Vector Type, or Vector Shapes, Vegas will properly interpret them on import. The .psd files will be opened with all visible layers flattened. Alpha channel will be retained and can be enabled (with several interpretation options) in the Vegas media properties dialog.

Importing Graphics into the System

Vegas opens supported still image files like any other file type. You can adjust the alpha channel interpretation in the media properties dialog. You can also save the alpha channel settings so that any file with the exact same parameters you subsequently open will use the same alpha interpretation.

Exporting Video Frames from Your System?

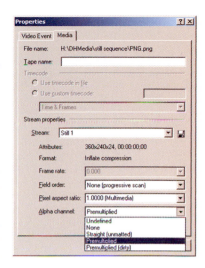

Vegas can save a timeline snapshot .png (with alpha). Set the Vegas Preview window to project size, best quality, cue to the frame you want to capture, apply any needed processing (filters, de-interlace etc), and Vegas will save a pixel aspect corrected still (either a .png w/alpha, or a low quality .jpeg). Timeline snapshots are WYSIWYG—what you see in the Vegas preview window is what you will see when you open the file in Photoshop for editing. In Photoshop you may need to check that the correct pixel aspect ratio was assigned (Image>Pixel Aspect Ratio).

General Tips On Usage

Rendering using the "Best" video rendering quality setting will produce the cleanest results, as the highest quality scaling algorithms are used. Render time will likely increase using "Best", so it is a good idea to do a test render using the "Good" setting—in many cases this will look excellent and require less render time.

If you are zooming in on still images in a Vegas project, and notice flickering or "combing artifacts" in the moving image, you may want enable the reduce interlace flicker (event switch). There is no one setting that produces perfect results under any circumstance, so some experimentation is often needed to obtain the perfect look.

Author

David Hill has been involved with Vegas since 1999 and continues to work on Vegas with an exceptionally talented team of developers at Sony Pictures Digital Networks' Media Software.

GLOSSARY

Special thanks to Glen Stephens, from Tools for Television, for help writing the glossary.

8-bit color 256 different colors per channel.

16-bit color 65,536 different colors per channel.

24-bit color 16.7 million different colors per channel.

32-bit color 4.3 billion different colors per channel.

action-safe area The action-safe area of an image is the outer box of the safe grid. All action taking place on screen should be composed inside this area, or it will not be seen when viewed on a television set.

Actions Scriptable macros within Photoshop that allow you to record your steps in the design process and easily repeat those steps multiple times. Actions can be assigned to f-keys and used to batch process files. Virtually all menu commands and processes are available to be recorded as actions.

additive color model A color model that creates white when the primary colors of the model are added together. For example, adding red, green, and blue in the RGB model will create white.

Adjustment Layer A layer that is placed above an art layer that creates adjustments to the layers below it. Adjustments can be levels, curves, color balance, hue saturation, and many others. Adjustment layers provide a nondestructive way of altering your image.

Adobe Acrobat Adobe Acrobat software lets you convert any document to an Adobe Portable Document Format (PDF) file. Anyone can open your document across a broad range of hardware and software, and it will look exactly as you intended—with layout, fonts, links, and images intact.

Adobe After Effects Adobe After Effects software delivers a comprehensive set of tools to efficiently produce motion graphics and visual effects for film, video, multimedia, and the Web. You can explore unlimited creative possibilities with precise control while working in a 2D or 3D compositing environment.

Adobe Illustrator Adobe Illustrator software defines the future of vector graphics with groundbreaking creative options and powerful tools for efficiently publishing artwork on the Web, in print, everywhere.

Adobe ImageReady Adobe Image Ready is an application by Adobe Systems that prepares Photoshop images and others for Web output. Image Ready provides support for GIF animations, rollovers, and a variety of other Web-based graphic applications. It was discontinued with the release of Photoshop CS3.

Adobe Photoshop Elements Photoshop Elements is the replacement application for Photoshop LE from Adobe Systems. Photoshop Elements provides an excellent platform for editing images. Photoshop Elements is a thinned-out version of Photoshop that provides many of the similar functions as Photoshop, but lacks in the complexity of control that is available in the full version of Photoshop.

Adobe Premiere Pro Delivering strong hardware support, Adobe Premiere software is an adaptable video editing tool. Premiere Pro allows you to work more productively with Real-Time Preview. You can also take advantage of the Adobe Title Designer, MPEG-2 export, DVD authoring, powerful audio tools, and more.

Adobe Type Manager Adobe Type Manager is an application by Adobe Systems that manages the fonts in your system and allows you to activate fonts and sets of fonts quickly and easily. This application has been discontinued. You should look for an alternative for type management.

aliasing Aliased images are images that have a rough or jagged edge to them. This is caused by the fact that all raster or bitmapped images are created from tiny square pixels, which inherently cannot create perfectly smooth edges.

anti-aliased images Images that have a smooth appearance to their edges. Anti-aliasing is achieved by varying the opacity of the pixels on the outer edge of the object, giving the appearance of a smooth edge. Different tools in the palette window have an anti-aliasing option, such as the Marquee tool and the Text tool. Your images will look smoother and cleaner if you have this option turned on. Anti-aliasing introduces the problem of the background color within your image being visible around the edges of your graphic when your graphic is keyed.

Align Linked Align Linked allows you to link a series of layers and align the contents of each layer to the parent layer. This is the same function as left, right, or center aligning text in a word processor.

alpha channel An alpha channel is the fourth channel in an RGB image. This channel is used to key out certain portions of your graphic. The alpha channel acts as a cookie cutter to remove portions of the image and replace them with underlying video. In most video systems, any area in the alpha channel that is white will show the graphic when keyed, and any area that is black will pass video through. Some systems, however, such as Avid systems, reverse the black and white areas. This is referred to as an inverse alpha channel. Alpha channels also support varying levels of opacity in an image. Shades of gray in an alpha channel show areas of the graphic as partially transparent. The closer to white the gray area is, the more opaque the graphic is for the corresponding pixels, and the closer to black the gray is, the more transparent the corresponding pixels are.

anamorphic D1 and DV video signals can be shot for playback in a 16:9 format. Anamorphic 16:9 is video that is squeezed horizontally so that when it is played back in 16:9 mode, it is stretched back to its original size to display a normal-looking image.

aspect ratio An aspect ratio is the general size of a given video format. For example, NTSC has a 4:3 aspect ratio so that all television sets are four units wide for every three units tall.

ATSC The Advanced Television Standards Committee (ATSC) is the governing body that sets the standards for HDTV.

Bezier curve A Bezier curve is the curve created in Photoshop using the Pen tool that creates vector-based artwork. Bezier curves are the foundation for artwork created in Adobe Illustrator.

bitmap See raster graphics.

blending modes Modes used in Photoshop to mathematically blend a layer with visible layers beneath it.

BMP A BMP is a standard Windows image format on DOS and Windows-compatible computers. BMP format supports RGB, indexed color, grayscale, and bitmap color modes. You can specify either Windows or OS/2® format and a bit depth for the image. For 4-bit and 8-bit images using Windows format, you can also specify RLE compression.

brightness Brightness is how light or dark a color is. It is independent from saturation.

Button mode A mode available in the Actions palette that displays all of your actions as buttons. Actions can be executed by clicking these buttons. When in Button mode, color labels and keyboard shortcuts are visible on the buttons.

Calculations command This command lets you blend two individual channels from one or more source images. You can then apply the results to a new image or to a new channel or selection in the active image.

Camera Raw The Adobe Camera Raw dialog box lets you open raw images. These files contain all of the raw data captured by the digital camera.

CCIR 601 DV and D1 signals are both NTSC non-square pixel video formats. However, CCIR-601 (sometimes called D1) is 720×486 pixels while the DV, or digital video standard, is 720×480 pixels, 6 fewer than the D1 standard. If this difference is not addressed in your designs, your graphics may not look correct when output to video.

Character palette The Character palette allows you to edit text attributes such as font size, kerning, leading, line spacing, as well as the font name and color.

clipping path An image clipping path is a path set in Photoshop that lets you isolate certain portions of an image and make everything else transparent when the image is printed or placed in another application.

CMYK The CMYK color mode is used primarily in the print world. It stands for cyan, magenta, yellow, and black (or key). The images in this color mode are comprised of these four colors. Logos that you receive for your broadcast graphics will most likely be in the CMYK color mode. These need to be converted to RGB before they can be used. Menu: Image>Mode>CMYK Color Pasting them, or simply moving them to your broadcast graphic will automatically convert them to an RGB color mode.

codec, Animation Codec stands for compressor decompressor. The animation codec is a codec used to encode QuickTime movies in an uncompressed file. This is the highest quality codec you can use that is the most compatible with other systems.

codec, None When you choose to render a clip without a codec, you are rendering at a quality higher than an animation codec with virtually no compression.

color gamut Color gamuts are the range of colors that a particular graphics system can display. All hardware differs in ability to reproduce colors. RGB and CMYK are different color spaces that represent different color gamuts. However, color gamuts go far beyond that. Macintosh and Windows systems have slightly different color gamuts as well. And most important, computer and televisions have very different color gamuts. Inevitably, colors may tend to change when viewed on different systems.

Color Picker The Adobe Color Picker in Photoshop allows you to select foreground and background colors to be used in your images. Colors can be selected using Lab, HSB, RGB, CMYK, and HEX settings, or simply by clicking on a given color.

color swatches The Swatches palette is a place to store frequently used colors. You can store any combination of colors in the Swatches palette and save them to swatch files for easy color cataloging.

composition A composition in After Effects is similar to a canvas in Photoshop in that it is made up of multiple layers. A project can have multiple compositions, and a composition can have multiple layers, which can include other compositions.

Conditional Mode Change This is a command that allows you to batch convert a series of images to a given color mode, depending on its original color mode. For example, you can tell the dialog to convert all open images with a CMYK or grayscale color mode to an RGB color mode, leaving all other images untouched.

Constrain Proportions Constrain Proportions means to equally scale height and width proportionally to each other. This prevents an image from being stretched when it is resized.

contours You can use contours to shape the appearance of an effect over a given range in the Drop Shadow, Inner Shadow, Inner Glow, Outer Glow, Bevel and Emboss, and Satin effects when creating custom layer styles. For example, a Linear contour on a Drop Shadow causes the opacity to drop off in a linear transition, while a Custom contour can be used to create a unique shadow transition.

contrast See contrast ratio.

contrast ratio The contrast of an image is how many steps of gray exist between the white and black areas of the image. This is typically expressed in terms of a ratio. The typical contrast ratio for video is 40:1, meaning that the brightest part of an image can only be 40 times brighter than the darkest area. Some digital cameras with high-quality CCDs can reach a contrast ratio of 100:1.

Copy Merged Copy Merged copies a merged image of the visible layers in your Photoshop document to the clipboard.

crop Cropping an image decreases the canvas size of the image without scaling or resizing pixels.

D1 DV and D1 signals are both NTSC non-square pixel video formats. However, D1 (sometimes called CCIR-601) is 720×486 pixels while the DV, or digital video standard, is 720×480 pixels, six fewer than the D1 standard. If this difference is not addressed in your designs, your graphics may not look correct when output to video.

DCS The Desktop Color Separations format is a variation of the standard EPS format. It is for saving color separations of CMYK images. This format has no uses for video applications.

De-interlace filter A filter that removes the interlaced scan lines of an image captured from a video card using either duplication or interpolation.

Defringe command The Defringe command replaces the color of any fringe pixels with the colors of nearby pixels containing pure colors (those without background color). For example, if you select a yellow object on a blue background and then move the selection, some of the blue background is selected and moved with the object. Defringe replaces the blue pixels with yellow ones.

Desaturate command The Desaturate command converts a color image to a grayscale image in the same color mode. For example, it assigns equal red, green, and blue values to each pixel in an RGB image to make it appear grayscale. The lightness value of each pixel does not change. This command has the same effect as setting Saturation to −100 in the Hue/Saturation dialog box.

Direct Selection tool This tool allows you to select individual points in a path for further manipulation.

DNG The Adobe Digital Negative format is a standardized file format introduced by Adobe. It is meant to be a unified way to store several different Raw camera file formats.

dots per inch (dpi) This is considered the resolution of your image, and it is a measurement of the number of dots or pixels displayed per unit. This is referred to as dpi. The screen resolution or dpi of video is often expressed as 72 dpi (although this is inaccurate as it is really pixels per inch or ppi).

duotone This mode creates two-color grayscale images using two inks. Images must first be grayscale before converting to duotone.

DV DV and D1 signals are both NTSC non-square pixel video formats. However, D1 (sometimes called CCIR-601) is 720×486 pixels while the DV, or digital video standard, is 720×480 pixels, six fewer than the D1 standard. If this difference is not addressed in your designs, your graphics may not look correct when output to video.

dye-sublimation printer A printer that uses colored film that is heated and impressed onto the paper as a vapor to achieve color images. Dye-sub printers have better printing quality than ink-jet printers because they are continuous tone and undithered.

EPS The Encapsulated PostScript (EPS) language file format can contain both bitmap and vector graphics in RGB, Lab, CMYK, indexed color, duotone, grayscale, and bitmap color modes. It is a widely supported format in the print world. When asking for logo files, an Illustrator file (.ai) or an EPS file created in a vector program is desirable. When opening an EPS file containing vector graphics, Photoshop converts the vector graphics to pixels. There are no advantages to the EPS format for video applications.

Equalize command The Equalize command redistributes the brightness values of the pixels in an image so that they more evenly represent the entire range of brightness levels. When you apply this command, Photoshop finds the brightest and darkest values in the composite image and remaps them so that the brightest value represents white and the darkest value represents black. Photoshop then attempts to equalize the brightness; that is, to distribute the intermediate pixel values evenly throughout the grayscale.

Export The Export command opens several specialized commands including Video Preview.

Eye icon The Eye icon turns the visibility on and off for a given layer or channel. Turning the eyeball off will hide the layer or channel, and turning the eyeball on will show it.

Fade Filter command The Fade Filter command allows you to fade the effect of a filter that has been applied based on percentages. It also gives you the option to apply a blend mode to the filter that was applied. Under Photoshop CS3 you can also click on Edit Blending Options icon if a Smart Filter was used.

Feather The Feather function allows you to smooth or soften the edges of a selection.

field All NTSC television signals are made up of 60 fields per second. Television signals are made up of horizontal lines stacked from the top of your television screen to the bottom. NTSC is made up of 525 lines of video. Showing all of the odd lines (1, 3, 5, 7, 9, etc.) at once is one field. Showing all even lines (2, 4, 6, 8, etc.) at once is the other field. It takes two fields of video to make one frame. PAL is made up of 625 lines of video, and interlaces the images the same as NTSC does, only with more lines. This creates an interlaced image, interlacing fields to create frames of video. Fields can create problems when video stills are brought into Photoshop. These lines are visible on your computer monitor and need to be removed by de-interlacing the image.

fill signal The fill signal is the RGB graphic portion of an image. This is the image that you want your viewers to see. The fill signal fills the image where the key signal allows it to pass. This signal is derived from the color information of your graphic.

Filmstrip The Filmstrip format is used for movie files created by Adobe Premiere. Every frame of video is saved to one file, which you can open in Photoshop for rotoscoping. This generally does not produce smooth results because you lack the ability to keyframe or 'tween items. If you change resolution, delete alpha channels, or alter the color mode, you won't be able to save it back to Filmstrip format. For more information, look in your Premiere owner's manual.

FireWire FireWire is the brand name for IEEE 1394, a high-performance serial bus for connecting devices such as hard drives and cameras to your computer. Apple computer lead the development of FireWire in 1986.

frame All NTSC television signals are made up of 30 frames per second. All PAL television signals are made up of 25 frames per second. Frames of video are essentially a series of still images flashed on the screen in rapid succession to create the illusion of movement. Two fields of video make up one frame.

Full Screen Mode The Full Screen Modes in Photoshop allow you to set the entire screen to your canvas, hiding the desktop in the background. You have up to three full-screen modes available.

GIF The Graphics Interchange Format (GIF) was originally developed by online service provider CompuServe. (If you remember them, add one point to your Geek IQ.) This format displays 8-bit or indexed-color graphics and images in HTML documents on the Internet. Because of its small color range and compressed images, this format is not very useful for video editing.

Gradient Fill Layer You fill an area with a gradient by dragging in the image with the gradient tool selected. The starting point (where the mouse is pressed) and ending point (where the mouse is released) affect the gradient appearance, depending on the gradient tool used. Gradients will be applied only to selected areas within your image.

Gradient Map The Gradient Map command maps the equivalent grayscale range of an image to the colors of a specified gradient fill. If you specify a two-color gradient fill, for example, shadows in the image map to one of the endpoint colors of the gradient fill, highlights map to the other endpoint color, and midtones map to the gradations in between.

Group Multiple layers in a document can be grouped into a folder. This can assist with organization of complex files as well as allow masking of the grouped layers.

halftone Images that are created where detail and tone values are represented by a series of evenly spaced dots in varying size and shape.

Hardness This command controls the size of the brush's hard center. Type a number, or use the slider to enter a value that is a percentage of the brush diameter.

HDRi High Dynamic Range imaging allows for a wide range of image data to be captured and accessed. They generally work in 32-bits per channel mode and are often referred to as float.

HDTV HDTV stands for High Definition Television and is an emerging video standard. HDTV has a 16:9 aspect ratio. It also has a variety of standards including interlaced signals, progressive signals, and a variety of sizes (either 720 or 1080 horizontal lines.) The two most common HDTV formats are 720p and 1080i. The p refers to a progressive video format and the i refers to an interlaced video format. HDTV formats are set by the Advanced Television Standards Committee (ATSC).

History palette The History palette is a road map of the work that you do in Photoshop. Each change that you make to your image is stored in the History palette. This is useful for going back to previous states of your image or for creating a new image from a specific history state. You can also paint from one history state to the image using the History Brush.

HSB HSB is a color model that generates colors based on the hue, saturation, and brightness of a given color.

hue Hue is the color reflected from or transmitted through an object. It is measured as a location on the standard color wheel, expressed as a degree between 0° and 360°. In common use, hue is identified by the name of the color such as red, orange, or green.

image size Image size is the size of a given image, which is determined by the resolution (dpi) and physical dimensions of the canvas.

import Importing allows you to bring a variety of different elements into an open image in Photoshop or to a new image. You can import anti-aliased PICTs, PDF images, annotations, and PICT resources. TWAIN imports allow you to import images directly from a scanner or digital camera.

indexed color The indexed color mode is limited to 256 colors. This color mode is most commonly used with GIF images and Web graphics. Because the number of colors is limited for each image, file sizes remain small. Images that you incorporate into your broadcast designs from the Web will most likely be in this format. These images need to be converted to the RGB color mode before they can be used. Menu: Image>Mode>Indexed Color

intellectual property An intellectual property is any product of the human intellect that is unique, novel, and non-obvious (and has some value in the marketplace). Examples include an idea, an invention, an expression or literary creation, a process, presentation, or a formula.

interlacing Interlacing is combining fields of video to create frames of video.

Inverse command The Inverse command is used to convert a selection to its exact opposite. If you have a selection in the shape of a circle and you inverse the selection, you now have a selection of everything but the circle.

Invert command The Invert command inverts the colors in an image. You might use this command to make a positive black-and-white image negative or to make a positive from a scanned black-and-white negative. When you invert an image, the brightness value of each pixel in the channels is converted to the inverse value on the 256-step color values scale. For example, a pixel in a positive image with a value of 255 is changed to 0, and a pixel with a value of 5 is changed to 250.

IRE IRE is the unit of measurement set forth by the Society of Motion Picture Television Engineers (SMPTE) that measures the overall brightness of your analog video signal. 100 IRE is pure white, 0 IRE is black.

JPEG The Joint Photographic Experts Group (JPEG) format is used to display continuous-tone images (such as photos) on the Web. Most digital cameras use JPEG because it provides excellent compression; the maximum setting provides comparable quality to much larger files. The JPEG format supports RGB, CMYK, and grayscale color modes, but does not support alpha channels. JPEG is a lossy compression and should not be used as a storage or production file format. If you are using it as a source format, be sure to set the digital camera to maximum quality.

kerning Kerning is the process of adding or subtracting space between specific letter pairs. You can control kerning manually, or you can use automatic kerning to turn on the kerning built into the font by the font designer.

key signal The key signal is the grayscale image that is sent to a hardware device that tells it what portions of an image to pass video through, and what portions of the fill signal should be visible. This signal is derived from the alpha channel or a matte.

L*a*b color In Photoshop, Lab mode (the asterisks are dropped from the name) has a lightness component (L) that can range from 0 to 100. In the Color Picker, the a component (green-red axis) and the b component (blue-yellow axis) can range from +128 to −128. In the Color palette, the a component and the b component can range from +120 to −120. Lab color is the intermediate color model Photoshop uses when converting from one color mode to another.

Layer Styles Sometimes known as Layer Effects, Layer Styles allow you to add drop shadows, glows, bevels, and a variety of other effects to any layer in Photoshop. Once Layer Styles have been applied to a layer, they can be removed or edited without permanently altering the contents of the layer.

Layers Layers in Photoshop act like separate images within a given canvas that contain image and opacity information. Layers are visually stacked one on top of another and are used to hold shapes, text, images, and any other element within your designs.

Levels The Levels dialog box lets you correct the tonal range and color balance of an image by adjusting intensity levels of the image's shadows, midtones, and highlights. The Levels histogram serves as a visual guide for adjusting the image's key tones.

lightness Lightness is used in the hue saturation and replaces color operations. Lightness moves a given color closer to white as it is increased, and closer to black as it is decreased.

linear key A linear key is a key that is achieved using an alpha channel or matte. This type of keying provides the greatest amount of flexibility. Linear keys allow for soft anti-aliased edges, partially transparent portions of your graphic, graphics that fade, drop shadows, and edge glows. Linear keys look to the alpha channel for the opacity level of each corresponding pixel in the image. Most video systems and software packages will support linear keys. If the system you are using does support them, use them. Your keys will be cleaner and more accurate with linear keys than with any other method of keying.

lines per inch Screen frequency is the number of printer dots or halftone cells per inch used to print grayscale images or color separations. Also known as screen ruling or line screen, screen frequency is measured in lines per inch (lpi) or lines of cells per inch in a halftone screen.

link Layers can be linked in Photoshop by selecting a layer and activating the chain icon on other layers that you wish to link to the parent layer. Layers that are linked can be moved in one operation, moved to layer sets, or deleted as a group.

load selection You can load the selection of a layer, channel, or layer mask. This operation reads the transparency of a layer or the selection that is represented by a channel or layer mask. You can load the selection of an element under the select menu, or by ⌘+clicking (*ctrl*+clicking) on the layer, channel, or mask.

lossless compression A method of compressing an image where detail is not lost in the compression process.

lossy compression A method of compressing an image where detail is lost in the compression process. JPEG, TIFF, and PDF are examples of file formats that support lossy compression.

luminance key A luminance key is a key that is achieved using the black background of an image. Luminance keys are very limiting and do not provide a great deal of creative control over how your graphics are keyed over video. Luminance keys do not allow for anti-aliased edges or partially transparent portions of your image. Luminance keys should only be used if your system does not support linear keys. Graphics that are luminance-keyed need to be placed on superblack.

LZW compression LZW (Lemple-Zif-Welch) lossless compression; supported by TIFF, PDF, GIF, and PostScript language file formats. Most useful for images with large areas of single color.

macro A small script or routine that automatically repeats a series of operations within an application. Actions are macros that can be recorded and played in Photoshop.

matte A matte does the same thing as an alpha channel. They both create key signals for a visual element. Mattes are typically not attached to the object for which they are creating a key signal. Mattes are separate files or footage applied to another clip or image. Alpha channels are typically attached to the element for which they are creating a key signal.

merge Combining the elements within multiple layers to a single layer. Merging layers is a destructive function in Photoshop.

moiré Moiré patterns are caused from tight, highly contrasting patterns of objects in your video. The effect is a vibrating rainbow pattern over the top of your video.

multi-session disc A session on a CD or DVD includes a lead-in area, a program area (data or audio tracks), and a lead-out area. A multi-session disc is one that has multiple sessions on one disc. Each session has its own lead-in, content and lead-out area, and is linked together with other sessions. Disc recorders that support multi-session recording must also support this feature. In terms of optical storage, this allows the capability of storing more data on a previously recorded recordable media.

Navigator palette The Navigator palette provides a thumbnail representation of your current canvas and allows you to zoom in and move your visible area around easily.

non-square pixels Pixels that are native to your computer are all square. However, pixels in a few television signals are not, because the image dimensions of the file do not fit in a 4:3 aspect ratio defined by the NTSC. Therefore, they are squeezed taller to fit all the needed pixels into the aspect ratio.

The National Television System Committee, otherwise known as the NTSC, has set the standard that television, as we know it today, has a 4:3 aspect ratio, excluding HDTV, which is 16:9. This means that the size of a television image is three units high for every four units wide.

Video hardware that uses the 640×480 dimension standard is in a 4:3 aspect ratio. 640×480 images have an aspect ratio of 4:3, which means that the square pixels on your computer stay square once converted in your video hardware. This is the easiest system to design for because you don't have to convert your images before going out to video.

However, video hardware that outputs 601 video (sometimes called D1) has a size of 720×486, which does not work out to a 4:3 ratio. This introduces the problem between square and non-square pixels. Because the 720×486 image must fit within a 4:3 aspect ratio, the pixels in that image are not square. They are taller than they are wide, roughly 0.9 to 1. Therefore, images created on your square-pixel computer monitor may look stretched out vertically when they go to NTSC video and stretched out horizontally on PAL video. The same holds true for DV images. They are 720×480, which is not a 4:3 aspect ratio, either.

NTSC NTSC stands for the National Television Standards Committee. This is the governing body that sets the standards for video signals in the United States and North America. It states that video signals in the United States must be in a 4:3 aspect ratio and must be 30 frames/60 fields per second, excluding HDTV.

NTSC color filter This filter restricts the gamut of colors to those acceptable for television reproduction to prevent oversaturated colors from bleeding across television scan lines.

opacity Opacity is a measurement of how opaque or transparent the pixels in your layers are. An opacity setting of 100 will make the elements in your layer completely opaque, and an opacity setting of 0 would be completely transparent.

OpenEXR The OpenEXR format is used by the visual effects industry for high dynamic range images. It was developed by Industrial Light and Magic and was released under an open source license. The format supports multiple lossless or lossy compression methods. It is designed to supports both 16-bit and 32-bit images. Its primary benefit is that it allows for over 30 stops of exposure (which gives it incredible range of lights to dark). For much more information, see http://www.openexr.com/about.html.

OpenType font OpenType is a font format for scalable (outline) files that extends the existing font file format used by Microsoft Windows and Apple Macintosh. OpenType was developed jointly by Microsoft and Adobe and allows an Adobe file to be part of a TrueType font file. Prior to OpenType, Adobe did not support TrueType fonts as well it did its own font format, Type 1, for printers that use PostScript. PostScript is an industry-standard printer formatting language for higher-quality and more sophisticated printers. OpenType is also known as TrueType Open v. 2.0.

Options bar The Options bar is the bar that sits at the top of your monitor directly under the Application menu. This palette allows you to set the options for all of the tools that are available in the tool palette.

orphan When laying out text, an orphan is a stranded word on a line by itself. This is something that you want to avoid. Work to balance out word spacing and wrapping so that this doesn't happen.

out of gamut A gamut is the range of colors that a color system can display or print. Different color models include a different set or range of colors. Colors that are represented in one color model may not exist in another. These colors would be considered out of gamut.

overscan Televisions crop the edges of your visuals because of a condition called overscan. The edges of a television set are covered partially by the case of the television, and the ray gun inside the television that generates the image will slightly overshoot the surface of the viewable area of the TV. This keeps unwanted portions of a video signal from being visible to the viewer. However, this will also cut off portions of your signal that you want to be seen. Using safe grids will help you monitor what will be kept and lost during transmission.

Some video monitors have a feature called underscan, which will cause the image on the monitor to be squeezed down so that all of the image can be seen on screen. This is not an accurate representation of what the audience will see when they watch your program.

PAL PAL is the most common video format used outside of North America. PAL video signals are a 4:3 aspect ratio and are 25 frames/50 fields per second.

panning A camera movement that adjusts the composition of a shot from right to left. Often photos are taken from Photoshop into After Effects (or another compositing application) so that they can be panned. Be sure you have extra pixel information so you can pan or zoom.

Pantone Used for printing solid-color inks, the Pantone Matching System includes 1114 solid colors. To select a color, use a Pantone color guide printed on coated, uncoated, and matte stocks.

Paragraph palette You can use the Paragraph palette to set formatting options such as alignment and line spacing for a single paragraph, multiple paragraphs, or all paragraphs in a type layer.

Paste as Pixels The Paste as Pixels command allows you to rasterize a vector object in your clipboard and paste the resulting pixels into your image.

Paste Into The Paste Into command will paste the contents of the clipboard into the selection of the active layer as opposed to creating a new layer for the pasted object.

PCX The PC Paintbrush format is used by PC-compatible computers. The format is designed to match the standard VGA color palette. PCX supports RGB, indexed color, grayscale, and bitmap color modes, but does not support alpha channels. It is commonly a compressed file and supports bit depths of 1, 4, 8, or 24. Because of its small color range and compressed images, this format is not very useful for video editing.

PDF The Portable Document Format is an amazing, cross-platform, cross-application file format. PDF files accurately display and preserve fonts, page layouts, and both vector and bitmap graphics. You can also transfer Photoshop's annotation notes (both text and audio) into the PDF. The Photoshop PDF format is the only one that Photoshop can save, and it supports layers and other Photoshop features. You do not need to flatten to save a PDF file. This file can then be transferred to others for review and comment using Adobe Acrobat or viewed with the free Acrobat Reader. This is an excellent format for review purposes, but will not be understood by all video-editing applications.

Pen tool The Pen tool allows you to create Bezier curves for vector objects or paths in Photoshop.

PICT file The Macintosh Picture format is widely used by video editors. Its popularity can be traced back to many editing packages,

which historically required graphics to be in the PICT format.

Its popularity has suffered as other options became available, but the technology behind the format still makes it the best format for video. The PICT format supports RGB images with a single alpha channel, and is very effective at compressing large areas of solid color. This compression results in huge file savings for alpha channels, which are mostly black or white.

When saving, be sure to pick 32-bit pixel resolution. On the Mac platform, you have choices of additional JPEG compression. Avoid these because they cause import problems on PCs, and the file savings are not worth the quality loss.

PICT resource file The PICT resource is a PICT file that is contained in a Mac OS file's resource fork. This format is often used to create startup screens for software. While similar to a plain PICT file, avoid it. Resource files generally confuse video editing applications. You can edit a PICT resource file by importing it into Photoshop.

Pixar file The Pixar format is designed for high-end 3D applications. It supports RGB and grayscale images with a single alpha channel. If you also create 3D animation, you may use this format.

pixels per inch (ppi) The number of pixels displayed per unit of printed length in an image, usually measured in pixels per inch.

Place You can use the File>Place command to place artwork into a new layer in an image. In Photoshop, you can place PDF, Adobe Illustrator, and EPS files. Starting with Photoshop CS3, the new object can be added as a Smart Object.

PNG The Portable Network Graphics format provides lossless compression for the Web. The PNG supports 24-bit images and with 8-bit transparency. Because only newer browsers support it (and the file sizes are bigger), you will not find it widely used. If you have to use a Web image in your video, look for a PNG.

PostScript font Each character (or to be more precise, each glyph) in a font has a shape, and there are various ways of describing that shape on a computer. PostScript fonts generally describe the outline of the shape and then color in the interior of that outline; this coloring process is called rasterizing.

PPI See pixels per inch.

pre-multiplied alpha channel A pre-multiplied alpha channel is an alpha channel that follows the edge of your graphic material exactly. This is the type of alpha channel that Photoshop will output from your images. The potential problem from this type of alpha channel is that you run the risk of the background color of your image being present on the edges of your graphic. This is caused by the anti-aliasing that Photoshop does to your images. The edges of your image are partially transparent to give them a smoothing effect. However, this creates partially transparent edges on your alpha channel as well. This will allow part of the background color of your image to be visible when keyed. Some applications, such as After Effects, can address the problem of pre-multiplied alpha channels. You can tell the software that the image has a pre-multiplied alpha channel and it will un-multiply the background color from the edge pixels of your image.

primary colors Primary colors are the colors from which all other colors are made up. Red, green, and blue are the primary colors in the RGB color model; cyan, magenta, yellow, and black are the primary colors of the CMYK color model.

profile mismatch Color Settings lets you specify how Photoshop handles the files it opens and saves. It is especially important when opening files that have no embedded profile or that have a profile that doesn't match the current setup profile. Profile mismatch occurs when Photoshop encounters a file with an embedded profile that doesn't match the current setup profile. How Photoshop handles the mismatch depends on what you've set in the Profile Mismatch Handling section of the Color Settings dialog box.

progressive scan A progressive video signal is a video signal that does not have interlaced fields. Computer monitors, some HDTV standards, and some mini-DV cameras display progressive images. That means there are 30 full frames per second, not 60 fields, or half frames per second. Images that were shot in a progressive format are much cleaner and easier to work with inside the computer.

PSD The Photoshop format is the default file format. This format is the only format that supports all of Photoshop's features. Always save your design files in this format for maximum editing ability.

Quark Xpress Quark Xpress is a page layout application that is used for prepress and page layout for anything from simple brochures to entire books or other publications. These files cannot be opened by Photoshop, so be sure to ask the designer for all of the elements and a PDF file of the layout.

raster graphics Raster graphics, sometimes referred to as bitmapped graphics, use a grid of colors known as pixels to represent images. Each pixel is assigned a specific location and color value. For example, a circle in a raster image is made up of a mosaic of pixels in that location. When working with raster images, you edit pixels rather than objects or shapes. Raster or bitmap images are the most common electronic medium for continuous-tone images such as photographs, because they can represent subtle gradations of shades and color. Raster images are resolution dependent; that is, they contain a fixed number of pixels. As a result, they can lose detail and appear jagged if they are scaled larger.

rasterize Rasterizing is the process of converting vector images into bitmapped or pixel-based raster images.

Raw The Raw format is a flexible (and confusing) file format for transferring between applications and computer platforms. Essentially, a text file is written containing a stream of bytes describing the color information for the image. Every pixel is described in binary format. Avoid this format. It is not to be confused with the Camera Raw format.

resolution-dependent Resolution-dependent means that an image has a fixed resolution. Raster or bit-mapped images are resolution-dependent because they cannot be enlarged without losing resolution or clarity.

resolution-independent Resolution independent images, on the other hand, can be enlarged infinitely without losing any resolution or image quality. Vector-based artwork is considered resolution-independent.

Revert command The Revert command will discard any unsaved changes in your current image and return the image to the state in which it was last saved.

RGB The RGB color mode is the one used for television graphics. All graphics that are displayed on video systems need to be created in or converted to the RGB mode first (Menu: Image>Mode>RGB Color). All colors in the RGB color mode are made from a combination of red, green, and blue. These are the primary colors used to create color images on television. Other color modes will not work for video. The Channels palette in an RGB image will have a Red channel, a Green channel, and a Blue channel. It is best to design in the RGB color space because all of the filters in Photoshop work in RGB mode.

Rubber Stamp tool The Rubber Stamp tool is now called the Clone Stamp tool. The Clone Stamp tool takes a sample of an image that you can then apply over another image or part of the same image. Each stroke of the tool paints on more of the sample.

Rubylith mask Traditional color of masks used in printing.

run length encoding Lossless compression; supported by some common Windows file formats.

safe grid A grid that shows you what areas of your image will be safe and what areas of your image will be lost when transferred to video. Overscan on television sets will cut off approximately 10% of the edges of your image. All of the action within a given shot must be within the action-safe area, and all of the titles or graphics of an image must stay inside the title-safe area.

saturation Saturation is the intensity of a color. A saturated blue has a lot of blue in it; an unsaturated blue has very little blue in it.

Save selection as channel This command will take the active selection in your image and store the selection as channel in your Channels palette. You also have the option of saving the selection as a channel in other open images.

Scitex file The Scitex Continuous Tone format is used for high-end print work on Scitex computers. This format needs special scanners and rasterizing formats, and is designed for output of high-quality print such as magazines and art prints. While you may receive this format, you will never need to save in it for video output.

scratch disk This is the physical hard drive that Photoshop uses to write information to when RAM becomes full.

SCSI SCSI stands for small computer serial interface, and it is a serial bus on computers that allows the connection of external hard drives or scanners. SCSI is starting to phase out and be replaced by USB and FireWire.

sepia tone Conversion of a black-and-white image in silver to sepia (a brownish gray to dark olive brown) by metallic compounds. Sepia was the most common tone used, and was used in black-and-white prints of films for special sequences to enhance the dramatic or pictorial effect.

skew Skewing an image is vertically or horizontally distorting an image. This can be accomplished with the Free Transform tool.

slices Slices are dividers in Photoshop that allow you to prepare or cut up an image for Web deployment. Each slice you create in your Photoshop image can be saved as a separate file with an associated HTML file for the Web.

SLR Camera A single lens reflex (SLR) camera is a still camera where the viewfinder is actually looking through the lens at the exact same image that will be exposed to the film.

Smart Filters Starting with Photoshop CS3, you can apply filters to Smart Objects. These filters are applied as Smart Filters, which leave the filter editable even after it has been first applied.

Smart Object Smart Objects were first introduced in Photoshop CS2. They allow you to embed a full-resolution raster image or a vector image into a layer. Additionally, several layers can be grouped into a new Smart Object. This adds greater flexibility when scaling or modifying a layer.

Snap When Snap is enabled, your selections and drawing tools will snap to a combination of guides, grids, selections, and document bounds. Under the View>Snap to... command, you can select what Photoshop will snap to.

Snapshot command The Snapshot command lets you make a temporary copy (or snapshot) of any state of the image. The new snapshot is added to the list of snapshots at the top of the History palette. Selecting a snapshot lets you work from that version of the image.

Sponge tool The Sponge tool subtly changes the color saturation of an area. In grayscale mode, the tool increases or decreases contrast by moving gray levels away from or toward the middle gray.

square pixels Pixels that are native to your computer are all square. However, pixels in a few television signals are not, because the image dimensions of the file do not fit in a 4:3 aspect ratio defined by the NTSC. Therefore, they are squeezed taller to fit all the needed pixels into the aspect ratio.

The National Television System Committee, otherwise known as the NTSC, has set the standard that television, as we know it today, has a 4:3 aspect ratio, excluding HDTV, which is 16:9. This means that the size of a television image is three units high for every four units wide.

Video hardware that uses the 640×480 dimension standard is in a 4:3 aspect ratio.

640×480 images have an aspect ratio of 4:3, which means that the square pixels on your computer stay square once converted in your video hardware. This is the easiest system to design for because you don't have to convert your images before going out to video.

However, video hardware that outputs 601 video (sometimes called D1) has a size of 720×486, which does not work out to a 4:3 ratio. This introduces the problem between square and non-square pixels. Because the 720×486 image must fit within a 4:3 aspect ratio, the pixels in that image are not square. They are taller than they are wide, roughly 0.9 to 1. Therefore, creating images on your square pixel computer monitor may look stretched out vertically when they go to NTSC video and stretched out horizontally on PAL video. The same holds true for DV images. They are 720×480, which is not a 4:3 aspect ratio, either.

straight alpha channel A straight alpha channel is an alpha channel that does not follow the edge of your graphic material. An example would be an image of a green circle. Instead of the shape of the circle being determined by the color information of the graphic, it is defined by the alpha channel. The graphic would look like a solid green canvas, and the alpha channel would be in the shape of a circle.

This allows the edges of the color to extend outside of the alpha channel, giving you a much cleaner key without the chances of a thin black or white line around the edge of the circle. This is the preferred type of alpha channel. However, Photoshop cannot calculate this for you. If you want to obtain this type of alpha channel out of Photoshop, you need to plan your design ahead of time to be this way. To achieve this kind of alpha, you must place a solid color layer into your background that matches the color of your glow/drop shadow/ soft edge.

After Effects is one application that can take an image file with an alpha channel and turn the image into a new file with a straight alpha channel. Note: When referring to a straight alpha channel, the alpha channel is actually no different than any other alpha channel; it is the color information in your image that is different.

subtractive color model A color model that creates black when the primary colors of the model are added together. For example, adding Cyan, Magenta, Yellow, and Key (black) in the CMYK model will create black.

superblack Superblack is a level of black below 7.5 IRE, usually at 0 IRE. This is used for luminance keys. The areas of your image that you want to be keyed out should be superblack, and the areas of your image that are black that you want to keep should be at 7.5 IRE.

tablet A tablet is a secondary input device that uses a pen to control the computer as opposed to a mouse. This is extremely useful in Photoshop because it allows for pressure sensitivity and the feel of drawing with a pen instead of a mouse. Wacom is the most popular manufacturer of tablets.

TARGA file The TARGA format was designed for systems using Truevision video boards. It has become a standard format for PC users because it supports 24-bit RGB images (8 bits; 3 color channels), and 32-bit RGB images (3 color channels plus an alpha channel). Photoshop 7.0 shipped with a bug in its TARGA module that improperly saved the alpha channel. The free update to 7.0.1 or a separate TARGA download fixes this.

TIFF file The Tagged-Image File Format is a common cross-platform format that is supported by several applications. Several scanners can create TIFF files as well, and it is a more efficient format for saving non-layered images. The TIFF format supports RGB, CMYK, Lab, indexed color, and grayscale images with alpha channels. Photoshop can also save layers in a TIFF file; however, other applications only see the flattened version. TIFF is a good format for storing source photos.

title-safe area The title-safe area of an image is the portion of the image where all of the titles or graphics should be. This is the inner box on a safe grid. Any graphical elements that extend outside of the title-safe area run the risk of being cut off by the viewer's television set.

TOYO TOYO Color Finder 1050 consists of more than 1000 colors based on the most common printing inks used in Japan. The TOYO Color Finder 1050 Book contains printed samples of TOYO colors and is available from printers and graphic arts supply stores.

trackball A computer input device similar to a mouse. Instead of moving the mouse, you roll a ball in a cradle to make equivalent mouse movements. Trackballs provide more sensitivity and accuracy than a mouse, and some have four buttons that can be assigned to various functions.

tracking Tracking is the process of creating an equal amount of spacing across a range of letters.

TrueType font A scalable font technology that renders fonts for both the printer and the screen. Originally developed by Apple, it was enhanced jointly by Apple and Microsoft. TrueType fonts are used in Windows, starting with Windows 3.1, as well as in the Mac System 7 operating system.

Unlike PostScript, in which the algorithms are maintained in the rasterizing engine, each TrueType font contains its own algorithms for converting the outline into bitmaps. The lower-level language embedded within the TrueType font allows unlimited flexibility in the design.

Type Mask tool The Type Mask tool will create a selection of the shape of the text when type is entered as opposed to a color.

underscan Televisions crop the edges of your visuals because of a condition called overscan. The edges of a television set are covered partially by the case of the television, and the ray gun inside the television that generates the image will slightly overshoot the surface of the viewable area of the TV. This keeps unwanted portions of a video signal from being visible to the viewer. However, this will also cut off portions of your signal that you want to be seen.

Using safe grids will help you monitor what will be kept and lost during transmission. Some video monitors have a feature called underscan, which will cause the image on the monitor to be squeezed down so that all of the image can be seen on screen. This is not an accurate representation of what the audience will see when they watch your program.

Unsharp Mask filter Unsharp Mask locates pixels that differ from surrounding pixels by the threshold you specify and increases the pixels' contrast by the amount you specify. In addition, you specify the radius of the region to which each pixel is compared.

USB 1 USB stands for universal serial bus. USB 1 was the original version of USB that had a maximum data transfer rate of 12 mbits/second. USB is used primarily for connecting keyboards and mice to computers. However, there are USB scanners, cameras, and hard drives.

USB 2 USB stands for universal serial bus. USB 2 is a high-speed serial bus that has a maximum data transfer rate of 480 mbits/second. USB is used primarily for connecting keyboards and mice to computers. However, there are USB scanners, cameras, and hard drives.

Variations command The Variations command lets you adjust the color balance, contrast, and saturation of an image by showing you thumbnails of alternatives. This is a good method for beginners, but does not offer the precise control of the other adjustment methods.

vector graphics Vector graphics are made up of lines and curves defined by mathematical objects called vectors. Vectors describe an image according to its geometric characteristics. For example, a circle in a vector graphic is made up of a mathematical definition of a circle drawn with a certain radius, set at a specific location, and filled with a specific color. You can move, resize, or change the color of the circle without losing the quality of the graphic.

Vector graphics are resolution-independent; that is, they can be scaled to any size and printed at any resolution without losing detail or clarity. As a result, vector graphics are the best choice for representing bold graphics that must retain crisp lines when scaled to various sizes—for example, logos.

video filters Filters in Photoshop that are video-specific, such as De-interlace and NTSC colors.

Web Photo Gallery The Web Photo Gallery can be found under File>Automate. This function will automate Photoshop to generate a Web gallery of a folder of images on your machine. It will generate thumbnail, HTML files, and the full-size images. You can control the layout, image sizes, and content within the pages.

white point The white point of an image is a reference for what Photoshop believes to be the brightest portion of your image that is white. From this white point, Photoshop can adjust the color balance of your image. The white point is set in the levels or curves palette.

Wide Gamut RGB Wide Gamut RGB provides a very wide range of colors by using spectrally pure primaries. The downside is that most of the colors in this gamut cannot be displayed on standard computer monitors or printed. When editing a file, colors are often forced into the display space (clipped) and, consequently, your color adjustments may not appear as visible changes on the screen.

WORM disc WORM stands for Write Once Read Many. Any single-session CD-R would be considered to be a WORM disc.

YCC Color space developed by Eastman Kodak that defines colors by luminance (Y) and two levels of chrominance (C and C).

INDEX

Book Design

The chapter headings of this book were designed by Ben Miners, Bradley Grosh, and Sean Rodwell of Digital Vision.